Investing For Dummies
by Eric Tyson

P9-BAV-186

Sheet

Top Twenty Imperatives for Investing

1. **Saving is a prerequisite to investing.** Unless you have wealthy, benevolent relatives, living within your means and saving money are prerequisites to investing and building wealth.

2. **Risk and reward go hand in hand.** The way that people of all economic means make their money grow is to take risk by investing in ownership assets, such as stocks, real estate, and small business, where you share in the success and profitability of the asset.

3. **Be realistic about expected investment returns.** Over the long-term, 10 percent per year is about right for ownership investments. It is possible with running a small business to earn higher returns and even become a multimillionaire, but years of hard work and insight are required.

4. **Think long-term.** Because ownership investments are riskier (more volatile), you must keep your long-term perspective when investing in them. Do not invest money in such investments unless you plan on holding them there for a minimum of five years, and preferably a decade or longer.

5. **Match the time frame to the investment.** Selecting good investments for yourself involves matching the time frame you have to the riskiness of the investment. For example, for money that you expect to use soon — within the next year, for example — focus on safe investments such as money market funds. Invest your longer-term money mostly in growth investments.

6. **Diversify.** Diversification is a powerful investment concept that helps you to reduce the risk of holding more aggressive investments. Diversifying simply means that you should hold a variety of investments that perform differently in different market environments. For example, if you invest in stocks, invest worldwide, not just in the U.S. market. You can further diversify by investing in real estate.

7. **Ignore the minutiae.** Don't feel mystified by or feel the need to follow the daily gyrations of the financial markets. Ultimately, the prices of stocks, bonds, and other financial instruments are determined by supply and demand, which are influenced by thousands of external issues and millions of investors' expectations and fears.

8. **Allocate your assets.** Besides your individual investment choices, how you divvy up or allocate your money among major investments greatly determines your returns. The younger you are and the more money you earmark for the long-term, the greater the percentage you should devote to ownership investments. One rule of thumb is to subtract your age from 100 (or 120 if you want to take more risk) and invest the resulting percentage in ownership investments.

9. **Look at the big picture first.** Understand your overall financial situation and how wise investments fit within it. Before you invest, examine your debt obligations, tax situation, ability to fund retirement accounts, and your insurance coverage.

10. **Do your homework *before* you buy an investment.** You work hard for your money and many investments cost you to buy and sell. Investing is not a field where acting first and asking questions later works well. *Never* buy an investment based on an advertisement or a salesperson's solicitation of you.

...For Dummies: The Best Selling Book Series

BUSINESS AND
GENERAL
REFERENCE
BOOK SERIES
FROM IDG

Investing For Dummies®
by Eric Tyson

Cheat Sheet

11. **Keep an eye on taxes when choosing investments.** Take advantage of tax-deductible retirement accounts and understand the impact of your tax bracket when investing outside tax-sheltered retirement accounts.

12. **Consider the value of your time and your investing skills and desires.** Investing in stocks and other securities via mutual funds is both time efficient and profitable. Real estate investing and running a small business are the most time-intensive investments.

13. **Where possible, minimize fees.** The more you pay in commissions and management fees on your investments, the greater the drag on your returns. And don't fall prey to the thinking that "you get what you pay for."

14. **Don't expect to beat the stock market averages.** If you have the right skills and interest, your ability to do better than the investing averages is greater with real estate and small business than with stock market investing. The large number of full-time, experienced stock market professionals makes it next to impossible for you to choose individual stocks that will consistently beat a relevant market average.

15. **Don't bail when things look bleak.** The hardest time, psychologically, to hold onto your investments will be when they are down. Even the best investments go through depressed periods, which is the worst possible time to sell. Don't sell when there's a sale going on; if anything, consider buying more.

16. **Ignore soothsayers and prognosticators.** It's nearly impossible to predict the future. Your long-term investments should be based on selecting and holding good investments, not trying to time when to be in or out of a particular investment.

17. **Minimize your trading.** The more you trade, the more likely you are to make mistakes. You'll also suffer increased transaction costs and higher taxes (for non-retirement account investments).

18. **Hire by the hour.** If you feel the need to hire help, focus on experts who are selling their advice by the hour. Beware of conflicts of interest when you consider advisors to hire.

19. **You are what you read and listen to.** Don't pollute your mind with bad investing strategies and philosophies. The quality of what you read and listen to is far more important than the quantity. Learn in this book how to evaluate the quality of what you read and hear.

20. **Remember the following highest-return, lowest-risk investments.** Your personal life and health are far more important investments than the size of your financial portfolio.

IDG
BOOKS
WORLDWIDE

...For Dummies: The Best Selling Book Series

Praise for Eric Tyson

Here's what critics and readers have said about Eric Tyson's three previous national best-sellers:

"*Personal Finance For Dummies* is the perfect book for people who feel guilty about inadequately managing their money but are intimidated by all of the publications out there. It's a painless way to learn how to take control. My college-aged daughters even enjoyed reading it!"
— Karen Tofte, producer, National Public Radio's *Sound Money*

"*I own many finance and investment books — this is <u>by far</u> the best!*"
— Mike Dodge, Baltimore, MD

"Among my favorite financial guides are . . . Eric Tyson's *Personal Finance For Dummies.*"
— Jonathan Clements, the *Wall Street Journal*

"*The book was well-written, concise, inspirational, excellent for common folk, and doesn't send you running for a dictionary.*"
— Brian O'Connor, Bogota, NJ

"Smart advice for dummies . . . skip the tomes . . . and buy *Personal Finance For Dummies,* which rewards your candor with advice and comfort."
— Temma Ehrenfeld, *Newsweek*

"*Superb reference! Led to my being offered a job as a mortgage origina-tor. [The] bank said I was the 'most informed buyer' they ever sat with!!!*"
— K.A. Carney, Greensburg, PA

"Eric Tyson is doing something important — namely, helping people at all income levels to take control of their financial futures. This book is a natural outgrowth of Tyson's vision that he has nurtured for years. Like Henry Ford, he wants to make something that was previously accessible only to the wealthy accessible to middle-income Americans."
— James C. Collins, coauthor of the national bestseller *Built to Last;* Lecturer in Business, Stanford Graduate School of Business

"*Eric Tyson took a subject — finances — which has always intimidated me and made it manageable. Thanks!*"
— Margaret Holtje, North Sebago, ME

"You don't have to be a novice to like *Mutual Funds For Dummies*. Despite the book's chatty, informal style, author Eric Tyson clearly has a mastery of his subject. He knows mutual funds, and he knows how to explain them in simple English."
— Steven T. Goldberg, *Kiplinger's Personal Finance Magazine*

"I work with investments and have used this book to help some of my clients understand finances."
— Bryan Bailey, Mandan, ND

"*Personal Finance For Dummies* offers a valuable guide for common misconceptions and major pitfalls. It's a no-nonsense, straightforward, easy-to-read personal finance book. . . . With this book, you can easily learn enough about finances to start thinking for yourself."
— Charles R. Schwab, Chairman and CEO, The Charles Schwab Corporation

"Makes financial planning as easy as spending my paycheck."
— Tim Campbell, Green River, WY

"It can be overwhelming to keep up with the latest developments, which is why you might turn to the book *Mutual Funds For Dummies* by Eric Tyson. A light touch and the use of plenty of graphics help the pages fly by. This book is a primer for those who flinch when contemplating the 7,000 funds you can now buy."
— Brian Banmiller, Fox-TV

"A nice, easy-to-use format allowed me to skip useless data and glean only the information relevant to me."
— Steven A. Baffy, Trenton, MI

"Best new personal finance book."
— Michael Pellecchia, syndicated columnist

"I thoroughly enjoyed the honest, matter-of-fact, straightforward manner in which the book was written. I am grateful to you for providing me with a valuable resource for one of life's great drudgeries."
— Sven Hagen, Atlanta, GA

"Eric Tyson . . . seems the perfect writer for a . . . *For Dummies* book. He doesn't tell you what to do or consider doing without explaining the why's and how's — and the booby traps to avoid — in plain English. . . . It will lead you through the thickets of your own finances as painlessly as I can imagine."
— Clarence Peterson, *Chicago Tribune*

"Great book!"
— Cheryl Eichelkraut, Phoenix, AZ

"The best book I've ever bought!"
— David Clarke, Chicago, IL

"This book was written for real people."
— Lisa Timco, Westland, MI

"Personal Finance For Dummies is, by far, the best book I have read on financial planning. It is a simplified volume of information that provides tremendous insight and guidance into the world of investing and other money issues."
— Althea Thompson, producer, "PBS Nightly Business Report"

". . . amazingly you were even able to add humor to such a topic."
— Steve Stachling, Wausau, WI

"This book provides easy-to-understand personal financial information and advice for those without great wealth or knowledge in this area. Practitioners like Eric Tyson, who care about the well-being of middle-income people, are rare in today's society."
— Joel Hyatt, founder, Hyatt Legal Services, one of the nation's largest general-practice personal legal service firms

". . . very understandable, informative and enjoyable. . . . This should be required reading for every senior!"
— Barbara Greub, River Falls, WI

"*Personal Finance For Dummies* is a sane and useful guide that will be of benefit to anyone seeking a careful and prudent method of managing their financial world."
— John Robbins, founder of EarthSave, author of *May All Be Fed*

"Very informative, lighthearted. . . . I read it cover to cover."
— Lou Furry, Northampton, PA

"Worth getting. Scores of all-purpose money-management books reach bookstores every year, but only once every couple of years does a standout personal finance primer come along. *Personal Finance For Dummies,* by financial counselor and columnist Eric Tyson, provides detailed, action-oriented advice on everyday financial questions. . . . Tyson's style is readable and unintimidating."
— Kristin Davis, *Kiplinger's Personal Finance Magazine*

"I purchased copies for each of my children."
— M.G. Sher, Marblehead, MA

"I liked his holistic view. He placed money management in perspective to life's important considerations. Invaluable! I'd like to give a copy to each of my sons just starting their 1st jobs."
— Robin Ketchum, Norfolk, CT

"Fantastic. I wish I had it 20 years ago. I'll make sure my children get one."
— C.H. Day, Richmond, VA

"Presents complicated issues with simplicity, clarity and a touch of humor."
— *The Times-Picayune,* New Orleans, Louisiana

"This book is the first on finances that I have ever read that makes sense to me."
— Tony Toledo, Salem, MA

"Straightforward, readable. . . Tyson is an authoritative writer. . . ."
— *Orange County Register*

"Personal Finance For Dummies is a great book. It addresses everything and helps me feel secure about my finances."
— Phyllis Haber, Kansas City, MO

". . . among tax advice books is far and away the best. *Taxes For Dummies* s fun to read and teaches about the tax system itself. The book also provides excellent advice about dealing with mistakes — created by you or the Internal Revenue Service. And it talks about fitting taxes into your daily financial planning. In other words, it's a book you can use after April 15, as well as before."
— Kathy M. Kristof, *The Los Angeles Times*

"Taxes For Dummies *helped us save $500 on our tax return."*
— Bob and Diane Hayman, Mishawaka, IN

"Smart chapters — not just thumbnail sketches — for filling out forms."
— Susan Tompor, Gannett News Service

"Finally, a book about finance that I can understand!"
— Michael K. Owens, Knoxville, TN

"*Taxes For Dummies* will make tax preparation less traumatic. . . . It is a book that answers — in plain English, and sometimes with humor — many puzzling questions that arise on the most commonly used tax forms."
— Stanley Angrist, *The Wall Street Journal*

"I should never have brought this book into work — everyone wants to borrow it!"
— Maria Zografos, San Francisco, CA

". . . a witty, irreverent reference . . . And since laughter is good medicine, it most definitely is what it claims. But its focus on humor does not undermine its merit as a research tool. While the guide could be used just to answer individual questions, its friendly format is such fun that you may end up reading Eric Tyson's book from cover to cover. No kidding."
— *The New Orleans Times-Picayune*

"This book answered so many questions. Truly, I was completely illiterate financially — now I am becoming the family guru."
— Jean M., Holt, Missouri

"There are plenty of books out there that do the job, but if you're looking for one which explains the tax laws using plain English, with a dash of a sense of humor, the *Taxes For Dummies* is highly recommended. . . . *Taxes For Dummies* is the ideal guide for getting you through the Ides of April."
— Bill Peschel, *The Herald*

"It's great! It moves you to a mindset that allows you to control your finances — instead of them controlling you."
— Sabrina Karl, Madison, WI

"*Dummies* is a primer for those who are tired of making bad choices — or no choices at all — with their money."
— Barbara Tierney, *Smart Money by The Wall Street Journal*

"This book should be taught in every high school and college in America. Most people, like me, wait until they're in trouble before they get help."
— Gary Rzepka, APO AP Japan

TM

BUSINESS AND GENERAL REFERENCE BOOK SERIES FROM IDG

References for the Rest of Us!™

Do you find that traditional reference books are overloaded with technical details and advice you'll never use? Do you postpone important life decisions because you just don't want to deal with them? Then our *...For Dummies*™ business and general reference book series is for you.

...For Dummies business and general reference books are written for those frustrated and hard-working souls who know they aren't dumb, but find that the myriad of personal and business issues and the accompanying horror stories make them feel helpless. *...For Dummies* books use a lighthearted approach, a down-to-earth style, and even cartoons and humorous icons to diffuse fears and build confidence. Lighthearted but not lightweight, these books are perfect survival guides to solve your everyday personal and business problems.

> *"More than a publishing phenomenon, 'Dummies' is a sign of the times."*
> — The New York Times

> *"A world of detailed and authoritative information is packed into them..."*
> — U.S. News and World Report

> *"...you won't go wrong buying them."*
> — Walter Mossberg, Wall Street Journal, on IDG's ...For Dummies™ books

Already, millions of satisfied readers agree. They have made *...For Dummies* the #1 introductory level computer book series and a best-selling business book series. They have written asking for more. So, if you're looking for the best and easiest way to learn about business and other general reference topics, look to *...For Dummies* to give you a helping hand.

TM

IDG BOOKS
WORLDWIDE

5/97

INVESTING FOR DUMMIES®

by Eric Tyson, M.B.A.

Financial Counselor, Syndicated Columnist, and
Author of five National Best-sellers, including
Personal Finance For Dummies® and
Mutual Funds For Dummies®

IDG BOOKS WORLDWIDE™

IDG Books Worldwide, Inc.
An International Data Group Company

Foster City, CA ♦ Chicago, IL ♦ Indianapolis, IN ♦ Southlake, TX

Investing For Dummies®

Published by
IDG Books Worldwide, Inc.
An International Data Group Company
919 E. Hillsdale Blvd.
Suite 400
Foster City, CA 94404
www.idgbooks.com (IDG Books Worldwide Web site)
www.dummies.com (Dummies Press Web site)

Library of Congress Catalog Card No.: 95-82349

ISBN: 1-56884-393-3

Printed in the United States of America

10 9 8 7

1B/RQ/RS/ZX/IN

Distributed in the United States by IDG Books Worldwide, Inc.

Distributed by Macmillan Canada for Canada; by Transworld Publishers Limited in the United Kingdom; by IDG Norge Books for Norway; by IDG Sweden Books for Sweden; by Woodslane Pty. Ltd. for Australia; by Woodslane Enterprises Ltd. for New Zealand; by Longman Singapore Publishers Ltd. for Singapore, Malaysia, Thailand, and Indonesia; by Simron Pty. Ltd. for South Africa; by Toppan Company Ltd. for Japan; by Distribuidora Cuspide for Argentina; by Livraria Cultura for Brazil; by Ediciencia S.A. for Ecuador; by Addison-Wesley Publishing Company for Korea; by Ediciones ZETA S.C.R. Ltda. for Peru; by WS Computer Publishing Corporation, Inc., for the Philippines; by Unalis Corporation for Taiwan; by Contemporanea de Ediciones for Venezuela; by Computer Book & Magazine Store for Puerto Rico; by Express Computer Distributors for the Caribbean and West Indies. Authorized Sales Agent: Anthony Rudkin Associates for the Middle East and North Africa.

For general information on IDG Books Worldwide's books in the U.S., please call our Consumer Customer Service department at 800-762-2974. For reseller information, including discounts and premium sales, please call our Reseller Customer Service department at 800-434-3422.

For information on where to purchase IDG Books Worldwide's books outside the U.S., please contact our International Sales department at 415-655-3200 or fax 415-655-3295.

For information on foreign language translations, please contact our Foreign & Subsidiary Rights department at 415-655-3021 or fax 415-655-3281.

For sales inquiries and special prices for bulk quantities, please contact our Sales department at 415-655-3200 or write to the address above.

For information on using IDG Books Worldwide's books in the classroom or for ordering examination copies, please contact our Educational Sales department at 800-434-2086 or fax 817-251-8174.

For press review copies, author interviews, or other publicity information, please contact our Public Relations department at 415-655-3000 or fax 415-655-3299.

For authorization to photocopy items for corporate, personal, or educational use, please contact Copyright Clearance Center, 222 Rosewood Drive, Danvers, MA 01923, or fax 508-750-4470.

 is a trademark under exclusive license to IDG Books Worldwide, Inc., from International Data Group, Inc.

About the Author

Eric Tyson, M.B.A.

Eric Tyson is a nationally recognized personal financial writer, lecturer, and advisor based in San Francisco, California. Through his work, he is dedicated to teaching people to manage their personal finances better and to successfully direct their own investments.

Eric is a former management consultant to businesses for which he helped improve operations and profitability. Before, during, and after this time of working crazy hours and traveling too much, he had the good sense to focus on financial matters.

He has been involved in the investing markets in many capacities for the past two decades. Eric first invested in mutual funds back in the mid-1970s, when he opened a mutual fund account at Fidelity. With the assistance of Dr. Martin Zweig, a now-famous investment market analyst, Eric won his high school's science fair in 1976 for a project on what influences the stock market. In addition to investing in securities over the past two decades, Eric has also successfully invested in real estate and started and managed his own business. He has counseled thousands of clients on a variety of investment quandaries and questions.

He earned a bachelor's degree in economics at Yale and an M.B.A. at the Stanford Graduate School of Business. Despite these impediments to lucid reasoning, he came to his senses and decided that life was too short to spend it working long hours and waiting in airports for the benefit of larger companies.

An accomplished freelance personal finance writer, Eric is the author of ...*For Dummies* best-sellers on Personal Finance and Mutual Funds and coauthor of Taxes, Home Buying and House Selling and is a syndicated columnist. His work has been featured and quoted in hundreds of national and local publications, including *Newsweek, Kiplinger's Personal Finance Magazine,* the *Los Angeles Times, Chicago Tribune, The Wall Street Journal,* and *Bottom Line/Personal,* and on NBC's *Today Show,* ABC, CNBC, PBS's *Nightly Business Report,* CNN, CBS national radio, Bloomberg Business Radio, National Public Radio, and Business Radio Network. He's also been a featured speaker at a White House conference on retirement planning.

To stay in tune with what real people care about and struggle with, Eric still maintains a financial counseling practice and is a lecturer of the Bay Area's (and perhaps the country's) most highly-attended money management course at the University of California, Berkeley.

ABOUT IDG BOOKS WORLDWIDE

Welcome to the world of IDG Books Worldwide.

IDG Books Worldwide, Inc., is a subsidiary of International Data Group, the world's largest publisher of computer-related information and the leading global provider of information services on information technology. IDG was founded more than 25 years ago and now employs more than 8,500 people worldwide. IDG publishes more than 275 computer publications in over 75 countries (see listing below). More than 60 million people read one or more IDG publications each month.

Launched in 1990, IDG Books Worldwide is today the #1 publisher of best-selling computer books in the United States. We are proud to have received eight awards from the Computer Press Association in recognition of editorial excellence and three from *Computer Currents'* First Annual Readers' Choice Awards. Our best-selling ...*For Dummies*® series has more than 30 million copies in print with translations in 30 languages. IDG Books Worldwide, through a joint venture with IDG's Hi-Tech Beijing, became the first U.S. publisher to publish a computer book in the People's Republic of China. In record time, IDG Books Worldwide has become the first choice for millions of readers around the world who want to learn how to better manage their businesses.

Our mission is simple: Every one of our books is designed to bring extra value and skill-building instructions to the reader. Our books are written by experts who understand and care about our readers. The knowledge base of our editorial staff comes from years of experience in publishing, education, and journalism — experience we use to produce books for the '90s. In short, we care about books, so we attract the best people. We devote special attention to details such as audience, interior design, use of icons, and illustrations. And because we use an efficient process of authoring, editing, and desktop publishing our books electronically, we can spend more time ensuring superior content and spend less time on the technicalities of making books.

You can count on our commitment to deliver high-quality books at competitive prices on topics you want to read about. At IDG Books Worldwide, we continue in the IDG tradition of delivering quality for more than 25 years. You'll find no better book on a subject than one from IDG Books Worldwide.

John Kilcullen
CEO
IDG Books Worldwide, Inc.

Steven Berkowitz
President and Publisher
IDG Books Worldwide, Inc.

Eighth Annual Computer Press Awards ➤ 1992

Ninth Annual Computer Press Awards ➤ 1993

Tenth Annual Computer Press Awards ➤ 1994

Eleventh Annual Computer Press Awards ➤ 1995

IDG Books Worldwide, Inc., is a subsidiary of International Data Group, the world's largest publisher of computer-related information and the leading global provider of information services on information technology. International Data Group publishes over 275 computer publications in over 75 countries. Sixty million people read one or more International Data Group publications each month. International Data Group's publications include: **ARGENTINA**: Buyer's Guide, Computerworld Argentina, PC World Argentina; **AUSTRALIA**: Australian Macworld, Australian PC World, Australian Reseller News, Computerworld, IT Casebook, Network World, Publish, Webmaster; **AUSTRIA**: Computerwelt Osterreich, Networks Austria, PC Tip Austria; **BANGLADESH**: PC World Bangladesh; **BELARUS**: PC World Belarus; **BELGIUM**: Data News; **BRAZIL**: Annuário de Informática, Computerworld, Connections, Macworld, PC Player, PC World, Publish, Reseller News, Supergamepower; **BULGARIA**: Computerworld Bulgaria, Network World Bulgaria, PC & MacWorld Bulgaria; **CANADA**: CIO Canada, Client/Server World, ComputerWorld Canada, InfoWorld Canada, NetworkWorld Canada, WebWorld; **CHILE**: Computerworld Chile, PC World Chile; **COLOMBIA**: Computerworld Colombia, PC World Colombia; **COSTA RICA**: PC World Centro America; **THE CZECH AND SLOVAK REPUBLICS**: Computerworld Czechoslovakia, Macworld Czech Republic, PC World Czechoslovakia; **DENMARK**: Communications World Danmark, Computerworld Danmark, Macworld Danmark, PC World Danmark, Techworld Denmark; **DOMINICAN REPUBLIC**: PC World Republica Dominicana; **ECUADOR**: PC World Ecuador; **EGYPT**: Computerworld Middle East, PC World Middle East; **EL SALVADOR**: PC World Centro America; **FINLAND**: MikroPC, Tietoverkko, Tietoviikko; **FRANCE**: Distributique, Hebdo, Info PC, Le Monde Informatique, Macworld, Reseaux & Telecoms, WebMaster France; **GERMANY**: Computer Partner, Computerwoche, Computerwoche Extra, Computerwoche FOCUS, Global Online, Macwelt, PC Welt; **GREECE**: Amiga Computing, GamePro Greece, Multimedia World; **GUATEMALA**: PC World Centro America; **HONDURAS**: PC World Centro America; **HONG KONG**: Computerworld Hong Kong, PC World Hong Kong, Publish in Asia; **HUNGARY**: ABCD CD-ROM, Computerworld Szamitastechnika, Internetto online Magazine, PC World Hungary, PC-X Magazin Hungary; **ICELAND**: Tolvuheimur PC World Island; **INDIA**: Information Communications World, Information Systems Computerworld, PC World India, Publish in Asia; **INDONESIA**: InfoKomputer PC World, Komputek Computerworld, Publish in Asia; **IRELAND**: ComputerScope, PC Live!; **ISRAEL**: Macworld Israel, People & Computers/Computerworld; **ITALY**: Computerworld Italia, Macworld Italia, Networking Italia, PC World Italia; **JAPAN**: DTP World, Macworld Japan, Nikkei Personal Computing, OS/2 World Japan, SunWorld Japan, Windows NT World, Windows World Japan; **KENYA**: PC World East African; **KOREA**: Hi-Tech Information, Macworld Korea, PC World Korea; **MACEDONIA**: PC World Macedonia; **MALAYSIA**: Computerworld Malaysia, PC World Malaysia, Publish in Asia; **MALTA**: PC World Malta; **MEXICO**: Computerworld Mexico, PC World Mexico; **MYANMAR**: PC World Myanmar; **NETHERLANDS**: Computer! Totaal, LAN Internetworking Magazine, LAN World Buyers Guide, Macworld Netherlands, Net, WebWereld; **NEW ZEALAND**: Absolute Beginners Guide and Plain & Simple Series, Computer Buyer, Computer Industry Directory, Computerworld New Zealand, MTB, Network World, PC World New Zealand; **NICARAGUA**: PC World Centro America; **NORWAY**: Computerworld Norge, CW Rapport, Datamagasinet, Financial Rapport, Kursguide Norge, Macworld Norge, Multimediaworld Norge, PC World Ekspress Norge, PC World Nettverk, PC World Norge, PC World ProduktGuide Norge; **PAKISTAN**: Computerworld Pakistan; **PANAMA**: PC World Panama; **PEOPLE'S REPUBLIC OF CHINA**: China Computer Users, China Computerworld, China InfoWorld, China Telecom World Weekly, Computer & Communication, Electronic Design China, Electronics Today, Electronics Weekly, Game Software, PC World China, Popular Computer Week, Software Weekly, Software World, Telecom World; **PERU**: Computerworld Peru, PC World Profesional Peru, PC World SoHo Peru; **PHILIPPINES**: Click!, Computerworld Philippines, PC World Philippines, Publish in Asia; **POLAND**: Computerworld Poland, Computerworld Special Report Poland, Cyber, Macworld Poland, Networld Poland, PC World Komputer; **PORTUGAL**: Cerebro/PC World, Computerworld/Correio Informático, Dealer World Portugal, Mac*In/PC*In Portugal, Multimedia World; **PUERTO RICO**: PC World Puerto Rico; **ROMANIA**: Computerworld Romania, PC World Romania, Telecom Romania; **RUSSIA**: Computerworld Russia, Mir PK, Publish, Seti; **SINGAPORE**: Computerworld Singapore, PC World Singapore, Publish in Asia; **SLOVENIA**: Monitor; **SOUTH AFRICA**: Computing SA, Network World SA, Software World SA; **SPAIN**: Communicaciones World España, Computerworld España, Dealer World España, Macworld España, PC World España; **SRI LANKA**: Infolink PC World; **SWEDEN**: CAP&Design, Computer Sweden, Corporate Computing Sweden, Internetworld Sweden, it.branschen, Macworld Sweden, MaxiData Sweden, MikroDatorn, Nätverk & Kommunikation, PC World Sweden, PCaktiv, Windows World Sweden; **SWITZERLAND**: Computerworld Schweiz, Macworld Schweiz, PCtip; **TAIWAN**: Computerworld Taiwan, Macworld Taiwan, NEW ViSiON/Publish, PC World Taiwan, Windows World Taiwan; **THAILAND**: Publish in Asia, Thai Computerworld; **TURKEY**: Computerworld Turkiye, Macworld Turkiye, Network World Turkiye, PC World Turkiye; **UKRAINE**: Computerworld Kiev, Multimedia World Ukraine, PC World Ukraine; **UNITED KINGDOM**: Acorn User UK, Amiga Action UK, Amiga Computing UK, Apple Talk UK, Computing, Macworld, Parents and Computers UK, PC Advisor, PC Home, PSX Pro, The Web; **UNITED STATES**: Cable in the Classroom, CIO Magazine, Computerworld, DOS World, Federal Computer Week, GamePro Magazine, InfoWorld, I-Way, Macworld, Network World, PC Games, PC World, Publish, Video Event, THE WEB Magazine, and WebMaster; online webzines: JavaWorld, NetscapeWorld, and SunWorld Online; **URUGUAY**: InfoWorld Uruguay; **VENEZUELA**: Computerworld Venezuela, PC World Venezuela; and **VIETNAM**: PC World Vietnam. 3/24/97

Dedication

Actually, before I get to the major thank yous, please allow me a *really* major thank you and dedication.

This book is hereby and irrevocably dedicated to my family and friends, as well as to my counseling clients and customers, who ultimately have taught me everything that I know about how to explain financial terms and strategies so that all of us may benefit.

Acknowledgments

Thanks to chief IDG Books honcho John Kilcullen for recruiting me into the fold and to Milissa Koloski and Kathy Welton for keeping me focused on writing needed books. Behind every good book (I trust, dear reader, you think that it is) is a great project editor — thank you, Mike Kelly, for your insights and attention to detail. Thanks also to Kelly Ewing for all her fine editing, to Gabriele Dahms and Andy Lewandowski for additional editorial and research help, and to Beth Jenkins, Sherry Gomoll, Kathie Schnorr, Gina Scott, Carla Radzikinas, and the rest of the fine folks in Production for making this book and all my charts and graphs look great! Thanks also to Stacy Collins, Kathy Day, and Maureen Watts for all their sound work behind the scenes, and to everyone else at IDG Books who contributed to getting this book done and done right.

And last but not least, a tip of my cap to the fine lot of technical reviewers who helped to ensure that I did not write something that wasn't quite right. These good folks included Ed Wholihan, McKinsey & Co. management consultant extraordinaire; Ken Fisher, investment manager and most informed stock market historian; Al Gobar, real estate investing guru; small business professor Pam Autrey of the University of Texas; and Dennis Ito, Bob Taylor, Madelyn O'Connell, and Marilyn Wilson from the worldwide tax and financial experts, KPMG Peat Marwick LLP. Thank you one and all!

Publisher's Acknowledgments

We're proud of this book; please register your comments through our IDG Books Worldwide Online Registration Form located at: http://my2cents.dummies.com.

Some of the people who helped bring this book to market include the following:

Acquisitions, Development, and Editorial

Project Editor: Michael Kelly

Media Development Manager: Joyce Pepple

Copy Editor: Kelly Ewing

Technical Editors: Pam Autrey, Ph.D., Kenneth L. Fisher, Alfred J. Gobar, Dennis Ito, Madelyn O'Connell, Robert Taylor, Ed Wholihan

Editorial Assistants: Constance Carlisle, Chris Collins, Ann Miller, Kevin Spencer

Production

Project Coordinator: Sherry Gomoll

Layout and Graphics: E. Shawn Aylsworth, Elizabeth Cárdenas-Nelson, Angela F. Hunckler, Todd Klemme, Jill Lyttle, Jane Martin, Carla Radzikinas, Anna Rohrer, Gina Scott, Deirdre Smith, Kate Snell

Proofreaders: Henry Lazarek, Christine Meloy Beck, Michelle Croninger, Gwenette Gaddis, Dwight Ramsey, Carl Saff, Robert Springer

Indexer: Anne Leach

General and Administrative

IDG Books Worldwide, Inc.: John Kilcullen, CEO; Steven Berkowitz, President and Publisher

IDG Books Technology Publishing: Brenda McLaughlin, Senior Vice President and Group Publisher

Dummies Technology Press and Dummies Editorial: Diane Graves Steele, Vice President and Associate Publisher; Mary Bednarek, Acquisitions and Product Development Director; Kristin A. Cocks, Editorial Director

Dummies Trade Press: Kathleen A. Welton, Vice President and Publisher; Kevin Thornton, Acquisitions Manager; Maureen F. Kelly, Editorial Coordinator

IDG Books Production for Dummies Press: Beth Jenkins, Production Director; Cindy L. Phipps, Manager of Project Coordination, Production Proofreading, and Indexing; Kathie S. Schutte, Supervisor of Page Layout; Shelley Lea, Supervisor of Graphics and Design; Debbie J. Gates, Production Systems Specialist; Robert Springer, Supervisor of Proofreading; Debbie Stailey, Special Projects Coordinator; Tony Augsburger, Supervisor of Reprints and Bluelines; Leslie Popplewell, Media Archive Coordinator

Dummies Packaging and Book Design: Patti Crane, Packaging Specialist; Lance Kayser, Packaging Assistant; Kavish + Kavish, Cover Design

♦

The publisher would like to give special thanks to Patrick J. McGovern, without whom this book would not have been possible.

♦

Contents at a Glance

Cartoons at a Glance

By Rich Tennant

page 156

page 358

page 396

page 54

page 77

page 209

page 375

page 346

page 7

page 293

Fax: 508-546-7747 • E-mail: the5wave@tiac.net

Table of Contents

. . . .

Introduction

• •

*1*f you've succeeded in accumulating some money to invest, congratulations! You've accomplished a feat that the majority of people in the world have not yet done. If you've decided to move to the next step — actually investing some of that money — congratulations again! You've come to the right place. *Investing For Dummies* is your one-stop investment reference and counselor, ready to prepare you for that sometimes thrilling, sometimes dangerous, and usually rewarding world of high — and not-so-high — finance.

In many parts of the "developing" world, life's basic necessities — food, clothing, shelter, and taxes — gobble up people's earnings. In "advanced" countries, such as the good old U.S.A., despite considerably higher incomes, most Americans save little, if any, money. We save less than 5 percent of our take-home income, while people in other industrialized countries, such as Japan, Germany, and Switzerland, save two to three times this amount!

Some Americans share the same struggle for basic necessities with people in developing nations. For many others, everything — eating out, new cars, hopping on an airplane for vacation — is a necessity. I've taken it upon myself in this book to help you recognize that investing — that is, putting your money to work for you — is a necessity, if you want to accomplish important personal and financial goals such as owning a home, starting your own business, helping your kids through college, retiring, and so on.

It has been said, and too often quoted, that the only certainties in life are death and taxes. To these two certainties I could add more, including being confused by and ignorant of investing. You may be tempted to look with anxiety-ridden eyes at those in the world around you who appear to be savvy when it comes to money and investing. I'd like to make two important points that are both factually correct and may help you feel better about yourself.

First, all of us start with the same level of financial knowledge — that is to say, with none! *No one* is born knowing this stuff! The only difference between those who know and those who don't is that those who know have invested their time and energy to learn. While it's true that financial learning begins in childhood, you've already blamed your parents for enough of your shortcomings. It's time to take charge of your own learning.

That brings me to my second point: Some of the people who you think are so smart or good at what they do are investing dummies. Consider Donald Trump, former sports stars Kareem Abdul-Jabbar and Bjorn Borg, and child actress sensation Shirley Temple. They all lost big money through bad investments and flawed investment strategies. They (and their advisors) did things that could have, and should have, been avoided. Trump borrowed too much and invested heavily in real estate in a small part of the country — in other words, he put too many eggs in one basket. Abdul-Jabbar got slam-dunked by limited partnerships, which you'll learn are ladened with outrageous sales commissions and ongoing fees. Shirley Temple's dad blew nearly the entire $3 million that she made tap dancing her way to fame in the movies. Borg was forced to file bankruptcy for the same reason Trump nearly did: He put too much money in one investment — clothing manufacturers — that headed south, an investing double-fault.

The Importance of Common Sense

With very few exceptions, the investing books that rocket onto bestseller lists are about how to make a fortune investing in individual stocks. These are usually written by a successful professional money manager or someone claiming to have developed a system to beat the system. Those who fall into the latter category often have another agenda, such as to sell you a newsletter or convince you to turn your investment dollars over to them to manage. As Nancy Reagan so eloquently put it, just say no. And don't waste your money on these books, either.

As for reading books about those who have publicly available and audited track records of success as investors — the Peter Lynches and Warren Buffetts of the investment world — we could perhaps learn something useful. Problem is, these folks don't write books that could help the rest of us. They're too busy engaged in other activities that are more lucrative and that they're better at. As for learning how to "beat the market" by reading such books, allow me to politely say, "It ain't gonna happen."

Although we may acknowledge and enjoy watching the extraordinary talent of Michael Jordan playing basketball, Bill Gates developing new computer technology, and Barbra Streisand or Bette Midler performing, let's not forget two important points. First, we could read 100 books about them and not develop their talents. Second, remember that each of these icons is supported by dozens and, in some cases, thousands of others for their successful performances.

There's no doubt that over long periods of time, investing in the stock market is a proven and sensible way to build wealth. However, when investing in the stock market, why waste your valuable time trying to learn second-, third-, or fourth-hand the strategies of the investment gods when you can hire them first-hand, at a low cost, through mutual funds? And why waste your time trying to select and manage a portfolio of individual stocks when you can replicate the market average returns (and beat the majority of professional money managers) through an exceptionally underrated and underused investment fund called index funds? Plus, you save yourself the heartache of disappointing returns.

As a financial counselor, I know from working with real live people of modest and immodest economic means that the typical best-selling investment books don't focus on the ways that these people build wealth. Quite simply, they increase their wealth by

✔ Living within their means and systematically saving and investing money, ideally in a tax-favored manner

✔ Buying and holding stocks, ideally through mutual funds

✔ Building their own small business or career

✔ Investing in real estate

That kind of investing is what this book is all about. I don't profess to be a guru, but I do have an eye for spotting, through firsthand experience, what works (and what doesn't) for ordinary, yet in many ways extraordinary, people like you!

Equally, if not more importantly, I help you understand and choose investments that fit with your personal and financial goals. Even if you can learn to beat the street, market, or whatever the heck they call the stock market, what good will it do you if you pay gobs more in taxes or don't realize your dreams?

How to Get the Most from This Book

Seriously, this stuff isn't rocket science. You see, I write this book hoping that you'll learn enough in these subject areas so that you won't need to hire people like me.

By all means, if you're dealing with a complicated, atypical issue, get competent professional help. But educate yourself first. As you'll learn from the mistakes that others have made, it's dangerous to hire someone if you yourself are financially challenged. If you do finally decide to hire someone, you'll be much better prepared by educating yourself, and you'll be more focused in your questions and better able to assess that person's competence.

This book will help to fill gaps in your investing knowledge. It is structured so that you can read it cover-to-cover, or you can dive into particular sections that most currently interest you. Here are the major parts:

Part I: Investing Fundamentals

Before you can confidently and intelligently choose investments, you need to be able to cut through the lingo and jargon and get to the heart of what invest-ments are and are not, and how they differ from one another. You'll learn about what rate of return you can reasonably expect to earn and how much risk you'll need to take to get it. You'll also clearly see how investments best fit into your overall financial aspirations and situation.

Part II: Stocks, Bonds, and Wall Street

I know that you probably don't want to trade in your day job for one where you'd need to wear a three-piece suit and need to know on what page of the daily *Wall Street Journal* you can find yield curves. But you *do* want to understand what the financial markets are and how you can participate in them without suffering too many abrasions and lacerations. You'll learn what stocks and bonds are all about and how to best buy them and build your fortune.

Part III: Real Estate

We all need places to live, work, and shop, so it makes sense that real estate can be a profitable part of your investment portfolio. Intelligently buying and managing real estate draws on many skills you may not have used in recent years. I'll show you what you need to know about the best ways to invest in real estate, and you'll get a crash course in mortgages, landlording, buying low and selling high, and taxes.

Part IV: Small Business

There's nothing small about the potential profits you can make from small business. The best news is that you can choose the way to invest in a small business that matches your skills and time. If you aspire to be the best boss you've ever had, you'll learn the right ways to start your own or buy someone else's small business. Or maybe you'd like to try your hand at spotting up-and-comers but don't want to be on the front lines — try investing in someone else's small business.

Part V: The Part of Tens

A staple of the *...For Dummies* books, these shorter chapters will build your investing knowledge further. You can learn about such topics as investing in collectibles and other odd investments, issues to consider when selling an investment, and resources to learn more about investing.

You'll also be pleased to know that this book has a super-useful index. If you're the kind of reader who jumps around from topic to topic rather than reading from cover to cover, you'll be pleased that the index highlights the page where an investing term is defined.

Icons Used in This Book

Throughout this book, icons help guide you through the maze of suggestions, solutions, and cautions. I hope you find that the following images make your journey through investment strategies smoother.

Denotes strategies that will enable you to build wealth faster and leap over tall obstacles in a single bound.

Indicates treacherous territory that has made mincemeat out of lesser mortals who have come before you. Skip this point at your own peril.

In the shark-infested investing waters, you'll find creatures who feast on novice waders, ready to take a bite out of a swimmer's savings. This icon notes when the sharks may be circling.

Companies, products, services, and resources that have proven to be exceptional over the years — in other words, resources I would or do use personally or would recommend to my friends and family.

Skip it or read it, the choice is yours. You'll fill your head with more stuff that may prove valuable as you expand your investing know-how, but you risk overdosing on stuff you may not need right away.

Demarcates an issue that requires more detective work on your part. Don't worry, I'll prepare you for your work so that you don't have to start out as a novice gumshoe.

I know this is something your parents always told you that promptly flew out your other ear, but this icon indicates something really, really important and don't you forget it!

Part I
Investing
Fundamentals

The 5th Wave   By Rich Tennant

"ANNUITIES? EQUITY INCOME? TAX-FREE MUNICIPALS? I SAY WE
STICK THE MONEY IN THE GROUND LIKE ALWAYS, AND THEN FEED
THIS GUY TO THE SHARKS."

In this part . . .

*L*ike a good map or aerial photograph, this part helps you see the big picture of the investment world. Here you discover the different types of investments, which investments are good and bad for a variety of different circumstances, and what return you can expect from various investments. And, as if that weren't enough, you also see how to make wise investing decisions that fit with your overall financial situation.

Chapter 1

Investments Defined

The first and only time that I met with George was at his home. He had written up his investments on a sheet of paper that had a faded look and smelled old. You'd probably best describe his home's furnishings as spartan. Probably from the years of family pets and children running around and on his living room couch, the stuffing was falling out of it. He owned a Philco television set, which I'm sure had a black-and-white picture, although I didn't see it on and didn't want to be nosy in asking. You'd never know that George was and still is a millionaire.

While I talked with George, the telephone rang, and after he said hello, he waited to find out who was calling with all the anticipation of a young child in line at an amusement park. Then his eyes really lit up as he realized it was his granddaughter, and she would soon be visiting.

George is a wealthy person in many ways. Nearly 80, he is in great health and appears to have lots of friends and family. He has enjoyed his career working in a manufacturing environment. George served his country in World War II and earned a Purple Heart.

Despite the fact that he never came close to earning a six-figure salary, he was able to retire at the age of 50. In addition to being with his close-knit family and friends, he spends his time on volunteer work and travel. Despite his significant financial wealth and his ability to save and invest wisely, George says of his money: "I know that I can't take it with me."

In his 20s and 30s, George worked overtime to come up with necessary cash to buy a couple of properties. He's owned real estate ever since. He also took about 10 percent of each paycheck and invested it into stocks.

George didn't have any advanced degrees in business or any other subject and hadn't even gone to college. He accumulated his wealth the old fashioned and best way, through hard work, savings, and common-sense investing.

George also didn't follow any gurus to divine the right time to sell or trade his investments. He did some homework, bought sound investments, and turned, so to speak, into an investing couch potato. "After all the time, trouble, and work to save up the money and then choose an investment, why would I want to sell it?" George asks. An excellent question that trigger-happy traders may ask themselves too late in life.

George's questions for me were whether his *portfolio* (his collection of investments) was properly balanced and what mutual funds he should invest in, given his tax situation. Upon hearing about my book, *Mutual Funds For Dummies* (IDG Books Worldwide), George agreed that meeting with me for advice once and then reading that book and a couple of others would make the best use of his time, money, and educational needs. You see, George was also smart enough to realize that consultants cost money and that you can learn a lot on your own if you get pointed in the right direction!

It's Not Brain Surgery

Not everyone views advisors the way that George does, largely, I think, because too many advisors try to perpetuate the need for their services. I'll never forget the lunch that I had several years ago with a tax attorney, Larry, whom I had heard on a local radio station. On the air, he seemed well-spoken and knowledgeable. He called himself "The People's Attorney." I wanted to learn more about tax attorneys and the world of radio, so I asked Larry to lunch.

After talking for a while, I asked Larry what he hoped to do with his work in the future and what his goals were. Without missing a beat, he said, "To make as much money as possible in as short a time as possible." He went on to explain that his practice didn't just focus on taxes, but he would "help" his clients with many other legal matters.

"The key, Eric," Larry said with an almost paternalistic tone in his voice, "is to work on anything that's an urgent matter. That way, the customer is willing to pay my hourly fee of $275."

Gulp!

Larry then offered me a proposition. If I directed all my clients' legal needs to him, he'd be happy to put me on a retainer — in other words, kick back money that he was earning from clients I was sending his way. We finished lunch and I went home with the beginnings of indigestion.

Over the next several weeks, I listened to Larry's radio show with fresh ears. I noticed a repeated and disturbing pattern. "The People's Attorney" was very, very short on specifics in response to callers' questions and often went out of his way to make things sound complicated.

One caller asked Larry about using a computer software program to create a will, to which Larry warned ominously, "Would you use a computer on yourself to perform brain surgery?! There are so many ways you can go wrong."

Well, preparing a will and making most investments aren't brain surgery, not even close. You can make intelligent, sound, wealth-building investing decisions using your common sense and some relatively simple strategies without obtaining input from advisors. Sadly, many advisors are out to maximize their profits — by keeping you in the dark and dependent on them — rather than your profits.

How Real People Build Wealth

Most books about investing and wealth building are about investing in individual stocks or "traditional vehicles" such as bank products and insurance. Despite the fact that the only people I know who have gotten wealthy lending money are bankers, some investing books devote many chapters to banks.

Then there are the scores of stock market books each year. More books have been written about how to get rich in the stock market than any other type of financial book. Few are worth reading. Many (too many, from my perspective) books are written by authors with an agenda (they want to manage your money or sell you a high-priced market-timing newsletter) other than to provide honest education and practical advice.

It has occurred to me in recent years, as the U.S. stock market continues to reach one record high after another, that some people are worried about investing their money in stocks with stock prices at such a seemingly high level. It seems as if these folks only know about bank accounts or U.S. stocks. Whether U.S. stock prices are too high is debatable and an issue I'll take up later in this book.

The stock market

The stock market is not a bad way to build wealth. That's what Thomas has done over the years. At the age of 75, he is the proud owner of a more than $1.2 million portfolio. Thomas had worked for 30 years as a pressman for a newspaper, from which he retired in his early 50s. When he retired he was making about $9,000 per year. "I never had a college education but always made sure to save and invest money each month and watch it grow," says Thomas.

No B.A.s, M.B.A.s, M.D.s, or Ph.D.s are required to make money in the stock market. If you can practice some simple lessons, such as making regular and systematic investments and investing in proven companies and funds while minimizing your investment expenses and taxes, you'll be a winner.

But I don't believe that you're going to be able to "beat the markets," and you're certainly not going to beat the best professional money managers at their own, full-time game. In this book, you'll learn time-proven, nongimmicky methods to make your money grow in the stock market and other financial markets. (I explain how in Part II.)

Real estate

Another method that people use to build wealth is to invest in real estate. Owning and managing real estate is like running a small business. You need to satisfy customers (tenants), manage your costs, keep an eye on the competition, and so on. Some methods of real estate investing are more time intensive than others, but many are proven ways to build wealth.

John, who works for a city government, and his wife, Linda, a computer analyst, have built $1.5 million in investment real estate *equity* (the difference between the property's market value and debts owed) over the past two decades. "Our parents owned rental property, and we could see what it could do for you by providing income and building wealth," says John. Investing in real estate also appealed to John and Linda because they didn't know anything about the stock market, so they wanted to stay away from it. The idea of *leverage* — making money with borrowed money — on the real estate also appealed to them.

John and Linda bought their first property, a duplex, in 1971, when their combined income was $20,000 per year. Every time they moved to a new home, they kept the prior one and converted it to a rental. Now in their mid-40s, John and Linda own seven pieces of investment real estate and are millionaires. "It's like a second retirement having several thousand in monthly income from the real estate," says John.

As with running your own business, John readily admits rental real estate is not without its hassles. "We haven't enjoyed getting calls in the middle of the night, although we have people who can help with this when we're not available. It's also a pain dealing with finding new tenants," he says.

Overall, John and Linda figure they've been well rewarded for their time spent and money invested. It's also allowed them to live in a nicer home than they otherwise could afford.

Ultimately, to make your money grow much faster than inflation and taxes, you must absolutely, positively do at least one thing: Take some risk. Any investment that has real growth potential also has shrinkage potential! You may not want to or have the stomach to take the risk. Don't despair; I discuss lower-risk investments in this book as well. You'll learn all about risks and returns in the next chapter.

Small business

I know people who have hit investing "home runs" by owning or buying a business. Unlike the stock market, most people work at running their business full-time, increasing their chances of doing something big financially with it. If you try investing in individual stocks, by contrast, you're likely to be working at it part-time and competing against professionals who do it practically around the clock. (Imagine you and your 20-handicap golf game going up against the likes of Greg Norman or Jack Nicklaus, and you have some idea of the disadvantage you start with.)

A decade ago, Calvin set out to develop a corporate publishing firm. Because he took the risk in starting the business and has been successful in slowly building it, today, in his early 40s, he enjoys a net worth in excess of $2 million and could retire if he wanted to.

Even more important to many business owners, and the reason that financially successful entrepreneurs such as Calvin don't call it quits once they've amassed a lot of cash, are the non-financial rewards — including the challenge and fulfillment of operating a successful business.

Sandra has worked on her own as an interior designer for 18 years. She worked in fashion previously, as a model and then as a retail store manager. Her first taste of interior design was redesigning rooms at a condominium project. "I knew when I did that first building and turned it into something wonderful and profitable that I loved doing this kind of work," says Sandra.

Today, Sandra's firm specializes in the restoration of landmark hotels, and her work has been written up in dozens of magazines. "The money is not of primary importance to me . . . my work is driven by a passion . . . but obviously it has to be profitable," she says. Sandra has also had the fun and enjoyment of designing hotels in many parts of the U.S. and overseas, including one in Japan.

Most small business owners (myself included) are quick to point out that the entrepreneurial life is not a walk through the rose garden. (Well, actually, it does have its share of thorns.) Emotionally and financially, entrepreneurship is sometimes a roller coaster. In addition to the financial rewards, however, small business owners can enjoy seeing the impact of their work and knowing that it made a difference. Calvin's and Sandra's firms combined have created 25 new jobs.

Not everyone needs to be sparked by a eureka-type idea to profit from small business. Other ways into this world include buying an existing business and investing in someone else's budding enterprise. I'll talk more about evaluating and buying a business later in the book so that you better your chances of investing in the next Starbucks, and not the next Café Sludge.

How the world's wealthiest got that way

Most people wouldn't mind being comfortably well off, but do you really need hundreds of millions of dollars, or a billion dollars, or more!? Odds are you won't have to answer that question. But if you want to build wealth, observing how the world's wealthiest have done it is enlightening.

Not surprisingly, the champions of wealth around the globe have done it largely through owning a piece (or all) of a successful company they (or others) have built. Take the case of Bill Gates, founder and chief executive officer of Microsoft — and college dropout. Microsoft is the world's largest producer of software that runs on personal computers. DOS and Windows, the two primary PC operating systems, and Word, which is the word-processing software that I'm using to write this book, are all Microsoft products.

Every time I, or millions of other people, buy a personal computer with one of these Microsoft packages, or simply go out and buy or upgrade a Microsoft software package, Microsoft makes more money. As the largest stockholder in the company, Gates, and other Microsoft shareholders, stand to make more as increasing sales and profits drive up the stock's price. Microsoft's profits and stock price have skyrocketed several thousand percent since the company first issued shares of stock in the company back in 1986.

In addition to their own businesses, the well-to-do have built their nest eggs and mansions by also investing in real estate and the stock market. And, of course, some people come into wealth the old-fashioned way: They inherit it. Even if your parents are among the rare ones, and you expect them to pass on big bucks to you, you need to learn how to invest your money intelligently. Investing as the big boys and girls do is a smart move as long as you understand and manage the risks.

The Major Players

The investment field is filled with a lot of jargon. There are literally tens of thousands of different investments. Unfortunately, for the novice, and even for experts who will be honest with you, the name of the investment or company is just the tip of the iceberg. Underneath each of these investments lurks a veritable mountain of details.

If you wanted to and had the ability, you could make a full-time endeavor out of analyzing financial statements, talking to the business's employees, customers, suppliers, and so on. That's why you must be realistic and selective about choosing your investment spots. If you're like most people, you have limited time on this here Earth.

I don't want to scare you off from investing just because some people do it on a full-time basis. Making wise investments need not take a lot of your time. If you know where to get high-quality information and purchase good, managed investments, you can do the things that you're best at and have more free time for other fun stuff.

An important part of the process of making wise investments is knowing when you know enough to do things well on your own versus when you should hire others to help you. For example, when investing in foreign stock markets, it makes far more sense to hire a good money manager, such as through a mutual fund, rather than going to all the time, trouble, and expense of trying to pick individual stocks on your own. Throughout the book, I'll explain when it may make sense to obtain advice or hire help.

So let's take a machete to all this high and dense foliage. I'll clear a path so that you can identify the major and important landmarks and what each of the investments are good for.

Ownership investments

If you want your money to grow and don't mind a bit of a roller-coaster-type ride from time to time in the value of your investments, ownership investments are for you. Stocks are an example of an ownership investment. Stock represents shares of ownership in a company.

If you'd like to share in the growth and profits of companies such as Microsoft, you can! You simply buy shares of their stock through a brokerage firm. As you'll discover in Chapter 6, however, just because Microsoft makes money in the future, there's no guarantee that the value of your stock will increase. It could decrease. But at least the next time you call Microsoft up and fork over $35 for technical support, you'll have some small satisfaction that you'll be indirectly profiting.

You can pick and choose which stocks you'd like to own and buy them through a broker. Some companies today even sell stock directly to investors, allowing you to bypass brokers altogether. You can also invest in stocks via a stock mutual fund, where a fund manager decides which stocks to buy.

Investing in real estate or running a small business also allows you to participate in the success and growth of the economy and in specific businesses or property. As opposed to buying stock through a brokerage firm or mutual funds, these ownership investments offer you more of a hands-on opportunity to manage something.

If you don't have lots of time, don't give up on these routes. You can invest in real estate that others manage or in other people's small businesses, where you may choose to participate little or not at all.

If you understand and are comfortable with the risks, and take sensible steps to diversify (don't put all your eggs in the same basket), ownership investments are the key to building wealth. In order to accomplish typical longer-term financial goals, such as retiring, the money that you save and invest will need to grow at a healthy clip. If you dump it all in bank accounts paying only a few percent per year in interest, you're likely to fall short of your goals.

Not everyone needs to make their money grow, of course. For example, suppose you inherit a significant sum and/or maintain a restrained standard of living and work your whole life simply because you enjoy doing so. It's possible that you may not need to take the risks to go for a potentially faster growth investment. You may be more comfortable with *safer* investments, such as paying off your mortgage faster than necessary. Chapter 3 helps you think through some of these issues.

Lending investments

The other major type of investments are those in which you lend your money. Suppose that like most people you keep some money in your local bank — most likely in a checking account but perhaps also in a savings account or certificate of deposit (CD). No matter what type of bank account you place your money in, you are lending your money to the bank.

How long and under what conditions you are lending your bank the money depends on the specific bank and account you are using. With a CD, you commit to lend your money to the bank for a specific length of time — perhaps six months. In return, the bank pays you a higher rate of interest than if you put your money in a bank account offering immediate access. (You may demand termination of the CD early; however, you will be penalized.)

As you later discover, bonds are another type of lending investment. When you purchase a bond that has been issued by the government or by a company, you agree to lend your money for a predetermined period of time and receive a particular rate of interest. A bond may pay you 6 percent interest over the next four years, for example.

Lending investments are all the same in that instead of directly sharing in the ownership of a company or other asset, such as real estate, you are lending your money to some organization that in turn is investing it. If you lend your money to Microsoft through buying one of its bonds that matures, say, in 10 years, and Microsoft quintuples in size over the next decade (or year, as the case may be), you won't share in its growth. Microsoft's stockholders and employees will reap the rewards of the company's success, but as a bond-holder, you won't.

Most people keep far too much of their money in lending investments where they are effectively allowing others to reap the rewards of the growth in our economy. Although lending investments appear safer because you know in advance what return you will receive, they aren't that safe. The long-term risk of these seemingly safe money investments is that your money will grow too slowly to enable you to accomplish your personal financial goals.

Cash equivalents

Cash equivalents are any investment that can quickly and without great cost be converted into cash. Of course, cash in your wallet qualifies. With most checking accounts, for example, you can write a check or withdraw cash by visiting a teller — either the live or the mechanical automated type.

Money market mutual funds are another type of cash equivalent. Investors, both large and small, have hundreds of billions of dollars in money market mutual funds because the best ones have higher yields than bank savings accounts. Why should you sacrifice 1, 2, 3, or 4 percent of "free" yield? The reason more than a few bank savers do sacrifice this yield is that they think money market funds are risky — they're not. Money market mutual funds generally invest in ultra-safe things such as short-term bank certificates of deposit, U.S. government-issued treasury bills, and commercial paper issued by the most creditworthy corporations.

The yield advantage of a money market fund almost always widens when interest rates increase because banks move about as fast as molasses on a cold winter day to raise savings account rates. When interest rates rose in 1988 and 1989, for example, the rates on money market funds followed, rising from

The double whammy of inflation and taxes

It's reassuring to many investors that bank accounts and bonds pay a decent return. Earning a few percent sure beats losing some or all of your money in a risky investment.

The problem is that money in a savings account, for example, that pays 3 percent, is not actually earning 3 percent on your money. It's not that the bank is lying — it's just that your investment bucket has some holes in it.

The first hole is taxes. When you earn interest, you must pay taxes on it (unless the money is invested inside a retirement account, in which case you pay taxes at a later date when you withdraw the money). If you're a moderate income earner, you'll end up losing about a third of your interest to taxes. Now your 3 percent return is down to 2 percent.

But the second hole in your investment bucket is even bigger than the first: inflation. While a few products become cheaper over time

(computers, for example), most goods and services increase in price. Inflation in the U.S. is running right around 3 percent per year. Inflation depresses the purchasing power of your investment's returns. If you subtract the 3 percent "cost" of inflation from the remaining 2 percent after payment of taxes, I'm sorry to say that you've actually *lost* 1 percent on your investment.

To recap: For every dollar you invested in the bank a year ago, despite the fact that the bank paid you 3 pennies of interest, you have to pay a penny of that in taxes, and you lost another 3 pennies to inflation, so you are left with only 99 cents of real purchasing power for every dollar you had a year ago. In other words, thanks to the inflation and tax holes in your investment bucket, you can buy *less* with your money now even though you've had it invested for a year (unless you're going out to purchase a computer).

around 6 percent to 9 percent. The average rate on bank savings accounts remained level during this period at around 5 percent. In 1994, as Yogi Berra once said, it was déjà vu all over again. When interest rates headed north again, money market fund yields increased from 3 percent to nearly 6 percent while bank savings accounts were stuck under 3 percent.

One reason people keep too much money in traditional bank accounts is that the local bank branch office makes the cash seem more accessible. Money market mutual funds, however, offer many quick ways to get your cash. You can write a check (most funds stipulate the check must be for at least $250) or call the fund and request that they mail or wire you money.

By all means, keep your checking account at the local bank so that you can write smaller checks to pay your cable television, phone, and utility bills. Having local access to an ATM for fast cash withdrawals is also a plus. But get that extra money that's snoozing away in your bank savings account, for example, into a higher-yielding money market mutual fund! Even if you have just a few thousand dollars, the extra yield will more than pay for the cost of this book. If you're in a high tax bracket, you can also use tax-free money market funds (see Chapters 7 and 8 to learn more about money market funds).

What Is Investing?

You have money and you put it some place — this is investing. If you put the money in your mattress, which some people did during the Great Depression in the U.S. in the early 1930s, you've chosen an investment that pays no interest and is subject to theft and fire! Why did people choose such an investment? Banks were failing, and the stock market fell out of bed. At the time, the mattress was a reasonable place to invest. (An even better place was in government-backed bonds that appreciated in value as inflation ebbed.)

Investing is a process of making choices. Whether your money is in the bank, a mattress, or a relative's business, you are the one ultimately responsible for deciding where it gets invested.

Some or even all of your money may be invested in things out of default or for reasons that are not in your current and long-term best interests. Perhaps you hold investments

- In a "parking place" until you figure out what to do with your money. Today, the equivalent of the mattress is a bank account. When most people receive money, it goes into the local bank account. There it may sit for years on end.

- Sold to you by a broker or financial advisor. Many people hold investments that they don't understand, and the investments may not be appropriate for their financial situation and goals. Perhaps you're already a student of the investing school of hard knocks and have lost money on poor investments ravaged by high commissions and fees.

- Based on your previous circumstances. While your situation may change slowly from year to year, it may differ greatly from where you were five or ten years ago. Maybe you bought investments that made sense for you when you were in a much lower tax bracket. Perhaps you have less time to track and monitor your holdings now and your investment holdings are time intensive.

- That you inherited. What made for a good investment for your parents, grandparents, and so on doesn't necessarily make sense for you. And who says what they held is a good investment? You can love the person and honor their memory, and still be analytical about the investments they left you.

Chapter 3 shows you how to choose and construct an investment portfolio that fits with your financial situation and goals.

Futures and options are not investments

Suppose you think that IBM's stock is a good investment. You're impressed with the direction that the management team is taking, and you like the new personal computers and other products and services the company is offering. Profits seem to be on a positive trend; everything's looking up.

You could go out and buy the stock — suppose it's currently trading at around $100 per share. If the price rises to $150 in the next six months, you've made yourself a 50 percent profit ($150-$100=$50) on your original $100 investment. (Of course, you'd have to pay some brokerage fees to buy and then sell the stock.)

But rather than buying the stock outright, you could buy what are known as *call options* on IBM. A call option gives you the right to call away shares of IBM under specified terms from the person selling you the call option. You might be able to purchase a call option that allows you to exercise your right to buy IBM at, say, $120 per share in the next six months. For this privilege, you might pay $3 per share.

If IBM's stock price skyrockets to, say, $150 in the next few months, the value of your options allowing you to buy the stock at $120 will be worth a lot — at least $30. You can then simply sell your options, which you bought for $3 in this example, at a huge profit — you've made a 10-times return (1,000 percent) on your money.

While this talk of fat profits sounds much more exciting than simply buying the stock directly and making far less money from a price increase, there are two big problems with options. First, if you hold the call option the full six months, and IBM's stock price goes nowhere or rises a little, the option will expire worthless, and you'll lose all — that is, 100 percent — of your investment. In fact, if IBM's stock is trading at $120 or less at the time the option expires, the option will be worthless.

Second, when you buy a call option, you're not investing in IBM as a long-term investment — a call option represents a short-term gamble (in this example, over the next six months) on IBM's stock price. IBM could expand its business and profits greatly in the years and decades ahead, yet the value of the call option hinges on the ups and downs of IBM's stock price over a very short period of time. If the stock market happens to dip in the next six months, IBM might get pulled down as well, despite the company's improving financial health.

To the individual, *futures* are a similar type of gambling instrument that deal mainly in commodities such as heating oil, corn, wheat, gold, silver, and pork bellies. Futures have a delivery date in the not-too-distant future. (Do you really want 5,000 bushels of wheat delivered to your home? Or worse yet, 5,000 pork bellies!) You also can place a small down payment — around 10 percent — toward the purchase, which greatly leverages your "investment." If prices fall, you'll need to put up more money to keep from having your position sold.

My advice: Don't gamble with futures and options. The only real use that you should (if ever) have for these *derivatives,* so called because their value is "derived" from the price of other securities, is to hedge. (That's what some companies use them for.) Suppose you hold a lot of a stock, for example, that has greatly appreciated, and you don't want to sell now because of the tax bite. Perhaps you'd like to postpone selling the stock until next year as you plan on not working in that year, or you expect the government to lower the tax rate on capital gains. You could buy what's called a *put option,* which increases in value when a stock's price falls. Thus, if the stock price does fall, the rising put option value offsets some of your losses. This way you can postpone selling without exposing yourself to the risk of a falling stock price.

The Underrated Keys to Investing Success

We live in a society that likes to build up gurus. I'm not going to argue that some people aren't more expert than others in what they do for a living. Clearly, in the world of investing, the most successful investors earn much better returns than the worst ones.

But what may surprise you is that by following some relatively simple rules, you can end up much closer to the top of the investing performance heap than the bottom. In fact, you can beat many of the full-time investing professionals. Here are some commonly overlooked keys to achieving your full investing potential.

Save

I know plenty of high-income earners, including more than a few who earn six figures annually, who have little to invest. I also know many people, such as Thomas and George whom you met earlier in the chapter, who built significant personal wealth despite having modest-paying jobs. The difference: the ability to save what you earn.

If you're not a high-income earner, it's tempting to think you can't save. Even if you are a high-income earner, you may think that you'll be better able to save more if you can bump up your income. Although this may be true, this way of thinking is a crutch. It justifies spending most of what you earn and saving little now. If you need help coming up with more money to invest, see my first book, *Personal Finance For Dummies* (IDG Books Worldwide).

Participate in the riskier stuff

Saving money is half the battle. The other half is making your money grow. Over long time periods, earning just a few percent more makes a big difference in the size of your nest egg. Earning inflation-beating returns is easy to do if you're willing to invest in stocks, real estate, and small businesses. Figure 1-1 shows you how much more money you'll have in 25 years if you can earn investment returns greater than the rate of inflation (which is currently running at 3 percent).

As you see in Chapter 2, ownership investments (stocks, real estate, and small business) have historically generated returns greater than the inflation rate by 6 percent or more, while lending investments (savings accounts and bonds) tend to be 0 to 2 percent above inflation.

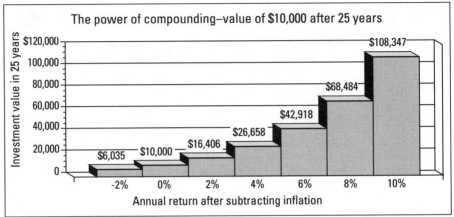

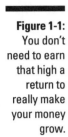

Figure 1-1:
You don't
need to earn
that high a
return to
really make
your money
grow.

Avoid high commissions and fees

You've probably heard the expression, "You get what you pay for." In the world of investing, more often than not, what you pay for is subtracted from and depresses your returns — and your spirits.

Many of the best investments can be had without paying sales commissions. Historically, if you've invested through banks or brokers that derive commissions from what they sell, you may not have realized that. Nor have the bankers or brokers been likely to help you realize that.

Don't panic

Battered, collapsed, plunging, pounded. Whenever the U.S. stock market drops more than a few percentage points in a short period, it attracts a lot of attention, which leads to concern, anxiety, and, in some cases, panic.

I remember when the Loma Prieta earthquake struck the San Francisco Bay Area, my home, in 1989. I had just left an office building in San Francisco's financial district when the ground started to shake, rattle, and roll. My first panicked thought as I looked at all of the glass-windowed skyscrapers towering over me was that I would be found buried under several feet of shattered glass. Although an unpleasant thought, it wasn't original. I had heard this scenario explained by others. Although the quake was scary, the only thing I lost that day was a bit of my courage — and a little more of my hair, I'm sure!

Immediately following the earthquake, some of my East Coast friends and family thought the entire Bay Area was in ruins, based on early TV coverage. Television news programs typically played a few minutes' worth of tape showing a collapsed freeway near the city of Oakland, several partially collapsed and fiery buildings in the Marina district of San Francisco, and a fallen portion of the upper deck of the Bay Bridge that connects the two cities. Over and over and over again, these segments were played.

Now I don't want to diminish the tragedy, loss of life, and damage done by this earthquake. However, watching these news programs throughout the week following the quake, you'd never have known that more than 99 percent of the Bay Area was just fine, except for people with shaken nerves and a few broken vases. Fewer people died as a result of the earthquake than die every day driving in cars on U.S. highways and streets.

When the financial markets suffer earthshaking events, some investors worry that their investments are in a shambles. As with earthquakes, the media is often to blame because of its hyping short-term events and blowing them out of proportion to entrance viewers and listeners. History has shown that financial markets recover; it's just a question of time. If you're in investments for the longer-term, then the last six weeks — or even last couple of years — is a short period. And a mountain of evidence and studies demonstrate that no one can predict the future, so there's little use in your trying to base your investment plans on your or others' predictions. In fact, you could lose more money by trying to time the markets.

A big danger that larger-than-normal market declines hold is that they may encourage decision-making based on emotion rather than logic. Just ask anyone who sold *after* the stock market collapsed in 1987 — the U.S. stock market dropped 35 percent in a matter of weeks in the fall of that year. Since then, it has more than tripled!

I remember following the daily gyrations of the stock market more than two decades ago when, as a high school student, I did a science fair project that attempted to discover what caused the market to fluctuate. My interest developed because my father, who had lost his job during the recession that began in 1973, found himself in the new position of investment manager of his own money. His former employer gave him a chunk of money that, at the time, represented virtually all of his long-term money for retirement.

Dad started trading individual securities through a broker and soon found himself in a rapidly dropping market. I'll never forget the day we drove to see the broker in person because the market, as measured by the Dow Jones Industrial Average, was down more than 20 points — which at that time was a lot because the Dow was around 700. To make a long story short, Dad sold out most of his stock holdings, with his broker's encouragement and blessing, pretty much near what turned out to be, in retrospect, one of the better buying opportunities of this century.

My dad, a self-educated mechanical engineer, is a smart man — I'm not just saying that because of his familial linkage to me. But he sold his stock for the wrong reasons. He didn't need the money at the time for some other purpose;

he sold out of fear of losing more. Stocks, like real estate, have historically been solid places to invest for long-term growth. They are not appropriate investments if you need to use your money in, say, the next five years or so.

Give up the guru search

Stock market declines, like earthquakes, bring all sorts of prognosticators, soothsayers, and self-anointed gurus out of the woodwork, particularly among those in the investment community with something to sell, such as newsletter writers. The words may vary but the underlying message does not: "If you had been following my sage advice, you'd be much better off now."

People spend far too much of their precious time and money in pursuit of a guru who can tell them when and what to buy and sell. Peter Lynch, the former manager of the Fidelity Magellan fund, amassed one of the best long-term stock market investing track records. His stock-picking ability allowed him to beat the market averages by just a few percent per year. He says you can't time the markets and acknowledges knowing many pundits who have been right "once in a row" in predicting the future course of the stock market.

According to the *Hulbert Financial Digest*, investment newsletters that attempt to time the market have largely underperformed the broad market averages, some by a wide margin. According to *Hulbert*, the *Granville Market Letter*, for example, would have lost 96 percent of your investment dollars had you followed its advice over the past ten years. The very few that have bettered the market averages have done so only by a meager 0.5 percent per year or so over the past decade. And *none* have beaten the national average over the past 15 years.

Don't believe everything you read or hear

Individuals in search of financial reporting used to have it much simpler. You could subscribe to publications such as *Kiplinger's* magazine for general money issues and a metropolitan newspaper for daily financial quotes. The hard-core, upscale investor got the *Wall Street Journal* daily.

Today's consumer of personal finance information faces overload. You can't pick up a newspaper or magazine or go channel surfing on cable or radio without bumping into articles, stories, segments, and entire programs devoted to personal finance issues. In just the past several years, three new money magazines have been launched: *Worth,* published by the mutual fund behemoth Fidelity, *SmartMoney* by the editorial staff of the *Wall Street Journal,* and *Bloomberg Personal Finance* by Bloomberg Business News, which is partly owned by Merrill Lynch. On the information superhighway, you can research and trade all sorts of securities and talk to other cyberspace users on topics ranging from asset allocation to zero-coupon bonds. The daily newspapers have made a big push to initiate and beef up their personal finance coverage.

Why is everybody and his brother in the media trying to help us with our money? Has money become that much more complicated, or are we becoming a money-obsessed society? And with all this financial information and advice around, how do you discern the good from the bad?

Many factors have caused the explosion in financial information and advice that the media is offering. Some are obvious. Global competition and rapid changes in technology are causing turmoil as most industries undergo dramatic changes in much shorter periods of time. Although jobs are plentiful for many with particular training and skills, fear of job loss and financial instability run high. Economic change and widespread cynicism about the ability of Social Security to provide a reasonable retirement income to baby boomers has caused many to seek financial planning help.

Ironically, the failure of the "financial planning" industry to meet the needs of those looking for help is one of the reasons why so many consumers seek financial information and advice elsewhere. "The high attraction to books and computer programs is because consumers are worried about planners' agendas," says Barbara Roper, director of investor protection at the non-profit Consumer Federation of America.

Roper was the author of CFA's report, *Financial Planning Abuses, A Growing Problem,* which documented that 85 percent of financial planners earn some or all of their income from commissions from products they sell. The small number of fee-based advisors primarily manage money for the affluent. "Financial planning for middle-income consumers still tends to be extremely sales driven, which creates a substantial conflict of interest," says Roper. And fee-based planners who also manage money have their own conflicts of interest. They have a bias against recommending strategies, such as paying off a mortgage or investing in real estate or a small business, that take money away from them to manage.

This inability to find objective financial help is all the more frustrating as individuals face increasingly complex choices. More employees are being forced to take responsibility for saving money for their retirement *and* deciding how to invest it. In the past, more employers offered pension plans. In these plans, the employer set aside money on behalf of employees and retained a pension manager to decide how to invest it. All employees had to do was learn what level of benefits they had earned and when they could begin drawing a monthly check. With today's plans, 401(k)s for example, employees need to be educated about how much they need to save and how to invest it. In addition to becoming a retirement planner and investment allocator, consumers face a dizzying number of financial products, such as mutual funds, that are marketed and distributed directly.

With the tremendous increase in the coverage of personal finance issues, more and more journalists are writing about increasingly technical issues. Some of the coverage provides good information and advice. Unfortunately, there is also some incorrect and wrong advice. The core of these problems is that many journalists are writing articles giving advice in areas that they themselves are not expert in. In many fields, such as medicine or the law, we wouldn't be so willing to take advice from nonexperts.

The short length of newspaper and magazine articles can easily lead writers to oversimplify complex issues. For example, many of the pieces on mutual funds focus mostly on a fund's returns and investment philosophies. Little, if any, space is devoted to the risks or tax consequences of investing in recommended funds.

Scores of articles horrify parents with the expected cost of a college education. The typical advice: Start saving and investing early so that you don't have to tell Junior that you can't afford to send him to college. Completely overlooked and ignored are the tax and financial aid consequences of the recommended investment strategies. For example, if parents don't take advantage of tax-deductible retirement accounts and save instead outside them, they not only pay more in taxes but they also qualify for less financial aid. Sound financial planning decisions require a holistic approach that acknowledges that people have limited money and must make these sorts of tradeoffs.

Consider the gaffe made by an article that ran in *Money* magazine in June 1987, a piece entitled, "Where to get safe, high yields." The title itself should have been a red flag: It's impossible to find a *safe,* high yield. To get high yields, by definition, you must be willing to accept more risk. In the *Money* article, three of the recommended investments were limited partnerships (LPs) sold through commission-based brokers. These products' high commissions and ongoing fees doomed even the luckiest of investors to mediocre or dismal investment returns.

The *Money* article even asserted that investors could earn returns as high as 18 percent per year on some LPs. Students of the financial markets know that the best ownership investments, such as stocks and real estate, return no more than 10 to 12 percent per year over the long haul. To expect more is to hold unrealistic expectations.

Marshall Loeb, former managing editor of *Money,* in his book, *Marshall Loeb's Money Guide,* written four years after the infamous *Money* piece, said, "For most investors who don't have the skill to do the necessary research, limited partnerships are just too risky." Although an improvement over the poor *Money* magazine advice of four years prior, Loeb still missed the mark. The point isn't risk. In fact, limited partnerships, like other bundled investments such as mutual funds, are only as risky as the component investments they hold. The major issue is cost. Even financially unsophisticated types would take a pass if they knew that broker-sold limited partnerships took 15 percent of their up-front investment for commissions and other start-up expenses, as well as 3 percent per year in operating fees. Another issue is lack of liquidity. LP investors typically don't have access to their money for 7 to 10 years.

The dangers of financial advice on the radio

Some of the worst financial advice you can obtain is brought to you, not surprisingly, for "free." Nationally, thousands of radio stations have financial and money talk shows. Because listeners don't pay for these shows, the ability to sell advertising time drives who and what gets on the air.

Some of these shows are "hosted" by an expert who is nothing more than a financial salesperson. The first, and sometimes only, motivation for wanting to do the show is to pick up clients. Consider that a broker who reels in just one big fish a month — a person with $300,000 to invest — can easily generate commissions totaling $15,000 by selling investments with a 5 percent commission.

But it can get worse than that, as evidenced by the case of Sonny Bloch, a New York radio "personality" who was indicted for fraud in 1995. The Securities and Exchange Commission has alleged that Bloch was receiving kickbacks from investment brokers for endorsing some pretty crummy investment products on his nationally syndicated radio show. The SEC also filed a complaint against Bloch for defrauding investors of millions of dollars to supposedly purchase some radio stations. Instead, according to the SEC, Bloch and his wife used hundreds of thousands of dollars to purchase a condominium. Partners in a precious metals firm, "DeAngelis Brothers Collectibles," that Bloch regularly endorsed on the air, were arrested for theft and ended up in bankruptcy. Again, Bloch was accused of receiving kickbacks.

I know from personal experience in the media what too many radio stations are looking for in the way of hosts of financial programs. The host's integrity, knowledge, and lack of conflict of interest don't matter. Willingness to work for next to nothing helps: One radio station program director told me that she liked the broker she had doing a financial talk show because the broker was willing to work for so little compensation from the radio station. Never mind the fact that the broker rarely gave useful advice and made the world of investing out to be so complicated that you needed a trusted advisor always by your side. The program director told me, "We're in the entertainment business."

Historically, one way that journalists have attempted to overcome this technical gap in their knowledge is to interview and quote financial experts. Although this may add to the accuracy and quality of a story, journalists who are themselves not experts sometimes have trouble discerning among the self-anointed experts. A classic example of this problem was the media exposure that author Charles Givens used to receive. In addition to appearing on *Oprah, Donahue,* and many other programs, Givens became a darling of the media and the public following unprecedented, consecutive three-day appearances on the NBC *Today Show.*

"When Charles Givens talks, everyone listens," said Jane Pauley, then cohost of the NBC *Today Show.* Bryant Gumbel, the other cohost, said of Givens, "Last time he was here, the studio came to a complete stop. . . . Everyone started taking notes, and I was asking for advice." Givens was regularly holding court on the talk show circuit with the likes of Larry King, Oprah Winfrey, and Phil Donahue.

The Givens case highlights some of the media's inability to distinguish between good and bad experts. In his books, it's relatively easy for the financially sophisticated to see the dangerous, oversimplified, and biased advice that Givens offers. In his first best-seller, *Wealth Without Risk,* Givens recommended investing in limited partnerships and provided a phone number and address of a firm, Delta Capital Corporation in Florida, through which to buy the partnerships. Those who bought these products ended up paying hefty sales commissions and owning investments worth half or less of their original value. Besides the problematic partnerships he recommended, court proceedings against Givens in a number of states have uncovered that he owned a major share of Delta Capital.

Other investing advice from Givens that gives cause to pause: In his chapters on investing, you're told that the average yearly return you'll earn investing in mutual funds will be 25 percent per year or 30 percent on discounted mortgages. The reality: An investor would have been fortunate to earn half of these inflated returns.

So how did Givens get on all of these national programs? A shrewd publicist combined with show producers who either didn't read his books and/or were themselves financially illiterate. Talk shows and many reporters often don't take the time to check out people like Givens. I know this for a fact because I've been on dozens of radio and television programs and understand how they work. Most of the time, the books are never read. Producers often decide to put someone on the air on the basis of a press kit.

In addition to not doing their homework on their sources, daily financial press reports tend to cause people to be shortsighted. If six-month charts weren't cause enough for investors to lose sight of the long-term, today it's not uncommon for daily newspaper charts that show the stock market's movements at 30-minute intervals throughout the previous day. This focus on the "noise of the day" causes nervous investors to make panicked, emotionally based decisions, such as selling *after* the stock market crashed in the fall of 1987.

So what's an otherwise intelligent person who wants to learn more but doesn't want to be overloaded with information to do? Educate yourself and be selective. If you're considering subscribing to financial publications, go to the library first and review some old issues. Was the information and advice useful and error-free? The more you learn, the better able you will be to separate the wheat from the chaff. Shy away from those that purport to be able to predict the future — few can and those who can are usually busy investing and managing money.

Read bylines and biographies and get to know writers' strengths and weaknesses. Ditto for the entire publication. Any writer or publisher can make mistakes. Some make many more than others — follow their advice at your own peril. Start by evaluating advice in the areas that you know the most about. For example, if you're interested in investing in Microsoft or Intel and are reasonably familiar with the computer industry, find out what the publications are saying about technology investments.

And remember that you're not going to outfox the financial markets because they are reasonably efficient. So spend your time seeking out information and advice that helps you to flesh out your goals and develop a plan with specific recommendations. I hope that you find one of my books to be one of those sources.

Chapter 2

Risks and Returns

- -

In This Chapter

▶ What are the risks?

▶ How can you reduce risk and still earn good returns?

▶ How much can you expect your investments to return?

▶ How much do you want or need your investments to return?

- -

*E*verywhere you turn there are risks; some are just more apparent than others. Risks are also misunderstood. For example, some people who fear flying don't understand statistically how much safer it is than driving to the airport. When a plane goes down, however, it's big news; dozens — and, in some cases, hundreds — of nice people, who probably weren't under the influence or engaging in otherwise reckless behavior, perish.

Meanwhile, the handful of people who die on the road in each of hundreds of towns and cities daily is less noticed. If you're a white-knuckle flyer, consider how much more dangerous your car or taxi ride to the airport is than your actual plane trip. Statistically, you are approximately 40 times more likely to die in a motor vehicle than in an airplane.

Then there are other more imponderable risks. A deadly virus such as Ebola could mutate and kill millions. A generation ago, the prospect of AIDS surely would have been an equally frightening prospect. In recent years, scientists have had increasing concern about a large asteroid or comet crashing into Earth. Staying indoors and not traveling to avoid a killer virus would appear extreme. When you figure out how to avoid the giant asteroid, let me know! Worry, worry, worry. I suppose if you had billions of dollars like Saddam Hussein, you could build an elaborate underground fortress.

Risks, Risks Everywhere

While some of us like to live life to its fullest and take "fun" risks — how else can you explain triathletes, mountain climbers, parachuters, and bungee jumpers — most people seek to minimize risk and maximize enjoyment in their lives. You would be mighty unhappy living a life that sought to eliminate risks, and you likely wouldn't succeed anyway.

A couple of silly examples illustrate. Every day, you speak with lots of people, many face to face. Every time you come near another human being, you risk getting sick from the "cloud" of germs that results from their breathing and speaking. If you wanted to minimize the risk of others infecting you with cold and flu viruses, you could walk around with a surgical mask over your mouth or only talk with others over the phone, through the mail, or on the Internet.

If you're like most people I know, you probably won't give up those in-person, one-on-one interactions — they're, well, more personal and fun. On the other hand, you're probably not going to go out of your way to get too close to someone with a fever and runny nose. (Hopefully, sick people are considerate enough to keep their distance.)

Another risk that most of us have to deal with in one form or another is the risk of losing our lives at the hands of another. Crime seems to be everywhere today. To preserve your life and reduce your risk of serious injury, you could barricade yourself inside your home and install a world-class alarm and camera-based external surveillance system. While a small number of people choose to (and can afford to) take these extreme measures, most people feel that this leads to a reduction in the quality of their lives. What about going outside occasionally to walk on the beach or gaze up at the stars or watch the sun set?

While you don't want to become a hermit, you don't want to subject yourself to big risks. Driving an expensive convertible with the top down through the crime-ridden part of town at 1 a.m. probably ranks as a not-so-smart risk to take. So too would be refusing to turn over your wallet to a criminal with a gun, yet people continue to do so, and some end up in the morgue.

Here's a real life example to show that risks can be more complicated and interactive. Consider the fact that some runners like their sport because of the cardiovascular and health benefits. Yet best-selling author Jim Fixx (his *The Complete Book of Running* got me hooked on running at a young age) dropped dead of a heart attack while running, at the young age of 52. While he appeared to understand some of the health benefits of running, his diet was another matter. In a chapter entitled, "Eating to Run: Good News if You Really Love Food," Fixx leads off by describing a meal he enjoyed before he had one of his best runs ever: "an enormous lunch: two hamburgers, French fries, and a milk shake." In addition to his artery-clogging diet, other risks that couldn't be controlled worked against Fixx. He had a family history of heart disease.

Now I'm not trying to depress you, but I am trying to make some important points. You can't live without taking risks. There is no such thing as risk-free activities or ways of living. You can minimize but never eliminate risks. Some methods of risk reduction aren't palatable because of the reduction in quality of life. Risks are also composed of several factors, as Fixx's case highlights.

In the world of investments, risks similarly abound. All investments carry risk. As with your day-to-day life, some risks are much more apparent than others.

The best way to reduce investment risk is to "buy" yourself some "insurance" via diversification. Diversification simply means that you place your investment dollars into various investments that perform differently under particular economic circumstances. Worriers may be the best at diversifying since they can easily conjure up calamities!

Market value risk

Let's start with some obvious risks. While the stock market can help you build wealth, most people recognize that it can plunge quite a bit — 10, 20, 30 percent or more in no time. If you invest $5,000 today, your investment may shrink to $4,000 or less. That doesn't feel good; it feels like risk — and it is. Your investment can shrink in value!

If you think the U.S. stock market crash that occurred in the fall of 1987 was a big one (the market plunged 36 percent in a matter of weeks), consider these massive plunges in the U.S. stock market over the past 100-plus years, listed in Table 2-1, which were all worse than the 1987 crash:

Table 2-1	Depressing U.S. Stock Market Declines
Period	*Size of Fall*
1929-1932	89% (ouch!)
1937-1942	52%
1906-1907	49%
1890-1896	47%
1919-1921	47%
1901-1903	46%
1973-1974	45%
1916-1917	40%

Real estate has exhibited similar annoying tendencies to be downright unruly. Although it generally has been a terrific long-term investment, various real estate markets have gotten clobbered from time to time.

U.S. housing prices took a tumble of nearly 25 percent from the late-1920s to the mid-1930s. When the oil industry collapsed in the Southeast in the early-1980s, real estate got clobbered. Later in the 1980s, the northeastern U.S. became mired in a severe recession, and real estate prices plummeted by 20 to 40 percent in many areas.

The West Coast continued to enjoy rapid economic growth in the late 1980s — some areas in Los Angeles, San Diego, and the San Francisco Bay Area witnessed housing appreciation of 50 percent or more just between 1987 and 1989. But the recession finally caught up with most of the left coast, particularly California, by 1990. From peak to trough, prices dropped 20 percent or more in most areas by 1995.

Then there's the Japanese real estate market crash that began around the time of the California market collapse. Property prices in Japan have fallen about 60 percent since the market's peak!

After reading this section, you may want to keep all your money in the bank — after all, at least you know you'll earn a few percent every year, and you won't have to be a non-stop worrier. No one you know has ever lost 20, 40, 60, or 80 percent of their bank-held investment in a few years.

However, if you pass up on the stock and real estate markets simply because of the potential risk, you miss out on a historic, time-tested method of building substantial wealth. I'll show you the generous returns these investments usually yield. The following sections suggest some simple things you can do to lower your investing risk and help prevent your portfolio from suffering a huge fall.

Diversify, diversify, diversify

Markets rarely crash all at the same time. For example, when the U.S. stock market crashed in the fall of 1987, many foreign stock markets dropped far less or not at all. So if you had spread your money across many different stock markets, your portfolio wouldn't have suffered nearly as much as if you had it all in U.S. stocks.

Investors who are concerned about the health of the U.S. economy, government, and dollar can reduce their investment risk by investing overseas. Most large U.S. companies do business overseas, so when you invest in U.S. stocks, you may get some international investment exposure there. You can also invest in international stocks, ideally via mutual funds.

Liquidity

The term *liquidity* simply refers to how long until, and at what cost, an investment can be converted into cash. The money in your wallet is considered perfectly liquid — it's already cash, and it costs you nothing to get it into cash.

Suppose you have money invested in a handful of stocks. While you can't easily sell these on a Saturday night, any day the financial markets are open (normal working days), you can sell most stocks quickly through a broker for around 1 to 2 percent of the total sales amount. You pay a higher percentage to sell if you use a high-cost broker or if you have little to sell.

Real estate generally is much less liquid than stock. It takes time to prepare property for sale, and if you want to get a property's fair market value, it may take weeks or months to find a buyer. Selling costs (agent commissions, fix-up expenses, and closing costs) can easily approach 10 percent of the home's value.

A privately-run small business is among the least liquid of the better investments you can make. Selling such a business typically takes longer than selling most real estate.

So that you won't be forced to sell one of your investments that you intend to hold for longer-term purposes, keep an emergency reserve of three to six months expenses in a money market account. Also consider investing some money in bonds, which pay higher than money market yields without the high risk or volatility that comes with the stock market.

Of course, investing overseas can't totally protect you. There's not much you can do about a global economic catastrophe. If you're going to worry about that risk, then you should probably be worried about that huge meteor crashing into Earth as well. Maybe there's a way to colonize outer space....

Diversifying your investments can involve more than just your stock portfolio, however. Likewise, you can diversify by holding some real estate investments. Some real estate markets actually appreciated in the late 1980s while the U.S. stock market was in the doghouse.

Check your time horizon

Investors worried that the stock market might take a dive and take their capital with them should first consider the time period they plan to stay invested. In a one-year time period in the stock and bond markets, anything can happen (see Figure 2-1). History has shown that once in every three years that you invest in the stock and bond markets, you will lose money — that's the bad news. But the good news is that you make money, sometimes substantial, two-thirds of the time.

While the stock market is more volatile in the short-term than the bond market, stock market investors earn far better long-term returns than do bond investors (see the "Stock returns" section later in this chapter). Remember, however, that bonds generally outperform keeping your money in a boring old bank account.

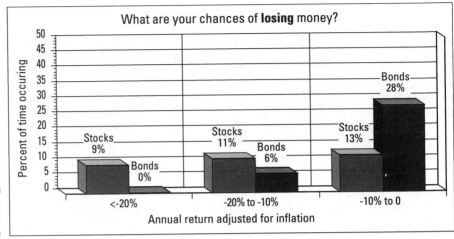

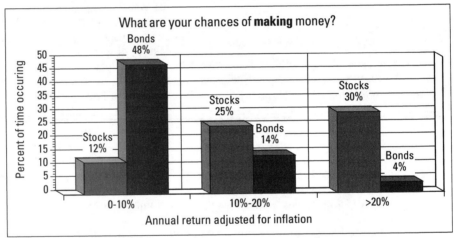

Figure 2-1:
What are
the odds of
making or
losing
money in
the U.S.
markets? In
a single
year,
anything
can happen,
but you win
far more
than you
lose (and
win bigger
with stocks).

The risk of a stock or bond market fall becomes less of a concern the longer the time period you plan to invest. In fact, over any 20-year time span, U.S. stock market investors have never lost money, even after subtracting for the effects of inflation (see Figure 2-2).

Pare down holdings in bloated markets

Perhaps you've heard the expression, "Buy low, sell high." While I don't believe that you can time the markets, that is, predict the most profitable time to buy and sell, it's not all that difficult to spot a greatly overpriced market. Throughout the book, I show you some simple yet powerful methods to measure whether a particular investment market is fairly valued, a good value, or overpriced.

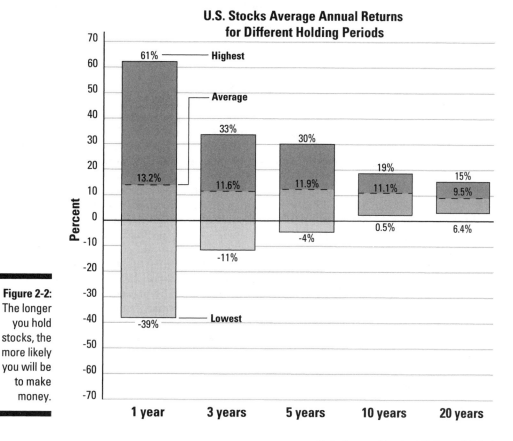

**U.S. Stocks Average Annual Returns
for Different Holding Periods**

Figure 2-2:
The longer
you hold
stocks, the
more likely
you will be
to make
money.

Data Source: Standard & Poors 500 index

You want to avoid overpriced investments for two important reasons. First, if and when these investments fall, they may fall farther and faster than investments more fairly priced. The second reason to avoid overpriced investments is that you can always find other investments that offer high potential returns.

Ideally, you want to avoid having a lot of your money in markets that appear overvalued. Practically speaking, this doesn't mean that you should try to sell all your holdings in that type of investment with the vain hope of buying them back at a much lower price. But you may benefit from the following strategies:

✔ **Focus investment of new money elsewhere.** As you save new investment money, put it into investments that offer better value. Thus, without selling any of your seemingly expensive investments, they become a smaller portion of your total holdings. If you hold investments outside tax-sheltered retirement accounts, this approach offers the benefit of allowing you to avoid incurring taxes from selling investments that have appreciated.

> ✔ If you need to raise money to live on, such as in retirement or for a major purchase, sell the expensive stuff. So long as the taxes aren't too onerous, it's better to sell high and lock in your profits.

Individual investment risk

Not only can a downdraft put an entire investment market on a roller-coaster ride but even healthy markets can produce losers. Since the early 1980s, the U.S. stock market has more than quintupled in value — one of the greatest bull markets in history. You'd never know it, though, looking at these losers.

Consider a company now called Navistar, which has undergone enormous transformations in the past two decades. This company used to be called International Harvester and manufactured farm equipment, trucks, and construction and other industrial equipment. Today, it mostly makes trucks.

As recently as late 1983, this company's stock traded at over $140 per share. Now a skeleton of its former self, it's hovering around $11 per share, as of this book's printing. That's more than a 90 percent drop in a little more than a decade. Lest you think that's a big drop, this company's stock traded as high as $455 per share in the early 1970s! Figure 2-3 shows that it's dropped 97 percent in the past two decades. If a worker retired from this company in the early 1970s with $200,000 invested in the company stock, the retiree's investment would be worth about $6,000 today!

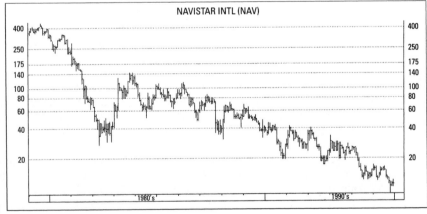

Figure 2-3: It hasn't been a bull market for every company.

Source: Telescan, Inc.

"Okay," you say, "I would have been smart enough to avoid sinking my money into a company that made farm equipment — heck, I knew we were in the industrial age and heading into the information and technology age! Any old idiot could have made money by following the right trends."

Consider this handful of mine fields in the computer industry alone. Cray Research is a global company that manufactures high-speed computer systems. A $10,000 investment in Cray in early 1987 would now be worth about $1,400.

Or how about Data General, a company that plays in the lucrative software industry, as well as the hardware part of the computer field? After trading as high as $76 in 1985, this stock fell off a cliff, plunging more than 95 percent to just $3 $1/2$ per share by 1990.

More than a few investors, large and small, rode the Digital Equipment roller coaster. Once considered a blue chip company, Digital Equipment's share value has been clobbered in the years since 1987. From a high of nearly $200 per share, it dropped nearly 91 percent in the next seven years.

Even "Big Blue," IBM, considered the corporate equivalent of the Rock of Gibraltar, has done poorly over the past decade. After climbing to a high of 175 $7/8$ in 1987, IBM plunged nearly 77 percent in just six years. (IBM paid a reasonably healthy dividend of about 4 percent over the years, but this too was cut and now is running at about 1 percent annually.)

Despite their price levels being determined more by overall market trends than what specifically happens with the property, individual real estate properties can also suffer. In California, for example, the prices of properties built on landfill were rocked by the earthquakes of recent years that highlighted the dangers of building on poor soil. So too in the early 1980s in the Times Beach, Missouri, and Love Canal, New York, communities, real estate values were beset by carcinogenic toxic waste contamination. Ultimately, many property owners in these areas were compensated for their losses by the federal government, as well as some real estate agencies that didn't disclose known contaminations.

Former residents of these communities that were evacuated for clean-up can take solace from the soothing words of syndicated radio show host and all around know-it-all Rush Limbaugh. In his book, *The Way Things Ought to Be,* Limbaugh says, "We closed down a whole town — Times Beach, MO — over the threat of dioxin. We now know there was no reason to do that. Dioxin at those levels isn't harmful. . . ." This is the same man who, according to the media watchdog group, Fairness and Accuracy in Reporting, made the following remark about global warming on his radio show in 1992: "Even if the polar icecaps melted, there would be no rise in ocean levels. . . . After all, if you have a glass of water with ice cubes in it, as the ice melts, it simply turns to liquid and the water level in the glass remains the same." Any student of science knows that the majority of our planet's ice is on land (ever hear of Antarctica, Rush?). If that ice melted, sea levels would rise by dozens of feet — a real catastrophe for many coastal communities. (In case you're wondering, I'm an independent voter.)

Not as easy as Peter Lynch likes us to believe

Maybe you like Peter Lynch's approach of only investing in companies that you can understand. For this reason, Lynch, the former manager of the famous Fidelity Magellan mutual fund, liked to invest in restaurant stocks. In his book, *Beating the Street*, Lynch reasoned, "If it's a choice between investing in the state-of-the-art computer chip and the state-of-the-art bagel, I'll take the bagel every time."

Lynch gushes with enthusiasm for restaurant chains and their stocks: "Every region of the country has been the incubator for one of these small town successes that went on to capture the stomachs and wallets of the country: Luby's, Ryan's, and Chili's in the Southwest...Shoney's and Cracker Barrel in the Deep South, Sizzler and Taco Bell in the Far West."

Students of the markets know that technology stocks have led the stock market boom of recent years. If you bought into Lynch's methods, you might also have been more than disappointed with his restaurant stock selections. Sizzler, for example, has fallen on hard times with the heightened competition in the restaurant business. From a high of 22 ½ in 1988, Sizzler has plunged almost 89 percent. Shoney's has never

fully recovered from the drubbing it took in the 1987 crash. After peaking over $33 per share in early 1987, its stock plunged under $7 per share within a year. It then bounced back to the $25 range before falling again to a low of $10 in 1995.

In his book, Lynch enthusiastically recommended Au Bon Pain, an East Coast chain of croissant and coffee shops. "Here you get...a ham-and-cheese-filled croissant for lunch, or a chocolate-filled croissant for lunch, all in less than three minutes."

And then a heart attack on Monday.

Besides suffering with a not easily remembered or pronounced name (unless you speak French), Au Bon Pain, like many other food chains, has been subject to intense competition. Coffee houses are springing up faster than weeds after a hot and thunderstorm-filled July. I'm not saying that this chain won't do well in the long term, but selecting good stocks isn't simple or safe. Since Lynch's book was written in early 1993, Au Bon Pain's stock has slid about 70 percent — from about $25 per share to its present $7 per share. And this during a period when the U.S. stock market rocketed ahead more than 100 percent.

The following sections suggest some simple things that you can do to lower the risk of individual investments upsetting you.

Due diligence

Some catastrophes can be avoided by doing your homework. When you purchase real estate, a whole host of inspections can save you from buying a pig in a poke. With stocks, examining some measures of value and the company's financial condition and business strategy can reduce your chances of buying into an overpriced company or one on the verge of major problems. You find out how to do your homework in Parts II, III, and IV of this book.

Diversify

Investors who seek growth invest in securities such as stocks. Placing significant amounts of your capital in one or a handful of securities is risky, particularly if they are in the same industry. To reduce this risk, purchase stocks in a variety of industries and companies within each industry.

Hire someone to do the investing for you

Increasing numbers of investors are turning to mutual funds, which offer professional management and oversight as well as diversification. Stock mutual funds typically own 25 or more securities in a variety of companies in different industries. You discover in Part III how you can invest in real estate in a similar way, that is, by leaving the driving to someone else.

Purchasing power risk

When Ethel retired at the age of 60 in 1980, she was more than satisfied with her retirement income. She was receiving an $800-per-month pension and $1,200 per month from money she had invested in long-term bonds. Her monthly expenditures amounted to about $1,500 so she was able to save a little money for an occasional trip.

Fast forward 15 years. She's still receiving $800 per month from her pension but now only $900 per month of investment income from some certificates of deposit. Ethel bailed out of bonds during the roller-coaster bond market of the early 1980s. Her monthly expenditures now come to about $2,400, and she has been using her investment principal at a good clip. She's terrified of outliving her money.

Ethel has reason to worry. She has 100 percent of her money invested without protection for increases in the cost of living. Although her income felt comfortable in the beginning of her retirement, it doesn't at age 75, and she could easily live another 15 or more years.

The erosion in the purchasing power of your investment dollars can, over longer time periods, be as bad as or worse than the effect of a major market crash. Table 2-2 shows the effective loss in purchasing power of your money at various rates of inflation and over differing time periods.

Table 2-2	Inflation's Corrosive Effect on Your Money's Purchasing Power			
Inflation rate	10 years	15 years	25 years	40 years
2%	-18%	-26%	-39%	-55%
4%	-32%	-44%	-62%	-81%
6%	-44%	-58%	-77%	-90%
8%	-54%	-68%	-85%	-95%
10%	-61%	-76%	-91%	-98%

Skittish investors may desire to keep all their money in bonds and money market accounts. The risk in this strategy is that your money will not grow enough over the years in order for you to accomplish your financial goals. In other words, the lower the return that you earn, the more you need to save to reach a goal. A 40-year-old seeking to accumulate $500,000 by age 65 would need to save $722 per month if she earns a 6 percent annual return but only needs to save $377 per month if she earns 10 percent per year. Younger investors should pay the most attention to the risk of generating low returns, but so too should younger senior citizens. At the age of 65, you should recognize that a portion of your assets may not be used for a decade or more from now.

Ironically, some people feel safe keeping much of their money in low yielding Treasury bonds issued by the U.S. federal government. Lending your money to the government has some patriotic value, but it certainly is not 100 percent risk-free. Remember that the federal government has nearly $5 trillion total debt outstanding, which is being added to at the rate of hundreds of billions of dollars per year. As budget debates highlight, there are no simple, acceptable solutions to stemming this problem. That's one of the reasons that the U.S. dollar has been pounded in foreign exchange markets over the past decade.

Hyperinflation

You think 6, 8, or 10 percent annual inflation rates are bad? How would you like to live in a country that experienced that rate of inflation in a day?! As you discover in Chapter 4, high rates of inflation are caused by too much money in circulation chasing after too few goods.

Excessive rates of inflation — dubbed *hyperinflation* — are usually caused by a government that has run amok with the nation's currency and money supply. Over the decades and centuries, hyperinflation has wreaked havoc in more than a few countries.

What happened in Germany in the late 1910s and early 1920s demonstrates how bad it can get. Consider that during this time period, prices increased nearly one billion-fold!!! You read that right — what cost 1 Reichsmark (that was the German currency in those days) at the beginning of this mess eventually cost nearly 1,000,000,000 Reichsmarks. People had to cart around so much currency at times that they needed shopping-type carts to haul it. Ultimately, this inflationary burden was too much for the German society, fueling the rise of the Nazi party and Adolf Hitler.

In just the past decade, a number of South American countries, such as Argentina, Bolivia, and Brazil, have gotten themselves into a hyperinflationary mess. In the mid-1980s, Bolivia's yearly inflation rate exceeded 10,000 percent. Argentina and Brazil have consistently had inflation rates of several hundred percent per year in recent years, as have Peru and Nicaragua. Other countries worldwide recently experiencing price increases annually in excess of 100 percent include Vietnam, Poland, and Ukraine.

Governments often try to slap on price controls to prevent runaway inflation (Richard Nixon did this in the U.S. in the 1970s), but the underground economy, known as the *black market,* usually prevails. Some have argued that the U.S. is in danger of a hyperinflationary spiral because of the burden of the U.S. federal government debt. Just since 1980, the federal government's outstanding debt has ballooned more than 500 percent from $914 billion to about $5 trillion (that's $5,000 billion). In recent years, the U.S. inflation rate has remained quite low — hovering around 3 percent — but the deficit problem has not changed.

Career risk

Your ability to earn money is likely your single biggest asset, or at least one of your biggest assets. Most people achieve what they do in the working world through education and hard work. By education, I'm not simply talking about what one learns in formal schooling. Education is a lifelong process. I've learned far more about business from my own front-line experiences and those of others than I've learned in educational settings. I also read a lot. Later in the book, I recommend books and other resources I've found most useful.

If you don't continually invest in your education, you risk losing your competitive edge. Your skills and perspectives can become dated and obsolete. That doesn't mean you should work 80 hours a week and never do anything fun. But it does mean that part of your "work" time should always involve updating and building on your skills. The best organizations are those that recognize this fact and invest in their workforce through training and career development. Just remember to look at your own career objectives, which may not be the same as your company's.

How Much Can You Make?

Most of us are greedy. The real Adam Smith called this the invisible hand; we tend to look out for ourselves before others. Why should it be any different with investments? Investors expect, indeed they demand, to earn a fair return on their investments. Since investors have lots of choices about where they can invest their money, if a particular type of investment doesn't appear to be offering a high enough rate of return, investors will put their money elsewhere.

In Chapter 5, you see that some investors invest their money with a rear view mirror — they chase after investments that have recently performed strongly, assuming and hoping the trend will continue. This is a dangerous proposition because it often leads investors into investments that have already had their run and may be peaking. Perhaps you've heard that the goal of investing is to buy low, sell high. Chasing investments that have performed very well recently can lead to buying high.

What is return?

When you invest money, the money that you invest is commonly referred to as *principal* (this has nothing to do with the quality lacking in disreputable financial advisors who sell inferior investments because it brings them hefty commissions, which is spelled p-r-i-n-c-i-p-**le**).

When you make investments, you have the potential to make money a variety of different ways. If you've ever had money in a bank account that pays *interest,* you know that the bank pays you a few percent in exchange for your allowing them to keep your money (which the bank turns around and lends to some other person or organization at a much higher rate of interest). The rate of interest is also known as *yield.* So if a bank tells you that its savings account pays 3.00 percent interest, the bank may also say that it is yielding 3.00 percent. Interest rates or yields are usually quoted on an annual basis.

If a bank pays interest monthly, for example, the bank will also likely quote a *compounded effective annual yield.* If the bank is paying you interest each month instead of once per year, that means that once the first month's interest is credited to your account, that *interest* starts earning interest as well. So the bank may say that the account pays 3.00 percent, which compounds to an effective annual yield of 3.04 percent.

When you lend your money directly to a company — which is what you're doing when you invest in a bond issued by a corporation — you also receive interest. Bonds, as well as stocks, which are shares of ownership in a company, fluctuate in value once they are issued.

When you invest in a company's stock, you hope that the stock increases in value, that is, appreciates. Of course, a stock can decline, or depreciate, in value. This change in market value is part of your return from a stock or bond investment:

$$\frac{\text{Current investment value} - \text{Original investment}}{\text{Original investment}} = \text{Appreciation or depreciation}$$

For example, if one year ago you invested $10,000 in a stock (you bought 1,000 shares at $10 per share) and the investment is now worth $10,500 (each share is worth $10 \frac{1}{2}$), your investment's appreciation is

$$\frac{\$10,500 - \$10,000}{\$10,000} = 5\%$$

But stocks can also pay *dividends,* which are a bit like the interest on a bank account. Dividends are the company's way of sharing some of its profits with you as a stockholder. Some companies, particularly those that are small or growing rapidly, choose to reinvest all of their profits back into the company. Of course, some companies don't turn a profit, so there's not much to pay out! These dividends should be factored into your return as well.

So suppose in the previous example that, in addition to the stock appreciating $500 to $10,500, it also paid you a dividend of $200 ($2 per share). Here's how to calculate your total return:

$$\frac{\text{Dividends} + \text{Current investment value} - \text{Original investment}}{\text{Original investment}} = \text{Total return}$$

Or, to apply it to the example

$$\frac{\$200 + \$10,500 - \$10,000}{\$10,000} = 7\%$$

Factoring in appreciation, dividends, interest, and so on, helps an investor calculate what's known as *total return*. This single figure tells you the grand total of what you made (or lost) on your investment.

After-tax returns

Well, you may be happy that your stock has given you a 7 percent return on your investment, but now I've got some bad news: Unless you held this investment inside a tax-sheltered retirement account, you'll owe tax on your return. Specifically, dividends and appreciation of investments that you sell are taxed.

If you're in a moderate tax bracket, these taxes probably run in the neighborhood of 35 percent (federal and state). So if your investment returns 7 percent before taxes, you'll be left with a return of 4.55 percent after taxes.

Often, people make investing decisions without considering the tax consequences of their moves. This is a big mistake. What good is making money if the government takes a lot of it away. In the next chapter, you learn how to make tax-wise investing decisions that fit with your overall personal financial situation.

Psychological returns

Profits and tax avoidance are powerful motivators in the choice of investments. However, as with other life decisions, there's more to the process than the bottom line. Some people want to have fun with their investments. Of course, they don't want to lose money or sacrifice a lot of potential returns. There are less expensive ways to have fun.

The psychological rewards are compelling reasons why some people choose to invest in individual stocks, real estate, or a small business. These investments are more tangible and, well, fun.

Be honest with yourself about why you're choosing the investments that you are. Allowing your ego to get in the way can be dangerous. Are you investing in individual stocks because you really believe that you can do better than the best full-time professional money managers? Chances are that you won't be able to beat the professionals, but there's nothing wrong with investing in stocks of your own choosing if you enjoy the activity for the fun of it. Do you like investing in real estate more because of the gratification of being able to drive by and show off your properties to others than because of its investment rewards? I know that these are not easy questions to answer, but they're worth considering, especially if seeking fun and gratification through your investments means lower returns.

Savings and money market account returns

Ideally, you should be keeping as little money as possible in your bank checking account, for the simple reason that your bank is likely paying you next to nothing (or actually nothing) in interest on this account. (Of course, your checking account should allow you unlimited check writing and ATM access to your money.)

You'll want to keep your extra cash awaiting investment (or an emergency) in a safe place, one that does not get hammered by the sea changes in the financial markets. However, there's no reason you shouldn't earn a healthier rate of return than the paltry amount of a bank checking account.

By default and for convenience, many people keep their extra cash in a bank savings account. While the bank offers the U.S. government's backing via the Federal Deposit Insurance Corporation (FDIC), it comes at a high price. As of this writing, many banks are paying a near microscopic 2 to 3 percent on their savings accounts.

A far better place to keep your liquid savings is in a money market mutual fund. As discussed in Chapter 1, these are the safest types of mutual funds around and, for all intents and purposes, are equivalent in safety to a bank savings account. However, the best money market funds pay higher yields than a bank savings account. Unlike a bank, a money market mutual fund will tell you how much they are skimming off for the cost of managing your money. If you're in a higher tax bracket, tax-free versions of money funds exist, as well.

If you don't need immediate access to your money, treasury bills or bank certificates of deposit are worth considering. Usually issued for terms such as 3, 6, or 12 months, you'll surely earn more in one of these than a bank savings account. The drawback is that you'll incur a penalty or fee to get your investment back before the term expires.

Bond returns

When you choose to lend your money to the federal government or corporations for longer periods of time, you buy a bond. When you buy a bond, you should expect to earn a higher yield or interest rate than you would on a money market or savings account. You're taking more risk, after all. Companies can and do go bankrupt, in which case you may lose some or all of your investment.

Generally, you can expect to earn a higher return when you buy bonds that are

- ✔ Longer-term
- ✔ Lower credit quality

Wharton School of Business professor Jeremy Siegel has tracked the performance of bonds and stocks all the way back to 1802 (most return data begins with the 1920s). Although you might say that what happened in the 19th century has little relevance to the financial markets and economy of today, the last seven decades of this century are a relatively small slice of time. The data is presented in Figure 2-4 so that if you'd like to give more credibility to the recent numbers, you may.

Note that, although the rate of inflation has increased since the Great Depression, bond returns have not. Long-term bonds have slightly higher returns in recent years than short-term bonds.

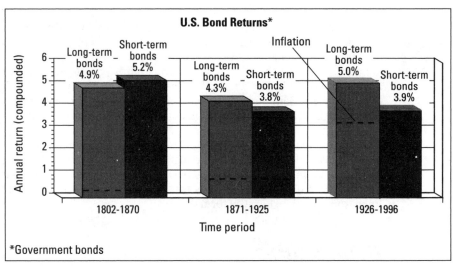

Figure 2-4:
A historical view of bond performance: Inflation has eroded bond returns more in the past seven decades.

Stock returns

A tremendous amount of data exists regarding stock market returns. In fact, in the U.S. markets, data going back nearly two full centuries documents the fact that stocks are a terrific long-term investment. The returns that investors have enjoyed from stocks have been remarkably constant from one generation to the next.

Going all the way back to 1802, the U.S. stock market has produced an annual return of 8.1 percent (compounded) while inflation has grown at 1.3 percent per year. Thus, after subtracting for inflation, stocks have appreciated 6.8 percent faster than the rate of inflation.

The U.S. stock market returns have consistently and substantially beaten the rate of inflation over the years (see Figure 2-5).

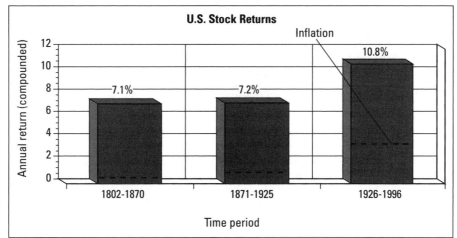

Figure 2-5:
History tells
us that
stocks are a
terrific
consistent
investment.

As you discover in more detail in Chapter 5, stocks are generally classified by the size of the company. Small company stocks are not stocks issued by physically small companies — they are simply stocks issued by companies that haven't reached the size of corporate behemoths such as IBM, AT&T, or Coca-Cola. The Standard & Poor's 500 index tracks the performance of 500 large company stocks in the U.S. The Russell 2000 index tracks the performance of 2,000 smaller company U.S. stocks.

Small company stocks have outperformed larger company stocks during the past seven decades. As measured by the Russell 2000, small company stocks have produced compounded annual returns of 12.5 percent versus 10.7 percent for the large company S&P 500 index. However, most of this extra performance is due to just one high-performance time period, from the mid-1970s to the early 1980s. If you eliminate this time period from the data, small stocks actually have under-performed larger company stocks.

Also, beware that small company stocks can get hammered in down markets. For example, during the Great Depression, small company stocks plunged more than 85 percent between 1929 and 1932 while the S&P 500 fell 64 percent. In 1937, small company stocks plummeted 58 percent; the S&P 500 fell 35 percent. And in 1969–1970, small company stocks fell 38 percent while the S&P 500 fell just 5 percent.

Stocks don't just exist in the U.S., of course (see Figure 2-6). More than a few U.S. investors seem to forget this. As discussed earlier in the chapter, one advantage of buying and holding overseas stocks is that they don't always fall when U.S. stocks drop. In other words, they help to diversify a portfolio.

In addition to diversification, investing overseas has proven profitable. The investment banking firm, Morgan Stanley, tracks the performance of stocks in both economically established countries and so-called emerging economies. As the name suggests, countries with emerging economies are "behind" economically but show promise of healthy rates of growth and progress.

For example, between 1986-1995 Morgan Stanley's EAFE (which stands for Europe, Australia, and Far East) index of foreign stocks appreciated at a rate of 17.9 percent per year. And emerging market stocks performed even better. This compares quite favorably with the U.S. stock market, which averaged 13.9 percent per year during this time period.

Countries have a lot in common with companies. Smaller ones can exhibit more explosive rates of growth. Once a company or country reaches a large scale, because of its sheer size, lower rates of growth are more common. Faster growing countries tend to have faster rising stock prices.

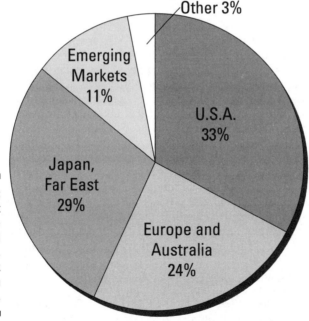

Total Value of Stocks Worldwide

Figure 2-6: Stocks exist around the world, and the U.S. stock market is in the minority.

In the years following World War II, the U.S. economy grew at a healthy clip —
output per person, after subtracting the effects of inflation, grew 2.2 percent per
year. Since the early 1970s, our growth rate has slowed substantially and in
recent years has been averaging just 1.2 percent annually.

Compare that rate to the growth rates over the past decade enjoyed by the
economies of these smaller countries:

Chile	6.1%
China	6.5%
Hong Kong	5.3%
Korea (South)	8.1%
Malaysia	5.7%
Singapore	6.1%
Thailand	8.4%

Source: World Bank

Real estate returns

Over the years, real estate has proven to be about as lucrative as investing in
the stock market. This fact makes sense because, ultimately, growth in the
economy, in jobs, and in population fuels the demand for real estate.

Consider what has happened to the U.S. population over the past two centuries.
In 1800, a mere 5 million people lived within our borders. In 1900, that figure
grew to 76.1 million, and today it's about 265 million. All these people need a
place to live, and so long as there are jobs to go around, the income from jobs is
largely what fuels the demand for housing.

Businesses and people have an annoying tendency to cluster in major cities and
suburban towns. Although some people are willing to commute, most people
and businesses locate near airports and major highways. Thus, real estate
prices in and near major metropolises and suburbs appreciate the most.
Consider the areas of the world that have the most expensive real estate prices:
Hong Kong, Tokyo, San Francisco, Los Angeles, New York, Boston. . . . What all
these areas have in common are lots of businesses and people and limited land.

Contrast these areas with the many rural parts of the U.S., such as in the
Midwest and South where real estate is a veritable bargain because of the
abundant supply of buildable land and relatively low demand for housing.

Investing in small private companies

Unlike the stock market, where lots of historic rate of return data exists, data on the success, or lack thereof, that investors have had with investing in privately held companies is harder to come by. Intuitively, investing in a small private company is riskier than investing in a large utility company. Thus, you would expect investors to demand a higher long-term rate of return from investing in smaller, riskier companies. Unlike a publicly traded stock you can sell quickly, private small company investments are also highly illiquid.

Smart venture capitalist firms operate a fun and lucrative business: They identify and invest money in smaller, start-up companies that they hope grow rapidly and eventually go public. Venture capitalists allow outsiders to invest with them via limited partnerships. To gain entry, you generally need $1 million to invest. I never said this was an equal opportunity investment club!

Venture capitalists, also known as general partners, typically skim off 20 percent of the profits and also charge limited partnership investors a hefty 2-3 percent annual fee on the amount they have invested. The return that's left over for the limited partnership investors isn't stupendous. According to Venture Economics, a firm that tracks limited partners returns, over the past ten years, venture funds have averaged annual returns of just 10 percent, almost exactly what stock market investors have earned on average this century. Over the last decade, U.S. stock market investors simply buying a Standard & Poor's 500 index fund earned 14.4 percent. You find out about the advantages of index funds in Chapter 8.

The general partners that run venture capital funds are, of course, making more than the limited partners. Estimates of the general partners' returns range from 17-18 percent to as high as 30 percent at the most successful firms.

You can attempt to do what the general partners do in venture capital firms and invest directly in small, private companies. You're quite likely to be investing in much smaller and simpler companies. Earning venture capitalist returns isn't easy to do. If you think you're up to the challenge, you find out about the best ways to do this in Chapter 14.

How Much Do You Need or Want to Earn?

This may seem like an extraordinarily stupid question to ask, but it's not! Few people *don't* want to earn a high return. But as you've discovered in this chapter, while investing in stocks, real estate, or small privately-held business can produce high, long-term returns, it is with greater, short-term risk.

Some people can't stomach the risk. Others are at a time in their lives when they can't afford to take great risk. If you're near or in retirement, your portfolio and nerves may not be able to wait a decade for your riskier investments to recover after a major stumble. Perhaps you have sufficient assets to accomplish your financial goals and are more concerned with preserving what you do have, rather than risking it to grow more. Most people don't have this problem.

If you work for a living, odds are you need and want to make your investments grow at a healthy clip. If your investments grow slowly, you may fall short of your goals of owning a home or retiring or changing careers.

The next chapter will help you with the important issue of making investing decisions that fit with your financial goals and situation.

Chapter 3
Investing Prerequisites

● ●

In This Chapter
▶ Investing in debt management
▶ Planning what you're going to do with your life
▶ Making more money by reducing your taxable income
▶ Insuring your valuables, and your kids' financial aid eligibility
▶ Learning about the big picture: asset allocation

● ●

*Y*ou want to know how to earn healthy returns on your investments without getting clobbered, right? Who doesn't? Although you generally must accept greater risk to have the potential for earning higher returns (see Chapter 2), I'm going to tell you about some free lunches in the world of investing.

I know you're itching to dive into making some double-digit return investments. But if I told you to get your financial house in order first, you'd say "Yuck!" and likely close the book. The truth is that rearranging your finances and learning some simple personal financial management concepts will pay off big for you in the decades ahead. You have a right to be skeptical about free lunches — but you're about to see that opportunities you likely have overlooked in managing your personal finances can be simple to access.

Establish an Emergency Reserve

Warren owned a home in which he lived and an investment property that he rented in the Pacific Northwest. He felt, and appeared to be, financially successful. But then Warren lost his job, a not uncommon occurrence given corporate America's downsizing mood, accumulated sizable medical expenses, and had to sell his investment property to come up with cash to tide himself over.

Like Warren, you never know what life will bring, so it makes good financial sense to have a liquid reserve of cash to meet unexpected expenses. You likely don't have to have tens of thousands of dollars languishing in a low interest bank account. If you have a sister who works on Wall Street as an investment banker or a loaded and understanding parent, they can be your emergency reserve. Ask them now how they feel about that.

If you don't have a financial safety net, you can end up selling an investment that you've worked hard for. Selling some investments costs big money in terms of transaction costs as well as taxes. Like Warren, you don't want to get forced out of a good investment. Warren never got around to purchasing another investment property and missed out on 300 percent-plus appreciation over two decades. Between the costs of selling and taxes, selling the investment property cost Warren about 10 percent of its sales price.

Make sure you have quick access to about six months' worth of living expenses. Keep this in a high-yielding money market fund (see Chapter 8). You may also be able to access cash quickly by borrowing against your employer-based retirement account or against your home equity. Warren didn't have enough equity in his home to borrow or other sources — a wealthy sister for example. That's why he was stuck selling his investment property.

Diminish Your Debts

Yes, it's boring to pay down debts, but doing so makes your investment decisions less difficult. Here you are spending all this time finding out about investing when, if you have debts, paying them off may be your best high-return, low-risk investment. Which debts it makes sense to pay off depends on the interest rate you are paying and on your investing alternatives.

Heave-ho the high-interest stuff

Many folks have credit-card or other consumer debt, such as auto loans, that costs 8, 9, or 10-plus percent per year in interest. Paying off this debt with your savings is like putting your money in an investment with a guaranteed *tax-free* return equal to the rate you pay on the debt.

For example, if you have credit-card debt outstanding at 15 percent interest, paying off that debt is the same as putting your money to work in an investment with a certain 15 percent tax-free annual return. Because the interest on consumer debt is not tax deductible, you actually need to earn more than 15 percent investing your money elsewhere in order to net 15 percent *after* paying taxes. It's highly unlikely that you will be able to earn such high investing returns, and in order to even have a chance, you'll be forced to take great risk.

Consumer debt is hazardous to your long-term financial health because it encourages you to borrow against your future earnings. I often hear people say, "I can't afford to buy most new cars for cash — look at how expensive they are!" That's true, new cars are expensive, so set your sights lower and buy a good used car that you can afford. Then invest the money you'd otherwise be paying on an auto loan into some good investments.

Borrowing via credit cards, auto loans, and the like is also one of the most expensive ways to borrow. Banks and other lenders charge higher interest rates for consumer debt than for debt for investments, such as real estate and business. The reason: Consumer loans are riskiest for a lender.

It may make sense to use consumer debt if you're financing a business. If you don't have home equity, personal loans through a credit card or auto loan may actually be your lowest-cost source of small business financing (see Chapter 13 for more details). Again, for it to be worthwhile, you must expect to earn a higher return than the interest costs.

Moderate your mortgage

Paying off your mortgage quicker may make sense, too. This financial move isn't as clear as paying off high-interest consumer debt because mortgage interest rates are generally lower and the interest is tax-deductible. When used properly, debt can help you accomplish your financial goals and make you more money in the long run. Borrowing to buy a home generally makes sense. Over the long-term, homes should appreciate in value.

If your financial situation has changed or improved since you first needed to borrow, you should reconsider how much mortgage debt you need or want. Even if your income hasn't escalated, or you don't inherit vast wealth, your frugality may allow you to pay down some of your debt sooner than the lender requires. Whether paying down debt sooner makes sense for you depends on a number of factors, including your other investment options and goals.

Financially, what matters in deciding whether to pay down your mortgage faster is your mortgage interest rate versus your investments' rates of return (which I define in Chapter 2). Suppose you have a fixed-rate mortgage at an interest rate of 8 percent. To come out ahead financially, if you're making investments instead of paying down your mortgage more quickly, your investments need to produce an average annual rate of return before taxes of 8 percent.

"But I don't want to give up those tax deductions"

While it's true that mortgage interest is usually tax-deductible, don't forget (because if you do, you're sure to end up in trouble with the IRS) that you must also pay taxes on investments held outside retirement accounts. You can purchase tax-free investments, such as municipal bonds (discussed in Chapter 7), but over the long haul, these investments won't earn a higher rate of return than the cost of the mortgage. Other types of lending investments, such as bank savings accounts, CDs, and other bonds, are highly unlikely to pay a high enough return either.

And don't assume that those mortgage interest deductions are that great. Just for being a living, breathing human being, you automatically qualify for the so-called standard deduction on your federal tax return. In 1997, this standard deduction was worth $4,150 for single filers and $6,900 for married people filing jointly. If you have no mortgage interest deductions — or less than you used to — you may not be missing out on as much of a write-off as you think. (Not to mention that joy of having one less schedule to complete on your tax return!)

If you're a high-income earner, you may not be able to fully deduct your mortgage interest on your tax returns. If your *adjusted gross income* (taxable income from all sources before subtracting itemized deductions and personal exemptions) exceeds $121,200 in 1997, you start to lose some of your mortgage interest deduction. You lose mortgage interest deductions by 3 percent times the amount that your adjusted gross income exceeds $121,200. You can lose up to 80 percent of your mortgage interest deduction, in fact. High-income couples are more likely to be affected by this provision, because the $121,200 threshold is the same for couples as it is for single filers. This rule is another part of the marriage penalty you've perhaps heard about.

Besides the most common reason of lacking the funds to do so, other good reasons to *not* pay off your mortgage any quicker include the following:

- ✔ **You're taking full advantage of contributing to retirement accounts, such as 401(k)s, IRAs, and Keoghs.** Paying off your mortgage faster has no tax benefit. Putting additional money into a tax-deductible retirement plan, however, can immediately reduce your federal and state income tax burden. The more years you have until retirement, the greater the benefit you get by investing in retirement accounts. Thanks to the compounding of your retirement account investments without the drain of taxes, you can actually earn a somewhat lower rate of return on your investments than you're paying on your mortgage and still come out ahead. (I discuss retirement accounts in detail later in this chapter.)

- ✔ **You're willing to invest in more growth-oriented, volatile investments, such as stocks and real estate.** In order for you to have a reasonable chance of earning more on your investments than it's costing you to borrow on a mortgage, you must be aggressive with your investments. As discussed in the previous chapter, stocks and real estate have produced annual average rates of return of about 8 to 10 percent. You can earn even more in your own small business or by investing in others' businesses.

Remember, you have no guarantee of earning these high returns in the future, and growth-type investments can easily drop 20 percent or more in value over a year or two.

Some investors like to leverage (borrowing to have more to invest) their investments. Paying down a mortgage ties up more of your capital, reducing your ability to make other attractive investments. To more aggressive investors, paying off the house seems downright boring — the financial equivalent of watching paint dry.

✔ **Paying down the mortgage depletes your emergency reserves.** Psychologically, some people feel uncomfortable paying off debt more quickly if it diminishes their savings and investments. You probably don't want to pay down debt if it depletes your financial safety cushion. Make sure that you have access — through a money market fund or other sources, a family member, for example — to six months' living expenses.

Finally, don't be tripped up by the misconception that somehow you'll be harmed more by a real estate market crash if you pay down your mortgage. Your home is worth what it's worth — its value has *nothing* to do with your debt load. Unless you're willing to walk away from your home — and send the keys to the bank, a.k.a. default — if real estate prices collapse, you suffer the full effect of a price decline, regardless of your mortgage size.

Set Your Financial Goals

Although you may be saving money only because it's what Mom and Dad told you was the right thing to do or because it makes you feel good, odds are that you're saving with some purpose in mind. Common financial goals include saving for retirement, a home purchase, starting your own business, and so on.

You may want to be saving and investing money for different purposes simultaneously. For example, when I was in my 20s, I was putting money away towards retirement, but I was also saving a stash so that I could hit the eject button from my job in management consulting. I knew that I wanted to pursue an entrepreneurial path and that in the early years of starting my own business, I couldn't count on as stable or as large an income as I had in consulting.

I invested the two "pots" of money — one for retirement, the other for my small business cushion — quite differently. As I discuss later in the chapter, you can afford to take more risk with money that you don't plan on using in the near term. So with my retirement money, I invested the bulk of it in stocks — actually stock mutual funds (explained in Chapter 8).

With the nest egg I was saving for the start-up of my small business, I took an entirely different tack. I had zero desire to put this money in risky stocks — what if the market plummeted just as I was ready to leave the security of my full-time job? Thus, I kept this money safely invested in a money market fund that paid a healthy rate of interest but didn't risk fluctuating in value.

Are your savings on track?

In order to accomplish your many financial and some personal goals, you need to save money. Yet many people haven't a clue what their *savings rate* is, that is, what percentage of their past year's income was saved and not spent. Maybe you already know that your rate of savings is low, nonexistent, or negative, and that you need to save much more. But part of being a smart investor involves figuring how much you should be saving to reach your goals.

You're better able to make the most of your money after you figure out how much you *should* be saving and set some goals. Now I should tell you that it's perfectly normal to not know what you want to be doing a decade or more from now. Besides, your goals and needs will evolve over the years. But that doesn't mean that you should just throw your hands up in the air and not make an effort to see where you stand today and think about where you'd like to be.

Another benefit of determining your savings rate is that you'll know better how much risk you need to take to accomplish your goals. Seeing the amount you need to save to achieve your dreams may encourage you to take more risk with your investments.

If you're consistently saving about 10 percent of your income during your working years, you're probably saving enough to meet your goals, unless you want to retire at a tender young age. On average, most people need about 75 percent of their preretirement income throughout retirement to maintain their standard of living. If you've never thought about your retirement goals, looked into what you can expect from Social Security, or calculated how much you should be saving for retirement, now's the time to do it. Pick up a copy of my first book, *Personal Finance For Dummies,* which goes through all the necessary details for retirement planning and a whole lot more.

Determine your investment likes and dislikes

You've got lots of good investing options — you can invest in real estate, the stock market, mutual funds, in your own business or someone else's, or you can pay down mortgage debt more quickly.

What makes sense for you depends on your goals, as well as your personal preferences. If you hate taking risks and detest volatile investments, paying down your mortgage, as recommended earlier in this chapter, may make better sense than investing in the stock market.

Boosting your savings rate

If you're one of the many people who isn't saving enough, you've got some homework to do. To save more, you need to reduce your spending, increase your income, or both. This isn't rocket science, but it's not easy to do.

For most people, reducing spending is the more feasible option. But where do you begin? First, figure out where your money's going. You may have some general idea, but you need to have facts. Get out your checkbook register, credit card bills, and any other documentation of your spending history and tally up how much you

spend on dining out, operating your car(s), paying your taxes, and everything else. After you have this information, you can begin to prioritize and make the necessary trade-offs to reduce your spending and increase your savings rate.

Earning more income may help boost your savings rate as well. Perhaps you can get a higher paying job or increase the number of hours you're willing to work. But if you're already working a lot, reining in your spending will be better for your emotional and economic well-being.

How would you deal with an investment that plunges 20 percent, 40 percent, or more in a few years or less? Some of the more aggressive investments discussed in this book can fall in a hurry. (I give many examples in Chapter 2.) You shouldn't go into the stock market, real estate, or a small business investment arena if such a drop is likely to cause you to sell low or make you a miserable wreck. If you haven't tried riskier investments yet, you may have to experiment a bit to see how you'll feel with your money in them.

A simple way to "mask" the risk of volatile investments is to diversify, that is, to put your money into different investments (see Chapter 2). Not watching prices too closely helps too — that's one of the reasons why real estate investors are less likely to bail out when the market declines. Stock market investors, unfortunately from my perspective, can get daily, even minute-by-minute price updates. Add in that with a quick phone call you can, in a flash, dump a stock, and you have all the ingredients for short-sighted investing.

Thou Shalt Fund Retirement Accounts

It's difficult for most people to save money. Don't make a tough job impossible by forsaking the terrific tax benefits that come from investing through retirement savings accounts. Contributions into these plans are generally federally and state tax-deductible. And once the money is invested inside these plans, the growth on your contributions is tax-sheltered as well.

The common mistake investors make is that they neglect to take advantage of these accounts in their enthusiasm to invest in "nonretirement" accounts. This can cost you hundreds, perhaps thousands, of dollars per year in lost tax savings. Add that loss up over the many years of working and saving, and, in the long-term, not taking advantage of these tax reduction accounts can easily cost you tens of thousands to hundreds of thousands of dollars. Ouch!

Don't miss those tax benefits

Taking advantage of saving and investing in tax-deductible retirement accounts should probably be your number one personal financial priority (unless you're still paying off high-interest consumer debt on credit cards or auto loans).

Retirement accounts should be called tax-reduction accounts — if they were called that, people might be more jazzed about contributing to them. Here's why. Suppose that you are paying about 35 percent between federal and state income taxes on your last dollars of income (see discussion later in the chapter to determine your tax bracket). For most of the retirement accounts described in this chapter, for every $1,000 you contribute, you save yourself about $350 in taxes in the year that you make the contribution.

Once money is in a retirement account, any interest, dividends, and appreciation grow inside the account without being taxed. You defer taxes on all the accumulating gains and profits until you withdraw the money down the road, which you can do without penalty after age 59 ¹/₂. In the meantime, more money is working for you, rather than the government, over a long period of time.

One of the "drawbacks" of investing heavily in real estate or small business is that this investing generally is done outside retirement accounts. Many people have made good money focusing on real estate and small business — just ask Bill Gates or Ross Perot if they have any regrets about focusing on their own businesses. Lesser mortals should be careful to not put too many of their investing eggs in non-retirement account baskets. Of the money you don't earmark for real estate or a small business investment, it's best to invest all that you can inside retirement accounts.

The longer you wait, the more painful it is

In order to take advantage of the tax savings that come with retirement savings plans, you must first spend less than you earn. Only then can you afford to contribute to these plans (unless you happen to have a stash of cash already from previous savings or inheritance).

The mistake people at all income levels make with retirement accounts is not taking advantage of them at a younger age. The sooner you start to save, the less painful it is each year to save enough to reach your goals because your contributions have more years to compound.

Each decade you delay approximately doubles the percentage of your earnings you should save to meet your goals. For example, if saving 5 percent per year in your early 20s gets you to your retirement goal, waiting until your 30s may mean socking away 10 percent, waiting until your 40s, 20 percent, and beyond that, the numbers get truly daunting.

If you enjoy spending money and living for today, that should motivate you to start saving sooner. The longer you wait to save, the more you ultimately need to save and therefore, the less you can spend today.

Governments are lousy investment managers

House Speaker Newt Gingrich and Congressional Republicans are wimps. For that matter, so are Democrats, who have been reluctant to touch the sacred cow of government programs: Social Security. In 1995, Gingrich and the Republicans touted their "Contract with America," which was supposed to get programs out of the government's hands. Yet this contract completely ignored Social Security, the second biggest component, nearly one-third of the federal government budget, that can be privatized.

By some projections, today's baby boomers will net an effective 1 percent annual return on the money they have paid into the system. For some, the rate of return will actually be negative. These are horrendous returns compared with the 10 percent return that the stock market has rewarded investors with this century, or even boring old bonds at 5 percent.

Regardless of your political orientation, it doesn't make sense for the federal government to be in the business of managing our retirement nest eggs because such an approach fails the common sense test. If you were leaving a job where you had some money in a retirement savings plan that you needed to roll over or you simply wanted to establish your own retirement investment plan, you would likely consider investing with the leading mutual fund companies, such as Vanguard, Fidelity, or T. Rowe Price. Why? Because of their experience and success with managing hundreds of billions of dollars of other people's and organizations' money. Would you ask our federal government, which has a total deficit outstanding of nearly $5 trillion and an annual shortfall approaching $300 billion, to manage your retirement money?! Social Security needs to be fixed before it allows the government to further live beyond its means. The federal government already owes the Social Security trust fund $400 billion. (Other countries have made the same mistake with systems similar to the U.S. Social Security system.)

While politicians have their heads stuck in the sand, the rest of us don't. Seventy-four percent of working Americans believe that the Social Security system is poorly managed, and of those, 79 percent believe that they can do a better job investing the money. If people really understood how poor the return is, these figures would be closer to 100 percent.

Social Security was conceived to fill a void. Congress passed the Social Security Act in 1935 to, among other things, ensure that older Americans have sufficient income for basic necessities, such as food, shelter, and clothing. The beauty of the system was that it was forced savings.

A privatized Social Security-type system would work as follows. First, the best aspect of Social Security — forced savings — would remain.

(continued)

(continued)

Future "forced retirement" contributions would go into approved investment management funds — mutual funds are an ideal vehicle. This raises the potential problem of some people investing their money poorly and not having enough or any money in retirement. Chile, a country that has successfully instituted a privatized Social Security-type system, dealt with this problem the same way company-provided 401(k) type retirement savings plans do. In Chile, workers must put away their forced savings of approximately 12 percent of salary into one of two dozen government-approved diversified investment funds.

Interestingly and somewhat depressingly, Chile's system was developed by professors at — you guessed it — American universities.

In order for an overhaul of the Social Security system to receive public support, all Americans would need to be assured that they would still receive Social Security benefits based on their previous contributions into that system. In other words, those already retired would continue to receive their promised benefits, those who have worked 20 years and are halfway to retirement age would receive half of the full expected benefit, and so on.

Retirement account investing options

If you earn employment income (or receive alimony), you have option(s) for putting money away in a retirement account that compounds without taxation until you withdraw the money. In most cases, your contributions into retirement accounts are tax-deductible.

If you work for a for-profit company, you may have access to a *401(k)* plan, which typically allows you to save up to $9,500 per year (for tax year 1997). Many nonprofit organizations offer *403(b)* plans to their employees. As with a 401(k), your contributions to these plans are federal and state tax-deductible in the year that they are made. The 403(b) plans often are referred to as *tax-sheltered annuities,* the name for insurance-company investments that satisfy the requirements for 403(b) plans. Nonprofit employees are generally allowed to contribute up to 20 percent or $9,500 of their salaries, whichever is less.

If you're self-employed, you can establish your own retirement savings plans. *Simplified employee pension individual retirement account (SEP-IRA)* plans allow you to sock away about 13 percent (13.04 percent, to be exact) of your self-employment income (business revenue minus expenses), up to an annual maximum of $24,000 (for tax year 1997). Each year, *you* decide the amount you want to contribute — no minimums exist.

Keogh plans are another retirement savings option for the self-employed. Keogh plans require a bit more paperwork to set up and administer than SEP-IRAs. The appeal of certain types of Keoghs is that they allow you to put away a greater percentage (20 percent) of your *self-employment income* (revenue less your expenses), up to a maximum of $30,000 per year.

Unlike SEP-IRAs, Keogh plans allow *vesting schedules,* which require employees to remain with the company a number of years before they earn the right to their retirement account balances. (If you're an employee in a small business, you *cannot* establish your own SEP-IRA or Keogh — that's up to your employer.)

If an employee leaves prior to being fully vested, the unvested balance reverts to the remaining plan participants. Keogh plans also allow for Social Security integration, which effectively allows those in the company who are high-income earners (usually the owners) to receive larger percentage contributions for their accounts than the less highly compensated employees. The logic behind this idea is that Social Security taxes and benefits top out after you earn $65,400 (for tax year 1997). Social Security integration allows higher-income earners to make up for this ceiling.

Please be advised, because I am now so doing, that with all types of self-employed retirement plans, employees need to be covered as well. As the owner of a small business, don't be deterred from keeping such a plan because employees may receive contributions as well. If you take the time to educate employees about the value and importance of using these plans to save for the future and reduce taxes, they'll see it rightfully as part of their total compensation package. In addition to the vesting schedules and Social Security discussed earlier in this chapter, many plans allow you to exclude employees from receiving contributions until they've completed a year or two of service.

If you work for a company that does not offer a retirement savings plan or if you've exhausted contributing to your company's plan, consider funding an *individual retirement account (IRA).* Anyone with employment (or alimony) income may contribute up to $2,000 each year to an IRA, or the amount of your employment or alimony income if it's less than $2,000 in a year. If you are a nonworking spouse, you're eligible to put up to $2,000 per year into a spousal IRA.

Your contributions to an IRA may or may not be tax-deductible. For tax year 1997, if you're single and your adjusted gross income is $25,000 or less for the year, you can deduct your IRA contribution. If you're married and file your taxes jointly, you're entitled to a full IRA deduction if your AGI (adjusted gross income) is $40,000 per year or less. In 1998, these income limits bump up to $30,000 and $50,000 respectively.

If you can't deduct your contribution to a standard IRA account, consider making a contribution to a new type of non-deductible IRA account called the Roth IRA (or IRA Plus). Single taxpayers with an AGI less than $95,000 and joint filers with an AGI less than $150,000 can contribute up to $2,000 per year to a Roth IRA. Although the contribution is not deductible, earnings inside the account are shielded from tax, and, unlike a standard IRA, qualified withdrawals from the account are free from income tax.

Retirement accounts are just a shell

When you establish a retirement account, you may not realize that the retirement account is simply a shell or shield that keeps the federal, state, and local governments from taxing your investment earnings each year. You still must choose what investments you want to hold inside this retirement account shell.

You may invest your IRA or other self-employed plan retirement account (SEP-IRAs, Keoghs) money into stocks, bonds, mutual funds, and even bank accounts. Mutual funds are an ideal choice, as they offer diversification and professional management (see Chapter 8).

Consider a nondeductible IRA only *after* you have exhausted the possibilities of contributing to retirement accounts that do provide an immediate tax deduction, such as 401(k)s, SEP-IRAs, Keoghs, and so on.

If you've exhausted contributing to IRA accounts and still want to put away more money into retirement accounts, consider *annuities,* which are contracts that are backed by insurance companies. If you, the *annuity holder* (investor), should die during the so-called *accumulation phase* (that is, prior to receiving payments from the annuity), your designated beneficiary is guaranteed to be reimbursed the amount of your original investment. This is not life insurance!

Annuities, like IRAs, allow your capital to grow and compound tax-deferred. You defer taxes until withdrawal. However, unlike an IRA that has a $2,000 annual contribution limit, you can deposit as much as you want in any year into an annuity — even a million dollars if you've got it! As with a Roth IRA, you get no up-front tax deduction for your contributions.

NOT FOR US!

Because annuity contributions are not tax-deductible, and because annuities carry higher annual operating fees to pay for the small insurance that comes with them, don't consider contributing to one until you've fully exhausted your other retirement account investing options. Because of their higher annual expenses, annuities make sense generally if you have about 15 or more years to go until you need the money. Annuities are *not* appropriate if you are already in retirement or near retirement.

Understand the Tax (B)rackets

Funding retirement accounts can help keep your current income taxes lower. Maximizing the amount of investing you do inside retirement accounts is generally a wise strategy. By doing so, you reduce the amount of your income currently taxable and shelter your investments' profits from taxation over time.

Some of the investing that you'll want to do, however, happens outside retirement accounts. When you're investing outside of tax-sheltered retirement accounts, the profits and distributions on your money are subject to taxation. So the type of non-retirement account investments that makes sense for you depends at least partly on your tax situation.

If you have money to invest, or if you're considering selling current investments that you hold, taxes should be an important factor in your decision. But tax considerations alone should not dictate how and where you invest your money. You should also weigh investment options, your desire (and the necessity) to take risk, personal likes and dislikes, and the number of years you plan to hold the investment.

 Consider how taxes affect investing in stocks and bonds. If you're in a high tax bracket, you should give preference to investments such as tax-free bonds and stocks with low levels of distributions, particularly dividends. Real estate and small business investments that you expect to appreciate are tax-wise choices as well. If you're in a lower tax bracket, avoid tax-free bonds because you'll end up with less of a return than in higher-yielding taxable bonds.

Determining your tax bracket

You may not know it but the government charges you different tax rates for different parts of your annual income. You pay less tax on your *first* dollars of earnings and more tax on your *last* dollars of earnings. For example, if you're single and your taxable income totaled $35,000 during 1997, you paid federal tax at the rate of 15 percent on the first $24,650 of taxable income and 28 percent on income above $24,650 up to $35,000.

Your *marginal tax rate* is the rate of tax that you pay on your *last* or so-called *highest* dollars of income. In the example of a single person with taxable income of $35,000, that person's federal marginal tax rate is 28 percent. In other words, he or she effectively pays a 28 percent federal tax on his or her last dollars of income — those dollars earned between $24,650 and $35,000. (Don't forget to factor in state income taxes that most states assess.)

Your marginal tax rate allows you to quickly calculate additional taxes that you would pay on additional income or the amount of taxes that you save by contributing more into retirement accounts or by reducing your taxable income (for example, by choosing investments that produce tax-free income).

Table 3-1 shows the 1997 federal tax rates for singles and for married households filing jointly.

Table 3-1	1997 Federal Income Tax Rates	
Singles Taxable Income	**Married Filing Jointly Taxable Income**	**Federal Tax Rate**
Less than $24,650	Less than $41,200	15%
$24,650 to $59,750	$41,200 to $99,600	28%
$59,750 to $124,650	$99,600 to $151,750	31%
$124,650 to $271,050	$151,750 to $271,050	36%
More than $271,050	More than $271,050	39.6%

What's taxed and when to worry

Interest that is paid on bank accounts, bonds, and dividends paid by stocks are all generally taxable. The exception is the interest paid on some types of bonds. U.S. Treasury bonds, for example, pay interest that is state tax-free. Municipal bonds, which are issued by state and local governments, pay interest that is federally tax-free and also state tax-free to residents in the state the bond is issued. (I discuss bonds in Chapter 7.)

If this sounds complicated, you might want to go ahead and pop an aspirin before we cover taxation on your *capital gains*, which is the *profit* (sales minus purchase price) on an investment. Investments held less than one year generate *short-term capital gains*, which are taxed at your normal marginal rate. Profits from investments held longer than 18 months are *long-term capital gains*, on which taxes are capped at 20 percent for those in a tax bracket of 28 percent or higher, and 10 percent for those in the 15 percent tax bracket. If your investment is held between 12 and 18 months, then your capital gains tax is capped at 28 percent.

For investments purchased after December 31, 2000 and then held longer than five years, the long-term capital gains rate drops to 18 percent for those in the 28 percent tax bracket and 8 percent for those in the 15 percent bracket.

Here are some good strategies to reduce the taxes on investments exposed to taxation:

> ✔ **Use tax-free money market and bonds.** If you're in a high enough tax bracket (federal 28 percent to 31 percent, or higher), you may find that you come out ahead with tax-free investments. Tax-free investments yield less than comparable investments that produce taxable earnings. But because of the difference in taxes, the earnings from tax-free investments *can* end up being greater than what you're left with from taxable investments. In order to do the comparison properly, subtract what you will pay in federal as well as state taxes from the taxable investment.

✔ **Invest in tax-friendly stocks.** Companies that pay little in the way of dividends reinvest more of their profits back into the company. If you're investing outside of a retirement account, unless you need income to live on, minimize your exposure to stocks with dividends. Be aware that low-dividend stocks tend to be more volatile.

Investing in index funds is a great way to include tax-friendly stocks in your portfolio. *Index funds* are mutual funds that invest in a relatively fixed portfolio of securities, such as stocks and bonds. They don't attempt to beat the market. Rather, they invest in the securities to mirror or match the performance of an underlying index, such as the Standard & Poor's 500 (see Chapter 5). Although index funds cannot beat the market, they have several advantages over actively managed funds. Because index funds trade less, they tend to produce lower capital gains distributions. For mutual funds held outside tax-sheltered retirement accounts, this reduced trading effectively increases an investor's total rate of return. Index fund investors also benefit from the reduced trading in the form of lower brokerage commissions. Also, because significant ongoing research need not be conducted to identify companies to invest in, index funds can be run with far lower operating expenses. All things being equal, lower brokerage and operating costs translate into higher shareholder returns (see Chapter 8 to find out more about mutual funds and indexing).

✔ **Invest in small business and real estate.** The growth in value of a business and real estate asset is not taxed until the asset is sold. Even then, with real estate, you often can roll over the gain into another property so long as you comply with tax laws. However, the current income that a small business and real estate produces is taxed as ordinary income.

Short-term capital gains (investments held less than one year) are taxed at your ordinary income tax rate. This is another reason that you shouldn't be trading or flipping your investments quickly (within 12 months).

Protect Your Assets

Work, work, work.

Save, save, save.

Invest, invest, invest.

If you're the thrifty, hard-working sort, you may actually be at risk of making a catastrophic investing mistake: not properly protecting your assets.

That's the mistake that Manny, a successful entrepreneur, made. Starting from scratch, he built up a successful million-dollar manufacturing operation. He invested a lot of his own personal money, as well as sweat, into building the business over 15 years.

Avoid these investments with their supposed "tax savings"

Brokers and financial planners who work on commission will try to sell you numerous investments that they claim offer big tax advantages. A limited partnership (LP) is a good example of a bad investment these salespeople push. Limited partnerships invest in real estate and a variety of businesses, such as cable television, health care, and technology-related companies. Although some of the companies that LPs invest in are sound, the only sure thing about investing in LPs is that you won't earn the best possible returns for your money because of high sales commissions and ongoing management fees.

Commissions, which are immediately deducted from your investment, can run 10 percent or more. Annual management fees can also be steep, running up to 3 percent per year. The best *no-load* (commission-free) mutual funds charge 0.2 percent to 1 percent per year for comparable investments.

LPs also have poor liquidity — you must typically wait 7 to 10 years until the partnership investments are sold to access your investment dollars. If you need to sell before then, you may be able to sell through the informal secondary market, but you'll receive pennies on the dollar.

Another investment that many salespeople love to pitch is cash value life insurance. Life insurance that combines life insurance protection with an account that has a cash value is usually known as *universal, whole,* or *variable life.*

Life insurance with a cash value is, at best, a mediocre way to invest money and, at worst, a terrible mistake, especially if you haven't exhausted contributing money to retirement accounts. Retirement savings plans, such as 401(k)s, 403(b)s, SEP-IRAs, and Keoghs, give you an immediate tax deduction for your current contributions in addition to growth without taxation until withdrawal.

The only real advantage cash value life insurance offers is that, if it's properly held in a trust, for people who expect to have substantial estates at their death, the proceeds paid to your beneficiaries can be free of estate taxes. Cash value life insurance is one of many ways, and generally far from the best way, to reduce your estate tax problems. Pick up a copy of *Taxes For Dummies* (IDG Books Worldwide) to find out more about minimizing estate taxes.

Then one day, catastrophe struck: An explosion ripped through the building, and the ensuing fire destroyed virtually all the firm's equipment and inventory, none of which was insured. The explosion seriously injured several workers as well, including Manny, who didn't carry disability insurance. Ultimately, Manny had to file bankruptcy.

As with investing your money, the decision as to what amount of insurance to carry is somewhat a matter of your desire and ability to accept financial risk. Some risks are not worth taking. Don't overestimate your ability to predict in advance what accidents and other bad luck may befall you. Here's what you need to protect yourself and your assets:

- **Major medical health insurance.** I'm not talking about one of those policies that pays $100 a day if you need to go into the hospital, or cancer insurance, or that $5,000 medical expense rider on your auto insurance policy. I know it's unpleasant to consider, but you need a policy that pays for all types of major illnesses and major expenditures. A $5,000 rider may pay for the first day or two and is hardly catastrophic coverage. Don't waste your money on these narrower, small-dollar coverage policies.

- **Adequate liability insurance on your home and car to guard your assets against lawsuits.** America is home to lots of lawyers — about three quarters of a million! You should have at least enough liability insurance to protect your *net worth* (assets minus your liabilities/debts), or ideally, twice your net worth.

   If you run your own business, get insurance for your business assets if they are substantial, such as in Manny's case. Also consider professional liability insurance to protect against a lawsuit. You may also want to consider incorporating (see Chapter 13).

- **Long-term disability insurance.** What would you (and your family) do to replace your income if a major disability prevents you from working? Even if you don't have dependents, odds are that *you* are dependent on you. Most larger employers offer group plans that have good benefits and are much less expensive than coverage you'd buy on your own. Also, check with your professional association for a competitive group plan.

- **Life insurance if others are dependent on your income.** If you're single or your loved ones can live without your income, skip it. If you need coverage, buy term insurance, which, like your auto and home insurance, is pure insurance protection. The amount of term insurance you should buy largely depends on how much of your income you want to replace.

- **Death contingency plan.** At a minimum, most people need a simple will to delineate to whom they would like to leave all their worldly possessions. If you hold significant assets outside retirement accounts, you may also benefit from establishing a living trust, which keeps your money from filtering through the hands and open wallets of probate lawyers. (Probate is another reason during your working years to shelter more of your money inside retirement accounts.) Living wills and medical powers of attorney are useful to have in case you're in a medically difficult state.

   If you have substantial assets, doing some estate planning is wise to minimize estate taxes and ensure the orderly passing of your assets to your heirs.

In my experience as a financial advisor, whereas many people are lacking particular types of insurance, others have unnecessary policies. Many people also keep very low deductibles. Remember, insure against potential losses that would be financially catastrophic for you and don't waste your money to protect against smaller losses. (See my first book, *Personal Finance For Dummies*, to discover the right and wrong ways to buy insurance, what to look for in policies, and where to get good ones.)

Tread Carefully while Investing for College

Many well-intentioned parents want to save for the children's future educational expenses. The mistake they often make, however, is putting money in accounts in their child's name (in so-called *custodial accounts*) or saving outside retirement accounts in general.

Why is this a problem? First, you receive no tax deduction on your contributions to these accounts, whereas your retirement account contributions are not only tax-deductible in the year made but also compound tax-deferred.

The second problem with underfunding retirement accounts is that the more money you accumulate outside tax-sheltered retirement accounts, the less assistance you're likely to qualify for from federal and state financial aid sources. Don't make the additional error of assuming that financial aid is only for the poor. Many middle-income and even some modestly affluent families qualify for some aid, which can include grants and loans available even if you're not deemed financially needy.

How you invest affects Junior's aid

Under the current financial needs analysis that most colleges use in awarding financial aid, the value of your retirement plan is *not* considered an asset. Money that you save *outside* retirement accounts, including money in the child's name, is counted as an asset and reduces your eligibility for financial aid.

Therefore, it does not make sense to forgo contributions to your own retirement savings plan(s) in order to save money in a non-retirement account for your children's college expenses. When you do, you pay higher taxes both on your current income and on the interest and growth of this money. In addition to paying higher taxes, you are expected to contribute more to your child's educational expenses.

How to pay for college

If you keep stashing away money in retirement accounts, it's reasonable for you to ask how you'll actually pay for education expenses when the momentous occasion arises. In most cases, even if you have some liquid cash that can be redirected to your child's college bill, you will, in all likelihood, have to borrow some money. Only the affluent can truly afford to pay for college with cash.

One good source of money is the equity in your home. You can borrow against your home at a relatively low interest rate, and the interest is generally tax-deductible. Some company retirement plans, for example, 401(k)s, allow borrowing as well.

A plethora of financial aid programs allow you to borrow at reasonable interest rates. The Unsubsidized Stafford Loans and Parent Loans for Undergraduate Students (PLUS), for example, are available, even when your family is not deemed financially needy. Only Subsidized Stafford Loans, on which the federal government pays the interest that accumulates while the student is still in school, are limited to those students deemed financially needy.

In addition to loans, a number of grant programs are available through schools and the government, as well as through independent sources.

You can apply for the federal government programs by completing the Free Application for Federal Student Aid (FAFSA). Grants available through state government programs may require a separate application. Specific colleges and other private organizations, including employers, banks, credit unions, and community groups, also offer grants and scholarships.

Many scholarships and grants don't require any work on your part — simply apply for such financial aid through colleges. Other programs need seeking out — check directories and databases at your local library, your kid's school counseling department, and college financial aid offices. Also try local organizations, churches, employers, and so on, because you have a better chance of getting scholarship money through these avenues.

Your child can work and save money during high school and college. In fact, if your child qualifies for financial aid, he or she generally is expected to contribute a certain amount to education costs from employment during the school year or summer breaks and from savings. Besides giving your gangly teen a stake in his or her own future, this training encourages sound personal financial management down the road.

If you're affluent enough that you expect to pay for your cherub's full educational costs, investing through custodial accounts can save you a bit on taxes. Prior to your child reaching age 14, the first $1,300 of interest and dividend income is taxed at your child's income tax rate rather than yours. After age 14, *all* income generated by investments in your child's name is taxed at your child's rate. Tax savings notwithstanding, I would politely like to raise a concern about your "generosity." Other generous parents' experience suggests that some kids don't value the education and money as much if it's all coming out of your pocket. Consider having them share in a portion of the cost.

If you plan to apply for financial aid, it's a good idea to save non-retirement account money in your name rather than in your children's names (custodial accounts). Colleges expect a greater percentage of money in your child's name (35 percent) to be used for college costs than money in your name (6 percent).

Hold off on putting any money into an Education IRA, a new savings vehicle created by Congress in 1997. In theory, Education IRAs sound like a great place to park some college savings: You can make non-deductible contributions of up to $500 per child per year, and investment earnings and account withdrawals are free of tax so long as the funds are used to pay for college costs. However, it's not yet clear how college financial aid officers are going to treat these accounts. Financial aid experts predict that the money will be treated either as a child's asset, which reduces financial aid by 35 percent for each dollar in the child's name, or as a pre-paid tuition plan, which reduces aid dollar for dollar. In other words, funding an Education IRA could undermine your child's ability to qualify for financial aid. Wait until the fall of 1998; by then we'll have a better idea of how colleges are going to handle these new accounts.

Also, be aware that your family's assets, for purposes of financial aid determination, also include equity in real estate and businesses you own. Although the federal financial aid analysis no longer counts equity in your primary residence as an asset, many private (independent) schools continue to ask parents for this information when making their own financial aid determinations. Thus paying down your home mortgage more quickly instead of funding retirement accounts can harm you financially. You may end up with less financial aid and pay more in taxes.

If you keep up to 80 percent of your investment money in stocks (diversified worldwide) with the remainder in bonds when your child is young, you should maximize the money's growth potential without taking extraordinary risk. As your child is making his or her way through the later years of elementary school, begin to make the mix more conservative — scale back the stock percentage to 50 or 60 percent. Finally, in the years just before entering college, you should have the stock portion whittled down to about 20 percent or so.

Diversified mutual funds, which invest in stocks in the U.S. and internationally, and bonds are an ideal vehicle to use when investing for college. Be sure to choose funds that fit with your tax situation if you invest in funds in non-retirement accounts.

Allocate Your Investments

A final and important consideration before I set you loose in the wild and woolly world of investing is how to mix up a great recipe of investments. Common sense suggests that you don't want to put all your eggs in one basket. As I discuss in Chapter 2, diversifying your investments helps buffer your portfolio from being sunk by one or two poor performers. By investing in different types of stocks, real estate, bonds, and so on, while some investments are periodically in the doghouse, others are rising to the occasion.

The younger you are, and the more years you have until you plan on using your money, the greater amount of your longer-term investment money should be in growth (ownership) vehicles, such as stocks, real estate, and small business. As I discuss in Chapter 2, the attraction of these investments is the potential to really make your money grow. The risk: The value of your portfolio can plunge from time to time.

The younger you are, the more time your investments have to recover from a bad fall. In this respect, investments are a bit like people. If a 30-year-old and an 80-year-old fall on a concrete walkway, odds are better that the younger person will fully recover. Older people who sustain such falls are sometimes disabled and have difficulty walking for years.

An old rule of thumb says to subtract your age from 100 and invest the resulting number as a percentage of money to place in growth (ownership) investments. So if you're 35 years old

$100 - 35 = 65\%$ of your investment money can be in growth investments.

If you want to be more aggressive, subtract your age from 120:

$120 - 35 = 85\%$ of your investment money can be in growth investments.

These tips are only rules of thumb and apply to money you're investing for the long-term (ideally for 10 years or more). For money that you need to use in the shorter-term, such as within the next several years, more-aggressive growth investments are not appropriate. See Chapters 7 and 8 for other investing ideas.

No hard and fast rules show you how to allocate the 85 percent earmarked for growth investments among specific investments, such as stocks and real estate. Part of how you decide to allocate your investments depends, for example, on what types of investments you want to focus on. As I discuss when I cover the stock market in Chapter 5, diversifying in stocks worldwide should be prudent as well as profitable.

Part II
Stocks, Bonds, and Wall Street

In this part . . .

Stocks, bonds, and mutual funds are the core financial market instruments that investors play with these days. But what the heck *are* these devices, and how can you invest in them, make some decent money, and not lose your shirt? Here you find out how and where to evaluate and buy these securities and how to comprehend the mind-numbing jargon the money pros use.

Chapter 4

How the Financial Markets Work

*P*erhaps on the evening news you've viewed the floor of the New York Stock Exchange, located at the corner of Broad and Wall Streets in lower Manhattan. Hundreds of darkly dressed men (primarily) mill about in a relatively unhurried manner, despite being in one of the world's largest markets for trading shares of company stock.

One hot summer day when my wife and I were visiting New York, I dragged her to see the floor of the exchange. You can't actually go out onto the floor, but you can view it from a visitor's observation deck. As with many popular things in the Big Apple, to get to the observation area, like sheep, you must wait in a long, single-file line. After enduring this ritual, you're then stuffed into a cramped elevator, cattle-style, and transported to the viewing area. A maze of exhibits greets the elevator passengers, who, like hamsters, must first wander around before finally reaching the narrow corridor that overlooks the floor. So that you can't toss a paper airplane or your gum onto this shrine of capitalism, the corridor is glass enclosed. There's enough space for people to stand half a dozen deep. If you're lucky, you may get to the front of the pack for a short time and actually see something.

After all this waiting and navigating, my wife said to me, "This is boring. . . ." As so often has occurred in our marriage, she was right — you don't see a whole lot at this exchange or other stock exchanges, even on a day when the market is plunging. The real action is at the companies that issue stocks and other securities, such as bonds, and that's where our journey begins.

Imagine You're a Company

Imagine that you run your own business — many people do or want to (see Part IV). Suppose that you make something, anything. A friend of mine, Liz, initially made necklaces and pins out of her home as a hobby. Her friends complimented her on the jewelry, so she began making some for them. Eventually, she started selling them to some local retail stores.

Now, suppose a large retail department store chain like Macy's contacted you to sell them thousands of the necklaces and pins so that you had to contract for big-time manufacturing help. Newspapers and magazines begin featuring your work, and lots of retailers are lining up for your creations.

The money begins to roll in, so you're in the big time now. At some point, you may want to raise more money, known as *capital* in the financial world, to expand and afford your growing company's needs, such as hiring more employees, buying computer systems, and purchasing manufacturing equipment.

You have two major money-raising options when you go into the financial markets: issuing stocks or issuing bonds. A world of difference exists between these two major securities, both from the perspective of the investor as well as from the issuing company (which in this case I'll call Liz's Distinctive Jewelry), as the following explanations illustrate.

- ✔ **Bonds are loans that a company must pay back.** Rather than borrowing money from a bank, many companies elect to sell *bonds,* which are IOUs to investors. The primary disadvantage, from a company's perspective, is that this money must be paid back with interest. On the other hand, the business doesn't have to relinquish ownership when borrowing money. Companies are also more likely to issue bonds if the stock market is depressed. A low stock market means that companies aren't able to fetch as much for their stock.

- ✔ **Stocks are shares of ownership in a company.** Some companies choose to issue stock to raise money. Unlike bonds, the money raised through a stock issue is not paid back because it's not a loan. When stock is bought by the public (people like you and me), it continues to be held and traded among outside investors. (Although companies may occasionally choose to buy their own stock back, usually because they think it's a good investment, they are under no obligation to do so. If a company does a stock buyback, the price the company pays is simply the price the stock is currently trading for, which can be less than an investor paid.)

  Even though a company relinquishes some of its ownership when it issues stock, it allows its founders and owners to sell some of their relatively illiquid private stock and reap the rewards of their successful company. Many growing companies also prefer stock issues because they don't want the cash drain that comes from paying loans (bonds) back.

So how do companies decide whether to issue debt or equity? Companies that meet the requirements (discussed in Chapter 5) to sell stock on one of the exchanges try to do what is in their best interests. If the stock market is booming and new stock can be sold at a premium price, companies opt to sell more stock. On the other hand, if investors don't believe a company has good growth prospects and interest rates are relatively low, the company may lean toward selling bonds instead. Ultimately, companies seek to raise capital the lowest cost way they can, so they'll elect to sell stocks or bonds based on what the finance folks tell them is the cheaper option.

From your perspective as a potential investor, you can make more money in stocks than bonds, but stocks are generally far more volatile in the short-term (see Chapter 2).

Going public

Suppose that Liz's Distinctive Jewelry is going to issue stock for the first time, which is called an *initial public offering (IPO)*. If Liz decides to go public, she works with *investment bankers,* who, like real estate agents trying to sell homes, help companies decide when and at what price to go public. (It should be noted that most investment bankers don't like being compared to real estate agents, but the successful ones in both professions make big bucks getting a percentage of every deal they do. Both investment bankers and real estate agents must determine their merchandise's asking price.)

Suppose further that the investment bankers believe that the company can raise $50 million by issuing stock. When a company issues stock, the price per share that the stock is sold for is somewhat arbitrary. The amount that a prospective investor is willing to pay for a particular portion of the company's stock depends upon the company's profits and future growth prospects. Companies that are producing higher levels of profits and growing faster can generally command a higher sales price for a given portion of the company.

Consider the following ways investment bankers can structure the IPO:

Price of Stock	Number of Shares Issued
$5	10 million
$10	5 million
$20	2.5 million

In fact, Liz's Distinctive Jewelry can raise $50 million in an infinite number of ways, thanks to varying stock prices. If the company wants to issue the stock at a higher price, then the company has fewer shares to sell.

A stock's price per share by itself is meaningless in evaluating whether to buy a stock. Ultimately, what investors are willing to pay for a company's outstanding stock depends greatly on the company's financial condition. If Liz's Distinctive Jewelry is producing annual earnings (profits) of $3 million and companies comparable to Liz's have stock outstanding that sells at 10 times earnings, then Liz's stock in the market should be worth about $30 million.

$$\frac{\text{The value of a company's stock}}{\text{relative to (divided by) its earnings}} = \text{its } \textit{price-earnings ratio}$$

In the case of Liz's Distinctive Jewelry, here are the numbers:

What it takes to go public

Not just any company can go public and issue stock. When most U.S. companies go public, their stock is listed and traded in the over-the-counter market, known in the trade as the OTC or NASDAQ, which stands for National Association of Securities Dealers Automated Quotation system. (Whew!) NASDAQ provides computer quotes to brokers around the country trading in these stocks. More than 33,000 small companies currently trade on the OTC. Of the approximately 33,000 companies traded on the OTC, about 5,000 are currently listed and actively traded on the NASDAQ computer system. To get listed on NASDAQ, a company needs to have *annual profits* (revenue less expenses) of $750,000 or more, assets of at least $4 million, a minimum of 400 shareholders, and value of stock outstanding of at least $1 million.

The other 28,000 or so OTC stocks are the riskiest and most dangerous stocks to invest in, because the financial requirements to be listed are nil. You won't find these small-company OTC stock prices listed in the financial section of even the best business papers. And that may be a good thing if you're trying to teach your kids about investing, because you may have difficulty explaining how a company such as Rick's Cabaret, a Houston-based chain of topless bars, made the list!

The American Stock Exchange (AMEX) typically attracts somewhat larger companies' stocks. To be listed on the AMEX, a company must have a stock market value of outstanding shares of at least $2.5 million and 250,000 shares issued. About 900 companies are listed on the AMEX.

The oldest and largest of all stock exchanges in the U.S. is the New York Stock Exchange (NYSE). To be listed on the NYSE, companies need to be even larger than on the AMEX. Stock outstanding must total at least 1.1 million shares, be worth at least $18 million, and be backed by a company with annual profits of $2.5 million.

While many company owners like to take their companies public to cash in on their stake, not all owners want to go public, and not all who do are happy that they did. Among the numerous drawbacks of being a public company are the burdensome financial reporting requirements, such as production of quarterly earnings statements and annual reports. These documents not only take lots of time and money to produce but also can reveal competitive secrets. Some companies also harm their long-term planning ability because of the pressure and focus on short-term corporate performance that comes with being a public company.

$$\frac{\$30 \text{ million}}{\$3 \text{ million}} = 10$$

In the next chapter, I talk more about price-earnings ratios and what influences stock prices.

When most investors purchase stocks or bonds today, they don't receive the actual paper certificate demonstrating ownership. Stocks and bonds are often held through brokerage accounts, and the brokerage firm holds the certificate on your behalf. It's beneficial to hold your securities through a brokerage account because most brokers charge an extra fee to issue certificates. I discuss other reasons to hold your securities through a brokerage account later in this chapter.

Where to find the prices of stocks and bonds

Most major newspapers print a listing of the prior day's stock prices (unless you live in an area with a late afternoon paper that publishes that day's activity). Figure 4-1 is typical of the daily price quotes carried in local newspapers.

SAN FRANCISCO EXAMINER

Stock	Div	PE	Sales 100s	Hi	Lo	Last	Net chg.
Clorox	2.12	20	321	78⅜	77⅛	77⅝	+⅝
Coachm	.28	10	246	22⅜	21¾	22⅜	+¼
CoastSv		**30**	**2009**	**31**	**29¾**	**31**	**+1¼**
Coastal	.40	17	6568	35¾	34⅛	35⅜	+1⅛
CstlPhys			324	14	13¾	13¾	-⅛
Coastcst		14	308	10½	10¼	10½	+⅛
CocaCl	.88	36	13922	80⅛	78⅜	79⅜	+⅞
CocaCE	.05	40	402	29	28⅝	28⅞	-¼
CCFemsa	.10	e 19	551	20	19¾	19¾	-¼
Coeur	.15		846	18⅞	18½	18¾	+¼
CohenST	.96	a	191	13⅛	12⅞	13⅛	+¼
Colemn		19	122	35½	35⅜	35⅜	-¼
ColgPal	1.88	65	3530	74¾	73¼	74¾	+½
CollAik		3	1178	6⅞	6⅝	6¾	
ColBgp	.90	10	138	30⅝	30	30⅝	+½
ColHln	.58		509	7⅞	7¾	7¾	
Collntln	.96		342	11⅛	10⅞	10⅞	
CollHI	.70		154	7⅛	7	7	
CollnvG	.63		314	10	9⅞	10	
ColMu	.51		505	6¾	6⅝	6¾	+⅛
ColonPT	1.90	21	472	25⅝	25½	25½	+¼
Coltec		11	891	12	11¾	11¾	-¼
ColumGas		9	2007	43⅞	43⅜	43⅝	+¼
ColHCA	.12	24	7593	53⅛	52⅜	52½	-⅝
Comdsc s		14	856	23¾	23	23⅛	+⅜
Comed pfT	2.12		242	25⅝	25⅜	25⅜	-⅛
Comeric	1.40	11	1208	37⅛	36⅞	37	
CmceGp	.24	7	221	21⅝	21½	21½	-¼
CmcFdl	.10	p 17	372	36¾	36¼	36¾	+⅜
CmclTek	.54	f 12	535	18¼	17¼	17¾	+¼
CmclMtl	.48	9	271	24⅜	23¾	23¾	+⅛
CmclNL	1.16	12	93	13⅛	12⅞	13	
ComHlSy		18	1175	34⅞	34	34	-⅞
CPsyc	.01	e 12	831	12	11½	11½	-⅜
CompUSA		22	3076	38½	36¾	36¾	-⅛
ChileTel	2.91	e	284	77⅜	76¾	77⅛	-⅜
Compaq		14	37982	50½	49	49¼	+⅞
CmpAsc s	.13		6187	64½	62⅝	62¾	-1⅛
CompSci		33	1028	74⅝	73½	73¾	-⅞
CmpTsk	**.10**	**18**	**133**	**20⅜**	**19⅜**	**20⅜**	**+⅞**
Cmptvsn	**.04**	**26**	**2537**	**12½**	**11¾**	**12⅜**	**+⅝**
Comsat	.78	27	1367	20	19¾	19⅞	-⅛
CsatCap pf	2.03		366	25⅛	25	25	-⅛

Stock	Div	PE	Sales 100s	Hi	Lo	Last	Net chg
Domtar			612	7⅜	6⅞	7⅛	-¼
Donaldsn	.28	17	74	24⅞	24⅝	24⅝	-¼
DonLJ n	.13	p	377	32¼	32	32⅛	+⅛
Donlley	.72	20	5865	40	37¾	37¾	-1½
Dover s	.60	17	1441	37⅜	37⅛	37¼	-⅛
DowCh	3.00	10	9283	71⅜	70⅝	70¾	-⅜
DowJns	.92	20	677	39⅞	39⅝	39¾	+¼
Dravo		37	725	11⅞	11¾	11⅞	
Dressr	.68	20	25284	23⅝	22⅞	23⅝	+⅝
DryStG	.75		622	9⅜	9⅛	9¼	+⅛
DryStrt	.67		711	9⅝	9½	9½	-⅛
DrySM	.62		926	9¼	9⅛	9¼	+¼
DuPont	2.08	13	8100	69⅜	67⅞	69¼	+1¼
DufPUtil	.72		2599	9	8⅞	8⅞	
DufPUC	1.18		490	14⅛	13⅞	14⅛	+¼
DukeP	2.04	14	1082	46½	46	46⅜	+¼
Duke pfA	1.59		108	25	24	24	-¼
DukeRlty	1.96	21	321	30¼	29⅞	30¼	+⅜
DunBrd	2.64	17	2223	63¼	62¼	63⅛	+1
Duracel	1.04	28	3426	54⅞	53¾	53⅞	+¼
DutyF	.20	26	224	14⅞	14½	14½	-⅛
Dycom		11	283	5⅞	5½	5⅝	-⅛
Dyersbg	.04	10	139	4⅝	4⅝	4⅝	
E							
ECC Int		10	344	10⅜	10	10	-¼
EGG	.56	a 19	207	19½	19¼	19½	+¼
EMC		13	6943	17½	17¼	17¼	-⅛
ENI n			4002	32¼	31¾	32¼	+⅜
EQK Rt			129	1¾	1⅝	1⅝	
EstANG	1.60	e	138	15⅜	15¼	15⅜	+⅛
EastEn	1.48	f 13	371	33⅝	33¼	33½	+⅜
EastUtl	1.60	15	885	23⅜	23⅛	23⅛	-¼
EastChm	1.68	f 10	2161	66⅛	65	65⅜	-⅞
EKodak	1.60	27	10075	70⅜	68¾	70⅛	+1⅜
Eaton	1.60	11	1959	55⅜	54¾	54⅞	+⅛
Echlin	.82	15	2863	38¼	37¾	37⅞	+¼
Eckerd		15	3911	42⅜	42⅛	42¼	+¼
Ecolab	.50	22	206	29½	29¼	29⅜	-¼
vjEdisBr	.73	j	715	2⅛	2	2⅛	
Edwards	.64	f 11	1181	25⅝	25¼	25⅜	-¼

Figure 4-1: If you're lucky enough to live in a city that still has an afternoon paper, you can review that day's stock market activity.

Source: The San Francisco Examiner

The *Wall Street Journal* is the most widely-read daily business paper that publishes stock and bond prices daily. Figure 4-2 shows you the additional detail this larger daily business publication offers.

Let's take a look at one of the listings. Check out the second line where you see General Motors, the largest U.S. automaker. The first two columns indicate the high ($53 3/8) and low ($36 1/8) trading prices for General Motors during the past 52 weeks.

Next to the name of the company, you see the trading symbol, GM, which is the code that brokers use to look up the price on their computer-based quotation systems, described later in this section.

General Motors

	52 Weeks					Yld		Vol				Net
	Hi	Lo	Stock	Sym	Div	%	PE	100s	Hi	Lo	Close	Chg
s	53⅜	40½	GenMills	GIS	1.88	3.6	22	2807	52¾	51¾	52	− ¼
	53⅜	36⅛	GenMotor	GM	1.20f	2.5	7	21549	49⅜	48½	48⅝	+ ¼
	46¼	34¾	GenMotor E	GME	.52	1.2	24	6130	43⅝	42⅞	43⅛	...
	42¾	31	GenMotor H	GMH	.92	2.2	16	3000	42½	42	42½	+ ½
	65⅞	53¾	GenMotor depC		3.25	5.2	...	333	62½	61¾	62	− ⅛
	26¾	22¼	GenMotor pfD		1.98	7.6	...	52	26	25¾	26	+ ⅛
	28½	24¾	GenMotor pfG		2.28	8.2	...	58	28	27¾	27⅞	+ ⅛
	28¼	24¾	GenMotor pfQ		2.28	8.4	...	60	27¼	27	27⅛	+ ⅛
	3⅝	**2⅛**	**GenPhysics**	**GPH**	**.24**	**8.0**	**...**	**367**	**3⅛**	**2⅞**	**3**	**+ ¼**
	31	23¾	GenPubUtil	GPU	1.88	6.5	11	760	29¼	28¾	28⅞	− ¼
	138⅜	104½ ♣	GenRe	GRN	1.96	1.5	15	2178	133⅞	132⅛	133	+1
	42½	31	GenSignl	GSX	.96	2.6	53	1344	37	36⅜	36½	− ⅛
	4½	1⅝	Genesco	GCO		...	dd	1406	4⅜	4¼	4¼	...
	32½	23¼	GenesisHlth	GHV		...	25	337	30⅛	28⅞	29⅜	− ½
	18	7⅛	GenevaSteel	GNV		...	dd	394	8⅝	8½	8⅝	+ ⅛
	8⅝	4⅛ ♣	GenRad	GEN		...	16	330	8	7⅝	7⅝	− ¼
	40⅜	33⅞	GenuinePart	GPC	1.26	3.3	16	3452	38⅜	37⅞	38¼	+ ⅜
	31⅝	23½	Geon	GON	.50	1.7	16	778	28¾	28½	28¾	+ ⅛
	43¼	26⅝	GeorgiaGulf	GGC	.16e	.5	7	4771	33⅞	33¼	33¼	− ½
	95¾	64¼	GaPacific	GP	2.00	2.2	11	7579	90½	89¼	89⅝	+ 1½
n	27⅞	24¾	GA PwrCap pfA		2.25	8.1	...	63	27⅞	27⅝	27⅞	+ ⅛
▲	101¼	86	GaPwr pf		7.72	7.6	...	z340	102	102	102	+ ¾
	103¼	88	GaPwr pfB		7.80	7.7	...	z280	101	101	101	+ 1⅝
	24½	19¾	GaPwr pfL		1.62e	7.6	...	19	21½	21⅜	21⅜	− ¼
	27¼	24⅛	GaPwr pfO		2.13	8.1	...	22	26½	26⅜	26 29/64	− ⅛
▲	26	21¾	GaPwr pfQ		1.99	7.7	...	8	26⅛	25¾	25¾	...
	25¾	22	GaPwr pfR		1.94	7.6	...	7	25½	25⅜	25⅜	...
	17⅝	11⅞	GerbSci	GRB	.32	1.9	23	103	17½	17⅛	17¼	− ⅜
	8½	6¾	EmergGerFd	FRG	.12e	1.5	...	2010	8⅛	7⅞	8	+ ¼
	12½	10⅝	GermanyFd	GER	.84e	6.8	...	343	12⅜	12⅛	12⅜	+ ⅛
	13½	11⅛	NewGermnyFd	GF	.06e	.4	...	663	13½	13¼	13⅜	+ ⅛
	8⅞	2⅝	GerrityOil	GOG		...	dd	149	3⅞	3⅝	3⅝	− ⅛
	16⅛	10	GerrityOil dep pf		1.50	12.2	...	20	12¼	12¼	12¼	− ⅛
	13¼	10⅝	GettyPete	GTY		...	20	82	11⅞	11⅜	11¾	...
	11⅛	5⅝	GIANT Gp	GPO		...	2	11	6⅞	6⅞	6⅞	...
	9¼	6⅝ ♣	GiantInd	GI	.15e	1.9	38	71	8	8	8	+ ⅛
s	46⅛	34¼	Gillette	G	.60	1.4	26	9365	44⅛	43⅜	43¾	...
	10⅛	6½	GlamisGld g	GLG	.06	...	...	1250	7⅝	7⅜	7½	...

Figure 4-2: A typical stock page listing from the *Wall Street Journal.*

Reprinted by permission of the Wall Street Journal
© 1995. Dow Jones & Company, Inc.
All Rights Reserved Worldwide.

The next column, DIV, indicates the current dividend, which in this case is $1.20 per share, that the company is paying yearly to shareholders. (Most companies actually divide this up and pay one-quarter of their total annual dividend every three months). If you look up the 'f' in the explanatory notes section, you see that the company recently increased its dividend. Companies generally increase dividends after profits have increased nicely. Don't buy a stock because its dividend has increased. Remember, it's old news.

Yld % indicates the effective yield the dividend is producing. The effective yield is calculated simply by dividing the dividend rate ($1.20) by the current stock price ($48 $^5/_8$). Thus, GM shareholders can expect to receive a dividend worth about 2.5 percent of the current stock value. So even if the stock treads water and is the same price a year from now, so long as the dividend isn't cut, the shareholders earn 2.5 percent — a rate comparable to many bank saving's accounts today — on their investment.

PE (the price-earnings ratio), as explained in the "Going Public" section earlier in this chapter, measures the price of GM's stock relative to the company's earnings or profits. You can find out more about PEs in Chapter 5.

Vol 100s indicates the number of shares, in hundreds, that traded during the previous day's trading. Just add two zeros, and you know that GM stock traded 2,154,900 shares. Given the price per share, that means that about $100 million worth of GM stock traded hands. Although that may sound like a lot, it's not — some large companies with actively traded stocks can easily have billions of dollars of their stock change hands in one trading day.

Hi, Lo, and Close show, respectively, the highest and lowest prices the stock traded at during the day and the final trade or closing price.

Net Change is simply how this closing price compares with the prior day's closing price. Because GM was up $^1/_4$ to 48 $^5/_8$, we can surmise that it closed the previous day at 48 $^3/_8$. The net change is calculated by subtracting the previous day's closing price from the current day's.

Now you know how to read the stock pages! I explain reading the bond listings in Chapter 7, where I dig into bonds in detail.

Getting security prices other ways

If you're hooked up, you can obtain security price quotes from any of the major online computer services, such as America Online, CompuServe, Prodigy, and so on. To do so, you need the security's trading symbol.

If you hold securities in a brokerage account, you should be able to call the brokerage firm (often on an 800 number at their expense) and get quotes over the phone. As with the computer online services, you need a security trading symbol to get this information. Good brokerage firms have resources available for their employees to look up the trading symbols — it just means a little more time on the phone with them while they do so.

For a real thrill, you can stop by a local brokerage office and see the current stock quotes whizzing by on a long, narrow screen on a wall (see Figure 4-3). Stock market channels on cable television often have this ticker-tape screen running by on the bottom of your television tube. Many brokerage firms also have publicly accessible terminals that look a lot like a personal computer on which you can obtain current quotes for free.

Figure 4-3:
Stock quotes whiz by on a brokerage firm's electronic screen.

Source: Charles Schwab & Co., Inc.

Brokerage firms: dealers in stocks, bonds, and palmistry

You generally purchase stocks and bonds through a brokerage firm. Like a private country club, the major stock exchanges sell a limited number of memberships, known as *seats,* to brokerage firms. The cost of a membership on the exchanges fluctuates over time based on supply and demand. Over the past decade, the price of a seat on the New York Stock Exchange has bounced around $500,000.

When a brokerage firm buys a seat on an exchange, the firm gains entry to the exchange floor and can place trades on their customers' behalf. So when you call a brokerage firm and place a trade to buy or sell a stock or bond, the brokerage firm in turn relays your request to its representatives on the floor of the exchange. (Many of the trades placed by the public, because of their small size, are actually done via computer.)

All brokerage firms are not created equal

It's sometimes hard to believe or imagine, but just one generation ago, all the major brokerage firms were basically alike. Prior to 1975, all brokerage firms charged the same fee, known as a *commission,* to trade stocks and bonds. Commissions were regulated by the *Securities and Exchange Commission (SEC),* the federal government agency responsible for overseeing investment firms and their services.

Beginning May 1, 1975 — May Day — brokerage firms were free to compete with one another on price, like companies in almost all other industries. Most of the firms in existence at that time, such as Prudential, Merrill Lynch, E.F. Hutton, and Smith Barney, largely continued with business as usual, charging relatively high commissions.

However, a new breed of brokerage firms, dubbed *discount brokers,* was born. These firms charge substantially lower commissions, typically 50 to 75 percent lower, than the other firms. Today, discount brokers abound and continue to capture the lion's share of new business. San Francisco-based Charles Schwab & Company is the nation's largest discount broker. Other major discount brokerage firms include Quick & Reilly, Waterhouse Securities, and Fidelity.

Discount brokers can place your trades at a substantially lower price because they have much lower overhead. Discount brokers tend not to rent the most swank, downtown office space — complete with mahogany paneled conference rooms — that they can find in order to impress customers. Discounters also don't waste tons of money employing economists and research analysts, who largely produce worthless forecasts and predictive reports (at least that's what many objective studies have proven).

Specialists execute trades and make big bucks

Although not officially recognized until the Exchange Act passed after the Great Depression, the specialist system of trading actually began on the New York Stock Exchange around 1865. A *specialist* (and his or her firm) is a member of the exchange, owns a seat, and is the focal point for trading in a listed stock. Getting into this specialist's club requires a lot of money, in order to make a market in the securities the specialist is responsible for, and selection by the Board of Governors of the Exchange.

In most stocks, all trading centers around one specialist (several dozen stocks have two specialists). Specialists are responsible for maintaining a continuous and stable market in the stocks that they handle. Specialists perform numerous functions, which earn them megabucks. First, they execute the trades that brokers place with them by matching up buy and sell orders — in other words, they, too, earn a commission or cut of every deal.

Second, specialists themselves can trade and hold stock positions in their own accounts. It is in this capacity that a few people and studies have raised questions about the specialist's potential for conflicts of interest in their work. Specialists can only trade for their own accounts when all the orders from other investors have first been fulfilled. Thus, specialists can only step in and buy for or sell from their own accounts when an excess of sell or buy orders exists.

Although you may expect specialists to be decimated by buying and selling when others don't want to, you'd be wrong. Although specialist firms are not required to disclose the profits from their own investment accounts, several studies of periods of high market volatility demonstrate that specialists profit handsomely. For example, when President John F. Kennedy was assassinated on November 22, 1963, the stock market plunged. The next day, the market opened sharply higher. A House Subcommittee investigation found that specialists didn't step in to buy shares during the heavy selling on the 22nd until after they allowed prices to plummet, rather than attempting to support prices.

Prior to the 45 percent stock market drop in 1973 and 1974, specialists made near-record use of a trading technique known as *short-selling,* which enables an investor to profit by first selling the stock and later rebuying it when stock prices go down.

Economist Milton Friedman said the following in *Newsweek* in 1968: "Private monopolies seldom last long unless they can get governmental assistance in preserving their monopolistic position. In the stock market, the SEC both provides that assistance and shelters the industry from antitrust action." What he said was more true then than today — retail brokerage firms in those days all charged the same commissions to the investing public. But the specialist system is still in place today, and recent data show that specialists are still making piles of money.

In addition to lower commissions, another major benefit of using a discount broker is that their brokers generally work on salary. Working on salary removes a significant conflict of interest that continues to get commission-paid brokers and firms, such as Prudential, Smith Barney Shearson, Merrill Lynch, and Dean Witter, into trouble. Though many of these firms today purport to perform financial planning, the reality is that commission-paid brokers are no different than other salespeople, whether the product is cars, copy machines, or computers. They are salespeople. People who sell on commission to make a living aren't inherently evil, it's just that you shouldn't expect to receive holistic, in-your-best-interest, investing counsel from commission-paid salespeople.

One of the many sales tactics of high-commission brokerage firms is to try to disparage discounters by saying things such as, "You'll receive poorer service or no service from discounters." My own experience and that of others suggest that in many cases, discounters actually offer better service. High-commission firms, for example, used to argue that discount customers got worse trade prices when they bought and sold. This assertion is a bogus argument, because all brokerage firms use a computer-based trading system called DOT for the smaller retail trades. Trades are processed typically in 20 seconds.

High-commission brokers also say that discounters are only "For people who know exactly what they are doing and don't need any help." This statement is also false. Many of the discounters offer help, including assistance with filling out paperwork and access to independent research reports. And as I show you in Chapter 8, you can buy no-load (commission-free) mutual funds that make investing decisions for you.

Within the discount brokerage business, *deep discounters* are known as firms that offer the lowest rates but fewer frills and other services. Generally, deep discounters don't have local branch offices, like big discounters, or offer money market funds with the highest yields. Major deep discounters include Jack White & Company and Brown & Company. Be careful of some deep discounters that offer bargain commissions but stick it to you in other ways, such as high fees for other services or low interest rates on money awaiting investment.

Markets & Economics 101

We've made it to the moon, created powerful computer chips smaller than your fingernail, and cranked out $100 hightops with air inflatable insoles that allow pimply-faced, gangly teenagers and wannabe athletes to aspire to the heights of Michael Jordan. But those who are honest with you will admit that we still haven't figured out exactly how to predict what the financial markets and the economy will do in the years ahead.

Tens of thousands of books, millions of articles, and enough Ph.D. dissertations to fill a major New Jersey landfill have been written about these topics. You can spend the rest of your life reading all this stuff, and you still won't get through it. Don't do it — it would be an enormous waste of human potential! So that you can make informed investing decisions, in this section I explain what you do need to know about what makes the financial markets and economy work.

Better to keep your securities in a brokerage account?

Sometimes people hold stock and bond certificates themselves — this practice used to be more common among your parents' and grandparents' generations. The reason: During the Great Depression, many brokerage firms failed and took people's assets down with their sinking ships. Since then, various reforms have greatly strengthened the security of money and securities you hold in a brokerage account.

Just as the FDIC insurance system backs up money in bank accounts, the SIPC (Securities Investor Protection Corporation) provides insurance to investment brokerage firm customers. The base level of insurance is $500,000 per account. However, many firms purchase additional protection — some as high as $25 million total!

Brokerage firms don't often fail these days, but unlike during the Depression, SIPC protects you if they do. The SIPC coverage, of course, doesn't protect you against a falling stock market. If you invest your money in stocks, bonds, or whatever that plunge in value, that's your problem!

Besides not having to worry about losing your securities if a brokerage firm fails, another good reason to hold securities with a broker is so that you don't lose them, literally! Surprising numbers of people — the exact number is, of course, unknown — have lost stock and bond certificates. Those who realize their loss can get them replaced by contacting the issuing firms, which takes a good deal of time. But as with future goals and plans, some certificates are simply lost, and owners never realize their loss. This financial fiasco sometimes happens when people die and their heirs don't know where to look for the certificates or what securities their loved ones held.

Another reason to hold your securities in a brokerage account is that it cuts down on processing all those dividend checks. For example, if you own a dozen stocks that each pay you a dividend quarterly, you'll be receiving, endorsing, and otherwise dealing with 48 separate checks. Some people like doing this — they say it's part of the "fun" of owning securities. My advice: Stick all your securities in one brokerage account into which dividends are paid. Brokerage accounts offer you the ability to sweep these payments into a reasonably good yielding money market fund. Some firms, such as Charles Schwab, Fidelity, and Jack White, even allow you to reinvest stock dividends into purchasing more shares of that stock at no charge.

When you purchase stock through a brokerage firm today, you can ask them to issue you the certificate. Most charge a fee ranging from $15 to $40 for this service, because it's an administrative pain in the butt. I don't see any benefit to getting the certificates, unless you like marveling at the artwork on them.

Rah! Rah! Capitalism!

I'll start with the economy. In America, we live in a capitalistic (a.k.a. free market) society. Have you ever stopped to think what that means? What it really means is that you have a tremendous (although not unlimited) amount of economic freedom.

If you want to start your own business, you can. That's not to say that you don't have to deal with obstacles, such as being able to afford the start-up stages and dealing with regulatory red tape. Most American entrepreneurs will tell you that one of their greatest business frustrations is dealing with all the various government agencies. In addition to the long lists of licenses that you need to obtain for certain businesses, you may have to deal with zoning and planning offices regarding how you expect to use a location for your business, other state and local agencies if you decide to incorporate, and still more government folk to comply with the myriad tax laws of the land.

Whine, whine, whine.

Go to a socialist country if you want to see really red, red tape and lack of economic opportunity and mobility. Socialism, in contrast to capitalism, is an economic system best summed up by its 19th-century promoters, Karl Marx and Friedrich Engels: "Abolish all private property."

Lenin transformed Marx's and Engels' socialist theory into a political system known as communism. In communism, the government largely controls and owns organizations that provide what people need. Over time, various countries in Europe, the former Soviet Union (Russia), and China have tried to make communism work. As is old news by now, increasing parts of the world are becoming more capitalistic. (Please note that just as the labels Republican and Democrat are somewhat meaningless, increasingly so too are labeling particular countries' economies capitalistic or socialistic.)

What did these systems in were the low standard of living in communist countries, long waits in lines to purchase goods, poor health care, and so on. But, of course, Ronald Reagan and George Bush like to take some (or maybe all?) of the credit for winning the Cold War.

What's good and not-so-good about capitalism

I came from a family that pulled itself up by its own bootstraps. My parents didn't have a college education, yet were able to own a decent home and retire comfortably in their 60s after many years of hard work, which included raising three children who went to Ivy League colleges. Despite this fact, we all turned out all right, I think.

My brother, sister, and I are all entrepreneurs. My brother operates a thriving veterinary clinic, my sister a computer consulting firm, and then there's me. I'm continuing to do what I love to do — teach others about sound financial management. Through books, teaching, and counseling work, I've been able to fulfill a career dream.

I feel fortunate because if I were living in a country like Russia or China, I wouldn't have been able to do the things that I have and had the enjoyment that my work and living in a free society have brought me. That's the good side of capitalism — people who have some smarts and who are willing to roll up their sleeves and work hard can carve out a standard of living that many people around the world long for.

But, like any system, capitalism has its warts. First, the free markets can be ruthless. People lacking particular skills (in some cases, through no fault of their own, but because of their lack of access to opportunities while growing up) get left behind or worse. Famous economist John Maynard Keynes, who is noted for, among other things, clearly seeing some of the flaws of free markets, said, "The outstanding faults of the economic society in which we live are its failure to provide full employment and its arbitrary and inequitable distribution of wealth."

Another "problem" with capitalism is that, left to their own devices, some companies and the heads of them seek to maximize profits and ignore other important matters, such as ethics and the negative impact their business practices may have on customers, the environment, and so on. In describing some of the less savory businessmen of his time, Abraham Lincoln said in 1837, "These capitalists generally act harmoniously and in concert, to fleece the people."

Some companies do bad things in the pursuit of profits. Some opponents of any type of government regulation seem to forget this. Some companies sell products that have been proven to harm users and other innocent bystanders. Tobacco and gun manufacturers come to mind. Even Malcolm Forbes, founder of one of the world's most pro-business, anti-big government magazines, said, "I'd say capitalism's worst excess is in the large number of crooks and tinhorns who get too much of the action."

But just because a company or person makes a great amount of money compared with others doesn't mean that they are doing less good than those who aren't. I have to disagree with people such as Ayn Rand, author of *The Fountainhead*, who said, "Capitalism and altruism are incompatible; they are philosophical opposites; they cannot co-exist in the same man or in the same society." Baloney. My favorite examples of successful capitalists are those who have succeeded in business and accomplished a lot of good; you meet some of these people later in this book. When America is at its best as a country, we do both capitalism and altruism well!

Maximize profits: Higher stock prices will follow

Most companies' goal is to make money, or *profits*. Profits are simply the difference between what a company takes in, *revenue,* and what it expends, *costs*. I say *most* companies, because many organizations' primary purpose is not to maximize profits. Nonprofit organizations, such as colleges and universities, are a good example. But nonprofits can't thrive and prosper without a steady flow of the green stuff.

Companies that are publicly traded on the stock exchanges are supposed to maximize profits — that's what their shareholders want. Higher profits make stock prices rise. Most private companies seek to maximize profits as well but have much more latitude to pursue other goals.

So what's the secret to maximizing profits? The key is to produce products and services for which the demand (ideally) greatly exceeds the supply. If you had made the mistake of majoring in economics like I did, one of the few useful things that you would have learned about are supply and demand curves. These important conceptual devices explain why products are priced the way that they are and why particular companies earn the profits that they do.

Following are ways that companies maximize profits:

- ✔ **Build a brand name.** Coca-Cola, for example, and many types of well-known beers rate comparably in blind taste tests to many generic colas and beers that are far cheaper. Yet, consumers (perhaps you) are willing to fork over more of your hard-earned loot because of the name and packaging. Companies build brand names largely through advertising and other promotion. (*...For Dummies* is a brand name, but *...For Dummies* books cost the same or less, in most cases, than the competition!)

- ✔ **Build a better mousetrap.** Some companies are able to develop or promote an invention or innovation that better meets customer needs. Consider the personal computer. In the "old days," if you wanted to write a business letter, report, or book like I am now doing, you did it on a typewriter. Editing was a wearisome, time-consuming process. If you made a mistake, you either started the page over or retrieved the "white-out." Personal computers revolutionized the way people write and edit their work. Of course, computers aren't better in all ways — you can possibly lose an entire document due to a major computer glitch. Your home has to burn to the ground or your dog go on a paper-eating rampage for that to happen with your typed papers!

- ✔ **Open new markets to your products.** Many successful U.S.-based companies, for example, have been stampeding into foreign countries to sell their products. Although some adaptation is usually required to sell the product overseas, selling an already proven and developed product or service to new markets increases a company's chances for success.

✔ **Be in related businesses.** This is what has been causing the Antitrust Division of the Justice Department to challenge Microsoft's business strategies. Microsoft develops the operating systems, such as Windows and DOS, on which most personal computers run software. All the computer software, such as word-processing software, must run on and be compatible with the operating systems. Guess what — Microsoft is in the business of developing and selling "compatible" software as well.

✔ **Manage costs.** Smart companies control costs. Lowering the cost of manufacturing their products or providing their services allows companies to offer their products and services more cheaply. It may help fatten the bottom line. Sometimes, though, companies try to cut too many corners, and it comes back to haunt them in the form of dissatisfied customers — or even lawsuits based on a faulty or dangerous product.

✔ **Watch the competition.** Successful companies don't necessarily mimic the competition but keep an eye on what they're doing. If lots of competitors are targeting one part of the market, some companies target a less pursued segment, which, if they can capture it, may produce higher profits thanks to the reduced competition. It takes courageous and intelligent management to avoid following the herd.

Profitable companies use a host of other tactics to maintain and increase profits. Higher profits generally lead to higher stock prices. A healthier financial condition also increases a company's ability to pay interest on and repay its debt (bond) obligations.

Efficient markets?

Companies do their best to maximize profits and maintain a solid and healthy financial condition. Ultimately, the financial markets are the final judge of what a stock or bond issued by a company is worth. Trying to predict in advance what will happen to the stock and bond markets and individual securities has consumed many a market prognosticator.

In the late 1960s, somewhat to the chagrin of market soothsayers, academic scholars developed a theory called the *efficient market hypothesis.* This theory basically went as follows. Lots of investors collect and analyze all sorts of information about companies and their securities. If investors think that a security, such as a stock, is overpriced, they sell it or don't buy it. Conversely, if they believe that a security is underpriced, they buy it or hold what they already own. Because of the competition among all these investors, the price that a security trades at generally reflects what lots of informed, smart people think it's worth.

Therefore, the efficient market theory implies that trading in and out of securities and the overall market in an attempt to beat the market is a futile endeavor. Buying or selling a security because of new news is also fruitless. As Burton

Malkiel so eloquently said in his classic book, *A Random Walk Down Wall Street*, this theory "Taken to its logical extreme . . . means that a blindfolded monkey throwing darts at a newspaper's financial pages could select a portfolio that would do just as well as one carefully selected by the experts."

Malkiel added, ". . . financial analysts in pin-striped suits don't like being compared with bare-assed apes." True enough, but the *Wall Street Journal* actually has been running a contest since the 1980s where every three months several of their staff writers "select" stocks to invest in by tossing darts at the tacked up financial pages. This randomly chosen portfolio is then compared to the stocks selected by esteemed money managers. Over the 62 contests that have occurred, the dartboard-selected portfolio (which is actually now chosen randomly via computer) has beaten the pros 25 times. In other words, the pros have won just 60 percent of the time — not very good considering that by chance alone they should be expected to win 50 percent of the time.

And — and this is an important and — the cost of hiring these professional money managers is left out of this comparison. Most professional money managers charge big bucks, and these fees erode the returns that they generate. If you factored in their hefty fees, the dartboard wins nearly half the time!

It is true that some money managers have been able to beat the markets. Doing so over a year or three years is not difficult. Over a decade or more, few can. Efficient market supporters argue that some of those who beat the markets, even over a ten-year period, do so because of luck. Consider that if you flip a coin five times, on some occasions, you'll get five consecutive heads. This coincidence actually happens, on average, once every 32 times you do five coin-flip sequences because of random luck, not skill. Consistently identifying, in advance, on which sequence you'll get five consecutive heads is not possible.

Strict believers in the efficient market hypothesis say the same of identifying the best money managers in advance. Some money managers, such as those who manage mutual funds, have publicly available track records. Inspecting those track records and doing other common-sense things, such as investing in funds that minimize your expenses, does improve your odds of doing a bit better than the market.

Various investment markets differ in how efficient they are. Though the stock market is reasonably efficient, most of the bond market is considered even more efficient. The real estate market is less efficient, because properties can be unique and you sometimes have less competition and access to information. If you are able to locate a seller who really needs to sell, you may be able to buy a property at a discount from what it's really worth. Small business is also less efficient. Entrepreneurs with innovative ideas and approaches can earn enormous returns.

One of the keys to building wealth is to focus your time and investment strategies in a way that reflects the realities of the investment marketplaces you're investing in. If you desire to earn superior returns, you're better off trying to invest on your own in less-efficient markets, such as real estate and small business. For most people who want to invest in the stock and bond markets, on the other hand, trying to beat the market averages and the best professionals at stock and bond picking is a largely unproductive, but perhaps entertaining, endeavor.

Market overreactions can create buying opportunities. Efficiency notwithstanding, the financial markets, which reflect the collective forces of millions of buyers and sellers, can sometimes go to extremes. In the mid-1970s, pessimism ran rampant in this country. President Richard Nixon had resigned in disgrace, inflation and unemployment were spiraling upward, and the stock market had fallen out of bed. Smart investors took advantage. Throughout this book, I show you how to evaluate different investment markets to identify if they have gone to an extreme.

Interest rates, inflation, and the Federal Reserve

While not as exciting to some as sex, violence, and rock and roll, the course of interest rates, inflation, and the monetary policies set forth by the Federal Reserve captivate many investors' attention. For decades, economists, investment managers, and other often self-anointed gurus have attempted to understand these economic factors. Why? Because they seem to move the financial markets and the economy.

High interest rates are bad, low rates are good

Many businesses borrow money to expand. People like you and me, who are affectionately referred to as consumers, borrow money as well, to buy things such as homes. Interest rate increases tend to slow the economy. Businesses scale back on expansion plans, and some businesses that have to borrow to continue operation can't afford to and go under. Most individuals have limited budgets as well and have to scale back some purchases. Higher interest rates, for example, translate into higher mortgage payments for home buyers.

If high interest rates choke business expansion and consumer spending, economic growth slows, or the economy may actually shrink in size, possibly ending up in *recession*. The government-sanctioned definition of a recession is two consecutive quarters (six months) of declining total economic output.

The stock market usually develops a case of the queasies as corporate profits shrink. High interest rates usually depress many investors' appetites for stocks, as the yields paid on certificates of deposit, treasury bills, and other bonds increase.

Not everyone is unhappy with higher interest rates. If you locked in a fixed-rate mortgage on your home or on a business loan, your loan looks so much the better. Some retirees and others who live off the interest income on their investments are happy with interest rate increases as well. Consider back in the early 1980s, for example, when for each $100,000 that a retiree invested in bonds or certificates of deposit (CDs) paying 10 percent, the retiree was receiving $10,000 per year in interest or dividends.

A retiree purchasing the same bonds and CDs in the fall of 1993, however, saw dividend income slashed by about 50 percent, because rates on the same bonds and CDs were just 5 percent. So for every $100,000 invested, only $5,000 in dividend or interest income was paid.

If you're trying to live off the income produced by your investments, a 50 percent drop in that income is likely to cramp your life-style. So higher interest rates are better if you're living off of your investment income, right? Not necessarily.

The inflation and interest rate connection

Consider what happened back in the late 1970s and early 1980s. After the U.S. successfully emerged from a terrible recession in 1974, the economy seemed to be on the right track. But within just a few years, the economy was in turmoil again. The annual increase in the cost of living (known as the rate of inflation) burst through 10 percent on its way to 14 percent. The explosion in oil prices, which more than doubled in less than five years, was largely responsible for this increase.

Interest rates, which are what bondholders receive when they lend their money to corporations and governments, followed inflation skyward. Here's why inflation and interest rates usually move in tandem. If you knew that, because of the ravages of inflation, the dollars you were going to be paid back with a year later were going to buy much less than they do in the present, wouldn't you too demand more interest? That's why interest rates soared along with inflation in the late 1970s and early 1980s, breaking 15 percent in 1981.

The primary driver of interest rates is the rate of inflation. Interest rates were much higher in the early 1980s because we had double-digit inflation. If the cost of living was increasing at the rate of 10 percent per year, why would you, as an investor, lend your money (which is what you're doing when you purchase a bond or CD) at 5 percent? You and other investors wouldn't do such a thing, which is why interest rates were so much higher in the early 1980s.

In recent years, interest rates have been low because inflation has significantly declined since the early 1980s. So the rate of interest that investors could earn lending their money dropped accordingly. Although low interest rates reduce the interest income coming in, the corresponding low rate of inflation doesn't devour the purchasing power of your principal balance. That's why higher interest rates aren't necessarily better if you're trying to live off your investment income. So retirees shouldn't be happy with higher interest rates. See Figure 4-4 to see how interest rates and inflation have moved in tandem.

So what's an investor, who is depending on living off the income from his investments and is not getting enough because of the low level of interest rates, to do? A simple but psychologically difficult solution is to use up some of your principal to supplement your interest and dividend income. This practice is what is effectively happening anyway when inflation is higher — the purchasing power of your principal is eroded more quickly. You may also not have saved enough to meet your desired standard of living — that's why you may want to run a retirement analysis.

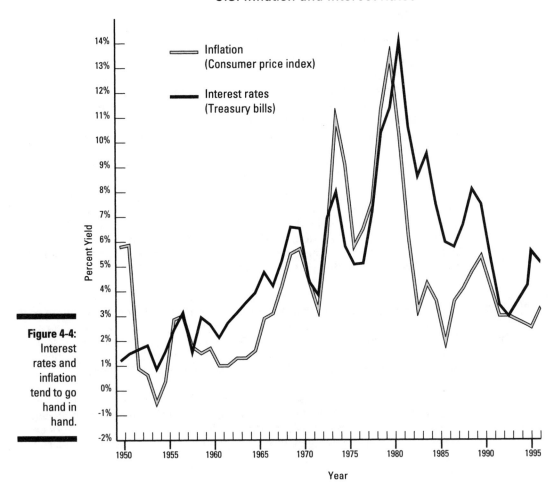

U.S. Inflation and Interest Rates

Figure 4-4:
Interest
rates and
inflation
tend to go
hand in
hand.

The role of the Federal Reserve

When the chairman of the Federal Reserve Bank speaks, an extraordinary number of people listen. When the 12 presidents from the respective Federal Reserve district banks and the seven Federal Reserve governors conduct their Federal Open Market Committee meetings behind closed doors eight times per year, most financial market watchers and the media want to know what the Federal Reserve has decided to do.

What exactly is the Fed, as it's known, and what does it do? The Federal Reserve tries to influence *monetary policy.* Yes, I know that is jargon, but that's the term you'll often hear thrown around. All this means is that the Fed tries to affect the amount of money or currency in circulation, known as the *money supply,* and the level of interest rates.

Before your eyes glaze over and you fall into a stupor such as those I endured when I made the mistake of choosing economics as one of two college majors (thankfully the other was in a real science: biology), let me quickly get you to a point of light. You see, money is no different than lettuce, computers, or sneakers. These products and goods cost you dollars to buy. The cost of money is the interest rate that you must pay to borrow it. And the cost or interest rate of money is determined by many factors that ultimately influence the supply of and demand for money.

This is where the Federal Reserve comes in. The Fed, from time to time and in different ways, attempts to influence the supply of and demand for money and the cost of money: interest rates. One of the ways the Fed attempts to do this is through raising or lowering the interest rates they charge banks to borrow money from them. The Fed also buys or sells government bonds from time to time.

Now the senior officials at the Fed readily admit that the economy is quite complex and affected by so many things, so it's very difficult to predict where it's heading. If it's so difficult to forecast and influence markets, then why does the Fed exist? The Fed officials believe that they can have a positive influence in creating a healthy overall economic environment: one in which inflation is low, and growth proceeds at a modest pace. If the economy expands too rapidly, inflation can escalate. On the other hand, Fedsters believe that if the supply of money is too restricted and interest rates too high, businesses won't be able to borrow and expand, and the economy will stagnate, or worse, actually shrink. So the Fed tries to keep everything just right!

Over the years, the Fed has come under attack for various reasons. Yale economist Edward Tufte's controversial book, *Political Control of the Economy,* argued that the Federal Reserve would, with a nudge of encouragement from the President, goose the economy. The Fed gooses the economy by loosening up on the money supply, which leads to a growth spurt in the economy, and a booming stock market, just in time to make the Prez look good. The consequences of inflation, conveniently, take longer to show up — not until after the election. In recent years, others have questioned the Fed's ability to largely do what they want without accountability.

TECHNICAL STUFF

How do the Federal Reserve chiefs invest?

Perhaps you've read headlines speculating about and documenting the Federal Reserve's moves to influence interest rates, inflation, and the economy. Fed officials have always been coy about tipping their hats and rarely give specifics, even when testifying before Congress. Current Fed Chairman Alan Greenspan is widely considered a master at such verbal obfuscation.

Wouldn't you love to know how the senior Fed officials invest their own personal money and when they refinance their mortgages and what type they get? Inquiring minds like to know, and I was curious, so I started asking some questions.

Getting Fed officials, who don't generally see themselves as part of the government or accountable to the public, to return phone calls is a challenge. But persistence pays off. Bob Parry, president and CEO of one of the regional Federal Reserve banks said to me of his investments, "It's pretty boring stuff. I don't have time to do research on individual securities, so I use mutual funds." Specifically, Parry says he uses a lot of index funds (see Chapter 8), which hold a relatively fixed basket of stocks or bonds that mirror a broad market index, such as the 500 large U.S. company stocks that make up the Standard & Poor's 500 index. Another Fed official I spoke with also says he uses index funds because, as a former stock and bond analyst, he learned that, "You can't easily beat the market."

Somewhat to my surprise, I discovered that the top brass at the Fed have few restrictions on the types of investments they may hold and when they can trade. Fed employees are prohibited from owning individual stocks or bonds of banks or dealers in government securities and are also prohibited from investing in government bonds. But no specific prohibitions prevent Fed officials,

for example, from dumping their bond holdings if they think interest rates are set to rise, loading up on them if the Fed is entering a period of looser credit, or dumping stocks and bonds altogether.

Interestingly, most senior Fed officials come into the Fed from the private sector where they were forecasters. Greenspan, for example, was a partner in the economics forecasting firm of Townsend and Greenspan. Despite earning a living for their predictions, surprisingly, most Fed officials dismiss their forecasting abilities *after* they join the Fed.

Some financial market pundits say not to underestimate the role of the Fed and its ability to signal its interest rate intentions to the financial markets. Others see the Fed as having less and less influence on the increasingly global financial markets and economy. Interest rates, they say, are ultimately determined by supply and demand, not the Fed.

How much Fed officials can divine the future remains an open question. As for timing your investments and trying to buy and sell based on publicly available information and anticipated Federal Reserve moves, if you can figure out a system, you should be a professional money manager. I don't know if Fed officials, who are privy to inside information, have been able to profit from their inside knowledge, but it would seem prudent for them to set up safeguards to prevent such an occurrence or the likely outcry from the uncovering of past occurrences. Requiring public disclosure of their personal trades, as corporate executives must do when trading their own companies' stock, is one solution. Another is for Fed officials, as other senior government officials must do, to place their investments in a blind trust during their years of work at the Fed.

Chapter 5

The Stock Market

● ●

In This Chapter

▶ Getting the inside scoop on The Market

▶ Buying low and selling high

▶ Shopping for stocks: how to's and how not to's

▶ Mastering the stock market's secrets

● ●

*T*he only reason to invest in the market is because you think you know something others don't.

> — R. Foster Winans, a former writer for *Newsweek* and the *Wall Street Journal,* who was later convicted of insider trading!

Unfortunately, the stock market has gotten a bad rap in some quarters. People liken investing in the stock market to gambling. "I deal in a big floating crap game, one that is played every weekday in the richest and most exclusive casino in the world: the New York Stock Exchange," says Richard Ney, a veteran stock market prognosticator.

In a real casino, the games — slot machines, poker, roulette, and so on — are all structured so that in aggregate, the casino owners siphon off a quite healthy slab (40 percent) of the money that people brought with them. The vast majority of casino patrons lose money, in some cases all of it. The few who leave with more than they came with are usually people who are lucky and are smart enough to quit while they are ahead.

I can understand why some individual investors, perhaps you, feel that the stock market is legalized gambling. The stock market seems mysterious — it has lots of jargon and supposed experts. When you do want to buy stocks, you generally need to do so through brokers, and you've maybe heard about how you can be shark bait for these commission-hungry folks. Brokers and financial advisors have many conflicts of interest. Most of them want to make the market out to be complicated. If you understand it too much and realize that their crystal ball has more than a few cracks in it, you'll find other and better ways that don't involve their services to invest your money in the stock market.

Stocks and Profits

So why bother with the stock market if it's so confusing and filled with people eager to separate you from your money. In Chapter 2, I discuss the potential risks and rewards of different investments. Shares of stock, which represent portions of ownership in companies, offer a way for people of modest and opulent means, and everybody in between, to build wealth by investing in companies.

The stock market is not a casino — far from it. A casino is a zero-sum game where for every dollar you win or lose, that dollar comes from the casino. In the stock market, as it appreciates over the years, which long-term history shows that it does, nearly everybody can win. I say nearly because even some people who are active in the market over many years manage to lose money because of easily avoidable mistakes, which I'll keep you from making in the future.

The fuel that powers stocks is the increasing profits that expanding companies hopefully produce. As you can see in Figure 5-1, over the years, corporate profits have been on an upward trajectory. It's not a straight line up but more like the path that a small bird takes when fighting to gain altitude in a fierce head wind. As I'm sure you know, the aerodynamics of the bird wins out. How many birds have you seen crash to Earth? But sometimes the bird hits an air pocket or spot of bad weather and loses some altitude.

And so it is with corporate profits. They, too, tend to trend up, but sometimes the economy hits a bad patch and profits fall. As with the bird, economies don't usually crash all the way back to ground zero. Yes, it's possible that if a huge meteor smashes into the Earth or a horrible, contagious virus spreads like wildfire, we could all be done for — people and companies might cease to exist and make a profit. In the meantime, why not share in the expansion of the economy and keep an optimistic view on life?

What is "The Market"?

So you invest in stocks to share in the spoils of capitalistic economies. When you invest in stocks, you do so through the stock market. What is the stock market? Everybody talks about The Market the same way they do a close personal friend. You know, they use the person's first name only, as if only one Tony exists in the world.

"The Market is down 37 points today."

"With The Market constantly hitting new highs, isn't now a bad time to invest in The Market?"

"The Market's up more than 30 percent thus far this year. It seems ready for a fall."

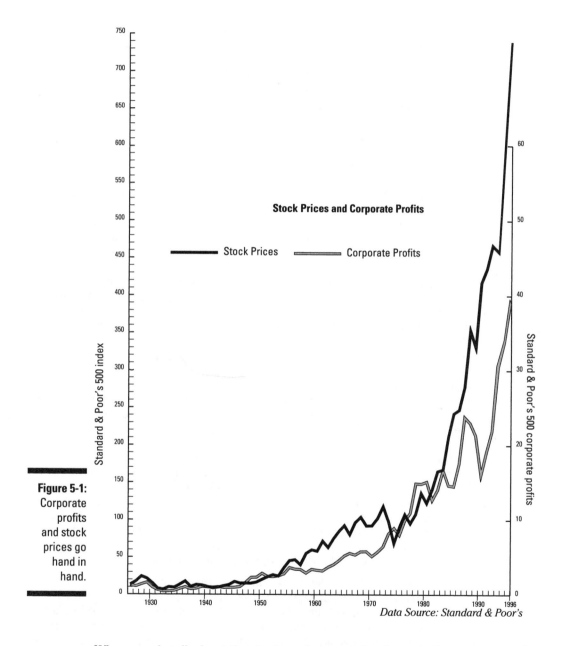

Figure 5-1:
Corporate
profits
and stock
prices go
hand in
hand.

When people talk about the stock market, you often hear similar statements. If you've ever lived near New York or talked with New Yorkers, you've perhaps heard them refer to The City. It's The City because people who use this phrase simply assume that you know what they're talking about: The City, as in New York City, or more specifically, Manhattan. Heaven forbid that anyone thinks that you are referring to Brooklyn or Staten Island!

When people talk about The Market, they're usually referring to the U.S. stock market. Even more specifically, they're speaking about the Dow Jones Industrial Average, created by Charles Dow and Eddie Jones. Dow and Jones, two reporters in their 30s, started publishing a paper you may have heard of — the *Wall Street Journal* — in 1889. Like its modern-day version, the *Wall Street Journal* reported current financial news. Dow and Jones also compiled stock prices of larger, important companies and created and calculated indexes to track the performance of the U.S. stock market.

So when people in the U.S. are talking about The Market, they not only are referring to the U.S. stock market but often even more specifically to the *Dow Jones Industrial Average (DJIA)*. This market index tracks the performance of 30 large companies headquartered in the U.S. The Dow 30 includes companies such as telecommunications giant AT&T, airplane manufacturer Boeing, soda pop maker Coca-Cola, oil giant Exxon, automaker General Motors, computer industry behemoth IBM, fast food king McDonald's, and retailer Sears.

The 30 stocks that make up the Dow aren't the 30 largest or the 30 best companies in America. They just so happen to be the 30 companies that senior staff members at the *Wall Street Journal* think reflect the diversity of the economy in the U.S. Some have criticized the Dow index for encompassing so few companies and for not being more diverse. The 30 stocks change over time as companies merge, decline, and rise in importance.

Just as Manhattan is not the only city to visit or live in, the 30 stocks in the Dow Jones Industrial Average are far from representative of all the different types of stocks you can invest in. Here are some other important market indexes and the types of stocks they track:

- **Standard & Poor's 500.** Like the Dow Jones Industrial Average, the S&P 500 tracks the performance of larger company U.S. stocks. As the name S&P 500 suggests, this index tracks the prices of 500 stocks. These 500 big companies account for about 70 percent of the total market value of the tens of thousands of stocks traded in the U.S. The Dow Jones stocks represent less than 20 percent of the total market value of U.S. stocks. Thus, the S&P 500 is a much broader and more representative index of the larger company stocks in the U.S. than is the Dow Jones Industrial Average.

- **Russell 2000.** This index tracks the performance of 2,000 smaller U.S. company stocks of varying industries. Small company stocks tend to move in tandem with larger company stocks. It's unusual for one to fall while the other is rising, although this happened in 1987 when the S&P 500 was up 5.2 percent and the Russell 2000 was down 8.8 percent. As I discuss in Chapter 2, smaller company stocks tend to be more volatile, often rising more when the stock market increases and falling more precipitously when the market declines.

- **Wilshire 5000.** Despite its name, the Wilshire 5000 index actually tracks the prices of about 6,000 stocks of U.S. companies of all sizes — small, medium, and large. Thus, this index is considered the broadest and most representative of the overall U.S. stock market.

✔ **Morgan Stanley EAFE.** Stocks don't just exist in the U.S. Morgan Stanley's EAFE index (EAFE stands for Europe, Australia, and Far East) tracks the prices of stocks in the other major countries of the world.

✔ **Morgan Stanley Emerging Markets.** This index follows the price movements of stocks in the less economically developed but "emerging" countries, which tend to concentrate in Southeast Asia and Latin America. These stock markets tend to be more volatile than those in established economies. During good times, emerging markets usually reward investors with higher returns.

You might hope that these are all the indexes you'll hear about, but literally hundreds of other indexes exist. But don't worry, you really don't need to know about the myriad other ones. You see, many companies, largely out of desire for publicity, develop their own indexes. If the news media reports on these indexes, the index developer effectively gets free advertising. Many of the other indexes out there essentially replicate the ones I've just discussed, which are considered the major and best ones to follow.

Indexes serve several purposes. First, they can quickly give you an idea of how particular types of stocks are faring and performing in comparison to other types of stocks. In 1993, for example, the S&P 500 was up 10.1 percent, but smaller company U.S. stocks, as measured by the Russell 2000 index, rose even more: 18.9 percent. The Morgan Stanley foreign stock EAFE index, by contrast, was up a whopping 33 percent, and its emerging markets index skyrocketed 74.9 percent in 1993! Every year is different: In 1995, the U.S. markets did better than the foreign markets.

Indexes also allow you to compare or benchmark the performance of your stock market investments. If you invest primarily in large company U.S. stocks, for example, you should be comparing the overall return of the stocks in your portfolio to a comparable index — in this case, the S&P 500.

Some other types of indexes you may hear about are more narrowly focused, such as those that track the performance of stocks in particular industries: advertising, banks, computers, drugs, restaurants, semiconductors, textiles, and utilities. Other countries, such as Japan, the United Kingdom, Germany, France, Canada, and Hong Kong, have stock indexes that track the performance of their own stock markets. It's dangerous to focus your investments in the stocks of just one or two industries or smaller countries. Thus I think you should ignore these narrower indexes.

How do I buy low and sell high?

Now that you know about the different types of stock markets, you may be wondering how to get rich and not get clobbered. Nobody wants to buy stocks before the markets take one of their big drops. Thousands of books have been written about how to get rich in the stock market by buying the best stocks cheaply and selling them when they become dear. It is with some trepidation that I embark on an explanation about how to buy low and sell high. As I discuss in Chapter 4, the stock market is reasonably efficient. What a company's stock is priced at normally reflects lots of smart people's assessment as to what is a fair price.

That's not to say that some investors don't have an ability for spotting good times to buy and sell particular stocks. But consistently doing so is very difficult. In fact, the investing public doesn't have such a great track record with buying low and selling high. Smaller investors have done somewhat the opposite — selling heavily *after* major declines and stepping up buying *after* major price increases.

As a percentage of household assets, the American public's ownership of stocks was below 20 percent after World War II before the stock market went on a bullish rampage. Stock ownership steadily increased until it peaked at about 36 percent of the public's financial assets in the late 1960s, when the market hit highs that it wouldn't break for nearly 15 years. When the market plunged in the mid-1970s, the public dumped stock and held less than 16 percent of its assets in stocks. During the 1980s and early 1990s, as the market has boomed, the public has been slow to increase stock ownership. Today's stock ownership is close to the average of the modern market.

The simplest and best way to make money in the stock market is to consistently and regularly feed new money into building a bigger portfolio. If the market does drop, your purchases will buy more. The danger in trying to time the market is that you may be "out" of the market when it appreciates greatly and "in" the market when it plummets.

Price-earnings ratios

Suppose I tell you that Liz's Distinctive Jewelry's stock is selling for $50 per share and another stock in the same industry, The Crafty Jeweler, is selling for $100. Which would you rather buy?

If you answered, "I don't have a clue because you didn't give me enough information," go to the head of the class! On its own, the price per share of a stock is meaningless.

While The Crafty Jeweler is selling for twice as much per share, suppose their profits are also twice as great per share. The level of a company's stock price relative to its earnings or profits per share helps you calibrate how expensively, cheaply, or fairly a stock price is valued.

$$\frac{\text{Stock Price Per Share}}{\text{Annual Earnings Per Share}} = \text{Price-earnings (P/E) ratio}$$

Earlier in the chapter, Figure 5-1 showed that stock prices and corporate profits tend to move like two dance partners in sync with one another. The *price-earnings (P/E) ratio* (say PE — the "/" isn't pronounced) compares the level of stock prices to the level of corporate profits.

P/E ratios can be calculated for individual stocks as well as entire stock markets. Take this practical example to see how P/Es can be used.

In recent years, many investors have been concerned that stock prices in the U.S. were getting into the nosebleed area. The U.S. stock market continued to hit one new high after another. In early 1997, the most widely quoted stock market indicator, the Dow Jones Industrial Average, broke 7,000. To many investors, that sounded like a mighty large number, especially given the fact that Dow was at 1,700 in 1987 and 1,200 as recently as 1984.

But the Dow at 7,000 was actually not at as high a level as it may appear. First, a lot of inflation had occurred over the years. In fact, adjusting for inflation, the Dow at 7,000 was actually just a bit higher than the level that it was way back in 1966. Another indicator that the U.S. stock market was not as expensive as it seemed was the price-earnings ratio of the market today versus where it has been historically. Over the past 100-plus years, the P/E ratio of the S&P 500 index has averaged about 14 (see Figure 5-2). It has varied as low as 6 and as high as 27. At the new heights achieved by the U.S. stock market in 1997, the S&P 500 P/E ratio was approximately 21, a bit higher than average but not way out of line.

Just because the larger company U.S. stocks have averaged P/Es of about 14, it doesn't mean that every individual stock will trade at such a P/E. Here's why. Suppose you have a choice between investing in two companies, Superb Software, which makes computer software, and Tortoise Technologies, which makes typewriters. If both companies' stocks are selling at a P/E of 15 and Superb Software's business and profits are growing 40 percent per year and Tortoises are remaining flat, which would you buy?

Because they are both trading at a P/E of 15, Superb Software appears to be the better buy. Even if it just continues to sell for 15 times earnings, its stock price should increase 40 percent per year as its profits do. Faster growing companies usually command higher price-earnings ratios, as shown in Table 5-1:

Table 5-1   Faster Growing Companies Tend to Sell at Higher P/Es

Company	*Recent P/E*	*Earnings Growth Past Five Years*
Barnett Banks	11	1%
Texaco	14	8%
Gillette	25	18%
Microsoft	41	45%

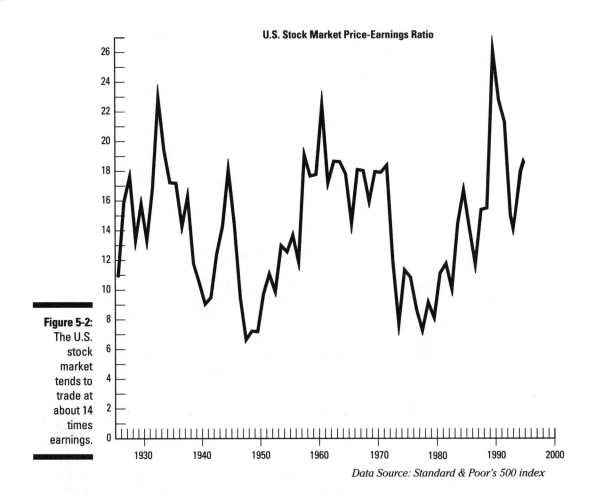

U.S. Stock Market Price-Earnings Ratio

Figure 5-2:
The U.S. stock market tends to trade at about 14 times earnings.

Data Source: Standard & Poor's 500 index

Just because a stock price or an entire stock market seems to be at a high price level doesn't necessarily mean that the stock or market is overpriced. Always compare the level of a stock to the level of that company's profits, or the overall market's price level to overall corporate profits. The price-earnings ratio captures this comparison. Faster growing and more-profitable companies generally sell for a premium — higher P/Es. Also remember that future earnings, which are difficult to predict, influence stock prices more than current earnings, which are old news.

Don't get swept up in times of speculative excess

Because the financial markets move as much on the financial realities of the economy as well as people's expectations and emotions (particularly fear and greed), I don't believe that you should try to time the markets. Knowing when to buy and sell is much harder than you think.

That said, you should be careful not to get sucked into investing lots of your money into aggressive investments that seem to be in a frothy state. Doing this is where people go wrong. Many people don't become aware of an investment until it's getting lots of attention. By the time everyone else is talking about an investment, it's often nearing or at its peak.

Health-care hype

Consider what happened with health-care stocks in the late 1980s. During most of the 1980s, health-care stocks largely tracked the overall U.S. stock market. But in the late 1980s, health-care stocks began to beat the rest of the pack. These companies' profits were doing well, but so too was most of the rest of corporate America.

Then in 1991, health-care stocks zoomed to the moon. Mutual funds that specialize in health-care stocks produced total returns of almost 64 percent in 1991. Consider that — 64 percent — for $10,000 invested, a year later investors had $16,400 to show for their efforts!!! In this century, the U.S. stock market has averaged returns of 10 percent per year. Health-care stocks went up six times that amount during 1991.

Health-care funds filled top performance charts in 1991. Four of the top 20 funds that year were health-care industry funds and many of that year's other top performers were loaded with health-care stocks. I remember that many people I spoke with at that time thought that health-care stocks were good investments. "With the continued aging of the population and soaring health-care costs, won't these companies be able to make the big bucks in the years ahead?" one person asked. "People always need health care, so profits will always grow," said another.

New money flooded into health-care stocks. At year-end 1990, the health-care stock mutual funds in existence reported $1.63 billion under management. A year later, nearly double this amount — $3.23 billion — of new money gushed into these funds. More than 40 percent of this new money flowed into Fidelity Investments, which ran three health-care-related sector funds at that time.

Fidelity spent gobs advertising the performance of these funds to lure in new and novice investors. Fidelity also charged its investors 3 percent for the privilege of being sucked into these funds at their peak.

In 1992 and 1993, the two years immediately following the flood of new money into health-care stocks, the average health-care stock fund dropped 1.1 percent in value, greatly underperforming the overall U.S. stock market, which rose more than 21 percent.

As returns proved so dismal during a continued boom in the stock market, investors have started to bail out. More than a billion dollars has flowed out of these funds in recent years.

The 1920s: dawn of the first modern consumer spending binge

The Dow Jones Industrial Average soared nearly 500 percent in a mere eight years from 1921 to 1929, the best bull market run that the U.S. stock market has ever seen. The country and investors had good reason for economic optimism. The "new" devices — telephones, cars, radios, and all sorts of electric appliances — were making their way into the mass market. The stock price of RCA, the radio manufacturer, for example, ballooned 5,700 percent during this great bull run.

Speculation in the stock market moved from Wall Street to Main Street. Investors during the 1920s could borrow lots of money to buy stock, through *margin borrowing*. Margin borrowing can still be done today — for every dollar you put up, you may borrow an additional dollar to buy stock with. At times during the 1920s, you could borrow nine dollars for every dollar you had in hand. The amount of margin loans outstanding swelled from $1 billion in the early 1920s to more than $8 billion in 1929. When the market plunged, margin calls forced margin borrowers to sell their stock, thus exacerbating the decline.

What's a bull and a bear?

If you read magazines or newspapers or listen to people talk about the stock market, you'll often hear reference to *bull* markets and *bear* markets. Maybe you know which one means a good market and which one means a bad market to be an investor in. But even if you do, you may be wondering where these silly terms came from.

It's hard to find agreement on the origin of these terms, but my favorite description comes from Robert Claiborne's *Loose Cannons and Red Herrings — A Book of Lost Metaphors*. The term bear, according to Claiborne, originates from a proverb that mocks a man who "sells the bearskin before catching the bear." Here's the connection to the stock market. When dealers in the stock market thought that the market had become too pricey and speculative, these dealers would sell stock that they hadn't yet "caught" (bought). These dealers were labeled "bearskin jobbers" and, later, "bears."

The practice that these bearish dealers were engaging in was *short selling*. They hoped that when they ultimately bought the stock that they had first sold, they could buy it back at a lower price. Their profit thus was the difference between what they sold it for and what they bought it for. Short selling is simply investing in reverse: You sell first and buy back later. The worst thing for a bear is if prices go up, and you must buy back the stock at a high price. As Claiborne said, "He who sells what isn't his'n, must buy it back or go to prison."

The bulls, according to Claiborne, were those who worked the "other side" of the street. They bought stocks with the hope and expectation that they would rise. Ben Travato, a man whom Claiborne describes as one prone to inventing colorful, but often inaccurate, etymologies, said that the bulls tossed stocks up in the air with their horns.

The steep run-up in stock prices was also due, in part, to market manipulation. Investment pools would buy and sell stock amongst one another, thus generating high trading volume in a stock, making it appear that interest in the stock was great. Also in cahoots with pool operators were writers who would dispense enthusiastic prognostications about said stock. (Reforms later passed by the Securities and Exchange Commission addressed these problems.)

Not only were members of the public largely enthusiastic, so too were those who should have known better. After a small decline occurred in September 1929, economist Irving Fisher said in mid-October, "Stock prices have reached what looks like a permanently high plateau." High? Yes! Permanent plateau? Investors wish!

On October 25, 1929, just days before all heck began breaking loose, President Herbert Hoover said, "The fundamental business of the country . . . is on a sound and prosperous basis." Days later, multimillionaire oil tycoon John D. Rockefeller said, "Believing that fundamental conditions of the country are sound . . . my son and I have for some days been purchasing sound common stocks."

By December of that same year, the stock market had dropped by more than 35 percent. General Electric President Owen D. Young said at that time, "Those who voluntarily sell stocks at current prices are extremely foolish." Actually not. By the time the crash had run its course, the market had plunged 89 percent in value in less than three years.

The magnitude of this steep decline in stock prices could not have been predicted or expected in the late 1920s. The economy went into a tailspin. Unemployment soared to more than 25 percent of the labor force. Companies entered this period with excess inventories, which mushroomed further once people slashed their spending. High overseas tariffs stifled American exports. Thousands of banks failed, as early bank failures triggered "runs" on other banks (no FDIC insurance existed in these days).

The 1960s weren't just about sex, drugs, and rock and roll

The U.S. stock market mirrored the climate of our country during this decade of change and upheaval. There were good years and bad years, but overall, the stock market gained. Unfortunately, the investors who were old enough to remember what happened to the stock market during the Great Depression were now dead or retired. The new investors and the majority of the investors during the 1960s were born after the go-go years of the 1920s or were still sucking on a pacifier then.

Consumer product companies' stocks were very popular and were bid up to stratospheric prices. When I say that, I mean that some stock prices were high relative to the company's earnings — our old friend, the price-earnings (P/E) ratio. Investors had seen such stock's prices rise for many years and thought that the good times would never end.

Take the case of Avon Products, which sells cosmetics door-to-door primarily with an army of women. During the late 1960s, Avon's stock regularly sold at a P/E of 50 to 70 times earnings (remember, the market average is about 14). After trading as high as $140 per share in the early 1970s, Avon's stock never got back on track. Now more than two decades later, Avon's stock price has never come close to its lofty levels. Its stock price has recently been around $70 per share, which is a more sane 18 times earnings.

When a stock such as Avon's sells at such a high multiple of earnings, two factors can lead to a bloodletting. First, the company's profits may continue to grow, but investors may decide that the stock isn't such a great long-term investment after all and not worth, say, a P/E of 60. Consider that if investors decide it's only worth a P/E of 30 (still a hefty P/E), the stock price would drop 50 percent to cut the P/E in half.

The second shoe that can drop is the company's profits or earnings. If profits fall, say, 20 percent, as Avon's did during the 1974–75 recession, the stock price will fall 20 percent, even if it were to continue selling for 60 times earnings. But when earnings drop, investors' willingness to pay an inflated P/E plummets along with the earnings. Growth companies and growth stocks don't have shrinking profits! So when Avon's profits finally did drop, the P/E investors were willing to pay plunged to 9! In less than two years, Avon's stock price thus dropped nearly 87 percent.

Avon was not alone in its stock price soaring to a rather high multiple of its earnings in the 1960s and early 1970s. Well-known companies such as Black & Decker, Eastman Kodak, IBM, Kmart (used to be called S. S. Kresge in those days), Polaroid, and Xerox sold for 60 to as much as 100 times earnings. All these companies, like Avon, are selling today at about the same or at a lower price than they achieved more than 20 years ago. Many other well-known and smaller companies sold at similar and even more outrageous premiums to earnings.

The Japanese stock market juggernaut

Lest you think that the U.S. had cornered the market on manias, overseas examples abound. A rather extraordinary one happened not so long ago — less than a decade — in the Japanese stock market.

After the crushing defeat suffered in World War II, Japan's economy was in a shambles. Two major cities — Hiroshima and Nagasaki — were destroyed and more than 200,000 killed when the U.S. dropped atomic bombs to "win" the war.

Out of the rubble, Japan emerged a strengthened nation that became an economic powerhouse on the par of the world's most successful economies. Over 22 years, from 1967 to 1989, Japanese stock prices rose an amazing 30-fold (3,000 percent) as the economy boomed. From 1983 to 1989 alone, Japanese stocks soared more than 500 percent.

Other maniacal manias in centuries long gone

I can fill an entire book with modern-day stock market manias. But bear with me as I roll back the clocks a couple of centuries to observe others, the first being England's South Sea bubble of 1719. King George backed the South Seas Company and acted as its governor. South Seas was not the kind of company that would have met today's socially responsible investor's needs. Initially, the South Seas Company focused on the African slave trade. Too many slaves died in transit, so it wasn't a lucrative business.

If you think government corruption is a problem today, consider what politicians of those days did without the scrutiny of a widely-read press. Politicos in Parliament bought tons of stock in the South Seas Company and even rammed through Parliament a provision allowing investors to buy stock on borrowed money. The stock of the South Seas Company soared from about £120 to more than £1000 in just the first six months in 1720.

After such an enormous run-up, the insiders realized that the stock price was greatly inflated and quietly bailed. Citizens were falling all over themselves to get into this surefire moneymaker. Other seafaring companies pursued the South Seas trade business, and the greedy politicians passed a law saying that only government-approved companies could pursue trade. The stocks of these other companies tumbled, and investor losses led to a chain reaction that prompted selling in the South Seas Company stock, which plunged more than 80 percent by the fall of that same year.

England wasn't the only European country to be swept up in an investment mania. Probably the most famous mania of them all was the tulip bulb (yes, those flowers that you can plant in your own home garden). A botany professor introduced tulips into Holland from Turkey in the late 1500s. Residents let a fascination with these bulbs turn into an investment feeding frenzy.

At their speculative peak, the price of a single tulip bulb was the equivalent of more than $10,000 in today's dollars. Many people sold their land holdings to buy more. Documented cases show people trading a bulb for a dozen acres of land! Laborers cut back on their work to invest. Eventually, tulip bulb prices came crashing back to Earth. A trip to your local nursery should show you what a bulb sells for today.

In terms of the U.S. dollar, the Japanese stock market rise was all the more stunning, as the dollar lost value versus Japan's currency, the yen. The dollar lost about 65 percent of its value during the big run-up in Japanese stocks. In dollar terms, the Japanese stock market rose an astonishing 8,300 percent from 1967 to 1989.

Investing in stocks in Japan was considered close to a sure thing, much like many California real estate investors said to me of their favorite investment when I moved to the Golden State in 1987. Increasing numbers of people became full-time stock market investors in Japan. Many of these folks were actually speculators, as borrowed funds were used heavily. As the Japanese real estate market had boomed in tandem with the stock market, real estate investors borrowed from their winnings to invest in stocks and vice versa.

Borrowing heavily was an easy thing to do as Japan's banks were awash in cash, and it was cheap, cheap, cheap to borrow. Investors could borrow money for a mere few percent. Property purchases by "established investors" could be made with no money down. Cash abounded from real estate as the price of land in Tokyo, for example, soared 500 percent from 1985–1990. Despite having $1/25$ as much land as the U.S., Japan's total land values at the close of the 1980s were four times that of all the land in the U.S.

Speculators also used futures and options to gamble on higher short-term market prices. Interestingly, selling short is not allowed in Japan. And given the strong Japanese currency, investors did their investing at home, so as to not lose out from devaluation of foreign currencies. This is one of the reasons why many Japanese investors had little sense about what investments were intrinsically worth.

Price-earnings ratios? Forget it. Speculators justified the high prices they paid for stocks by pointing out that the real estate many companies owned was soaring to the moon and making companies more valuable.

Price-earnings ratios on the Japanese market soared during the 1980s and ballooned to more than 60 times earnings by 1987, four times the U.S. market average. As I point out earlier in this chapter, such lofty P/Es were sometimes awarded hot stocks in the U.S. But the entire Japanese stock market, which included many mediocre and not-so-hot companies, had a P/E of 60-plus.

When Japan's version of AT&T, Nippon Telegraph and Telephone, went public in February 1987, it was met with such frenzied enthusiasm that its stock price was soon bid up to a stratospheric 300-plus price-earnings ratio. At the close of 1989, Japan's stock market, for the first time in history, had unseated the U.S. stock market in total market value of all stocks. And this happened despite the fact that the total output of the Japanese economy was less than half of that of the U.S.

Investors in the U.S. sometimes get concerned when dividend rates on stocks sink below 3 percent. In Japan, in the late 1980s, yields sank to a skeletal 0.5 percent.

Even some U.S. observers started to lose sight of the big picture and added to the rationalizations for why the Japanese markets weren't irrational. After all, it was reasoned, Japanese companies and executives were tightly knit and a "closed circle," investing heavily in stock of other companies they did business with. The supply of stock for outside buyers was thus limited as companies sat on their shares.

Corporate stock ownership went further, though, as stock prices were sometimes manipulated as they had been in the U.S. in the earlier part of this century. Speculators gobbled up the bulk of outstanding shares of small companies and traded shares back and forth with others they were in partnership with to drive up prices.

Company pension plans started dumping all (as in 100 percent) of their employees' retirement money into stocks with the expectation that stock prices would always keep going up. Someone else would always pay a higher price to buy stock.

BEWARE

The *New York Times* and Merrill Lynch said buy at the highs

One of the reasons that otherwise intelligent people get sucked into grossly overpriced investments near their peak is because organizations they think are in the know encourage them to do so. In October 1989, the *New York Times*, the paper of record, weighed in with an article on the Japanese market entitled "Japanese Market Watchers Not Worried." The piece argued in a fairly one-sided fashion and quoted many supporting sources saying that Japanese stock prices were on solid ground. The *New York Times* article said that Japanese financial executives did not expect a sustained downturn in the Japanese stock market. The head of trading at Nikko Securities, a large Japanese brokerage firm was quoted as saying, ". . . any drop would be temporary."

Of course, whom you interview and what facts you bring to bare have an enormous impact on the story to be told. What would one expect brokerage firms, which make all of their money by encouraging stock market investing, to say? Duh.

U.S. economist James Grant pointed out in his newsletter a couple of years earlier the silliness of high P/Es in some Japanese stocks being used to justify high P/Es elsewhere. Grant told of a Merrill Lynch brokerage analyst who recommended investing in Yasuda Trust, a Japanese bank. Yasuda's P/E at the time was a modest 63 compared to other bank stocks, which weighed in at nearly 100 times earnings. Over the next five years, investors who followed Merrill's advice were greeted with a 70-plus percent decline. Being a U.S. headquartered brokerage firm, Merrill should have known better. The desire to win more commissions clouded their judgment.

Less than three months after the *New York Times* weighed in with their "don't worry about high prices" piece on the Japanese stock market, the party ended with few of the invited guests ever told. The lights were shut off, the punch bowls emptied, and most people's cars stolen, so they couldn't even get home.

The collapse of the Japanese stock market was swift. After peaking at the end of 1989, the Tokyo market plunged nearly 50 percent in the first nine months of 1990 alone. By the middle of 1992, the worst was over, but Japanese stock investors who were diversified and hadn't borrowed were down nearly 65 percent — a plunge that the U.S. market hasn't experienced since the Great Depression. Japanese investors who borrowed lost everything and sometimes more. The total loss in stock market value was about $2.5 trillion, about the size of the entire Japanese annual output.

Several factors finally led to the bursting of the Japanese stock market bubble. Japanese monetary authorities tightened credit as inflation started to creep upward and concern increased over real estate market speculation. As interest rates began to rise, investors soon realized that they could earn 15 times more interest from a safe bond versus the paltry yield on stocks. (U.S. investors, concerned about our markets' recently low yield of 2.5 percent, would need to be tempted by a 37-plus percent yield for a similar situation!)

As interest rates rose and credit tightened, speculators were the first to be squeezed. Real estate and stock market speculators began to sell to pay off mounting debts. Higher interest rates, less available credit, and the already grossly inflated prices greatly limited the pool of potential stock buyers. The plunging stock and real estate markets fed on one another. Investor losses in one market triggered more selling and price drops in the other. The real estate price drop has been equally severe — equaling 50 to 60 percent or more in most parts of Japan since the late 1980s.

Psychologically, it is easier for many people to buy stocks *after* they've had a huge increase in price. Just as you shouldn't attempt to drive your car solely by looking through your rearview mirror, basing investments solely on past performance usually leads novice investors into overpriced investments. If many people are talking about the stunning rise in the market and new investors are piling in based on the expectation of hefty profits, take note.

I'm not saying to necessarily sell your current stock holdings if you see an investment market getting frothy and speculative. So long as you're diversified in stocks worldwide and hold other investments, such as real estate and bonds, the stocks you hold in one market should be but a fraction of your total holdings. Timing the markets is very difficult: How do you know how high is high and when it's time to sell, and then how low is low and when it's time to buy? And if you sell non-retirement account investments at a profit, you end up sacrificing a lot of the profit to federal and state taxes.

Roll out the fleet of shopping carts during a sale

Along with speculative buying frenzies come valleys of pessimism. Having the courage to buy when stocks are "on sale" can pay bigger returns.

In the early 1970s, interest rates and inflation escalated. Oil prices shot up as the Arab oil embargo choked off supplies, and Americans had to wait in long lines for gas. Gold prices soared, and the U.S. dollar got clobbered in foreign currency markets.

If the economic problems weren't enough to make most everyone gloomy, the U.S. political system hit an all-time low around this period as well. Vice President Spiro Agnew resigned in disgrace under a cloud of tax evasion charges. Then Watergate led to President Nixon's August 1974 resignation, the first presidential resignation in our history.

When all was sold and done, the Dow Jones Industrial Average had plummeted more than 45 percent from early 1973 until late 1974. Among the stocks that fell the hardest and furthest included those that were most popular and selling at extreme multiples of earnings in the late 1960s and early 1970s. (See "The 1960s weren't just about sex, drugs, and rock and roll," earlier in this chapter.)

Take a gander in Table 5-2 at the drops in these well-known companies and how cheaply these stocks were valued relative to corporate profits (look at the P/Es) after the worst market drop since the Great Depression.

Those who were too terrified to buy stocks in the mid-1970s actually had plenty of time to get on board and take advantage of the buying opportunities. The stock market did have a powerful rally and, from its 1974 low, rose nearly 80 percent over the next two years. But over the next half dozen years, the market backpedaled, losing much of its gains.

In the late 1970s and early 1980s, inflation continued to escalate well into double digits. Corporate profits plunged more and unemployment rose higher than in the 1974 recession. While some stocks dropped, others simply treaded water and went sideways for years after major declines in the mid-1970s. As some companies' profits increased, P/E bargains abounded (see Table 5-3).

When bad news and pessimism abound and the stock market has been clobbered, it's a much safer and better time to buy stocks by the truckload. You may even consider shifting some of your money out of your safer investments, such as bonds, and invest more aggressively in stocks. Investors feel during these times that prices can drop further, but if you buy and wait you'll be amply rewarded. Most of the stocks listed in the last several pages have appreciated 500 to 2,000-plus percent in the past 15 to 20 years.

Table 5-2	Stock Bargains Galore in the Mid-1970s		
Company	**Industry**	**Stock Price Fall from Peak**	**1974 P/E**
Abbott Laboratories	Drugs	66%	8
AIG	Insurance	67%	10
Avon	Cosmetics	87%	9
H&R Block	Tax preparation	83%	6
Chemical Bank	Banking	64%	4
Coca-Cola	Beverages	70%	12
Dayton-Hudson	Department stores	86%	4
Disney	Entertainment	75%	11
Dun & Bradstreet	Business information	68%	9
General Dynamics	Military	81%	3
Hilton Hotels	Hotels	87%	4
Humana	Hospitals	91%	3
Intel	Semiconductors	76%	6
Kimberly-Clark	Consumer products	63%	4
McGraw-Hill	Publishing	90%	4
Mobil	Oil	60%	3
PepsiCo	Beverages	67%	8
Pitney Bowes	Postage meters	84%	6
Polaroid	Photography	91%	12
Potlatch	Lumber and paper	66%	3
PPG Industries	Glass	60%	4
Quaker Oats	Packaged food	76%	6
Rite Aid	Drug stores	95%	4
Scientific-Atlanta	Communications Equipment	82%	4
Sprint	Telephone	67%	7
Tandy	Consumer electronic retailer	70%	5
Textron	Aerospace	80%	4
TRW	Electronics	83%	4
U.S. Shoe	Shoes	82%	4
Woolworth	Discount stores	86%	3

Table 5-3   More Stock Bargains in the Late 1970s and Early 1980s

Company	Industry	Stock Price Fall from Peak	P/E Late 70s/ Early 80s
Anheuser-Busch	Beer	75%	8
Avon	Cosmetics	86%	6
Campbell Soup	Canned Foods	36%	6
Coca-Cola	Beverages	61%	8
Colgate-Palmolive	Personal care	69%	6
Eastman Kodak	Photography	73%	7
General Electric	Consumer/industrial products	44%	7
General Mills	Food	44%	6
Gillette	Shaving products	74%	5
McDonald's	Fast food	46%	9
MMM	Consumer/industrial products	50%	8
Pacific Gas & Electric	Utility	52%	6
J.C. Penney	Department stores	80%	6
Procter & Gamble	Consumer products	46%	8
Ralston Purina	Pet food	49%	6
Rubbermaid	Rubber products	60%	7
Sara Lee	Food	60%	5
Schering Plough	Drugs	71%	7
Seagram	Alcohol	60%	7
Sears	Department store	76%	6
Tambrands	Feminine hygiene products	82%	7
Wells Fargo	Banking	50%	3
Whirlpool	Household appliances	63%	5
Xerox	Copiers	85%	5

Buying Stocks

So many stocks, so little time.

You can let a mutual fund manager or stockbroker do the picking for you. You can pick your own and possibly even buy stock direct from the issuing company.

I remember when I first moved to California and heard that rather than simply going to the grocery store to buy fruits and vegetables, you could go to a farmers' market. Farmers' markets brought the farmers to you. A number of California towns have a couple dozen small farming operations that set up shop for a few hours weekly and sell their stuff.

And if that isn't direct enough, you can go straight to some farms and pick your own. I remember the first time I did this — it was a blast, although several weeks later I was mighty tired of eating the apples and berries I had picked.

The next time I decided to drive out to these farms, the hour-plus drive in the hot, baking sun seemed a lot longer than I remembered. The produce prices, I noticed on this go-round, weren't that much less than our local supermarket charged. And I had to spend all my time and pick it myself, for goodness sakes — the farmers were saving on the labor costs! Then it dawned on me that their fruit pickers probably weren't paid all that much and were likely ten times more efficient (okay, maybe a hundred times more) than I. If I factored the costs of driving my car out to buy the fruit that I bought, it ended up costing about what I would pay at the store five minutes from my home.

Now some people would continue to drive out to the farms, perhaps even weekly, for the sheer joy and pleasure of selecting and picking their own produce in the heat and dust. But I've discovered that one of the values of the farmers and stores doing the choosing and work for me is that they are better at it.

When you go to invest in stocks, you have choices similar to those that you have when it comes time to go produce shopping. Picking your own stocks can be entertaining and educational. And few things are more gratifying and vindicating to the old ego than to see your stock choice double or better in price after you purchase it. As with picking your own produce though, don't forget to factor your time and expertise into the equation.

Stocks through funds

If you're busy and suffer no delusions about your expertise, you'll love stock mutual funds. If you can find your telephone, dial an 800 number, fill out some relatively simply application forms, and attach a check, you can invest in stocks through mutual funds.

Mutual funds are investment companies that take money from people like you and me and invest the money in securities, such as stocks and bonds. Stock mutual funds, as the name suggests, invest primarily or exclusively in stocks (some "stock" funds sometimes invest a bit in other stuff, such as bonds).

The advantages of stock mutual funds are many:

- ✔ **Diversification.** It would be prohibitively expensive to buy individual stocks on your own, unless you buy reasonable chunks (100 shares or so) of each stock. But to buy this amount of stock in, say, a dozen companies' stocks to ensure diversification, you need about $36,000 if the stocks you buy average $30 per share in price.

- ✔ **Professional management.** Even if you have big bucks to invest, mutual funds offer something you can't deliver: professional, full-time management. Look at it this way: Funds are a huge time-saver. It's Friday night — would you rather go to the local library and do some research on semiconductor and toilet paper manufacturers or enjoy dinner or a movie with family and friends? (I guess the answer to that question depends on who your family and friends are!)

  Mutual fund managers peruse a company's financial statements and otherwise track and analyze a company's business strategy and market position. The best managers put in more than a 40-hour work week and have lots of expertise and experience in the field.

- ✔ **Low costs — if you pick 'em right.** More than a few brokers and others with a vested interest in convincing you that mutual funds aren't a good way for you to invest will point out the high fees some funds charge. An element of truth rings here: Some funds are expensive, charging you a couple percent or more per year in operating expenses on top of hefty sales commissions.

  But just as you wouldn't want to invest in a fund managed by a novice with no track record, why would you want to invest in a high-cost fund? Contrary to the "You get what you pay for" notion often trumpeted by those trying to sell you something at an inflated price, many of the best managers are the cheapest to hire. Through a no-load (commission-free) mutual fund, you can hire a professional, full-time money manager to invest your $10,000 for a mere $20 to $100 per year. And if you have far less than this to invest, they'll still invest your money at a low cost: $2 to $10 per year if you invest $1,000.

As with all investments, mutual funds are not without drawbacks. First is the issue of control. If you're a control freak, you may be unnerved turning over your investment stash to a seemingly black box process where others decide when and in what to invest. My advice: Don't sweat it. You should be more nervous about the potential blunders you'll make investing in individual stocks of your own choosing or, even worse, those stocks pitched to you by a broker.

Taxes are another concern for investing in funds outside retirement accounts. Because the fund manager, and not you, decides when to sell specific stock holdings, some funds may produce somewhat high levels of taxable distributions. Fear not — simply select tax-friendly funds if taxes are a concern.

In Chapter 8, I talk about the wonderful world of mutual funds. They're a terrific, low cost, high-quality way to invest in stocks around the globe.

Buying individual stocks

More than a few investing books suggest and enthusiastically encourage people like you to do their own stock picking. The vast majority of people would be better off *not* doing this.

Why do I make this statement? Not because I don't think highly of you and your capabilities; I do. I've long been an advocate of people educating themselves and taking responsibility for their own financial affairs.

But taking responsibility for your own finances doesn't mean that you should do *everything* yourself. Remember my discussion about picking your own produce in the fields versus buying it closer to home? I challenge you to consider why you might prefer to invest in individual stocks of your own choosing. Table 5-4 includes some of the thoughts you may have on the subject:

Table 5-4	The Pros and Cons of Choosing Your Own Stocks
Good Reasons to Pick Your Own Stocks:	*Bad Reasons to Pick Your Own Stocks:*
You enjoy the challenge.	You think you can beat the best money managers. (If you can, you're in the wrong profession!)
You want to learn more about business.	You want more control over your investments, which you think will happen if you understand what companies you're investing in.
You have a substantial amount to invest.	You think mutual funds are for people who aren't smart enough to choose their own stocks.

Several popular investing books have tried to convince investors that they can do a *better* job than the professionals at picking their own stocks. Consider former mutual fund manager Peter Lynch's second book, *Beating the Street*. This is a title designed to attract the greedy side of our personalities. (It should be noted that the publisher, Simon & Schuster, also cranked out other financial titles, such as *Wealth Without Risk*.) Consider what Lynch says: ". . . an amateur who devotes a small amount of study to companies in an industry he or she knows something about can outperform 95 percent of the paid experts who manage the mutual funds. . . ."

Ninety-five percent, Mr. Lynch??? Quite a surprising statement from a man who made his living for more than a decade as a successful fund manager at Fidelity and today is a director at this largest of mutual fund companies. (Fidelity, it should be noted, also operates a brokerage division, which earns hefty profits off of stock traders.) And you're going to have to invest more than "a small amount of study." Lynch worked 80 hours a week at investing!

A Midwest investment club that claims to have beaten the market's returns by a wide margin wrote an investing book, *The Beardstown Ladies' Common-Sense Investment Guide.* This club's philosophy, like Lynch's, is to invest in companies whose businesses you are familiar with and you can understand. (I discuss this book in greater detail in Chapter 15.)

Although industry familiarity can, at times, supplement your choice of investment, it's dangerous to base your investment decisions solely on your own knowledge and gut feelings. Allow me to introduce you to a company that many people in Northern California invested in through this approach: Fresh Choice. The idea, and the restaurants based on it, is simple and understood by many. You enter their restaurants and walk down a serving line, where you can serve yourself salads and other fresh and healthy choices. A pasta bar, soups, breads, and even a self-service dessert bar greet hungry eyes. It's all you can eat for about seven bucks, and, because it's self-serve, you don't tip.

Fresh Choice went public in December 1992, with the cute trading symbol, SALD. Over the next few months, it traded at around $23 per share, which represented nearly a 60 times earnings (P/E) — a whopping figure.

With Americans trying to eat healthier, how could you go wrong? Brokerage analysts, many of whom work for firms that sold shares in Fresh Choice's initial public offering, engaged in a love fest for owning the stock. Almost every analyst who followed the stock recommended buying it during 1993 and the first half of 1994, during which time its stock price bounced around between $25 to $30 per share while earnings steadily grew:

- Montgomery Securities said "buy."

- Morgan Grenfell called it a "must own."

- Dain Bosworth said to "buy."

- Rauscher Pierce Refsnes rated it a "buy" and one of their "two favorite picks" in the restaurant business. The firm said the company was "uniquely positioned" and had a "unique concept."

- Seidler said, "We are excited by the growth prospects for Fresh Choice, and we project a five-year earnings per share growth rate of 35 percent. . . . We believe the stock represents a good value. . . ."

✔ Lead underwriter Alex Brown rated it a "strong buy" until July 1994, at which point it was merely downgraded to "buy." Prior to that time, Alex Brown said of Fresh Choice, ". . . an excellent company and an exciting concept."

In the second half of 1994, some major problems became apparent. Fresh Choice's expansion plan was poorly managed. Some new restaurants opened too close to existing ones and cannibalized sales. Even those new locations that weren't close seemed to cannibalize sales — it seemed that people who liked the idea had been driving a good distance to existing stores.

A warning sign that these analysts and investors should have heeded was that Fresh Choice refused to release same store sales, which would have allowed dissection of sales growth from existing stores versus the new locations that were opening. It's easy for an expanding company to increase sales by simply opening new locations. Meanwhile, existing locations can be suffering declining revenue, which is masked in the company's aggregate revenue figures. This is what was happening at Fresh Choice.

Also, outside the confines of Northern California, the chain also met with an audience not as attuned to the type of food Fresh Choice specialized in. The all-you-can-eat format, not surprisingly, attracted bigger eaters. People looking for less food, as many health-conscious eaters do, stayed away. As people tired of the same menu, the stores had difficulty retaining repeat customers.

As the company's profits sank, so too did the stock price. From a high of $32^1/_2$ in March 1994, Fresh Choice's stock price plunged 84 percent in the next year!

What's my point? Although it may seem that I'm trying to scare you away from buying individual stocks, I'm not. But picking "good stocks," even those that seem easy to understand, is not as easy as some people lead you to believe. It's not as simple as visiting a restaurant chain, liking it, and then sitting back and getting rich watching their stock zoom to the moon.

If you invest in stocks, I think you know by now that guarantees don't exist. But as with many of life's endeavors, you can buy individual stocks in good and not-so-good ways. In the next chapter, I explain how to research and trade individual stocks. But first, I should talk about other ways to buy stocks. I'll finish with other acceptable ways (don't forget about funds), but I don't want you to miss reading the worst ways in the next section. I don't want you to make the same mistakes that too many other investors who came before you have.

Buying stock "direct" from companies

Over the years, increasing numbers of companies are selling stock directly to the public. But before you get too excited about not paying any brokerage commissions to buy stock, you should be aware of the many hassles and drawbacks of these programs.

✔ **We're not talking big bucks here.** The vast majority of these companies allow you to buy stock from them without a trading fee only by reinvesting your dividends. These are known as *Dividend Reinvestment Plans* (sometimes referred to as DRIPs). Because dividends are typically only a few percent per year of the amount you have invested, the amount you're able to reinvest is minimal.

✔ **You're still going to incur fees to buy your first shares.** In order to enroll in a company's DRIP, you must first purchase a share through a broker. Most brokers have minimum trading fees of $30 or $40, so if you're buying a few shares, a huge percentage of your initial investment is going to commissions anyway.

✔ **Paperwork, paperwork, paperwork.** Every time you want to set up a DRIP, you must request and complete the company's application forms and you also must jump through the hoops of transferring your shares to them as well. If you go through the headache of doing so, say, a dozen times, you're then rewarded with receiving a dozen statements on a regular basis from each individual company. If you enjoy this sort of thing, I'm behind on my office filing and was wondering if you would be interested. . . .

✔ **Taxes, taxes, taxes.** These plans are really only feasible for non-retirement account investing, which unfortunately exposes all those dividends to federal and state income taxes. The fact that you're reinvesting the dividends is irrelevant from the standpoint of taxes because the investments are being held outside the shelter of retirement accounts. If you're still in your working years or otherwise in a high tax bracket, you don't want to increase your tax bill even more by investing in higher dividend paying stocks. Thus, DRIP stocks make no sense (see the discussion in Chapter 3 for how to pick investments with an eye on taxes).

✔ **Lack of control over when your sell orders are executed.** To sell your shares, you mail in a request to the company. If in the two weeks that it takes for your letter to get there and be processed the stock price plunges, you get whatever price is available on the day the order is finally processed.

✔ **DRIPs duplicate something you can more easily do through a discount broker.** A number of discount brokers, such as Charles Schwab, Fidelity, and Jack White, offer free stock dividend reinvestment for all types of accounts, including retirement accounts. Other discounters are likely to follow.

A small number of companies offer investors the ability to reinvest dividends as well as make additional stock purchases at a discount of 1 to 5 percent from the current market price of their stock. Buying stock at a discount gets me more excited than DRIPs, but many of the previously listed drawbacks still apply. The companies that offer such plans tend to be smaller, run-of-the-mill utilities and banks, so you're not going to build a diversified, high-quality portfolio this way.

I would skip these plans. If you want to buy good individual stocks, invest through your retirement accounts and in tax-friendly stocks outside your retirement accounts. Research for good companies through Value Line and pick your stocks on the basis of their merits (see Chapter 6 to discover how). If you want to have your dividends reinvested without cost, simply use one of the discount brokerage firms offering this service.

Ways not to buy individual stocks

You may be curious about other ways to buy individual stocks, and if they're in this section, it's because I enthusiastically *don't* recommend them. You can greatly increase your chances of success and earn higher returns by avoiding commonly made stock investing mistakes presented here.

Don't buy through commission-based brokers

Many investors make the mistake of investing in individual stocks through a broker who earns a living by working on commission. Firms such as Prudential, Smith Barney, and Dean Witter employ armies of such brokers.

The standard pitch of these firms and their brokers is that they have research departments that monitor and report on stocks. Their brokers, using this research, tell you when to buy, sell, or hold. Sounds good in theory, but this "research" and system have a lot of problems.

Brokerage firms happen to be in another business, which creates enormous conflicts of interest in producing objective reviews of companies. You see, these investment firms also solicit companies to help them sell new stock and bond issues. To gain this business, the brokerage firms need to demonstrate enthusiasm and optimism for the company's future prospects.

Brokerage analysts who, with the best of intentions, write negative reports about a company get clobbered in a variety of ways. Some firms have fired such analysts. Companies that the analysts have criticized exclude them from analyst gatherings about the company. Most investment firms don't even give analysts a chance to write such reports because it's an unwritten rule that analysts who know what's good for their career and their brokerage firm don't write such reports.

Though it's been known in the investment industry that such problems exist without documented proof, one firm got caught admonishing its analysts via a memo not to say negative things. As uncovered by *Wall Street Journal* reporter Michael Siconolfi, Morgan Stanley's head of new stock issues stated in a memo that the firm's policy had to be "no negative comments about our clients." The memo also stated that any analyst's changes in a stock's rating or investment opinion, "which might be viewed negatively" by the firm's clients, had to be cleared through the company's corporate finance department head.

Various studies of the brokerage firm's stock ratings have conclusively demonstrated that, from a predictive perspective, most of their research is barely worth the cost of the paper that it's printed on. Value Line, which is independent, beats them hands down. (I explain how to use Value Line in Chapter 6.)

Pass on initial public offerings

As explained in the previous chapter, when a company offers new stock to the investing public, it's called an initial public offering (IPO). If you had bought Microsoft's IPO back in the spring of 1986 and held on until today, you'd be a mighty happy camper, having made a return of nearly 7,000 percent! Similar tales abound for investors who scooped up shares of McDonald's and other companies that have grown into behemoth, multibillion dollar, worldwide enterprises.

So you'd like to buy shares of the next Microsoft and McDonald's. Good luck! Investors and brokers who tell you that they bought IPOs that became big successes have a lot in common with some people who go fishing. They'll tell you about the days that the fish were really biting and they landed some big catches. But you'll hear less or nothing at all about the hours and days where they caught nothing or small fry.

Even factoring in the Microsofts and McDonald's of the world, IPOs as a group are poor investments. You read that right! Two university professors, Jay Ritter and Timothy Loughran, went to the trouble of documenting the performance of the thousands of IPOs that have happened since 1970. Here's what they found:

Average annual return on the IPO stocks	5 percent per year
Average annual return on comparable stocks	12 percent per year

If you buy IPOs, you miss out on a lot of personal investing profits. Some firms' IPOs have done even worse. The worst brokerage firms' IPOs, according to a study done by *Forbes* magazine, are Merrill Lynch's and Smith Barney Shearson's.

Consider what happened with Boston Chicken, which was touted as the next McDonald's but was actually a turkey! Boston Chicken went public with a bang in November 1993, less than a full year after commencing operations. Though the stock was to be originally issued for $20 per share, it soared to more than $50 per share and closed its first day of trading up more than 142 percent to $48 1/2 per share. At its high of $51 per share, the company's stock was selling for an astronomical 364 times earnings.

Boston Chicken is a chain of restaurants (now named Boston Market) characterized by serving large and moderately priced, healthier home-cooked meals. The main menu offering is rotisserie chicken, which is supposed to be lower in

Is Netscape the next Microsoft?

In recent years, the hype over the Internet had reached a fevered pitch, and much like television and radio stocks were in the late 1920s, technology stocks had been red hot on the stock market in 1995. Well before Netscape went public in August 1995, it was dubbed the next Microsoft. Netscape makes software that allows computer users to access the truckload of stuff that's being shoveled onto the World Wide Web on the Internet. The company boasts a 70 to 90 percent market share. Netscape also provides software to the companies that put their stuff on the Internet. Netscape boasted former hot-shot executives from Silicon Graphics and McCaw Cellular and a supposed Bill Gates-style technology wunderkind in Marc Andreessen, who was all of 23 when he joined the company in early 1994.

Originally, the investment bankers who wanted to bring Netscape stock public planned to sell the company stock at $13 per share and later raised it to $28. On August 9, when the company went public, the demand to buy stock was stronger than the power of a 100-foot high tidal wave. The stock opened at $71 per share, the first opportunity that members of the general public had the opportunity to buy into the IPO, and soon zoomed to $74 3/4. (Only large institutional investors that buy lots of other investment banker IPOs can get shares of a hot IPO at the offering price, which in this case was $28.) Within months it skyrocketed to $174.

At the time it went public, Netscape had been in business for less than a year and a half and had only $16 million in revenues for the first half of 1995. Furthermore, the company was losing money. When the stock traded at $174 per share, Netscape had a total stock market value of an unbelievable $6.5 billion. This amount exceeded the market value of numerous companies — such as Quaker Oats, Charles Schwab, Clorox, Kmart, and Nordstrom — that have revenues of billions of dollars and profits of hundreds of millions of dollars and had been in business for a decade or more!

Unlike Netscape, most companies normally wait until they have several years under their belt and a track record of profits before going public. When Microsoft went public in 1986, it had turned a profit since 1982 and was selling for a P/E of around 20. (Microsoft earned a profit of $24 million on sales of $140 million the prior year.) Although Microsoft's stock initially sold for about three times its annual revenue after its IPO, within months of its IPO Netscape sold for an astounding 198 times revenue. (And Netscape was selling at a P/E of more than 400 times its 1996 estimated earnings.)

Many Netscape investors overlook Netscape's formidable competitors, including Microsoft. As for the company's astronomical market share, many investors didn't know that these market share numbers were based partly upon the number of free copies available of the company's software, which can be downloaded off the Internet.

Only time will tell if Netscape is the next Microsoft.

fat and calories than its fried counterpart. Dinner at Boston Market can also include veggies, salad, and the like. The company is also opening bagel stores à la Noah's.

The company's concept of healthier than fast food is hardly unique (witness my discussion of Fresh Choice earlier in this chapter), and how healthy their menu is is open to debate. The trend in the restaurant business is slowly moving away from fattier, cholesterol-laden foods — or at least dressing up the menu to make it appear healthier. Kentucky Fried Chicken changed their name to KFC in part to obfuscate the "fried" part of their offerings. My nutritionist friends tell me that chicken is still chicken, and many of the other Boston Market dishes are, well, not so healthy. KFC, interestingly enough, copied Boston Chicken's chicken offerings.

In little more than a year, Boston Chicken's stock price declined 47 percent from its November 1993 high. Since then, it has struggled back to about the price where investors like you and me could first jump into it. During this time, the U.S. stock market has done quite well, about doubling. Boston Chicken shareholders are still missing some feathers. Profits have increased, so the company's P/E is down to a more reasonable 22 times earnings.

If Boston Chicken experiences the kind of long-term growth and profitability that McDonald's has over the years, its stock will do well over the long term. Expecting this kind of success, however, is foolhardy. The company has been on an aggressive growth plan and has an experienced small company growth team that built Blockbuster Video. Smart managers can replicate their success in different businesses, but running a video store is indeed different than a restaurant.

Don't invest in IPOs. Rather than IPO standing for initial public offering, it's more apt to mean "it's probably overpriced." It's easy to see a decade later which companies dominate their industries and whose stocks rocketed skyward. Picking them in advance is a difficult task. Investing in IPOs has proven to be an overall losing stock market investing strategy. Not surprisingly, the most IPOs come to market when the market is high so that companies can maximize their take. Don't buy IPOs, and run from them as fast as you can in an overheated market. If you can get in on the ground floor of an IPO (buy at the offering price), that's a sign it's probably a turkey or a small, risky offering.

Don't buy penny stocks

Even worse than buying stocks through a broker whose compensation depends on what you buy and how often you trade is purchasing penny stocks through brokers that specialize in such stocks. As I explained in the previous chapter, more than 30,000 smaller company stocks trade on the over-the-counter market. Some of these companies are quite small and sport low prices per share ranging from pennies to several dollars, hence the name penny stocks.

If you remember or know of a fellow by the name of Robert Brennan, then you know that he is the granddaddy of this reptilian business. I won't bore you with all the details, except to say that after more than a decade of financial shenanigans, Brennan in June 1995 was at last ordered by a judge to pay investors more than $70 million for all the bad stuff that he did. Pending suits may lead to hundreds of millions of dollars in additional judgments against Brennan's companies. To understand what Brennan did is to understand the problems with other penny stock operators.

Here's how many of the penny stock brokers work. Many of these firms purchase prospect lists of people who have demonstrated a propensity for buying other lousy investments by phone. Brokers are taught to first introduce themselves by phone and then call back shortly thereafter with a tremendous sense of urgency about a great opportunity to get in on the "ground floor" of a small but soon to be stellar company. Not all of these companies and stocks have terrible prospects, although many do. But all of them are grossly overpriced. Just as you're not going to make good investment returns purchasing jewelry that's marked up 100 percent, you don't have a fighting chance to make decent money on penny stocks that the broker may be flogging with similar markups.

The individual broker who cons you into "investing" in such cheap stocks gains a big slice as a commission, which is why he will keep calling with "opportunities" until you send him a check. A number of firms, including Brennan's, are known for engaging in manipulation of stock prices and driving up prices of selected shares until the public is left holding the bag.

Many brokers in this business with a record of violations but an ability to sell have no problem gaining employment at other penny stock peddlers. The firms themselves may also be in the business of encouraging companies to issue new, overpriced stock, which their brokers can then flog to people like you.

I remember when Brennan ran his infamous "Come Grow With Us" television ads in the early 1980s in which he would hop out of a helicopter. Brennan was always nicely dressed and had a polished image. In addition to being in the penny stock trade, you may find it interesting to note that Brennan owned a horse race track and wanted to get into the casino business. All these businesses share the characteristic that they don't involve investing and the deck is stacked against gullible members of the public that they hoodwink into submission.

A twist on the penny stock game is the higher than necessary markups, of which market makers of NASDAQ stocks have been accused. While not 100 percent, the difference between buy and sell price has been documented to be much higher than for other exchanges. High markups on over-the-counter stocks (NASDAQ) is another reason not to dabble in smaller company stocks on your own. It's better to leave this type of investing to a professional money manager who can buy and sell stock at better prices than you can.

Don't buy broker-sold limited partnerships

At their peak, brokers, and brokers masquerading as financial planners, were selling more than $10 billion per year of these terrible investments. Prudential Securities sold more of these than any other organization and has suffered the most pain as a result, having to cough up hundreds of millions of dollars in lawsuits. I explain in Chapter 3 the fundamental problems (mainly outrageous commissions and fees) that drain your LP investment returns.

The Keys to Stock Market Success

Anybody, no matter their educational background, IQ, occupation, income, or total assets, can make good money by investing in stocks. Over long periods of time, expect to earn about 10 percent per year on average.

To maximize your chances of stock market investing success, do the following:

- ✔ **Don't try to time the markets.** It is next to impossible to anticipate where the stock market and specific stocks are heading. Stock market prices are determined by economic factors, which are influenced by thousands of elements, as well as human emotions. Be a regular buyer of stocks with new savings. Buy more when stocks are on sale and pessimism is running high.

- ✔ **Diversify.** Invest in stocks of different size companies in varying industries around the world. When assessing the performance of your investments, look at your whole portfolio at least once a year and calculate your total return, after expenses and trading fees.

- ✔ **Keep trading costs, management fees, and commissions to a minimum.** These represent a big drain on your returns. If you're investing through a broker or "financial advisor" who earns a living on commissions, odds are high that you're paying far more than you need to be and likely getting biased advice.

- ✔ **Pay attention to taxes.** Like commissions and fees, federal and state taxes are another major investment "expense" to minimize. Contribute to your tax-deductible retirement accounts. Invest your money outside of retirement accounts with an eye on taxes (see Chapter 3). Calculate your annual returns on *after*-tax basis.

- ✔ **Don't overestimate your ability to pick the big winning stocks.** One of the best ways to invest in stocks is through mutual funds (see Chapter 8), where you can hire an experienced, full-time money manager at a low cost to do all the investing grunt work for you. If you want to invest in individual stocks, stay clear of initial public offerings, particularly trendy, popular ones and ones issued during times of an overheated stock market.

Chapter 6

Researching and Trading Individual Stocks

*I*f you want to research companies and their stocks, you don't have to worry about having enough information to peruse. Your problem will be information overload. You can spend dozens of hours researching and reading information on one company alone. You gotta focus on where you can get the best bang for your buck and time.

Don't Reinvent the Wheel

If you were going to build a car, I bet that you wouldn't try to do it on your own (unless you were my father). You would likely see if you could obtain some sort of kit or plans drawn up by others who have done it many times.

You can do the same when it comes to picking individual stocks. The following publications offer good columns and commentary, sometimes written by professional money managers, on individual stocks: *Barron's, Business Week, Forbes, Kiplinger's,* and the *Wall Street Journal.*

Another way to discern what smart money managers are buying is to look at their portfolios. I'm not suggesting that you invade their privacy or ask rude questions. The best mutual fund managers are required to disclose at least twice a year what stocks are in their portfolio. You can request this information by calling the fund companies and asking them to send their most recent semiannual reports detailing their stock holdings. (See Chapter 8 to see the best stock mutual funds.)

Value Line

My next recommendation is to subscribe to or borrow from your local library a terrific publication that I've been acquainted with for more than two decades called the *Value Line Investment Survey.* The beauty of Value Line's service is that it condenses down to a single page the key information and statistics about a stock and the company behind the stock.

Value Line's securities analysts have tracked and researched stocks since the Great Depression. The track record of their analysis and recommendations is quite good, and the analysts are beholden to no one. Many professional money managers use Value Line as a reference because of how comprehensive it is.

Suppose you read or hear somewhere that Ford Motor Company is a good stock to buy. Their new car models are reportedly selling like gangbusters. And you look in the newspaper and are shocked to see that the stock is selling for a mere six times earnings (P/E ratio). Take a look at the most important elements of a Value Line page for Ford, shown in Figure 6-1.

1. **Business.** This section describes the various lines of business that Ford is in. You can see that Ford is the second largest U.S. auto manufacturer and sold nearly 22 percent of the cars and 31 percent of the trucks sold in the U.S. in 1994. Ford also is in the business of leasing and renting vehicles and making electronic equipment. In this section, you also can see that the senior executives and directors of the company own a decent share (9 percent) of the stock — it's good to see these folks have a financial stake in the success of the company. They'll be upset if the stock price plunges!

2. **Analyst assessment.** Each Value Line stock is followed by a securities analyst. Each analyst focuses on specific industries and follows a few dozen stocks. This section provides the analyst's summary and commentary of the company's current situation and future plans.

3. **Value Line's rating.** Value Line gives a numerical ranking for each stock's timeliness (expected performance) over the next year. One is highest, and five is lowest, and these extreme ratings are each awarded to only about five percent of all stocks. Two is above average and four below average, and each is given to about one-sixth of the ranked stocks. All remaining stocks, a little more than half the total ranked, get the average three rating.

   The safety rank works the same way, with one being best and denoting the least-volatile stocks and most-financially stable companies. Five is the worst safety ranking and is given to the most-volatile stocks and least financially stable companies.

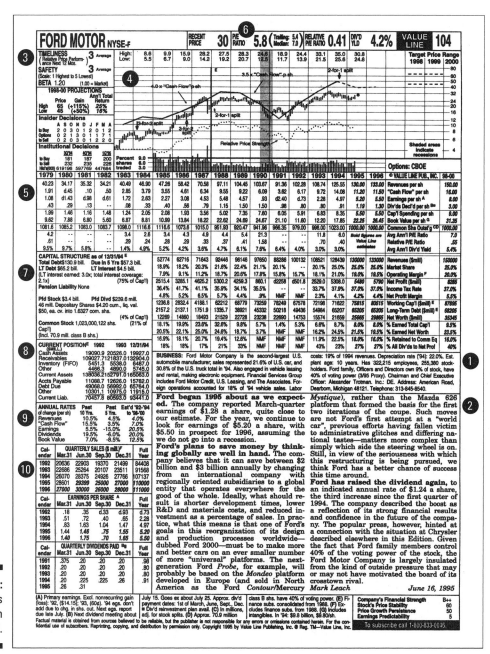

Figure 6-1: Value Line's report on Ford.

Though I've never been a fan of predictions and short-term thinking (one year is a very short period of time for the stock market), Value Line's system historically has done a good job. According to the *Hulbert Financial Digest,* which tracks the actual performance of investment newsletter recommendations, Value Line has the second best overall track record and has handily outperformed the market averages. That's not to say, however, that you should only consider investing in the highest-rated stocks, but it's a good place to start. Ford, as you can see, is not highly rated.

4. **Stock price performance.** The graph shows you how the stock price has performed over the past decade or so. The high and low stock price for each month is indicated by the highest and lowest point of the line on the graph. The year's high and low prices are indicated at the top of the graph.

   The graph also shows how the price of the stock has moved with changes in the company's cash flow. Cash flow is an important measure of a company's financial success and health. It's different than "net profits" reported for tax purposes. For example, the tax laws allow a company to take a tax deduction each year for the depreciation (devaluation) of the company's equipment and other assets. Although depreciation is good because it helps lower a company's tax bill, subtracting it from the company's revenue gives an untrue picture as to the company's cash flow (money coming in minus money going out). Thus, in calculating a company's cash flow, depreciation is not subtracted from revenue.

5. **Historic financials.** Here you can see 12 to 18 years of financial information on the company. For example, you can see from the earnings per share line that Ford's annual earnings or profits have been quite volatile. The company actually lost money during 1991–92 and 1980–82. Ford is considered a cyclical company. When difficult economic times hit, people slow their buying of new cars and Ford's profits plummet.

   Book value per share indicates the value of the company's assets, including equipment, manufacturing plants, and real estate, less any liabilities. Book value gives somewhat of a handle as to the amount the company can be sold for if it has a "going out of business sale." I say somewhat because the value of some assets on a company's books is not correct. For example, some companies own real estate, bought long ago, that is worth far more than is indicated on the company's current financial statements. Conversely, if Ford recently purchased some new assembly line equipment that it had to dump if it were liquidating its assets, it's likely that Ford would have to sell the equipment at a discount to entice a buyer.

   The book value of a bank, for example, can be misleading if the bank has made loans that aren't going to be paid back, and this fact hasn't yet been recognized on the bank's financial statements. All these complications with book value are why full-time, professional money managers exist. (If you want to delve more into a company's book value, you need to look at other financial statements, such as the company's annual report discussed in the "Annual reports" section later in this chapter.)

Market share indicates what portions of the industry that Ford has captured in a given year. It appears that Ford has, at least temporarily, reversed the slide in its market share of recent years.

A sustained slide in a company's market share is a dangerous sign, indicating that, for example, its customers are leaving for other companies that presumably are offering better products at lower prices. But that's not to say that you should avoid investing in a company with such problems. Compaq Computer, for example, had such difficulty in the 1970s but has totally kicked butt in the 1980s and 1990s. Identifying companies that are repositioning and strengthening their product offerings to reverse a market share slide can produce big profits for you as a stockholder.

6. **P/E ratio.** Here you can see, given Ford's recent stock price and earnings, that it's selling at a P/E of 5.8. Though quite low compared to the overall market, you can see here that this seemingly low P/E is not low for Ford. The median P/E of 7 tells you the approximate historic P/E this stock has sold for over the past decade.

   Although the overall market typically sells at a price-earnings ratio of about 14 times earnings (and was at 17 times earnings when this analysis of Ford was prepared), Ford sells for a much lower P/E. This lower P/E is because of the volatile earnings Ford experiences.

7. **Capital structure.** This section summarizes the amount of stocks and bonds that the company has outstanding. Remember that when a company issues these securities, it receives capital (money). What is most useful to examine in this section is the company's debt. If a company accumulates a lot of debt (as many governments have), the burden of interest payments can be a real drag on profits. If profits stay down for too long, debt can even push some companies into bankruptcy.

   Here you can see that Ford has approximately $131 billion in total debt outstanding and about $65 billion of that is in long-term debt. Long-term simply means debt that has to be paid back in more than a year. So how do you know if this is a lot, a little, or just the right amount of debt? Long-term interest earned compares Ford's annual profits to the yearly interest payments on its long-term debt. The 3.0x in Ford's case tells you Ford's most recent yearly profits can cover the interest payments on their long-term debt for about three years.

   Having a larger cushion to cover debt is more important when the company's business is more volatile. Ford's is quite volatile. Total interest coverage does a similar comparison of profits to interest owed for all debt that a company owes, not just long-term debt. Here you can see that Ford's annual profits cover approximately 2.1 years' worth of interest on all the company's debt. Warning signs for times interest earned numbers include a steep decline in this number over time and profits covering less than one year's worth of interest.

How to get Value Line reports

The least costly way to get Value Line pages on stocks that you're interested in is to visit your local library. Most libraries that have decent business sections subscribe to it.

If you want to have your very own copy of Value Line to read in the comfort of your own home, Value Line (800-634-3583) offers a 10-week trial subscription to their Value Line Investment Survey for $55. An annual subscription costs $590. At the start of your subscription, you receive a rather large binder divided into 13 sections with the most-recent reports on the 1,700 large- and medium-size company stocks this publication tracks. Every week, you receive a new packet of reports that replaces one of the 13 sections. Thus, at the end of 13 weeks, you have new reports on all the stocks.

The trial subscription is a great place to start because you get all the current reports plus the next 10 weeks' worth of updates for a reasonable fee. You can also see how much use you get out of the reports. The trial is available to each household once every three years.

Value Line also offers an expanded investment survey, which contains reports on 1,800 additional, smaller companies. Unlike the traditional Value Line pages, these pages include no analyst commentary or projections. A trial subscription to both the regular and expanded surveys costs $95. If you subscribe to the regular Value Line Investment Survey publication, you can subscribe to the expanded survey yearly for an additional $125.

If you simply want the Value Line report on one or two stocks, you may order single page reports from Value Line at a steep $12.50 each. Given the low cost of the trial, you may as well order the trial and receive all 1,700 reports. Ordering copies of single pages likely only makes sense if you've gotten a trial within the last three years and thus cannot order another trial for a while. You can try to interest a friend in the publication and have them order it for you!

8. **Current position.** This section provides a quick look at how the company's *current assets* (current meaning an asset that can be relatively easily sold and converted into cash within a year) compares with its *current liabilities* (debts due within the year). Trouble may be brewing if a company's current liabilities exceed or are approaching their current assets. In Ford's case, their current assets ($165,063 million) are about 1.77 times their current liabilities ($93,441 million) — a comfortable cushion.

Some financial analysts calculate what's known as the *quick ratio*, which ignores inventory when comparing current assets to current liabilities. If a company really must raise cash in a hurry, inventory may have to be dumped at a very low price. Thus, some analysts argue, inventory should be ignored as an asset.

9. **Annual rates.** This nifty section can save wear and tear on your calculator. Here, the good folks at Value Line have calculated rates of growth (or shrinkage) on important financial indicators, such as revenue and earnings (profits), over the past five and ten years. Value Line's projections for the next five years are also listed.

Projections can be highly unreliable, even from a research firm as good as Value Line. In most cases, the projections assume that the company will continue as it has in the most recent couple of years.

10. **Quarterly financials.** For the most-recent years, you can see an even more detailed quarterly breakout of sales and profits that may disclose changes masked by annual totals. You can also see the seasonality of some businesses. Ford, for example, tends to sell more cars in the spring quarter. Maybe that's because early tax filers who got large refunds run out to blow their IRS checks on a new car!

The information in Value Line reports is in no way inside information. Look upon these reports the same way you do a history book — useful background information that can keep you from repeating common mistakes. If you had simply bought Ford because you had renewed faith in the American auto industry and thought it was a steal at a P/E of 6, you likely would be disappointed. You've seen that Ford's low P/E is because its earnings plummet from time to time.

That's not to say that Ford isn't a good stock to buy. Value Line seems to think that Ford is an average stock, and who am I to disagree! If the U.S. economy grows quickly in the years ahead and Ford can lower their production costs through the use of more efficient manufacturing processes and technologies, Ford should do just fine. But if the U.S. suffers a severe recession, Ford's stock will likely perform poorly, although it likely won't be clobbered as badly as some high-flying stocks that are selling at high premiums today.

Annual reports

After you've reviewed the Value Line page on a company and you want to do more digging into financial documents, the next step is to ask yourself why. Why do you want to torture yourself so?

I successfully completed one of the supposedly better M.B.A. programs (Stanford's) and took more than my fair share of accounting and finance courses. Over the years, I've gotten to know investment managers and financial analysts who research companies. Although some financial documents are not that difficult to read (I'll show you how shortly), interpreting what they mean for the future of a company is not easy. Identifying trouble *before* other investors do is a skill that many professional investors haven't mastered — if you do, go manage other people's money!

All publicly traded companies are required to file certain financial documents annually. You should consider reviewing these documents more to enhance your understanding of a company's businesses and strategies rather than for the predictive value they provide.

The first such document companies produce that has useful information is the *annual report.* This yearly report provides standardized financial statements as well as management's discussion about what the company has been doing and what it plans to do. If you're a bit of a skeptical sort like I am, you may be thinking, "Aren't the company's officials going to make everything sound rosy and wonderful?"

To a certain extent yes, but not as badly as you may think. First, a large part of annual reports are the financial statements, which must be audited by an accounting firm. That doesn't mean that companies and their accounting firms can't legally structure the company's books to make them look rosier than they really are. And some companies have pulled the wool over their auditors' eyes who became accomplices in producing false financial figures.

Second, keep in mind that more than a few companies have been sued for misleading shareholders with inflated forecasts or lack of disclosure of problems. Responsible companies try to present a balanced and, of course, hopeful perspective in their annual reports. Most companies' annual reports are written by non-techno geeks, so you have a good shot at understanding them.

Financial and business highlights

The first section of most annual reports presents a description of a company's recent financial highlights and business strategies. This information can be useful in educating you as to what businesses a company is in and where a company seems to be heading. For example, in Figure 6-1 Value Line mentioned, without really detailing, that Ford was also in the business of manufacturing electronic equipment. The annual report can shed light on what this business is.

Enough about the auto industry for now, I'd like to expose you to another industry. As you may know, increasing growth in the U.S. economy is coming from service firms rather than from firms such as Ford that manufacture products. T. Rowe Price is a publicly traded investment company that also offers some decent mutual funds. A large part of its business is managing retirement account money for investors. In Figure 6-2, you can see that T. Rowe Price invests money for private accounts (institutions and wealthy individuals) as well as defined contribution — 401(k)-type plans — and IRAs. You can also read how the company is seeking to capture more of investors' retirement account assets.

ASSETS UNDER MANAGEMENT			
$75.4 BILLION AT DECEMBER 31, 1995		**$99.4 BILLION AT DECEMBER 31, 1996**	
Stock	61%	Stock	68%
Bond	22%	Bond	17%
Money Market	10%	Money Market	9%
Stable Value Contracts	7%	Stable Value Contracts	6%

Primarily as a result of these activities, net income rose $23 million, or 31%, from the prior-year level to a record of just under $100 million. After almost $20 million of stock repurchases and $24 million of dividends, stockholders' equity advanced to $346 million, another record. And, there is no long-term debt on the balance sheet.

Earnings per share also established an all-time high by increasing 28% — to $1.59 — in 1996. As has been true each year since T. Rowe Price became a public company, the dividend per share increased in 1996. The current $0.13 per-share rate is 24% higher than the prior quarterly amount and underlines our commitment to growth of dividends as a way of building value for our stockholders.

ASSETS UNDER MANAGEMENT

With the significant growth in AUM over the past two years, we think a comprehensive discussion of the asset composition might prove meaningful.

As the chart above shows, stock assets continued to represent a larger percentage of AUM in 1996, rising seven percentage points, or $21.4 billion, over the prior-year number. In total, the T. Rowe Price mutual funds accounted for $14.7 billion of the increase, including $8.6 billion in net cash flows, more than double the $3.9 billion record set in 1993. The Equity Income and International Stock Funds each contributed about $1.4 billion of net cash flows, followed by almost $1 billion in New Horizons and by over one-half billion in Science & Technology and Mid-Cap Growth. The New Horizons' rating in the top three is remarkable considering that it closed to most new investors in June of last year.

Of the 19 domestic stock funds which were in operation for all of 1996, 14 had total returns above 20%, and the other five were in double digits. With the exception of Japan, whose market was roiled by a number of problems, international equity funds also had favorable double-digit results. The ratio of international to domestic AUM, shown in the pie chart,

INTERNATIONAL VS. DOMESTIC AUM
DECEMBER 31, 1996

71% Domestic
29% International

Source: T. Rowe Price Associates, Inc.

Figure 6-2: T. Rowe Price's annual report explains who its customers are.

Balance sheet

The back portion of most annual reports is where you find the hard-core numbers. You can find many of these same numbers in Value Line reports except you get more specific details in the annual report. All annual reports contain a *balance sheet,* which is a snapshot summary of all the company's assets and liabilities. This report is prepared as of the last day of the company's year-end, which is typically December 31. Some companies have a fiscal year that ends at other times of the year.

A company's balance sheet is similar to a personal balance sheet. The entries, of course, look a little different because you likely don't own things like manu-facturing equipment. And you know if you read my *Personal Finance For Dummies* book that I'm against listing personal property, such as furniture and cars, as assets. (Are you planning on selling these things to raise money for retirement, home buying, and so on?) Figure 6-3 shows a typical balance sheet.

Assets

The assets section lists the following items that the company holds or owns that are of significant value:

- ✔ **Cash.** I think you know what cash is. Lest you think that these are stacks of bills sitting around in corporate vaults, rest assured that companies invest this money to earn interest. Many items are explained in more detail in explanatory notes that follow these financial statements. Note 1 explains that T. Rowe Price eats their own cooking — they keep their extra cash in their own money market funds.

- ✔ **Accounts receivable.** This is money that is owed to the company. The note explains that T. Rowe Price collects investment advisory fees for the funds that they manage. Just as your employer pays you at the month's end for your work during the entire month, the company is paid for services previously provided. If you're paid $4,000 monthly and you prepared your own personal balance mid-month, you can list salary of $2,000 as an asset because it is money due you that you haven't yet received.

  As companies grow, their receivables usually do too. Watch out for cases where the receivables are growing at a faster rate than the sales (revenue). This growth may indicate that the company is having problems with the quality of its product or pricing. Unhappy customers pay more slowly or demand bigger price discounts.

- ✔ **Investments.** In addition to cash, some companies may invest in other securities, such as bonds and stocks. Just as with your own personal situation, companies usually invest with money they don't expect to use in the near future.

CONSOLIDATED BALANCE SHEETS	DECEMBER 31	
	(in thousands)	
	95	**96**
ASSETS		
Cash and cash equivalents (Note 1)	$ 81,431	$ 114,551
Accounts receivable (Note 1)	55,841	73,239
Investments in sponsored mutual funds held as available-for-sale		
securities (Note 1)	121,606	143,410
Partnership and other investments (Note 8)	28,049	25,161
Property and equipment (Note 2)	60.222	101,207
Goodwill and other assets (Note 3)	18,194	21,266
	$ 365,343	$ 478,834
LIABILITIES AND STOCKHOLDERS' EQUITY		
Liabilities		
Accounts payable and accrued expenses (Note 5)	$ 27,287	$ 31,529
Accrued compensation and retirement costs	28,803	41,523
Income taxes payable (Note 4)	7,376	14,464
Dividends payable	6,036	7,484
Minority interests in consolidated subsidiaries	21,609	38,168
Total liabilities	91,111	133,168
Commitments and contingent liabilities (Notes 2 and 8)		
Stockholders' equity (Notes 5 and 8)		
Preferred stock, undesignated, $.20 par value - authorized and		
unissued 20,000,000 shares	—	—
Common stock, $.20 par value - authorized 100,000,000 shares		
in 1995 and 200,000,000 shares in 1996; issued 28,665,472		
shares in 1995 and 57,572,791 shares in 1996	5,733	11,514
Capital in excess of par value	2,912	7,823
Retained earnings	252,934	306,566
Unrealized security holding gains (Note 1)	12,653	19,763
Total stockholders' equity	274,232	345,666
	$ 365,343	$ 478,834

[23]

The accompanying notes are an integral part of the consolidated financial statements.

Figure 6-3:
The balance
sheet from
T. Rowe
Price's
annual
report.

Source: T. Rowe Price Associates, Inc.

✔ **Property and equipment.** All companies need equipment to run their business. This equipment can include office furniture and computers, as well as real estate they own. Manufacturing companies such as Ford Motor, discussed earlier in the chapter, also own machinery, such as the machinery Ford uses on an assembly line for making products.

Equipment becomes less valuable over time. This depreciation is taken by the company as a cost of doing business each year. Thus, even if a company ceases buying new equipment, this entry on the balance sheet gradually decreases as the depreciation is subtracted from the value of the equipment.

✔ **Goodwill and other assets.** One of the assets that doesn't show up on most companies' balance sheets is the goodwill they have. Companies work hard through advertising, product development, and service to attract and retain customers. Name brand recognition is a term you sometimes hear thrown around. Companies can't put a value on the goodwill they've generated, but when they purchase (acquire) another firm, some of the purchase price is considered goodwill. Specifically if a company is acquired for $100 million yet has a net worth (assets minus liabilities) of just $50 million, the extra $50 million is considered to have gone to goodwill. This goodwill then becomes an asset, which, like equipment, is depreciated or amortized over the years ahead.

"Other assets" is a catch-all category that can include some stuff that will make your eyes glaze over. For example, companies keep a different (yes, this is legal) set of books for tax purposes. Not surprisingly, companies do this because the IRS allows, in some cases, more deductions than what the company is required to show from an accounting standpoint on their financial statements. (If you were a company, wouldn't you want your shareholders, but not the IRS, to see gobs of profits?) The benefit of deferring taxes is treated as an asset until the IRS gets more of its share down the road.

Note: Manufacturing and retail companies also track and report *inventory,* which is simply product that has not yet been sold, as an asset. Generally speaking, as a business grows, so too does its inventory. If inventory grows more quickly than revenue, that growth may be a warning sign. This growth can indicate that customers are scaling back purchases and the company miscalculated and overproduced. It can also be a leading indicator of an obsolete or inferior product offering.

Liabilities

This section summarizes all the money that the company owes to others.

✔ **Accounts payable.** When companies make requests to purchase things for their business, sometimes they have time to pay the bills. As with inventory and accounts receivable, accounts payable generally increases with a company's increasing revenue.

If accounts payable is increasing faster than revenue, it can indicate a problem. On the other hand, that increase can also be a sign of good financial management. The longer you take to pay your bills, the longer you have the money in your pocket working for you.

✔ **Accrued compensation and retirement costs.** This line tallies money that the company is obligated to someday pay to its employees. For example, many larger firms maintain pension plans. These plans promise workers who retire with at least five years of service a monthly income check in retirement. Thus, the company must reserve this money that is owed and list it as a liability or debt that will someday have to be paid.

✔ **Income taxes payable.** Companies are in business to make a profit and as those profits are earned, a portion is supposed to be reserved to pay corporate taxes. As explained earlier, some of these taxes owed can be because of accounting differences between the company's financial statements and those filed with the IRS.

✔ **Dividends payable.** Not all companies pay dividends (see Chapter 4) to their shareholders. But those companies that do typically declare the dividend several weeks in advance of when the dividend is actually owed. During this interim period, the dividends promised but not yet paid are listed as a liability.

Stockholders' equity

The difference between a company's assets and liabilities is known as *stockholders' equity*. Stockholders' equity is what makes balance sheets always balance. When companies issue stock, for example, they receive cash, which is listed as an asset, for the stock sold.

Stock proceeds are divided between *par value* and *capital in excess of par value*. In the case of T. Rowe Price, the par value is $0.20 per share. Par values are arcane . . . and largely meaningless.

Income statement

The other big financial statement in an annual report is the income statement, an example of which is shown in Figure 6-4.

Revenue

Revenue is simply the money that the company receives from its customers as compensation for its products or services. Just as you can earn income from your job(s) as well as investments and other sources, a company can make money from a variety of sources as well. In the case of mutual fund provider T. Rowe Price, the firm collects fees (investment advisory and administrative) for the mutual fund investments that it manages on behalf of its customers as well as privately managed money for wealthy individuals and institutions. The company also receives income from its own money that it has invested.

CONSOLIDATED STATEMENTS OF INCOME			DECEMBER 31
			(in thousands, except per-share amounts)
	94	**95**	**96**
REVENUES (NOTE 1)			
Investment advisory fees	$ 290,071	$ 332,087	$ 451,307
Administrative fees	85,672	94,377	117,803
Investment and other income	6,635	12,835	16,960
	382,378	439,299	586,070
EXPENSES			
Compensation and related costs (Notes 5 and 6)	129,373	143,369	179,381
Advertising and promotion	31,201	34,843	58,291
Depreciation, amortization and operating rentals of			
property and equipment (Note 8)	24,993	30,247	38,112
International investment research fees	25,719	30,023	39,328
Administrative and general (Note 7)	49,899	57,124	83,487
	261,185	295,606	398,599
Income before income taxes and minority interests	121,193	143,693	187,471
Provision for income taxes (Note 4)	46,587	54,335	72,608
Income from consolidated companies	74,606	89,358	114,863
Minority interests in consolidated subsidiaries	13,455	12,900	16,410
Income before extraordinary charge	61,151	76,458	98,453
Extraordinary charge from early extinguishment			
of debt, net of income tax benefit (Note 7)	—	(1,049)	—
Net Income	$ 61,151	$ 75,409	$ 98,453
Earnings per share, which were reduced $0.01 per			
share in 1995 because of the extraordinary charge	$ 1.00	$ 1.24	$ 1.59

[24]

The accompanying notes are an integral part of the consolidated financial statements.

Figure 6-4:
T. Rowe Price's income statement.

Source: T. Rowe Price Associates, Inc.

Ideally, you want to see a steady or accelerating rate of growth in a company's revenues. If a company's revenue is growing more slowly, that raises the question why. Is it because of poor service or product performance, better competitor offerings, ineffective marketing, or all of the above?

For companies with multiple divisions or product lines, the annual report may detail the revenue of each product line in a later section. If it doesn't, check out some of the other financial statements recommended in the next section, "Other useful reports with funny names." Examine what's spurring, or holding back, the company's overall growth and what different businesses the company is operating in. One red flag is businesses that were acquired but don't really fit with the company's other business units. Large companies that have experienced stalled revenue growth sometimes, in desperation, try to "enter" new businesses through acquisition but then don't manage them well because they don't understand the keys to success in them.

 With retail stores, such as restaurant chains (for example, McDonald's) or clothing stores (such as The Gap), examine the change in revenue coming from opening new locations versus the change at existing locations, sometimes referred to as *same stores*.

Expenses

If only you got to keep all the income that you make. Just as personal income taxes, housing, food, and clothing expenses gobble up much of your personal income, company expenses use up much and sometimes all of a company's revenue.

Even healthy, growing businesses can get into trouble if their expenses balloon faster than their revenue. Well-managed companies stay on top of their expenses during good and bad times. Unfortunately, it's easy for companies to get sloppy during good times.

 It's particularly useful to examine each category of expenses relative to (in other words, as a percentage of) the company's revenue to see which are growing or shrinking. As a well-managed and financially healthy company grows, expenses as a percentage of revenue should decrease. As this happens in T. Rowe Price's case, profits as a percentage of assets under management increase.

Not all expense categories necessarily decrease. As you can see from T. Rowe Price's expenses, advertising spending increased significantly in 1996 as the company attempted to capitalize on investors' increased interest in mutual funds. Table 6-1 shows T. Rowe Price's expenses as a percentage of revenue during a recent three year period.

Table 6-1 T. Rowe Price's Expenses as a Percentage of Revenue			
Expense	*1994*	*1995*	*1996*
Compensation	33.8%	32.6%	30.6%
Advertising & P.R.	8.2%	7.9%	9.9%
Depreciation	6.5%	6.9%	6.5%
Int'l investment research	6.7%	6.8%	6.7%
Admin & General	13.1%	13.0%	14.2%

The net result of revenues increasing faster than expenses is a fatter bottom line. In T. Rowe Price's case, pre-tax income rose from 31.7 percent to 32.0 percent of revenue between 1994 and 1996. When you examine how a company's profits change relative to total revenue received, focus on operating income. Sometimes companies experience one-time events that can change profits temporarily. These one-time events are usually listed in the section under expenses. With T. Rowe Price, for example, you can see that in 1995 the company incurred a one-time charge for paying off a loan early.

Last, but not least, and of great importance to shareholders is the calculation of the earnings per share. Higher profits per share help fuel a higher stock price.

Other useful reports with funny names

In addition to annual reports, companies produce other financial statements that you may want to peruse. Some of these may be obtained from the company for free. In other cases, you have to pay a small fee.

10-Ks

10-Ks are an expanded version of an annual report. Most investment professionals read the 10-K instead of the annual report because the 10-K contains lots of data and business descriptions not in annual reports with little of the verbal hype sometimes found in annual reports. The 10-K is probably one of the most objective reports that a company publishes. If you're not intimidated by annual reports or want more meat, go for it!

Consider how much more you can learn about a business by taking a look at the New York Times Company's 10-K (Figure 6-5). For example, the 10-K shows that this company takes in more than 68 percent of its revenue from advertising and just 23 percent from selling subscriptions. The New York Times Company makes the vast majority of its money from publishing the *New York Times* newspaper and some other small newspapers, as well as some smaller magazines, such as *Golf Digest* and *Tennis*. So if you want to understand where this company's business is heading, you need to understand what is happening with the firm's advertising success.

CONSOLIDATED STATEMENTS OF INCOME			
Dollars and shares in thousands except per share data		Year Ended	
	December 29, 1996	December 31, 1995	December 31, 1994
REVENUES			
Advertising	$ 1,798,498	$ 1,672,598	$ 1,656,999
Circulation	593,627	551,985	545,854
Other	222,901	184,486	153,929
Total	2,615,026	2,409,069	2,356,782
COSTS AND EXPENSES			
Production costs			
Raw materials	364,237	368,152	304,360
Wages and benefits	557,543	537,159	529,701
Other	426,060	399,107	428,663
Total	1,347,840	1,304,418	1,262,724
Selling, general and administrative expenses	967,143	871,902	883,159
Impairment loss	126,763	-	-
Total	2,441,746	2,176,320	2,145,883
OPERATING PROFIT	173,280	232,749	210,899
Income from Joint Ventures	18,223	15,029	5,126
Interest expense, net of interest income	26,430	25,230	28,162
Net gain on dispositions	32,836	11,291	200,873
Income before income taxes	197,909	233,839	388,736
Income taxes	113,375	97,979	175,387
NET INCOME	$ 84,534	$ 135,860	$ 213,349
Average number of common shares outstanding	97,293	96,854	104,070
Per share of common stock			
Net income	$ .87	$ 1.40	$ 2.05
Dividends	.57	.56	.56

See notes to consolidated financial statements.

Figure 6-5:
The New York Times Company's 10-K.

Source: The New York Times Company

10-Qs

10-Qs provide information similar to the 10-K but on a quarterly basis. Figure 6-6 shows the New York Times Company's 10-Q. 10-Qs are worthwhile if you like to read a reasonably detailed discussion by management of the latest business and financial developments at the company. I recommend leaving the research to Value Line's analyst.

PART I. FINANCIAL INFORMATION

Item 1. Financial Statements

THE NEW YORK TIMES COMPANY

CONDENSED CONSOLIDATED STATEMENTS OF INCOME
(Unaudited)
(Dollars and shares in thousands, except per share data)

	For the Quarter Ended	
	March 30, 1997	March 31, 1996
	(13 Weeks)	
Revenues		
Advertising	$476,548	$431,617
Circulation	168,554	162,556
Other	47,359	33,402
Total	692,461	627,575
Production Costs		
Raw Materials	73,477	105,567
Wages and Benefits	153,172	136,834
Other	114,645	105,116
Total	341,294	347,517
Selling, General and Administrative Expenses	249,912	219,435
Total	591,206	566,952
Operating Profit	101,255	60,623
Income from Joint Ventures	1,315	4,682
Interest Expense, Net of Interest Income	8,318	6,438
Income Before Income Taxes	94,252	58,867
Income Taxes	42,413	26,153
Net Income	$ 51,839	$ 32,714
Weighted Average Number of Common and Common Equivalent Shares	101,066	97,653
Earnings Per Common and Common Equivalent Share	$.51	$.33
Cash Dividends Per Common Share	$.15	$.14

See notes to condensed consolidated financial statements.

Figure 6-6:
The New York Times Company's 10-Q.

Source: *The New York Times Company*

The financial data in these reports is unaudited and not of great use for the long-term investor. If you want to watch your investments like a hawk and try to be among the first to detect indications of financial problems (easier said than done), then these are required reading.

Many companies go back to restate their quarterly financials. Remember that these numbers haven't been approved by the accountants. Sometimes companies take their financial lump in one quarter to get problems behind them, so one bad quarter doesn't necessarily indicate a bad long-term trend.

Fundamental versus technical analysis

Throughout this chapter and the last, I've been talking a lot about the financial statements of a company — balance sheets, revenues, expenses, earnings, price-earnings ratios, and so on. Analyzing financial statements and making investing decisions based on them is known as fundamental analysis.

But another whole school of stock market analysts, known as technical analysts or technicians, exists. These folks like to examine chart patterns, volume, and all sorts of indicators that have little, if anything, to do with the underlying stock.

Technicians say things like, "Stock XYZ has a major support area at $20 per share" or "Stock ABC has broken out above $30 per share." It may be a bit extreme to say that all the technicians that have ever existed have never produced anything

of value. However, you can safely ignore this school of thinking. In fact, ignoring the techs will likely *increase* your stock market profits. Why? Because this way of thinking encourages a trader's, not an investor's, mindset.

Not surprisingly, most of the technicians come from one of two camps. Many techs work for brokerage firms and write weekly or monthly assessments of the entire stock market and some individual stocks. Recommendations and advice change over time, and the result is that you trade more. Curiously, these brokerage firms make more money the more you trade!

Investment newsletter writers are the other big advocates of this Ouija-board approach to investment management. Again, it's a great system for the newsletter writers to hook you on a $200-per-year monthly newsletter.

Proxies

The final corporate document you may be interested in reviewing is the annual *proxy statement,* which is sent out in advance of a company's annual meeting. The proxy statement contains some of the more important financial information and discussion found in the 10-K. It also contains information on other corporate matters, such as the election of the board of directors. Directors, who are usually corporate executives, lawyers, accountants, and other knowledgeable luminaries, serve as a sounding board, counselor, and sometimes overseer to the management team of a company.

The proxy statement becomes much more important when a company is facing a takeover or some other controversial corporate matter, such as the election of an alternative board of directors.

The proxy, shown in Figure 6-7, tells you who is serving on the board of directors as well as how much they and the executives of the company are paid. At annual meetings, where proxy statements are discussed, sometimes shareholders get angry and ask why the executives are paid so much when the company's stock price and business is underperforming the competition.

Compensation of Executive Officers

The following tables and discussion summarize the compensation for the fiscal year ended December 29, 1996, of the chief executive officer of the Company, each of the four other most highly compensated executive officers of the Company and one individual who was one of the four other most highly compensated executive officers during 1996, but resigned effective September 20, 1996.

Summary Compensation Table

(a)	(b)	(c)	(d)	(e)	(f)	(g)	(h)	(i)
					Long-Term Compensation			
		Annual Compensation			Awards		Payouts	
				Other Annual Compensation ($)[2]	Restricted Stock Awards ($)	Stock Options (#)	LTIP Payouts ($)[3]	All Other Compensation ($)[4]
Name and Principal Position	Year	Salary ($)[1]	Bonus ($)					
Arthur Ochs Sulzberger	1996	575,000	822,200	1,053	0	75,840	0	4,500
Chairman and Chief	1995	555,000	822,200	0	0	75,840	198,220	4,500
Executive Officer	1994	535,000	822,200[5]	8,248	0	100,000	336,300[5]	4,500
Russell T. Lewis[6]	1996	418,785	463,450	9,886	0	48,827	0	4,500
President and Chief Operating Officer								
Arthur O. Sulzberger, Jr.	1996	450,000	510,200	0	0	40,057	0	3,500
Publisher of *The New York Times*	1995	428,000	510,200	0	0	40,057	132,685	3,500
	1994	408,000	510,200	0	0	48,573	225,150	3,500
William O. Taylor	1996	421,289	368,364	7,466	0	40,057	0	0
Publisher of *The Boston Globe*	1995	407,019	161,777	9,107	0	40,057	0	0
	1994	397,000	153,451	10,917	0	48,573	0	0
David L. Gorham	1996	400,000	396,000	0	0	34,514	0	4,500
Senior Vice President	1995	358,000	364,000	1,092	0	34,514	109,480	4,500
Deputy Chief Operating Officer	1994	330,000	353,400	3,300	0	33,920	185,700	4,500
Lance R. Primis[7]	1996	485,000	499,350	5,855	0	0	0	3,590,340[8]
Former President and Chief	1995	460,000	665,800	13,338	0	48,827	149,345	4,500
Operating Officer	1994	435,000	665,800	0	0	70,000	241,838	4,500

Stock Performance Comparison Between S&P 500, The New York Times Company's Class A Common Stock and Peer Group Common Stock

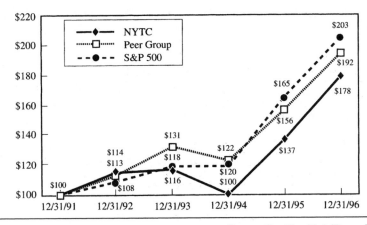

Source: The New York Times Company

Placing Your Trade through a Broker

Once you've decided to buy some stock, you generally need a broker (I explain in Chapter 5 a somewhat administratively hassled way to buy direct from some companies). As I explain in Chapter 4, discount brokers are the way to go. They take your orders and charge far less than conventional brokers who pay their brokers on commission.

Which discount broker is best for you depends on what you are looking for. In addition to fees, consider how important having a local branch office is to you. If you'd like to invest in some mutual funds as well, the following firms also offer access to good funds. In addition, they offer money market funds into which you can deposit money awaiting investment or proceeds from a sale and earn interest.

Here are my top picks and what is good and bad about each of them:

- ✓ **Fidelity (800-544-8666).** Fidelity is the nation's second largest discount brokerage firm and the largest mutual fund provider. Its strengths are 24-hour availability and approximately 100 branch offices located in most major cities. Fidelity also offers a number of good mutual funds, particularly those that focus on U.S. stocks. Fidelity's brokerage fees tend to be among the higher end of discount brokers.

- ✓ **T. Rowe Price (800-225-5132).** Like Vanguard (see below), T. Rowe Price also offers a solid family of no-load mutual funds that may also be purchased through their discount brokerage division. Their brokerage fees tend to be a bit less than Fidelity's. Branch offices are in Baltimore, Los Angeles, Tampa, and Washington, D.C., and hours are weekdays 8 a.m. to 10 p.m. EST.

- ✓ **Charles Schwab (800-435-4000).** Schwab is the nation's largest discount brokerage firm. Like Fidelity, their fees are among the highest for discounters, but the firm has 24-hour customer service and more than 200 branch offices if you like the in-person touch.

- ✓ **Vanguard (800-992-8327).** Vanguard is best known for their excellent family of no-load (commission-free) mutual funds, but their discount brokerage services have improved greatly in recent years. Their brokerage fees tend to be a bit lower than the more expensive discounters and comparable to T. Rowe Price's.

- ✓ **Jack White (800-323-3263).** White is the minimal-frills but deep discount discounter. White's brokerage fees are up to 50 percent or more below other discounters. Although it has only one office, located in the San Diego area, White does offer round-the-clock customer service (see Figure 6-8).

Source: Jack White & Company

Fidelity, Schwab, Vanguard, and White all offer mutual funds from many fund companies in addition to their family of funds, if they have one. In other words, you may purchase non-Fidelity mutual funds through Fidelity's brokerage department and non-Vanguard funds through Vanguard's brokerage service, for example. T. Rowe Price offers just their family of funds. Table 6-2 compares the fees for trading individual stocks through these recommended discount brokers.

All the firms shown in Table 6-2 offer an additional 10 percent discount when trading via your personal computer or Touch-Tone telephone.

Table 6-2	Fee Comparison for Discount Brokers		
Brokerage Firm	*100 Shares @ $15*	*200 Shares @ $20*	*500 Shares @ $30*
Fidelity	$55	$82	$127
T. Rowe Price	$46	$70	$107
Schwab	$55	$82	$127
Vanguard	$49	$69	$110
White	$36	$39	$48

After you decide which discount broker you want to use, call them up and request that they send you an account application package for the type of account you desire (non-retirement, IRA, Keogh, and so on). Complete the forms (call the firm's 800 number or visit a branch office if you get stuck) and mail or bring them back to the discounter.

When it comes time to place your order, simply call the discount broker and tell them what you want to do (or use your Touch-Tone phone to place your order). My advice is to place what's known as a *market order*. Such an order instructs your broker to buy you the amount of stock you desire, for example, 100 shares, at the current and best (lowest) price available.

Alternatively, you can try to buy at a specific price — for example, you can place a purchase order at $32 per share when the stock's last trade was $33 per share. This type of order is known as a limit order and is good for the day or good for four months or until canceled by you. You'd be hoping and gambling that the stock drops a little before it rises. I don't recommend that you try this tactic. If the stock simply rises from its current price of $33 per share or drops down to $32 $1/8$ before going on a big increase, you'll be kicking yourself. If you think the stock is a good buy, then go buy it. If you don't think it's a good buy, then don't buy it.

How to get even bigger discounts from brokers

Want even bigger discounts from the discounters? Don't get sucked into the firms that advertise free trading or ultra-low trading costs. You usually more than pay in other ways for these firms through low or nonexistent interest on money market balances or high fees elsewhere. Some firms, for example, charge hefty fees for lack of trading activity in your account.

If you're looking for low rates that really are low from a firm offering good service, then go with Jack White. But you may be surprised to hear that you can negotiate with the other more expensive discounters I've listed. Suppose you want to use Fidelity or Schwab because they have an office near you and you like their other services, but you want even lower fees.

You may be able to knock another 25 percent off these discounters' trading fees. Here's what you need to do. Ask to speak with the branch manager of the branch you plan on using. Make it clear when you call the company about opening an account that their earning your business is contingent on them giving you a further discount.

If you don't have a lot to invest or expect to place smaller trades (a few thousand dollars each), you're unlikely to get a bigger discount. Remember that it's a negotiation, and you have something they want — investment dollars. The more you have to invest, the bigger the potential discounts — perhaps as high as 25 percent.

Some firms have programs offering bigger discounts for active traders. Fidelity's is called Spartan Brokerage and Schwab's, Schwab 500. Both services offer 20 percent additional discounts for people who trade four times or more per month. If you qualify for these programs, you're probably doing too much trading and wasting money on brokerage commissions. Take a look at your long-term returns (after deducting trading costs), and see if all this trading is really helping you beat the market averages. I'd be surprised if you are over the long-term. Let me know if you are, and I'll tell you whom to send your resumé to to be hired as a full-time money manager!

Chapter 18 explains how to trade online inexpensively by using your computer.

One final word of advice. Try to buy stock in reasonable size chunks, such as 100 shares. Otherwise, commissions gobble a large percentage of the small dollar amount invested. If you don't have enough money to build a diversified portfolio all at once, don't sweat it. Diversify over time. Purchase a chunk of one stock after you have enough money accumulated and then wait to buy the next until you've saved up more money to invest.

If you want to learn more about analyzing companies, read the chapters in Part IV on small business.

The 5th Wave

By Rich Tennant

"I read about investing in a company called UniHandle Ohio, but I'm uneasy about a stock that's listed on the NASDAQ as UhOh."

Chapter 7

Only Bankers Get Wealthy Lending Money

· ·

In This Chapter

▶ Getting the most out of a bank

▶ Going with bonds: Which type is best for you?

▶ Making the individual bond versus bond mutual fund choice

▶ Understanding guaranteed-investment contracts and private mortgages

· ·

*I*n Chapters 1 and 2, I discuss the major types of investments and their potential risks and returns. *Lending investments* are those in which you are lending your money to an organization, such as a company or government, that typically pays you a set or fixed rate of interest.

If you really desire to make your money grow, lending investments are not for you. However, even the most-aggressive investors have a legitimate need for placing some of their money into lending investments. Table 7-1 shows some of the logic behind lending investments and when such investments make and don't make sense.

Table 7-1	The Logic of Lending Investments
Consider Lending Investments if . . .	*Consider Ownership Investments when . . .*
You need current income.	You don't need or want current income.
You need to access money within five years.	You're investing for the long-term (seven to ten-plus years).
Investment volatility makes you a wreck.	You don't mind/can ignore ups and downs.
You don't need to make your money grow.	You need growth to reach ambitious goals.

Lending investments are everywhere — at your local bank, brokerage, insurance and mutual fund companies, and even real estate and mortgage brokerage firms are pitching them. Lending investments you may have heard of include bank accounts (savings and certificates of deposits), treasury bills and other bonds, bond mutual funds, mortgages, and guaranteed investment contracts.

In this chapter, I talk you through these investments and tell you what's good and bad about each of them and when they should and shouldn't be used. I also tell you what to look for and look out for when comparing them.

So That's How They Pay for Big Bank Lobbies . . .

If you're like most people, your first investing experience was at your neighborhood bank where you established a checking and savings account. Depending on your family, this event may have happened as early as junior high school or as late as college or post college.

Because people's first experience with depositing money is at a local bank, when they begin to have some extra cash, it usually ends up for a time in the bank. Besides being where many of our parents first steered us financially, banks make us feel safe for a variety of reasons. At a relatively large branch, often within walking distance of your home or office, bank branches have vaults, security monitoring cameras, barriers in front of the tellers. Most of these latter accoutrements shouldn't make you feel safer about leaving your money with the bank — they are needed because of bank robberies! In this day and age with the preponderance and power of guns, you don't want to be in a bank lobby at the wrong time!

Large bank branches with all the trimmings cost a lot of money to operate. Guess where that money comes from? Of course, from you! That's one of the reasons the interest rates that banks pay is often so poor in comparison to equally safe alternatives.

What banks are good and not good for

I have a checking account at a local bank. I use that account to pay household bills and to access cash through automated teller machines. I keep enough money in my checking account to pay the bills and not a lot extra. I don't keep extra savings in the bank. You should think long and hard if you do. Bank savings accounts generally pay pretty crummy interest rates. In the next section, I tell you about a much better alternative to a bank savings account — a money market fund.

Some people are consoled by the Federal Deposit Insurance Corporation insurance that comes with bank accounts. It's true that if your bank fails, your account is insured up to $100,000. "So what," I say. Any Treasury bond is issued and backed by the federal government — that same, $5-trillion-debt-ridden organization that stands behind the FDIC. Plenty of other equally safe lending investments pay more.

Just because the federal government stands behind the banking FDIC system doesn't mean, in the event of a bank failure, that there is a 100 percent certainty you'll be paid back in full or paid back with dollars worth anywhere near what a dollar is worth today. Banks have failed and will continue to fail. Although you're insured for $100,000 in a bank, if the bank crashes, you'll likely wait quite a while to get your money back — and you'll probably settle for less interest than you thought you would get, too.

Any investment that involves lending your money to someone else or to some organization carries risk. That includes putting your money into a bank or buying a Treasury bond issued by the federal government. Although I'm not a doom-sayer, any student of history knows that governments and civilizations fail. It's not a matter of _whether_ they will fail; it's a question of _when_.

Other than savings accounts, banks also sell certificates of deposit (CDs). CDs are without a doubt the most overused bank investment around. The attraction is that you get a higher rate of return on a CD than on a bank savings account or money market fund. And unlike a bond, which I soon discuss, a CD's principal value does not fluctuate. Of course, CDs also give you the peace of mind afforded by the government's FDIC insurance program.

The reason that CDs pay higher interest rates than savings accounts is that you're committing to tie up your money for a period of time, such as 6, 12, or 24 months. The bank pays you 5 to 6 percent and then turns around and lends your money to people through credit cards, auto loans, and the like and charges the borrower an interest rate of 10-plus percent. Not a bad business, huh?

When you tie your money up in a CD, you're making a sacrifice. If you want it back before the CD matures, a hefty penalty (about six months' interest) is shaved from your return. With other lending investments, such as bonds and bond mutual funds, discussed later in this chapter, you can access your money without penalty and often at little or no cost.

In addition to penalties for early withdrawal, CDs yield less than a high-quality bond with a comparable maturity (for example, two, five, or ten years). Often, the yield difference is 1 percent or more, especially if you don't shop around and simply buy CDs from your local bank where you keep your checking account.

A final and perhaps fatal flaw of CDs comes from high-tax bracket investors purchasing them outside of retirement accounts. The interest on CDs is fully taxable at the federal and state levels. Bonds, by contrast, are available, if you desire, in tax-free (federal and/or state) versions.

TIP

You can earn higher returns and have better access to your money in bonds than in CDs. And bonds make especially good sense when you're in a higher tax bracket and would benefit from tax-free income on your non-retirement account investments.

CDs make the most sense when you know, for example, that you can invest your money for one year, after which you'll need the money for some purchase you expect to make. Just make sure that you shop around to get the best interest rate. If having the U.S. government insurance gives you peace of mind, take a look at Treasuries, which are discussed later in this chapter. Treasuries often pay more interest than the better CDs available.

Keep your savings in a money market fund

Keep your checking account at your local bank but not your extra savings, such as what you keep in bank savings accounts or — worse — in your checking account. Money market funds, which are a type of mutual fund (other common funds focus on bonds or stocks), are a great place to keep your extra savings. Money market funds are a higher yielding alternative to bank savings and bank money market deposit accounts.

Money market funds are unique among mutual funds because they do not fluctuate in value and maintain a fixed $1 per share price. As with a bank savings account, your principal investment in a money market fund does not change in value while you're earning dividends (same as the interest on a bank account). However, money market mutual funds offer several significant benefits over bank savings accounts. The biggest advantage is higher yields.

Money market mutual funds are able to pay higher yields because they don't have the high overhead that banks do. The most efficient mutual fund companies, such as Vanguard, T. Rowe Price, and USAA, don't have scads of branch offices on every street corner. Another reason that banks pay lower yields is that they know that many depositors, perhaps including you, believe that the FDIC insurance that comes with a bank savings account makes it safer than a money market mutual fund.

Another advantage of money funds over bank accounts is that money funds come in a variety of tax-free versions. So if you're in a high tax bracket (see Chapter 3), tax-free money funds offer something bank accounts don't.

Another useful feature that comes with money market mutual funds is the ability to write checks, without charge, against your account. Most mutual fund companies require that the checks that you write be for larger amounts — typically at least $250. They don't want you using these accounts to pay all your small household bills because checks cost money to process.

money market fund: offers checking

Money market funds are a good place to keep your emergency cash reserve of at least three to six months' living expenses. They're also a great place to keep money awaiting investment elsewhere in the near future. If you're saving money for a home that you expect to purchase soon (next year or so), a money fund can be a safe place to accumulate and grow the down payment. You wouldn't want to risk placing such money in the stock market, which can get clobbered in a relatively short period of time.

Just as you can use a money market fund for your personal purposes, you can open a money market fund for your business. I have one for my business. This account can be used for depositing checks received from customers and holding excess funds as well as for paying bills via the check-writing feature.

A few money funds, such as those offered with brokerage cash management accounts at firms such as Charles Schwab, Jack White, and Fidelity, allow checks to be written for any size amount and can completely replace a bank checking account. Money market funds that allow for unlimited check writing can be established and used for household checking purposes as well. (The brokerage firms that offer accounts with this capability downplay your ability to do this.) You can leave your bank altogether as these brokerage accounts often come with debit cards that can be used at bank ATMs for a nominal fee.

Higher yields, tax-free alternatives, and check writing. It almost sounds too good to be true. What's the catch? Good money market funds really don't have any, but you should know about an important difference between bank accounts and money market mutual funds. Money funds are not insured. As discussed earlier, bank accounts come with FDIC insurance that protects up to $100,000 you have deposited in a bank. So, if a bank fails because it lends too much money to people and companies that go bankrupt or abscond with the funds, you should get your money back.

The lack of FDIC insurance on a money fund shouldn't trouble you. Mutual fund companies can't fail because they have a dollar invested in securities for every dollar you deposited in their money fund. By contrast, banks are required to have available just 12 cents for every dollar you hand over to them.

It is possible that a money market fund's investments may decline slightly in value, which can cause the money fund's share price to fall below a dollar. A few cases have occurred where money market funds bought some bad investments. However, in each and every case, except one, the parent company running the money fund infused cash into the affected fund, thus enabling it to maintain the $1 per share price.

One money market fund did "break the buck." It didn't take money in from people like you or me but was run by a bunch of small banks for themselves.

The money market fund made some bone-headed investments. The share price of the fund declined by 6 percent, and the fund owners decided to disband the fund; they didn't bail it out, because they would be repaying themselves.

Stick with larger mutual fund companies if you're worried about the lack of FDIC insurance. They have the financial wherewithal and the largest incentive to save a floundering money fund. Fortunately, the larger fund companies have the best money funds anyway. More details about selecting and finding money funds can be found in the next chapter.

Bonds: Jargon for IOU

In the 1920s, Andrew Mellon said, "Gentleman prefer bonds." I've never figured out why, and I'm convinced that Mr. Mellon wasn't serious or sober when he said this. My observation is that conservative investors prefer bonds. (That's conservative when it comes to taking risk, not politics.) Otherwise aggressive investors seeking diversification or investing for a shorter-term financial goal also prefer bonds. The reason: Bonds offer higher yields than bank accounts without as great a volatility as the stock market.

A bond is similar to a certificate of deposit (CD). With a five-year CD, for example, a bank agrees to pay you a set interest rate, say, 6 percent. If all goes according to plan, at the end of five years of earning the 6 percent annual interest, you get back the principal that you originally invested.

Bonds work in a similar fashion. For example, you can purchase a bond, scheduled to mature five years from now, that is issued by a company such as the retailing behemoth Wal-Mart. A Wal-Mart five-year bond may pay you 7 percent. As long as Wal-Mart doesn't have a financial catastrophe, after five years of receiving interest payments on the bond, Wal-Mart returns your original investment to you. So, in effect, you're loaning your money to Wal-Mart (instead of the bank when you deposit money in a bank account).

The worst that can happen to your bond investment is that Wal-Mart's business goes into a tailspin and the company ends up in financial ruin — a.k.a. bankruptcy. If that happens, you may lose all of your original investment and miss out on some of the expected interest.

But bonds issued by high-quality companies, such as Wal-Mart, are quite safe — they rarely default. Heck, many companies have been around longer than you've been alive. Besides, even if every now and then a big company goes under, you don't have to invest all your money in just one or two bonds. If you own bonds in many companies, which can easily be done through a good bond mutual fund, and one bond unexpectedly takes a hit, it affects only a teeny tiny portion of your portfolio.

Why take the risk of a default? Because bonds pay higher interest rates than the bank. If you take extra risk and forsake that FDIC insurance, you should receive a higher rate of interest investing in bonds. Remember that when you invest in bank savings accounts and CDs, you're being paid less interest because of the overhead of the bank branches as well as the cost of the FDIC insurance.

What use are bonds?

Investing in bonds is a time-honored way to earn a better rate of return on money you don't plan to use within the next couple of years or more. As with other investments, stocks for example, bonds can generally be sold any day the financial markets are open. Because their value fluctuates, though, you're more likely to lose money if forced to sell your bonds sooner rather than later. In the short term, the bond market can bounce every which way; in the longer term, you're more likely to receive your money back with interest.

Bonds generally pay you more than bank savings and money market mutual funds but with a catch. As discussed later in this chapter, bonds are riskier than money market funds and savings accounts because their value can fall if interest rates rise. However, bonds tend to be more stable in value than stocks (the risk and return of bonds and stocks is covered in Chapter 2).

Don't put your emergency cash reserve into bonds — that's what a money market fund or bank savings account is for. But don't put too much of your longer-term investment money in bonds, either. As I show in Chapter 2, bonds are lousy investments for making your money grow. Growth-oriented investments, such as stocks, real estate, and your own business, are where you have the potential to build real wealth.

Here are some common financial goals and reasons why investing some money in bonds can make sense:

- ✔ **A major purchase** that won't happen for at least two years, such as the purchase of a home or some other major expenditure. Shorter-term bonds may work for you as a higher-yielding and slightly riskier alternative to money market funds.

- ✔ **Diversification.** Bonds don't move in tandem with the performance of other types of investments, such as stocks. In fact, in a terrible economic environment such as occurred during the Great Depression, bonds may appreciate in value if inflation is declining.

- ✔ **Retirement investments.** Bonds that have intermediate- to longer-term maturities may be appropriate while you're still working. When you invest in bonds as part of a longer-term investment strategy (such as for retirement), you should have an overall plan about how to invest your money, sometimes referred to as an *asset allocation strategy* (see Chapter 3).

Aggressive, younger investors should keep less of their retirement money in bonds than older folks who are nearing retirement.

✔ **Income-producing investments.** If you're retired or not working, bonds can be useful because they are better at producing current income than many other investments.

Bonds are not all created equal

Bonds aren't as complicated and unique as people, but they're certainly more complex than a bank savings account. And, thanks to some shady marketing practices by some investing companies and salespeople who sell bonds, you have your work cut out for you in getting a handle on what many bonds really are and how they differ from their peers. What follows are the major ways that bonds differ from one another so that you can make educated bond purchases.

To whom are you lending your money?

Bonds differ from each other according to what type of organization is issuing them — in other words, what kind of organization you're lending your money to. Here are the major options and when each may make sense for you.

Treasury bonds

Treasuries are IOUs from the biggest debtor of them all, the U.S. federal government. The types of Treasury bonds include Treasury bills (which mature within a year), Treasury notes (which mature between one and ten years), and Treasury bonds (which mature in more than ten years). These distinctions and delineations are arbitrary — you don't need to know them for an exam.

Treasuries pay interest that is state tax-free but federally taxable. Thus, they make sense for people interested in avoiding a high state income tax but not a high federal income tax bracket. However, most people in a high state income tax bracket also happen to be in a high federal income tax bracket. Such high tax bracket investors would be better off in municipal bonds (explained in the next section), which are federal and state tax-free.

The best use of Treasuries is in place of bank CDs. If you feel snug and secure with the federal government backing that comes with a bank CD, check out a Treasury bond. Treasuries that mature in the same length of time as a CD almost always pay the same or better interest rate. If you hunt around, you may stumble upon a bank that pays a slightly higher interest rate than a comparable Treasury bond. Just remember that bank CD interest is fully taxable, whereas a Treasury's interest is state tax-free. Unless you shop for a bank CD, you will likely earn a lower return on a CD than on a Treasury (see Table 7-2). I explain later in the chapter how to purchase Treasury bonds.

Table 7-2	Comparing Interest Rates on CDs versus Treasury Bills	
	6-Month Maturity	*12-Month Maturity*
Average of bank CDs	4.8%	5.0%
Best bank CDs	5.9%	5.7%
Worst bank CDs	3.2%	4.4%
Treasury bills	5.4%	5.6%

Note: Rates compared in the fall of 1995.

Municipal bonds

Municipal bonds are state and local government bonds that pay interest that's federally tax-free and state tax-free to residents in the state of issue. For example, if you live in New York and buy a bond issued by a New York government agency, you don't owe New York state or federal income tax on the interest.

The government organizations that issue municipal bonds know that the investors who buy municipals don't have to pay most or any of the income tax that normally would be required on other bonds — which means that the issuing governments can get away with paying a lower rate of interest.

If you're in a high tax bracket (31 percent or higher for federal tax) and you want to invest in bonds outside tax-sheltered retirement accounts, you should end up with a higher after-tax yield from a municipal bond (often called munis) than a bond that pays taxable interest. If you're in the 28 percent federal bracket, it's borderline whether you'll come out ahead with munis. At less than 28 percent, don't invest in munis.

Some people are concerned about the impact of the passage of a flat tax on their municipal bonds. Under some of the proposed versions of the flat tax, all interest earned on investments would not be taxed. Thus, muni bonds would lose their tax-free advantage versus other bonds. If such a flat tax were to pass, the price of municipal bonds, particularly longer-term ones, could fall significantly. Unless a Republican wins the White House in 1996, the passage of such a measure is considered remote. Even then, municipal bond holders aren't likely to take such a change lying down. That's why, like many radical proposed reforms in the tax laws, a flat tax is likely to end up in the scrap heap.

Corporate bonds

Corporate bonds are issued by companies such as McDonald's, Macy's, and IBM. Corporate bonds pay interest that's fully taxable. Thus, they are appropriate for investing inside retirement accounts. Only lower tax bracket investors should consider buying such bonds outside a tax-sheltered retirement account. Later in the chapter, I show you how to read the newspaper listing for such bonds. If you buy corporate bonds through a well-managed mutual fund, an approach I advocate, you won't need to read the newspaper listings.

International bonds

You can buy bonds outside the country you call home. If you live in the U.S., for example, most of the bonds just described can be bought from foreign issuers as well. International bonds are riskier to you because their interest payments can be offset by currency price changes.

While the prices of foreign bonds tend not to move in tandem with U.S. bonds and therefore offer some diversification value, foreign bonds are not a vital holding for a diversified portfolio. They are generally more expensive to purchase and hold than comparable domestic bonds.

Mortgage bonds

You remember that mortgage you took out when you purchased a home? Well, you can actually invest in that mortgage through purchasing a bond! Many banks actually sell their mortgages as bonds in the financial markets allowing other investors to invest in them. The repayment of principal on such bonds is usually guaranteed at the bond's maturity by a government agency, such as the Government National Mortgage Association (GNMA, a.k.a. Ginnie Mae) or the Federal National Mortgage Association (FNMA, a.k.a. Fannie Mae).

Convertible bonds

Convertible bonds are hybrid securities — they're bonds that you can convert into a preset number of shares of stock in the company that issued the bond. Although these bonds do pay interest, their yield is lower than nonconvertible bonds because convertibles offer you the upside potential of being able to make more money if the underlying stock rises.

Likelihood of being stiffed

In addition to who issues them, bonds differ from one another in terms of the creditworthiness of the issuer. Every year, billions of dollars worth of bonds default. You can minimize investing in bonds that default by purchasing high-credit quality bonds. Credit rating agencies, such as Moody's, Standard & Poor's and Duff & Phelps, rate the credit quality and likelihood of default of bonds.

The credit rating of a bond depends on the issuer's (company or government) ability to pay back its debt. Bond credit ratings are usually done on some sort of a letter-grade scale where AAA is the highest rating, with ratings descending through AA and A, followed by BBB, BB, B, CCC, CC , C, and so on. AAA and AA rated bonds are considered "high-grade" or "high-credit quality." Such bonds have little chance — a fraction of one percent — of default.

Bonds rated A and BBB are considered "general" grade or quality. Junk bonds (known more by their marketed name, *high yield*) are rated BB or lower. These bonds are more likely to default — perhaps as many as a couple of percent per year actually default.

You may be asking yourself why any right-minded investor would buy a bond with a low credit rating. Companies attract bond investors with lower-quality bonds by paying them a higher interest rate. The lower a bond's credit rating and quality, the higher the yield you can and should expect from such a bond. Poorer quality bonds, though, are not for the faint of heart.

In addition to paying attention to the credit quality of the bonds you're buying, make sure to diversify. Don't put all your money earmarked for corporate bonds into just one or two corporate bonds. Bond mutual funds are a great way to invest in bonds because they typically invest in dozens of bonds.

Maturity

Maturity simply means the time at which the bond pays you back — next year, in five years, in 30 years, and so on. You should care how long it takes a bond to mature. Why? Because a bond's maturity gives you a good (although far from perfect) sense of how volatile a bond will be if interest rates change.

Suppose that you are considering investing in two bonds that are issued by the same organization and both yield 7 percent. The bonds differ from one another only in when they will mature: One is a two-year bond and the other a 20-year bond. If interest rates were to rise just 1 percent (from 7 percent to 8 percent), the two-year bond would fall 2 percent in value whereas the 20-year bond would fall five times as much — 10 percent.

If you hold a bond until it matures, you get your principal back unless the issuer defaults. In the meantime, however, if interest rates fall, bond prices rise. The reason is simple. If the bond you hold is issued at say 7 percent and interest rates on similar bonds rise to 8 percent, no one (unless they don't know any better) will want to purchase your 7 percent bond. The value of your bond has to decrease enough so that it effectively yields 8 percent.

Bonds are generally classified by the length of time until maturity:

- ✔ **Short-term bonds** mature in the next few years.
- ✔ **Intermediate-term bonds** come due within three to ten years.
- ✔ **Long-term bonds** mature in more than 10 years and generally up to 30 years. Although rare, a number of companies issue 100-year bonds! A number of railroads did, as well as Disney and Coca-Cola in recent years. Such bonds are quite dangerous to purchase, especially if they are issued during a period of very low interest rates.

Most of the time, longer-term bonds pay higher yields than short-term bonds. You can look at a chart of the current yield of bonds plotted against when they mature — such a chart is known as a yield curve. At most times, this curve slopes upward. Investors generally demand a higher rate of interest for taking the risk of holding longer-term bonds. Most financial newspapers and magazines carry a current chart of the yield curve.

Individual bonds or bond mutual funds

You can invest in bonds in one of two major ways. You can purchase individual bonds or you can invest in a professionally selected and managed portfolio of bonds via a bond mutual fund.

Unless the bonds you are considering purchasing are easy to analyze and homogeneous (such as Treasury bonds), you're generally better off investing in bonds through a mutual fund. The first reason is diversification. You don't want to put all of your investment money into a small number of bonds that are issued by companies in the same industry or that mature at the same time. It's difficult to build a diversified bond portfolio with individual issues unless you've got a hefty chunk (at least $100,000) that you want to invest in bonds.

If you purchase individual bonds through a broker, you're going to pay a commission. In most cases, the commission is hidden. The broker quotes you a price for the bond that includes the commission. Even if you use a discount broker, though, these fees take a healthy bite out of your investment. The smaller the amount invested, the bigger the bite. On a $1,000 bond, the fee can equal up to 5 percent. Commissions take a smaller bite out of larger bonds — perhaps less than 0.5 percent if you use discount brokers.

The best reason to invest in bond funds instead of individual bonds is that you've got better things to do with your time. Do you really want to research bonds and go bond shopping? Bonds are boring! And bonds and the companies that stand behind them aren't that simple to understand. For example, did you know that some bonds can be "called" before their maturity date? Companies often call bonds to save money if interest rates drop significantly. After you purchase a bond, you need to do the same things that a good bond mutual fund portfolio manager needs to do, such as tracking the issuer's creditworthiness and monitoring other important financial developments.

A final reason to invest in bonds through a mutual fund is that it's cost-effective. Great bond funds are yours for a mere 0.2 percent per year in operating expenses. Selecting good bond funds isn't hard, as you discover in Chapter 8.

How to buy individual bonds

If you want to purchase a Treasury bond, the lowest-cost method is to do so directly through Federal Reserve. The Federal Reserve does not charge for accounts with less than $100,000 and charges $25 annually for accounts with more than $100,000 in Treasury bonds. Contact the Federal Reserve branch nearest you from the following list and ask them to mail you information to purchase Treasury bonds through their Treasury Direct program.

Atlanta, GA	404-521-8653	Memphis, TN	901-523-7171
Baltimore, MD	410-576-3300	Miami, FL	305-471-6497
Birmingham, AL	205-731-8708	Minneapolis, MN	612-340-2075
Boston, MA	617-973-3810	Nashville, TN	615-251-7100
Buffalo, NY	716-849-5000	New Orleans, LA	504-593-3200
Charlotte, NC	704-358-2100	New York, NY	212-720-6619
Chicago, IL	312-322-5369	Oklahoma City, OK	405-270-8652
Cincinnati, OH	513-721-4787	Omaha, NE	402-221-5636
Cleveland, OH	216-579-2000	Philadelphia, PA	215-574-6680
Dallas, TX	214-922-6770	Pittsburgh, PA	412-261-7802
Denver, CO	303-572-2470	Portland, OR	503-221-5932
Detroit, MI	313-964-6157	Richmond, VA	804-697-8372
El Paso, TX	915-521-8272	Salt Lake City, UT	801-322-7882
Houston, TX	713-659-4433	San Antonio, TX	210-978-1303
Jacksonville, FL	904-632-1179	San Francisco, CA	415-974-2330
Kansas City, MO	816-881-2883	Seattle, WA	206-343-3605
Little Rock, AR	501-324-8272	St. Louis, MO	314-444-8703
Los Angeles, CA	213-624-7398	Washington, D.C.	202-874-4000
Louisville, KY	502-568-9236		

Treasury bonds may also be purchased and held through brokerage firms and mutual funds. Brokers will typically charge a flat fee — $30 to $40 is reasonable — for buying a Treasury bond. Buying Treasuries through a brokerage account makes sense if you hold other securities through the brokerage account and like to be able to quickly sell a Treasury bond you hold. (Bonds bought and held through the Federal Reserve must first be transferred to a brokerage account if you want to sell them prior to maturity.)

The advantage of a mutual fund that invests in Treasuries is that it typically diversifies by holding Treasuries of differing maturities. No-load (commission-free) mutual funds can generally be bought and sold without a charge. Funds,

Assessing individual bonds you already own

If you already own individual bonds and they fit your financial objectives and tax situation, you can hold them until maturity because you've already incurred a commission when they were purchased; selling them now would just create an additional fee. When the bonds mature, the broker who sold them to you will probably be more than happy to sell you some more. That's the time to check out bond mutual funds (see the next chapter for how to buy bond funds).

Don't mistakenly think that your current individual bonds are paying the yield they had when they were originally issued (that yield is the number listed in the name of the bond on your brokerage account statement). As the market level of interest rates changes, the effective yield (the interest payment divided by the bond's price) on your bonds fluctuates as well to rise and fall with the market level of rates. So if rates have fallen since you bought your bonds, the value of those bonds has increased — which in turn reduces the effective yield that you're currently earning.

however, do charge an ongoing management fee. The Vanguard Group of mutual funds offers Treasury mutual funds with good track records and low management fees (see Chapter 8).

Purchasing other types of individual bonds, such as corporate and mortgage bonds, is a much more treacherous and time-consuming undertaking. Here's my advice for doing it right and minimizing the chance of a catastrophic mistake:

- ✓ **Don't buy through salespeople.** Brokerage firms that employ representatives on commission are in the sales business. Many of the worst bond investing disasters have befallen customers of such brokerage firms. Your best bet is to purchase individual bonds through discount brokers, such as Jack White, Quick & Reilly, Fidelity, and Charles Schwab (see Chapter 4).

- ✓ **Don't be suckered into high yields — buy quality.** Yes, junk bonds pay higher yields, but they also have a much higher chance of default. Nothing personal, but you're not going to do as good a job as a professional money manager at spotting problems and red flags. Thus, you're more likely to be left holding the bag when some of your junk bond purchases don't work out the way you expected. Stick with highly-rated bonds so that you don't have to worry about and suffer these unfortunate consequences.

- ✓ **Understand callability.** Many bonds, especially corporate bonds, can legally be called before maturity. What this means is that the bond issuer pays you back early, either because they don't need to borrow as much money or because interest rates have fallen and the borrower wants to issue new bonds at a lower interest rate.

  Be especially careful about purchasing bonds that were issued at higher interest rates than are currently prevailing. Such bonds are the first to be paid off early by the borrower.

- ✔ **Diversify.** Invest and hold bonds from a variety of companies in different industries. Doing so buffers you from changes in the economy that adversely affect one or a few industries more than others. Of the money that you want to invest in bonds, I wouldn't put more than 5 to 10 percent into any one bond. That means that you'll be holding anywhere from 10 to 20 bonds. This investing style is why you need a good chunk of change ($100,000-plus) to invest, given the size of most bonds and because high fees erode your investment balance if you invest too little.

- ✔ **Shop around.** Just as when you're buying a car, shop around for good prices on the bonds you have in mind. The hard part is doing an apples-to-apples comparison as different brokers may not be able to offer the same exact bond as other brokers. Remember that the two biggest determinants of what a bond should yield are when it matures and its credit rating.

Unless you're investing in boring, simple-to-understand bonds such as Treasuries, you are better off investing in bonds via mutual funds. One exception is if you absolutely, positively must get your principal back on a certain date. Because bond funds never mature, individual bonds with the correct maturity should best suit your needs. Consider Treasuries since they carry little, if any, default risk. Otherwise, you need a lot of money, time, and patience to invest well in individual bonds yourself.

Tracking individual bonds in the paper

Most daily newspapers don't publish the prices of individual bonds. Newspapers don't have a lot of interest in devoting what space they do have for securities prices for bonds. More business focused publications, such as the *Wall Street Journal,* provide bond pricing daily. You may also obtain bond prices over the phone by calling your broker. The following walks you through the bond listing for PhilEl (Philadelphia Electric) in Figure 7-1:

1. **Bond name.** This tells you who issued the bond. In this case, the issuer is a large utility company, Philadelphia Electric.

2. **Funny numbers after company name.** The first part of the numerical sequence here — 7 $^1/_8$ — refers to the original interest rate (7.125 percent) that this bond paid when it was issued. This interest rate is known as the coupon rate. The second part of the numbers — 23 — refers to the year that the bond matures, 2023 in this case.

3. **Current Yield.** This is arrived at by dividing the interest paid, 7.125, by the current price per share, $93. In this case, it equals, rounded off, 7.7 percent.

4. **Volume.** Indicates the number of bonds that traded this day.

5. **Close.** Shows the last price the bond traded at.

6. **Change.** How this day's close compares with the previous day's. In this case, this bond is up 2 $^1/_8$ points, a pretty healthy gain on a day that the overall bond market was up modestly. Some bonds don't trade all that often, so you

Philadelphia Electric

NEW YORK EXCHANGE BONDS

Quotations as of 4 p.m. Eastern Time
Tuesday, September 12, 1995

Volume $35,971,000

	Domestic Tue.	Domestic Mon.	All Issues Tue.	All Issues Mon.
Issues traded	357	354	366	364
Advances	200	159	202	167
Declines	89	130	95	132
Unchanged	68	65	69	65
New highs	38	31	39	32
New lows	2	1	2	1

SALES SINCE JANUARY 1
(000 omitted)

1995	1994	1993
$5,188,396	$5,277,981	$7,219,905

Dow Jones Bond Averages

-1994- High	-1994- Low	-1995- High	-1995- Low		---1995--- Close	---1995--- Chg.	---1995--- %Yld	--1994-- Close	--1994-- Chg.
105.61	93.56	103.75	93.63	20 Bonds	103.23	+ 0.13	7.12	97.60	+ 0.06
103.43	88.99	100.00	89.06	10 Utilities	99.51	+ 0.10	7.30	93.40	− 0.05
107.93	97.93	107.53	98.08	10 Industrials	106.95	+ 0.16	6.94	101.81	+ 0.18

CORPORATION BONDS
Volume, $35,617,000

Bonds	Cur Yld	Vol	Close	Net Chg.
ADT Op zr10	...	8	42¼	...
AMR 8.10s98	7.9	70	103	+ ⅛
AMR 9s16	8.4	68	107¾	+ 2
AMR 6⅛24	cv	49	103	− 1¼
ATT 4⅜96	4.5	145	98¼	− ⅛
ATT 4⅜99	4.6	20	95	+ ½
ATT 6s00	6.1	44	98⅝	...
ATT 5⅛01	5.4	45	94⅜	+ ⅝
ATT 7⅛02	6.9	311	103⅜	+ ⅛
ATT 6¾04	6.7	76	101¼	+ ⅝
ATT 7½06	7.1	33	106¼	+ ⅝
ATT 7¾07	7.2	10	107⅝	+ ⅛
ATT 8⅛22	7.8	531	104¾	+ ⅛
ATT 8⅛24	7.7	20	105¼	− ⅛
ATT 8⅝31	7.9	25	108⅞	+ ⅛
Actava 9⅞97	9.8	20	100¾	+ 1
Actava 9½98	9.6	58	99⅜	+ ⅜
AirbF 6¾01	cv	8	100	+ ½
AlskAr 6⅞14	cv	55	83½	+ ½
AlbnyInt 5¼02	cv	5	100¼	+ ¼
AlegCp 6½14	cv	82	108	+ ½
AlldC zr98	...	12	82⅜	+ ¼
AlldC zr09	...	105	36⅝	+ ⅛
Allwst 7¼14	cv	1	89	− ½
Alza zr14	...	25	38	− 1¼
AmBrnd 7½99	7.3	25	103	+ 1
AExC 6⅛00	6.2	10	99	...
AmHme 6⅞97	6.8	5	100½	...
Amsco 2002	cv	1	95¼	+ ¼
Ancp 13⅞02f	cv	2	40⅛	− ¼
AnnTaylr 8¾00	9.7	1694	90½	− 2½
Arml 11⅜99	10.8	10	105	+ ½
Arrow 5¾02	cv	2	170	...
Arvin 7½14	cv	10	101	...
AshInd 6¾14	cv	10	98½	+ 1
AutDt zr12	...	13	45⅜	− ⅝
Barnt 8½99	8.0	19	106	+ ½
Barnet 9⅞01	8.9	1	111	− ½
BellPa 7⅛12	7.2	35	98⅝	+ ⅛
BellPa 7½13	7.4	25	100¾	+ ¼
BellsoT 6½00	6.4	40	100⅞	− ¼
BellsoT 6¼03	6.4	95	98⅜	...
BellsoT 5⅞09	6.4	15	92⅛	+ ¼
BellsoT 7⅞32	7.5	20	104⅞	+ 1
BellsoT 7½33	7.4	50	100⅞	+ ⅞
BstBuy 8⅝00	8.7	112	99¾	+ ¼
BethSt 9s00	8.9	32	101⅜	− ⅛
BethSt 8⅜01	8.5	25	98⅝	− ⅛
BethSt 8.45s05	8.7	197	97⅛	− ⅜
Bevrly 7⅝03	cv	130	97⅛	− ⅜
BoisC 7cld	cv	25	101¼	− 5½
BoltBer 6s12	cv	27	126	− ½
Bordn 8⅜16	8.5	10	98½	− 1¼
BorgWS 9⅛03	10.1	60	90½	+ ¾
BwnSh 9¼05	cv	1	100½	− 1
BwnFer 6¼12	cv	63	101½	+ ¼

Bonds	Cur Yld	Vol	Close	Net Chg.
GMA zr15	...	168	233	+ 1¾
GMA 8¼16	8.0	124	102⅝	...
GnSgnl 5¾02	cv	400	104⅝	− ⅜
Gene 10⅜03	11.0	50	94	...
Genrad 7¼11	cv	30	89	+ 1½
GaPw 6⅛99	6.2	10	99½	+ ¾
Gerrity 11¾04	12.8	97	92	+ ⅜
Grancre 6½03	6.8	101	96	+ 1
Gulfrd 6s12	cv	7	99	+ ¼
Hallwd 7s00	9.4	15	74⅛	− ⅞
Hallwd na13½09	...	146	48	− ⅜
Hallw na13½09C	...	9	48	+ 8
Hlthso 9½01	9.1	25	104	+ ½
ICN 12⅞98	12.5	180	102⅞	− 2⅛
ICN Ph 8½99	cv	264	121	+ 1½
IMC Glb 6¼01	cv	40	110	+ 1
IRT Pr 7.3s03	cv	30	92½	+ ½
IllBel 7⅝06	7.5	38	101⅜	+ ⅛
IllPwr 8s23	7.9	35	101¾	+ 1½
InldStl 7.9s07	8.5	17	93	...
IBM 6⅜97	6.3	122	100⅝	− ⅛
IBM 6⅜00	6.4	110	100¼	+ ⅛
IBM 7¼02	7.0	194	104⅛	− ⅛
IBM 7½13	7.2	54	104⅜	+ ⅜
IBM 8⅜19	7.4	10	112¾	− ⅛
IntShip 9s03	9.0	41	99¾	+ 1
IntTch 9⅜96	9.3	5	100⅜	+ ⅜
KaufB 10⅜99	10.3	100	100½	− 2
KaufB 9⅜03	9.6	95	97½	...

Bonds	Cur Yld	Vol	Close	Net Chg.
PacTT 7¼08	7.3	30	100	...
ParCm 7s03A	7.5	30	93⅛	− ¾
ParCm 7s03B	7.5	5	93⅞	+ ⅞
Pathmk zr03	...	20	66½	− ⅜
Paten 8¼12	cv	69	88½	+ 2
PaylCsh 9⅛03	12.1	1128	75¾	− 1
PennTr 9⅝05	11.6	291	82¾	− ⅛
Pennzl 6½03	5.5	15	119¼	...
Pepsic 7⅝98	7.4	5	103⅝	− ⅛
PhilEl 7⅛23	7.7	15	93	+ 2⅛
PhilPt 7.92s23	8.0	75	99½	+ 1
Pier1 6⅞02	cv	80	104	+ 2½
PionFn 8s00	cv	10	128½	+ ¼
PotEl 5s02	cv	57	90	...
Primark 8¾00	8.6	15	101⅞	+ 1
PSEG 6½04	6.7	25	97¼	− ½
PSEG 7½23	7.6	102	99	+ 1⅜
RJR Nb 8s00	7.8	47	102½	+ ¾
RJR Nb 8⅝02	8.4	25	103⅛	...
RJR Nb 7⅝03	7.9	224	96¾	+ ¼
RJR Nb 8¾05	8.6	5	101⅞	+ ½
RJR Nb 8⅞07	8.7	52	101½	+ ½
RJR Nb 9¼13	9.1	84	101⅞	+ ½
RJR Nb 8.3s99	8.1	34	103	...
RJR Nb 8¾04	8.5	43	102½	+ ¼
Rallys 9⅞00	16.7	395	59	− 1
RalsP 9½16	9.1	34	103⅞	+ ⅛
RalsP 9⅜16	9.0	10	103¾	− ⅝
RalsP 8⅝22	8.0	40	108⅜	+ ⅞

Figure 7-1: Sample bond listings from the *Wall Street Journal.*

notice that some bonds were up and others were down on this day. The price movement of a given bond on a particular day is influenced by the demand of new buyers and the supply of interested sellers.

In addition to the direction of overall interest rates, the price of an individual bond is most affected by changes in the financial health of the company that stands behind it.

Other Lending Investments

Bonds, money market funds, and bank investments are hardly the only lending investments around. A variety of other companies are more than willing to take your investment dollars and pay you a relatively fixed rate of interest. In most cases, you're going to be better off staying away from the following investments.

Too many investing dummies get sucked into more sophisticated sounding lending investments. The bait: higher promised yields. Remember, remember, remember: Risk and return go hand in hand. Higher yields mean greater risk and vice versa. I help you work your way through other lending investments, from lower-risk to higher-risk ones.

Guaranteed-investment contracts

Guaranteed-investment contracts (GICs) are sold and backed by an insurance company. The allure of GICs is that your account value does not appear to fluctuate. Like a one-year bank certificate of deposit, GICs generally quote you an interest rate for the next year. Some GICs lock in the rate for longer periods of time, whereas others may change the interest rate up to four times per year.

The insurance company that issues the GIC actually invests your money mostly in bonds and maybe a bit in stocks. Like other bonds and stocks, these investments fluctuate in value — you just don't see it.

Typically once a year, you receive a new statement showing that your GIC is worth more, thanks to the newly-added interest. This statement makes nervous investors who can't stand volatile investments feel all warm and fuzzy.

The yield on a GIC is usually comparable to that available on a shorter-term, high-quality bond. Yet, the insurer invests in longer-term bonds and some stocks. The difference between what these investments generate for the insurer and what the GIC pays you in interest is profit to the insurer.

This difference can be huge and hidden. Unlike a mutual fund, which is required to report the management fee it is collecting and subtracting before your return is paid, insurers have no such obligations with a GIC. By having a return guaranteed in advance, you pay mightily — an effective fee of 2 to 4 percent per year — for the peace of mind in the form of lower long-term returns.

The high effective fees that you're being charged to have an insurer manage your money in a GIC aren't the only drawback. When you invest in a GIC, your assets are part of the insurer's general assets. Insurance companies sometimes fail, and although they often are merged into a healthy insurer, you can still lose money. The rate of return on GICs from a failed insurance company is often slashed to help restore financial soundness to the company. So the only "guarantee" that comes with a GIC is that the issuing insurer agrees to pay you the promised rate of interest so long as they are able!

Why companies offer GICs in their retirement plans

More than a few companies, in their retirement plans, offer GICs as an investment option. You may rightfully ask why because, as I've discussed, GICs are investments that leave a lot to be desired. I see GICs most often in companies where an insurer is already entrenched as the provider of the bulk of the company's retirement plan investment options. Insurers love GICs because they are so profitable — for them, that is.

But in some company retirement plans, GICs are the one and only investment option offered by an insurance company. Historically, companies were attracted to GICs as a defensive measure. GICs seemed so safe and conservative and made company officials who selected their retirement plan investment options feel safe. (More than a

few benefits and other corporate personnel who are responsible for establishing and maintaining these plans aren't exactly investing geniuses.)

Over the years, as more insurers have failed, including ones that appeared to be financially sound, the true risk of GICs is more apparent. As more people have discovered attractive alternative investment options such as mutual funds, which offer higher returns and low expenses, GIC's popularity has been waning. If your company's retirement plan doesn't offer good investment choices and has too many GIC-like investments, talk to your benefits department. You can also anonymously leave them a copy of this book so that they can better educate themselves!

Private mortgages

Earlier in the chapter, I discuss investing in mortgages similar to the one you take out to purchase a home. You can also invest directly in mortgages by loaning your money to people who need it to buy or refinance real estate. Such loans are known as mortgages or second mortgages.

Private mortgage investing appeals to investors who don't like the volatility of the stock and bond markets but aren't satisfied with the seemingly paltry returns on bonds or other common lending investments. Private mortgages seem to offer the best of both worlds — stock market like 10-plus percent returns without volatility.

Mortgage investments are often arranged by mortgage and real estate brokers, which is why you must tread carefully. It's not that these people are dishonest — most aren't — it's just that they have a vested interest in seeing the deal done. Otherwise the mortgage broker doesn't get paid for closing the loan, and the real estate broker doesn't get a commission for selling a property.

One broker who also happens to write about real estate wrote a newspaper column not so long ago describing mortgages as the "perfect real estate investment" and added that mortgages are a "high-yield, low-risk investment." If that wasn't enough to get you to whip out your checkbook, the writer/broker further gushed that mortgages are great investments because you have "... little or no management, no physical labor. ..."

You know by now that a low-risk, high-yield investment does not exist. Earning a relatively high interest rate goes hand in hand with accepting relatively high risk. The risk is that the borrower can default — which leaves you holding the bag. More specifically, you can get stuck with a property that you may need to foreclose on. And if you don't hold the first mortgage, you're not first in line with a claim on the property.

The fact that private mortgages are high risk should be obvious when you consider why the borrower is electing to obtain needed funds privately rather than through a bank. Put yourself in the borrower's shoes. As a property buyer or owner, if you can obtain a mortgage through a conventional lender, such as a bank, wouldn't you do so because banks generally give better interest rates? If a mortgage broker is offering you a deal where you can borrow money at 11 percent when the going bank rate is 8 percent, the deal must carry a fair amount of risk.

I would avoid these investments. If you must invest in such mortgages, you must do your homework on the borrower's financial situation. A banker doesn't lend someone money without examining a borrower's assets, liabilities, and monthly expenses. You shouldn't either. Be careful to check the borrower's credit and get a large down payment (at least 20 percent). This research is time-consuming. The best case to be a lender is if and when you're selling some of your own real estate and are willing to act as the bank and provide the financing to the buyer in the form of a first mortgage.

Also recognize that your mortgage investment also carries interest rate risk: If you need to "sell" it early, you'd have to discount it, perhaps substantially if interest rates have increased since you purchased it. And try not to lend so much money on one mortgage so that it represents more than 5 percent of your total investments.

If you're willing to lend your money to borrowers who carry a relatively high risk of defaulting, check out high-yield (junk) bond mutual funds instead. With these funds, you at least diversify your money across many borrowers, and you benefit from the professional review and due diligence of the fund management team. Also consider lending money to family members.

Mortgages, GICs, and CDs really do fluctuate in value

One of the allures of nonbond investments, such as private mortgages, GICs, and CDs, is that they don't fluctuate in value — at least not that you can see. Such investments appear safer and less volatile. You can't watch your principal fluctuate in value because you can't look up the value every day in the newspaper the way you can with bonds and stocks.

But the principal values of your mortgage, GIC, and CD investments really do fluctuate; you just don't see the fluctuations! As I explain earlier in this chapter, just as the market value of a bond drops when interest rates rise, so too does the market value of these investments, and for the same reasons. At higher interest rates, investors expect a discounted price on your fixed-interest rate investment because they always have the alternative of purchasing a new mortgage, GIC, or CD at the higher prevailing rates. Some of these investments are actually bought and sold (and behave just like bonds) among investors on what's known as a secondary market.

If the normal volatility of a bond's principal value makes you queasy, you could try not following your investments so closely!

Chapter 8

Mushrooming Mutuals

· ·

In This Chapter

▶ Why good funds work for you

▶ The secrets of successful fund investing

▶ Mixing up your own fund portfolio

▶ An inside look at the best stock, bond, and money market funds

· ·

*I*n the earlier chapters in this part, I explain all about stocks, bonds, and other common securities. If you understand these securities, then you can understand mutual funds. A *mutual fund* is just a big pool of money, from lots of investors like you and me, that the mutual fund manager uses to buy a bunch of stocks, bonds, and/or other assets (which I define in Chapter 1) that meet the fund's investment criteria.

When you invest in a fund, you buy shares and become a shareholder of the fund. Funds enable you to give your money to the best money managers in the country. Because good mutual funds take most of the hassle and cost out of figuring out which companies to invest in, they are one of the best investment vehicles, if not the best, ever created. They allow you to diversify your investments — that is, invest in many different industries and companies.

The different types of mutual funds can help you meet various financial goals. That's one of the reasons that investors have nearly $3 trillion invested in funds! You can use money market funds for something most everybody needs — an emergency savings stash of three to six months' living expenses. Perhaps you're thinking about saving for a home purchase, retirement, or future educational costs, so you're examining some stock and bond funds.

Many people plunge into mutual funds without looking at their overall financial situation. In their haste, such investors end up paying more taxes and neglect considering other valuable financial strategies. If you haven't taken a comprehensive look at your personal finances, you're not alone. Start by reading Chapter 3.

Why Funds Are (Often) Absolutely Fabulous

Funds are superior investment vehicles for people of all economic means and for accomplishing many financial objectives. Following are the main reasons you're best served investing in mutual funds rather than individual securities.

Professional management

Mutual funds are investment companies that pool your money with the money of hundreds, thousands, or even millions of other investors. The investment company hires a portfolio manager and researchers whose full-time jobs are to research and purchase suitable investments for the fund. These people screen the universe of investments for those that best meet the fund's stated objectives.

Typically, fund managers are graduates of the top business and finance schools in the country, where they learned portfolio management and securities valuation and selection. Many have additional investing credentials, such as the Chartered Financial Analyst's (CFA) degree. In addition to their educational training, the best fund managers typically have five or more years of experience in analyzing and selecting investments.

For most fund managers and researchers, finding the best investments is more than a full-time job. Fund managers do tons of stuff that you may not have the time or expertise to do. For example, fund managers analyze company financial statements; interview a company's managers to get a sense of the company's business strategies and vision; examine competitor strategies; speak with company customers, suppliers, and industry consultants; and attend trade shows and read industry periodicals.

In short, a mutual fund management team does more research, number-crunching, and due diligence than you could ever have the energy or expertise to do in what little free time you have. Investing in mutual funds helps your friendships and maybe even your sex life by freeing up time to read Dr. Ruth's *Sex For Dummies*. Don't miss the terrific time-saving benefits of fund investing!

Surprisingly cheap

Mutual funds are a cheaper, more communal way of getting the investing job done. When you invest your money in a good, efficiently managed mutual fund, it will likely cost you less than trading individual securities on your own. When fund managers buy and sell securities, they can do it for a fraction of the cost that you pay. Because mutual funds typically buy or sell tens of thousands of shares of a stock at a time, their transaction fees generally run 80 to 90 percent less per share than what you would pay to buy or sell a few hundred shares on your own.

Funds also spread the cost of research over thousands of investors. The most efficiently managed mutual funds cost less than 1 percent per year in fees (bonds and money market funds cost much less — in the neighborhood of 0.5 percent per year or less). Some of the larger and more established funds can charge annual fees as low as 0.2 percent per year — a mere $2 annual charge per $1,000 you invest. Such a deal!

Instant and extensive diversification

Diversification is a big attraction for many investors who choose mutual funds. Most funds own stocks or bonds from dozens of companies, thus diversifying against the risk of bad news from any single company or sector. It is difficult — and expensive — to diversify like that on your own, unless you have a few hundred thousand dollars and a great deal of time to invest. You need to invest money in about a dozen different companies in various industries to ensure that your portfolio can withstand a downturn in one or more of the investments.

Mutual funds typically invest in 25 to 100 securities, or more. Proper diversification increases the chances of the fund earning higher returns with less risk.

Although most mutual funds are diversified, some aren't. For example, some stock funds invest exclusively in stocks of a single industry (health care, for example) or country. I'm not a fan of these funds because of this lack of diversification and their typically higher operating fees.

For richer and poorer . . .

Most funds have low minimum investment requirements. Many funds have minimums of $500 or $1,000 or less. Retirement account investors often can invest with even less. Some funds even offer monthly investment plans, so you can start with as little as $50 per month.

Even if you have lots of money to invest, you also should consider mutual funds. Join the increasing number of companies with millions to invest who are using the low-cost, high-quality money management services that you can get from a mutual fund.

Different funds for different folks

Many people, including some financial writers, think mutual funds = stock market investing = risky. Wrong. The majority of money in mutual funds is not in the stock market. Choosing from a huge variety of mutual funds allows you to select the funds that take on the kinds of risks that you're comfortable with and that meet your financial goals. Following is a list of the three major types of mutual funds:

- ✔ **Stock funds.** If you want your money to grow over a long period of time (and you can put up with down as well as up years), select funds that invest more heavily in stocks.

- ✔ **Bond funds.** If you need current income and don't want investments that fluctuate as widely in value as stocks do, consider some bond funds.

- ✔ **Money market funds.** If you want to be sure that your invested principal does not drop in value because you may need to use your money in the short term, choose a money market fund.

Most investors choose a combination of these three types of funds to diversify and help accomplish different financial goals.

Banks and insurers are far more likely to fail

Hundreds of banks and insurance companies have failed in the past decade alone. Banks and insurers can fail because their *liabilities* (the money customers have given them to invest) can exceed their *assets* (the money they have invested or lent). For example, when a big chunk of a bank's loans go sour at the same time that its depositors want their money, the bank fails. That failure happens because banks typically have less than 15 cents on deposit for every dollar that you and I place with them. Likewise, if an insurance company makes several poor investments or underestimates the number of claims by insurance policyholders, it, too, can fail.

Such failures can't happen with a mutual fund. The situation in which the investors' demand for their investments (the fund's liabilities) exceeds the value of a fund's investments (its assets) simply cannot occur. Why not? Because the mutual fund's investors have purchased shares in the fund and the value of the fund's shares fluctuates as the securities invested in fluctuate in value. For every dollar of securities they hold for their customers, mutual funds have a dollar's worth of securities.

The worst that can happen with a fund is that if you want your money, you may get less cash than you originally put into the fund — but you won't lose all your investment. In fact, since the Investment Company Act of 1940 was passed to regulate the mutual fund industry, no fund has ever gone under. (One exception is a small money market fund run by and invested in by banks, which disbanded after losing a small portion of principal — see Chapter 7).

You may be interested to know that the specific stocks, bonds, and other securities that a mutual fund has bought are held at a *custodian,* a separate organization independent of the mutual fund company. The employment of a custodian ensures that the fund management company can't embezzle your funds or use assets from a better-performing fund to subsidize a poor performer.

Accessibility

What's really terrific about dealing with mutual funds is that they are set up for people who value their time and don't like going to a local branch office and standing in long lines. With funds, you can make your initial investment from the comfort of your living room by filling out a simple form and writing a check. Later, you can add to your investment by mailing in a check or by authorizing money transfers by phone from your other accounts, such as at a bank.

Additionally, most money market funds offer check-writing privileges. Many mutual fund companies also allow you to wire money back and forth from your local bank account; you can access your money almost as quickly through a money market fund as you can through your local bank.

Selling shares of your mutual fund is just as easy. Generally, all you need to do is call the fund company's toll-free 800 number. Some companies have representatives available around the clock, all year round.

The Keys to Successful Fund Investing

So I've explained why funds are a good investment vehicle to use. But not all funds are worthy of your investment dollars. Would you, for example, invest in a fund run by an 18-year-old who has never invested in his life? How about a fund that charges very high fees and has produced inferior returns in comparison to other similar funds? These are common sense questions, aren't they? You don't have to be an investing wizard to know the correct answers.

When you select a fund, you can use a number of simple, common-sense criteria to greatly increase your chances of investment success.

Minimize those fees

For a particular type of mutual fund (U.S. stocks, for example), dozens to sometimes hundreds of choices are available. The charges you pay to buy or sell a fund, as well as the ongoing fund operating expenses, have a big impact on the rate of return you earn on your investments.

Fund costs are an important factor in the return that you earn from a mutual fund. Why? Because fees are deducted from your investment returns and can attack a fund from many angles. All other things being equal, high fees and other charges depress your returns.

Avoid load funds

The first such fee to minimize are *sales loads,* which are commissions paid to brokers and "financial planners" who work on commission and are therefore also brokers who sell mutual funds. Commissions or loads generally range from 4 to 8.5 percent of the amount you invest.

Sales loads are an additional and unnecessary cost that is deducted from your investment money. You can find bucketfuls of outstanding no-load (commission-free) funds.

Brokers, being brokers, of course, sing the praises of buying a load fund, the pitfalls of no-loads, and even try to obscure the load altogether. Don't buy the pitch of the load fund salespeople. For example, brokers may tell you that the commission doesn't cost you because the mutual fund company pays them. Don't fall for this deception; it may be hidden somehow, but the commission always comes out of your investment dollars.

Brokers also love to say that load funds perform better than no-load funds. One reason, brokers claim, is that load funds supposedly hire better fund managers. Another lie. Absolutely no relationship exists between paying a sales charge to buy a fund and gaining access to better investment managers. Remember that the sales commission goes to the selling broker, *not* to the management of the fund. Objective studies demonstrate time and again that load funds not only don't outperform but in fact underperform no-loads. Common sense suggests why — when you factor in the higher commission and the higher average ongoing operating expenses charged on load funds, you pay more to own a load fund, so your returns are less.

Brokers also may argue that no-loads have hidden and higher fees than load funds. While it's true that some no-load funds may add miscellaneous marketing and operating fees, load funds also have to spend money to market themselves, both to brokers and to the investing public, like you and me. And the better no-load companies, such as those I recommend later in this chapter, benefit from the thousands of investors who call based on word-of-mouth or writers like me who recommend them.

Brokers also may imply that no-loads are for do-it-yourself types. People who need help buy load funds, they say. This either/or mentality permeates not only investment brokers sales spiels but also some of the financial writing in the mass media, where writers sometimes parrot what brokers say to them. If you need advice, you have other options. Brokers, not surprisingly, like you to believe that they are your only option. One other option is to hire a financial advisor and pay a one-time fee for his or her time to recommend specific no-load mutual funds.

Another problem with commission-driven load fund sellers is the power of self-interest. This issue is rarely talked about, but it is even more important than the extra costs you pay with load funds. When you buy a load fund through a salesperson, you miss out on the chance to get advice on other personal finance strategies. Maybe you're better off paying down your debts or investing in something entirely different. But, in my experience, salespeople almost never advise you to pay off your credit cards or your mortgage — or to invest through your company's retirement plan — instead of buying an investment through them.

Unfortunately, in recent years fund companies have come up with even craftier ways of hiding sales loads. Increasing numbers of brokers and financial planners are selling funds that they *call* no-loads, but these funds are *not* no-loads. In back-end or deferred sales load funds, the commission is hidden thanks to the different classes of shares, known as A, B, C, and D classes. You're told that as long as you stay in a fund for five to seven years, you need not pay the back-end sales charge that applies when you sell the investment. This claim may be true, but it's also true that these funds pay investment salespeople a hefty commission. The salespeople can receive their commissions because the fund company charges you exorbitant continuing operating expenses (which are usually 1 percent more per year than the best funds). So, one way or another, they get their commissions from your investment dollars.

Beware of high operating expenses

In addition to loads, the other costs of owning funds are the ongoing *operating expenses*. All mutual funds charge fees as long as you keep your money in the fund. The fees pay for the operational costs of running a fund, such as employees' salaries, marketing, servicing the toll-free phone lines, printing and mailing prospectuses (legal disclosure of the fund's operations and fees), and so on.

Because they're deducted before you're paid any return, a mutual fund's operating expenses are essentially invisible to you. The expenses are charged on a daily basis, so you don't need to worry about trying to get out of a fund at a particular time of the year before these fees are deducted. They're invisible, but the impact on your returns is very real.

Expenses matter on all types of funds, but they matter more on some and less on others. Expenses are critical on a money market mutual fund and very important on bond funds because these funds are buying securities that are so similar and so efficiently priced in the financial markets. With stock funds, expenses are a less important factor in picking a fund. However, don't forget that, over time, stocks have averaged returns of about 10 percent per year. So if one stock fund charges 1.5 percent more in operating expenses than another, you're giving up an extra 15 percent of your expected annual returns.

All types of funds with higher operating expenses, on average, tend to produce lower rates of return. This effect makes sense because operating expenses are deducted from the returns that a fund generates. Conversely, funds with lower operating costs can more easily produce higher returns for you than a comparable type of fund with high costs. Higher expenses mean a lower return to you.

A fund's operating expenses are quoted as a percentage of your investment. The percentage represents an annual fee or charge. You can find this number in a fund's prospectus, in the fund expenses section, usually in a line that says something like "Total Fund Operating Expenses." Or you can call the mutual fund's 800 number and ask a representative. Make sure that a fund doesn't appear to have low expenses simply because it is temporarily waiving them (you can find this out by asking the fund or looking in their prospectus at their fees).

Stick with funds that maintain low total operating expenses and that don't charge sales loads (commissions). Both types of fees come out of your pocket and reduce your rate of return. You don't need to pay a lot for the best funds. Many excellent commission-free money market, bond, and stock funds from fund companies, such as Vanguard, Fidelity, USAA, and T. Rowe Price, "cost" under 1 percent per year. Plenty of funds are also available for less than 0.5 percent per year in terms of their annual operating expense ratio.

Performance and risk

A fund's historic rate of return or performance is another important factor to weigh when selecting a mutual fund. Keep in mind, however, as all mutual fund materials must tell you, past performance is no guarantee of future results. In fact, many former high-return funds achieved their results by taking on high risk. Funds that assume higher risk should produce higher rates of return. But high-risk funds usually decline in price faster during major market declines. Thus, in order for a fund to be considered a *best* fund, it must consistently deliver a favorable rate of return given the level of risk that it takes.

The single biggest mistake investors make when choosing a mutual fund is over-emphasizing the importance of historic returns or past performance numbers. The shorter the time period, the greater the danger of using performance as an indicator of a good fund.

Although past performance *can* be a good sign, high returns for a fund, relative to its peers, are largely possible only if a fund is taking more risk. The danger of taking more risk is that it doesn't always work the way you'd like. The odds are very high that you won't be able to pick the next star before it vaults to prominence in the investing sky. You have a far greater chance of boarding that star when it's ready to plummet back to Earth.

In fact, if you had invested in the annual #1 top performing stock and bond funds over the last 15 years, 80 percent of these top performers subsequently performed worse, over the next three to ten years, than the average fund in their peer group! Two of these former #1 funds are actually the worst performing funds in their particular category.

Funds that make bogus comparisons

One clever way that mutual funds make themselves look better than other comparable funds is to compare themselves to funds that aren't, well, quite so comparable. The most common ploy is for a fund to invest in riskier types of securities and then compare their performance to funds that invest in less risky securities.

A classic example of this marketing is how the Fidelity Magellan fund has for years invested in smaller company stocks as well as international stocks. Yet, in Magellan's annual reports to its shareholders, the fund's performance has been compared to the Standard & Poor's 500 index of 500 large company U.S. stocks. This is not a fair comparison because smaller company stocks and international stocks are riskier and have outperformed the larger company U.S. stocks in the S&P 500 index over recent decades.

Magellan's not a bad fund, but it certainly is not as stellar as Fidelity's performance comparisons make it out to be. Many other funds with mediocre or worse performance records have made themselves appear near the top of their class through similar comparison games.

Always examine the types of securities that a fund invests in and make sure that the comparison funds or indexes invest in similar securities. See Chapters 5 and 7 for a discussion of the different types of indexes.

Stick with experience

Much is made of who manages a specific mutual fund. Although the individual fund manager is important, a manager is not an island unto himself. The resources and capabilities of the parent company are equally, if not more, important. Managers come and go, but fund companies don't.

Different companies have different capabilities and levels of expertise with different types of funds. Vanguard, for example, is terrific at money market, bond, and conservative stock funds, thanks to their low operating expenses. Fidelity has a lot of experience and success with investing in U.S. stocks.

A fund company has more or less experience than others, not only from the direct management of certain fund types, but also by hiring out. For example, some fund families contract with private money management firms that have significant experience. In other cases, private money management firms, such as PIMCO, Neuberger & Berman, Warburg Pincus, and Dodge & Cox, with long histories in private money management, offer mutual funds.

Buy index funds

Unlike other mutual funds, in which the portfolio manager and a team of analysts scour the market for the best securities, an index fund manager simply invests to match the performance of an index. *Index funds* are funds that are mostly managed by a computer. Managers invest an index fund's assets so as to replicate an underlying index, such as Standard & Poor's 500 index of 500 large U.S. company stocks.

Index funds deliver consistently good returns by keeping expenses low, staying invested, and not trying to jump around. Over ten years or more, index funds outperform about three-quarters of their peers! Most other so-called actively managed funds cannot overcome the handicap of high operating expenses that pulls down their funds' rates of return. Because significant ongoing research need not be conducted to identify companies to invest in, index funds can be run with far lower operating expenses.

The average U.S. stock mutual fund, for example, has an operating expense ratio of 1.4 percent per year (some funds charge expenses as high as 2 percent or more per year). That being the case, a U.S. stock index fund with an expense ratio of just 0.2 percent per year has an advantage of 1.2 percent per year over the average fund. A 1.2 percent difference may not seem like much, but in fact it is a significant difference. Because stocks tend to return about 10 percent per year, you're throwing away about 12 percent of your expected stock fund returns. (If you factor in the taxes you pay on your fund profits, these higher expenses gobble perhaps a quarter of your after-tax profits.)

With actively managed stock funds, a fund manager can make costly mistakes, such as not being invested when the market goes up, being too aggressive when the market plummets, or just being in the wrong stocks. An actively managed fund can easily underperform the overall market index that it is competing against. An index fund, by definition, can't. Index funds make great sense for investors who are terrified that fund managers may make big mistakes and greatly underperform the market.

Don't overestimate your ability to pick *in advance* the few elite money managers who manage to beat the market averages by a few percentage points per year in the long run. And then don't overestimate the pros' ability to consistently pick the right stocks. Index funds make sense for a portion of your investments, especially when investing in bonds and larger, more conservative stocks, where it's very difficult for portfolio managers to beat the market.

In addition to lower operating expenses, which help boost your returns, index mutual funds are tax-friendlier to invest in when you invest outside retirement accounts. Mutual fund managers of actively managed portfolios, in their attempts to increase their shareholders' returns, buy and sell securities more frequently. This trading increases a fund's taxable capital gains distributions.

Vanguard is the largest and best mutual fund provider of index funds because they have the lowest annual operating fees in the business. They have all types of bond and stock (both U.S. and international) index mutual funds.

Vanguard index fund

Mixing Up a Great Fund Recipe

Before you invest in funds, you should take a big-picture look at the rest of your finances. Be sure to read Chapter 3 first.

When investing money for the longer term, such as for retirement, you can choose among all the different types of funds discussed in this chapter. Most people get a big headache when they try to decide how to spread their money across those choices. The specific amount that you decide to invest in each of the different options is known as *asset allocation*. Asset allocation simply means that you decide what percentage of your investments you place — or *allocate* — into bonds versus stocks and into international versus U.S. stocks.

Many working folks have time on their side, and they need to use time to make their money grow. You may have two or more decades before you need to draw on some portion of your retirement account assets. If some of your investments drop a bit over a year or two — or even over five years — the value of your investments has plenty of time to recover before you retire.

Your current age and the number of years you must wait until you retire should be the biggest factors in your allocation decision. The younger you are and the more years you have before retirement, the more comfortable you should be with growth-oriented (and more volatile) investments, such as stock funds. (See Chapter 2 for the risks and historic returns of different investments.)

Table 8-1 lists guidelines for allocating money you've earmarked for long-term purposes, such as retirement. You don't need an M.B.A. to do this — all you need to know is how old you are and your desired level of risk.

Table 8-1	Asset Allocation for the Long Haul	
Your Investment Attitude	*Bond Allocation (%)*	*Stock Allocation (%)*
Play it safe	= Age	= 100 − age
Middle of the road	= Age − 10	= 110 − age
Aggressive	= Age − 20	= 120 − age

What's it all mean, you ask? Consider this example: If you're a conservative sort who doesn't like a lot of risk, but you recognize the value of striving for some growth to make your money work harder, you're a middle-of-the-road type. Using Table 8-1 if you're 35 years old, you may consider putting 25 percent (35–10) into bonds and 75 percent (110–35) into stocks.

Now divvy up your stock investment money between U.S. and international funds. Here's what portion of your "stock allocation" I recommend investing in overseas stocks:

- 20 percent (for play it safe)
- 35 percent (for middle-of-the-road)
- 50 percent (for aggressive)

If, for example, in Table 8-1, the 35-year-old, middle-of-the-road type is investing 75 percent in stocks, then about 35 percent of the stock fund investments (which works out to be around 25 percent of the total) can be invested in international stock funds.

So here's what the 35-year-old, middle-of-the-road investor's portfolio asset allocation looks like so far:

Bonds	25%
U.S. Stocks	50%
International Stocks	25%

Now take things a step further. Suppose that your investment allocation decisions lead you to want to invest 50 percent in U.S. stock funds. Which ones do you choose? As I explain later in this chapter, stock funds differ from one another on a number of levels. You have your growth-oriented stocks and funds and those that focus on value stocks. Small-, medium-, and large-company stocks and funds also invest in such stocks. These types of funds are explained later in the chapter. And then you have the decision about whether to invest in index funds (discussed in the previous "Buy index funds" section) versus actively managed funds that try to beat the market.

Generally, it's a good idea to diversify into different types of funds. You can diversify in one of two ways. Your first option is to purchase several individual funds, each of which focuses on a different style. For example, you can invest in a large-company value stock fund and in a small-company growth fund. I find this approach somewhat tedious. Granted, it does allow a fund manager to specialize and gain greater knowledge about a particular type of stock. But many of the best managers invest in more than one narrow range of security.

A second approach is to invest in a handful of funds (5–10), each of which covers several bases, and that together cover them all. Remember, the investment delineations are somewhat arbitrary, and most funds do more than just one type of investment. For example, a fund may focus on small-company value stocks but also invest in medium-size company stocks, as well as in some that are more growth-oriented.

As for how much you should use index versus actively managed funds, it's really a matter of personal taste. If you're happy as a clam (one that's still alive), knowing you'll get the market rate of return and that you can't underperform the market, there's no reason you can't index your entire portfolio. On the other hand, if you enjoy the challenge of trying to pick the better managers and want the potential to earn better than the market level of returns, don't use index funds at all. A happy medium is to do both. (You may be interested in knowing that John Bogle, founder of Vanguard and pioneer of index investment funds, has about 40 percent of his money invested in index funds.)

The Best Stock Mutual Funds

Earlier in this book, I made the case for why investing in stocks (also known as equities) is a good way to make your money grow. However, stock market investing carries risk as stocks sometimes plummet or otherwise can be depressed for a few years. Thus, stock mutual funds (also known as equity funds) are not a place for money you know you may need to protect in the next few years.

Unless you have a lot of money to invest, you're likely to buy only a handful of stocks. If you end up with a lemon in your portfolio, it can devastate your other good choices. If such a stock represents 20 percent of your holdings, the rest of your stock selections need to increase about 25 percent in value just to get you back to even.

Stock mutual funds reduce your risk by investing in many stocks, often 50 or more. If a fund holds 50 stocks and one goes to zero, you lose only 2 percent of the value of the fund if the stock was an average holding. If the fund holds 100 stocks, you lose 1 percent, while a 200-stock fund loses only 0.5 percent if one stock goes under. And a good fund manager is more likely to sidestep disasters than you are.

Another way that stock funds reduce risk (and thus their volatility) is that they invest in different types of stocks, such as growth stocks, or in the stock of larger, established companies. Some funds also invest in U.S. and international stocks. Different types of stocks don't always move in tandem. So if smaller-company stocks are being beaten up, larger-company stocks may be faring better. If U.S. stocks are in the tank, international ones may not be.

Stock mutual funds, as their name implies, invest in stocks. These funds are sometimes called equity funds — equity is another word for stocks. First, I talk about the different types you should know about or may hear about.

Stock funds and the stocks that they invest in usually are pigeonholed into particular categories based on the types of stocks they focus on. Categorizing stock funds often is tidier in theory than in practice, though, because some funds invest in an eclectic mix of stocks. Don't get bogged down in the names of funds — funds sometimes have misleading names and don't necessarily do what their names imply. What matters are the investment strategies of the fund and the fund's typical investments.

The first dimension on which a stock fund's stock selection differs is based on the size of the company — small, medium, and large companies — in which the fund invests. The categories with stocks are defined by the total market value (*capitalization*) of a company's outstanding stock. Small-company stocks, for example, are usually defined as stocks of companies that have total market capitalization of less than $1 billion. Medium-capitalization stocks have market values between $1 billion and $5 billion. Large-capitalization stocks are those of companies with market values greater than $5 billion. These dollar amounts are somewhat arbitrary.

Why care what size of companies a fund holds? Historically, smaller companies pay less dividends but appreciate more. They have more-volatile share prices but tend to produce slightly higher total returns. Larger companies' stocks tend to pay greater dividends and on average be less volatile and produce slightly lower total returns than small company stocks. Medium-size, as you may suspect, falls between the two. So investors looking for income as well as appreciation from their stock market investments can focus more on larger company stocks.

Stock fund managers and their funds are further categorized by those who invest in growth or value stocks. *Growth stocks* are companies that are experiencing rapidly expanding revenues and profits. These companies tend to reinvest most of their earnings in the company to fuel future expansion; thus, these stocks pay low dividends. Microsoft, for example, pays no dividends and reinvests most of its profits back into its business.

Value stocks are priced cheaply in relation to the company's assets, profits, and potential profits. It's possible that such a company is a growth company, but that's unlikely because growth companies' stock prices tend to sell at a premium compared to what the company's assets are worth.

Mutual fund companies sometimes use other terms to describe other types of stock funds. Aggressive growth funds tend to invest in the most growth-oriented companies and may undertake riskier investing practices, such as frequent trading. Growth and income funds tend to invest in stocks that pay decent dividends, thus offering the investor the potential for growth and income. Income funds tend to invest more in higher-yielding stocks. Bonds usually make up the other portion of income funds.

The components of a mutual fund's return

When you invest in stock mutual funds, you can make money in three ways. First, most stocks pay dividends. Companies hopefully make some profits during the year. Some high-growth companies reinvest most or all of their profits right back into the business. Many companies, however, pay out some of their profits to shareholders in the form of dividends (see Chapter 6). As a mutual fund investor, you can choose to receive these dividends as cash or reinvest them yourself by purchasing more shares in the mutual fund.

Unless you need the income to live on (if, for example, you've already retired), reinvest your dividends into buying more shares in the fund. If you do this outside a retirement account, keep a record of those reinvestments because those additional purchases should be factored into the tax calculations you make when you sell the shares.

The second way you make money with a stock fund is through capital gains distributions. When a fund manager sells stocks for more than he or she paid, the resulting profits, known as *capital gains,* must be netted against losses and paid out to the fund's shareholders. Just as with dividends, your capital gains distributions can be reinvested in the fund.

The final way you hope to make money with stock funds is via appreciation. The fund manager isn't going to sell all the stocks that have gone up in value. Thus, the price per share of the fund increases to reflect the gains in its stock holdings. For you, these profits are on paper until you sell the fund and lock them in. Of course, if a fund's stocks decline in value, the share price depreciates.

If you add together dividends, capital gains distributions, and appreciation, you arrive at the *total return* of a fund. Stocks, and the funds that invest in them, differ in the dimensions of these three possible returns, particularly with respect to dividends. Utility companies, for example, tend to pay out more of their profits as dividends. But don't buy utility stocks thinking you'll make more money because of the heftier dividends. Utilities and other companies paying high dividends tend not to appreciate as much over time because they aren't reinvesting as much in their businesses, and they're not growing.

Bond funds, discussed in the next section, can make you money from all three ways that a stock fund can. However, most of the time, the bulk of your return in a bond fund comes from dividends. With money market funds, also discussed later in the chapter, all your return comes from dividends.

Stocks and the companies that issue them are also divvied up based upon the location of their main operations and headquarters. Funds that specialize in U.S. stocks are not surprisingly called U.S. stock funds; those focusing overseas are typically called international or overseas funds.

Putting together two or three of these major classifications, you can start to appreciate all those silly and lengthy names mutual funds give to their stock funds. You can have funds that focus on large-company value stocks or small-company growth stocks. These categories can be further subdivided into more fund types by adding in U.S., international, and worldwide funds. So you can have international stock funds focusing on small company stocks or growth stocks.

You can diversify into different types of stocks by purchasing several stock funds, each focusing on a different type of stock. Two potential advantages result from doing so. First, not all of your money is riding in one stock fund and with one fund manager. Second, each of the different fund managers can look at and track particular stock investing possibilities.

Using the selection criteria I outline earlier in this chapter, the following sections describe the best stock funds worthy of your consideration. The funds differ from one another primarily in terms of the types of stocks they invest in. Keep in mind as you read through these funds that they also differ from each other in their tax-friendliness (see Chapter 3). If you're investing inside a retirement account, you don't need to care about tax-friendliness.

All-in-one funds

Balanced and asset allocation mutual funds, also known as hybrid funds, invest in a mixture of different types of securities. Most commonly, they invest in both bonds and stocks. These funds are usually less risky and less volatile than funds that invest exclusively in stocks; in an economic downturn, bonds usually hold up better in value than stocks do.

Hybrid funds make it easier for investors who are skittish about investing in stocks to hold stocks while they avoid the high volatility that normally comes with pure stock funds. Because of their extensive diversification, hybrid funds are excellent choices for an investor who doesn't have much money to start with.

Balanced funds generally try to maintain a fairly constant percentage of investment in stocks and bonds. Asset allocation funds, in contrast, normally adjust the mix of different investments according to the portfolio manager's expectations. Some asset allocation funds, however, tend to keep more of a fixed mix of stocks and bonds whereas some balanced funds shift the mix around quite frequently.

Although the concept of a manager trying to be in the right place at the right time and beating the market averages sounds good in theory, in reality most of these funds fail to best a buy and hold approach.

Because hybrid funds pay decent dividends from the bonds that they hold, they are not appropriate for some investors who are purchasing funds outside tax-sheltered retirement accounts. If you're in a higher tax bracket (that is, a federal tax bracket of 31 percent and higher), bonds that you purchase outside a retirement account should be tax-free. With the exception of the Vanguard Tax-Managed Balanced fund, which holds federally tax-free bonds, you should avoid the hybrid funds if you're in this situation. You can create your own hybrid portfolio by buying separate tax-friendly stock funds and tax-free bond funds (both discussed later in the chapter).

Here's my recommended short list of great balanced-type mutual funds (a list of phone numbers for the mutual funds recommended in this chapter is at the end of the chapter):

> Dodge & Cox Balanced
>
> Fidelity Asset Manager
>
> Fidelity Puritan
>
> Lindner Dividend
>
> T. Rowe Price Balanced
>
> Vanguard LifeStrategy funds
>
> Vanguard Star
>
> Vanguard Wellesley Income
>
> Vanguard Wellington

U.S. stock funds

Of all the different types of funds offered, U.S. stock funds are the largest category. To see the forest amidst the trees, remember the classifications I covered earlier in this section. Stock funds differ mainly in terms of the size of the companies that they invest in and in whether the funds focus on growth or value companies. Some funds do all these things, and some of these funds may invest a bit overseas.

The only way to know for sure where a fund is currently invested (or where the fund may invest in the future) is to ask. You can start by calling the 800 number of the mutual fund company that you're interested in. You also can read the fund's annual report. Don't waste your time looking for this information in the fund's prospectus, which doesn't give you anything beyond general parameters that guide the range of investments; it doesn't tell you what the fund is currently investing in or has invested in.

For mutual funds held outside retirement accounts, you gotta pay current income tax on dividends and capital gains that are distributed. (This is another reason that most investors, during their working years, are best off sheltering more money into retirement accounts.) If your circumstances allow you to have money to invest in stock funds outside retirement accounts, then by all means do it. But pay close attention to the dividend and capital gains distributions that funds make. I've indicated in the upcoming list which funds are tax-friendly.

Again, here's my short list of the best U.S. stock funds:

Brandywine

Columbia Growth and Columbia Special

Dodge & Cox Stock

Fidelity

Fidelity Contrafund (only buy for retirement accounts)

Fidelity Disciplined Equity

Fidelity Equity-Income (only buy for retirement accounts)

Fidelity Equity-Income II

Fidelity Low Priced Stock (only buy for retirement accounts)

Fidelity Stock Selector

Neuberger & Berman: Guardian, Partners, and Focus

T. Rowe Price Spectrum Growth

Vanguard Index Total Stock Market

Vanguard's Tax-Managed Capital Appreciation (tax-friendly)

Warburg Pincus Emerging Growth

No-loads with a load

Some mutual fund companies try to play it both ways. They sell load as well as no-load funds. Fidelity and Dreyfus, for example, sell both types of funds. Fidelity goes a step further. On many of their better stock funds, they charge a sales charge for non-retirement account investments. The logic behind this approach, from Fidelity's perspective, is that they expect retirement account investors to stay in a fund longer, thus providing a steady stream of fund management fees and profits.

If you're investing outside a tax-sheltered retirement account, I wouldn't purchase Fidelity's funds with sales charges. They're simply not worth it because you have plenty of other alternatives available. Also beware that Fidelity funds do lots of trading, so they tend to produce high rates of capital gains distributions — increasing the tax burden for non-retirement account investors.

International stock funds

For diversification and growth potential, funds that invest overseas should be part of an investor's portfolio that is invested in stocks. Normally, you can tell you're looking at a fund that focuses its investments overseas if its name contains words such as international, global, or worldwide.

As a general rule, you should avoid foreign funds that invest in just one country, regardless of whether that country is Australia or Zimbabwe, or anywhere in between. As with investing in a sector fund that specializes in a particular industry, this lack of diversification defeats the whole purpose of investing in funds. Funds that focus on specific regions, such as Southeast Asia, are better but still problematic because of poor diversification and higher expenses than other, more-diversified international funds.

If you want to invest in more geographically limiting international funds, take a look at T. Rowe Price's and Vanguard's offerings, which invest in broader regions, such as those investing just in Europe, Asia, and the volatile but higher-growth-potential emerging markets in Southeast Asia and Latin America.

In addition to the risks normally inherent in stock fund investing, international securities and funds are also subject to buffeting by changes in the value of foreign currencies relative to the U.S. dollar. If the dollar declines in value, that helps the value of foreign stock funds. Some foreign stock funds hedge against currency changes. Although this hedging helps reduce volatility a bit, it does cost money. I wouldn't worry about these things. Remember, you're investing in stock funds for the long haul. And in the long haul, your international stock funds' performances are largely driven by the returns generated on foreign stock exchanges, not currency price changes.

Here are my picks for diversified international funds that may meet your needs:

T. Rowe Price International Stock

Tweedy Browne Global Value

USAA Investment International (tax-friendly)

Vanguard International Growth (tax-friendly)

Warburg Pincus International Equity (tax-friendly)

Sector funds

Sector funds invest in securities in specific industries. In most cases, you should avoid sector funds. Investing in stocks of a single industry defeats a major purpose of investing in mutual funds — you give up the benefits of diversification. Also, just because the fund may from time to time be dedicated to a "hot" sector (different examples of these sector funds are often at the top of short-term performance charts), you can't assume that the fund will pick the right securities within that sector.

Another good reason to avoid sector funds is that they tend to carry much higher fees than other mutual funds. Many sector funds also tend to have high rates of trading or turnover of their investment holdings. Investors using these funds outside of retirement accounts will have to face the IRS for the likely greater capital gains distributions this trading produces.

The only types of specialty funds that may make sense for a small portion (10 percent or less) of your investment portfolio are funds that invest in real estate or precious metals. These funds can help diversify your portfolio because they can do better during times of higher inflation — which often depresses bond and stock prices. You can comfortably skip these funds because diversified stock funds tend to hold some of the same stocks as these specialty funds.

Real estate investment trusts (REITs) are stocks of companies that invest in real estate. REITs typically invest in properties such as apartment buildings, shopping centers, and other rental properties. REITs allow you to invest in real estate without the hassle of being a landlord. Just as it's a hassle to evaluate REIT stocks, you can always invest in a mutual fund of REITs.

REITs usually pay decent dividends. As such, they are not appropriate for people in a higher tax bracket investing money outside retirement accounts. Some good no-load REIT funds include Fidelity Real Estate and Cohen & Steers Realty Shares. (This latter fund can be purchased with a lower minimum initial investment through discount brokers.)

Another type of sector fund to consider is precious metals funds. Over the millennia, gold and silver have served as mediums of exchange or currency because they have intrinsic value and cannot be debased. These precious metals are used in jewelry and manufacturing.

As investments, gold and silver do well during bouts of inflation. For example, from 1972 to 1980, when inflation zoomed up in the U.S. and stocks and bonds went into the tank, gold and silver company stocks skyrocketed more than 500 percent. People were concerned that the U.S. government was going on a money-printing binge.

Generally over the long term, precious metals are lousy investments. They don't pay any dividends, and their price increases just keep you up with, but not ahead of, increases in the cost of living. Although investing in precious metals is better than keeping cash in a piggy bank or stuffed in a mattress, it's not as good as bonds, stocks, and real estate.

If you expect high inflation, or if you just want an inflation hedge in case you expect the end of civilization as we know it, stick with a gold fund. But these funds swing wildly in value and are not for the faint of heart or for the majority of your portfolio. Among the better precious metals funds are the Vanguard Gold Fund and the American Century Global Gold fund. Don't buy the bullion itself; storage costs and the concerns over whether you're dealing with a reputable company make buying bullion a pain. Also avoid futures and options, which are gambles on short-term price movements.

The Best Bond Funds

In the previous chapter, I discuss what bonds are and how different bonds vary from one another. Make sure to read that material before venturing into bonds.

When selecting bond funds to invest in, bond fund investors often are led astray as to how much they can expect to make in a bond fund. The first mistake is to look at recent performance and assume that that's what you're going to get in the future. Investing in bond funds based only on recent performance is tempting right after a period where interest rates have declined, because declines in interest rates pump up bond prices and, therefore, bond fund total returns. Remember that an equal but opposite force is waiting to counteract pumped-up bond returns — bond prices fall when interest rates rise.

Don't get me wrong: Past performance is an important issue to consider. In order for performance numbers to be meaningful and useful, you must compare bond funds that are comparable to each other (such as intermediate-term funds that invest exclusively in high-grade corporate bonds).

Because the market for bonds is pretty efficient, it's difficult for a bond fund manager to beat the market averages significantly over time. Much better numbers to look at when selecting a bond fund are the fund's *yield* — how much the fund currently pays in dividends — and the fund's annual operating expense ratio.

Bond mutual funds calculate their yield after subtracting their operating expenses. When you call a mutual fund company to ask for a fund's current yield, make sure that you understand what time period the yield covers. Fund companies are supposed to report to you the *SEC yield,* which is a standard yield calculation that allows for fairer comparisons among bond funds. The SEC yield reflects the bond fund's so-called yield to maturity. The SEC yield is the best yield to utilize when comparing funds because it captures the effective rate of interest an investor will receive looking forward.

Unfortunately, if you select bond funds based on yield, you're almost guaranteed to purchase the wrong bond funds. Bond funds and the mutual fund companies that sell them can play more than a few games of creative accounting to fatten a fund's yield. Such sleight of hand makes a fund's marketing and advertising departments happy because higher yields make it easier for salespeople and funds to hawk their bond funds. But remember that yield-enhancing shenanigans can leave you poorer. Here's what to watch out for:

✔ **Lower quality.** You may compare one short-term bond fund to another and discover that one pays 0.5 percent more and therefore looks better. However, it turns out that the higher-yielding fund invests 20 percent of its money in junk bonds, whereas the other fund is fully invested in high-quality bonds.

✔ **Longer maturities.** Bond funds usually can increase their yield just by increasing maturity a bit. If one long-term bond fund invests in bonds maturing on average in 12 years, while another fund is at 10 years for its average maturity, comparing the two is a classic case of comparing apples to oranges.

✔ **Giving your money back without your knowing it.** Some funds return a portion of your principal in the form of dividends. This move artificially pumps up a fund's yield but depresses its total return. When comparing bond funds to each other, make sure that you compare their total return over time (in addition to making sure that the funds have comparable portfolios of bonds).

✔ **Waiving of expenses.** Some bond funds, particularly newer ones, waive a portion or even all their operating expenses to temporarily inflate the fund's yield. Yes, you can invest in a fund that is having a sale on its operating fees, but you'd also buy yourself the bother of having to monitor things to determine when the sale is over. Bond funds engaging in this practice often end sales quietly when the bond market is doing well. Don't forget that if you go to sell a bond fund (held outside of a retirement account) that has appreciated in value, you owe taxes on your profits.

You can earn a higher yield from a bond fund in one of three major ways — by investing in funds that hold longer-term bonds, by investing in funds that hold lower-quality bonds, or by investing in funds that have lower operating expenses. After you've settled on the type of bonds you want, a bond fund's costs — its sales commissions and annual operating fees — are a huge consideration. Stick with no-load funds that have lower annual operating expenses.

Although hundreds of bond funds — an overwhelming number of choices — exist, not that many remain after you eliminate high-cost funds (those with loads and high ongoing fees), low-performance funds (which are often the high-cost funds), and funds managed by fund companies and fund managers with minimal experience investing in bonds.

Although it's not difficult to tell a good bond fund from a bad one, remember that it's important to be in the right category. Bond fund objectives and names usually fit one of three maturity categories — short, intermediate, and long term.

Also pay attention to the taxability of the dividends that they pay. If you're investing in bonds inside retirement accounts, then you want taxable bonds. If you're investing in bonds outside retirement accounts, the choice between taxable versus tax-free depends on your tax bracket (see Chapter 3).

The riskier the bonds a fund holds, the higher the yield of that fund should be. Generally speaking, bonds are riskier the longer their maturity and the lower the credit rating of their issuer. A higher yield is the bond market's way of compensating you for taking greater risk.

You should use the following funds only if you have reserved sufficient money in an emergency reserve. If you're investing money for longer-term purposes, particularly retirement, you should come up with an overall plan for allocating your money among a variety of different funds, including bond funds (see "Mixing Up a Great Fund Recipe," earlier in this chapter).

Be careful with actively managed bond funds

Some bond funds are aggressively managed funds. Managers of these funds have a fair degree of latitude to purchase and trade bonds that they think will perform best in the future. For example, if a fund manager thinks that interest rates will rise, he usually buys shorter-term bonds and keeps more of a fund's assets in cash. The fund manager may be willing to invest more in lower-credit-quality bonds if he thinks that the economy is going to improve and that more companies will prosper and improve their credit standing.

Aggressively managed funds gamble. If interest rates fall instead of rise, the fund manager who moved into shorter-term bonds and cash suffers worse performance. If interest rates fall because the economy sinks into recession, the lower-credit-quality bonds likely will suffer from a higher default rate and depress the fund's performance even further.

Some people think that it's not difficult for the "experts" to predict which way interest rates or the economy is heading. The truth is that economic predictions are difficult, and the experts are often wrong. Few bond fund managers have beaten a buy and hold approach. William Gross,

who manages the PIMCO bond funds, is one fund manager who has pretty consistently beaten the market averages by a bit.

But, remember that trying to beat the market can lead to getting beaten! Increasing numbers of examples have occurred in recent years of bond funds falling on their face after risky investing strategies have backfired. Interestingly, bond funds that charge sales commissions (loads) and higher ongoing operating fees are the ones more likely to have blowups. This result may be because these fund managers are under more pressure to try to pump up returns to make up for these higher fees.

It's fine to invest some of your bond fund money in funds that try to be best positioned for changes in the economy and interest rates. But remember that if these fund managers are wrong, you can lose more. Over the long term, you'll do best in efficiently managed funds that stick with an investment objective and that don't try to time and predict the bond market. Index funds that invest in a relatively fixed basket of bonds so as to track a market index of bond prices are a good example of this passive approach.

Short-term bond funds

Of all bond funds, short-term bond funds are the least sensitive to interest rate fluctuations. Their stability makes them the most appropriate bond funds for money that you want to earn a better rate of return on than a money market fund could produce for you. But, with short-term bond funds, you also have to tolerate the risk of losing a percent or two in principal value if rates rise.

Short-term bonds work well for money that you've earmarked for use in a few years, such as the purchase of a home or a car, or that you plan to withdraw from your retirement account in the near future.

Bond funds that pay taxable dividends are appropriate when you're not in a high tax bracket (less than or equal to 28 percent federal) and for investing inside retirement accounts. Good funds to consider include

Vanguard Short-Term Corporate Portfolio

PIMCO Low Duration (purchase through discount broker Jack White)

U.S. Treasury bond funds are appropriate if you prefer a bond fund that invests in U.S. Treasuries (which have the safety of government backing) or if you're not in a high federal tax bracket (less than or equal to 28 percent), but you *are* in a high state tax bracket (5 percent or higher). I don't recommend Treasuries for retirement accounts; they pay less interest than fully taxable bond funds.

Vanguard Short-Term Treasury

Vanguard Admiral Short-Term U.S. Treasury (higher yields if you have $50,000 to invest)

State and federally tax-free short-term bond funds are scarce. If you want shorter-term bonds, invest in these *federally* tax-free bond funds (the dividends on them are state taxable) if you're in a high federal bracket (31 percent and up) but in a low state bracket (less than 5 percent). If you live in a state with high taxes, also consider checking out the state and federally tax-free intermediate-term bond funds if you can withstand their volatility — see the next section. Another option is to use a state money market fund, covered later in this chapter in "The Best Money Market Funds."

Vanguard Municipal Short-Term Portfolio

Vanguard Municipal Limited-Term

Intermediate-term bond funds

Intermediate-term bond funds hold bonds that typically mature in a decade or so. They are more volatile than shorter-term bonds but can be more rewarding.

The longer you can own an intermediate-term bond fund, the more likely you are to earn a higher return on it than on a short-term fund, unless interest rates keep rising over many years.

As an absolute minimum, you should not purchase an intermediate-term fund unless you expect to hold it for three to five years — or even longer, if you can. Therefore, the money you put into such a fund should be money that you don't expect to use during that period.

Taxable intermediate-term bond funds to consider include

American Century-Benham GNMA

Dodge & Cox Income

PIMCO Total Return & Total Return III

USAA Federal Securities GNMA

Vanguard GNMA

Vanguard Index Total Bond Market

U.S. Treasury bond funds are appropriate if you prefer a bond fund that invests in U.S. Treasuries (which have the safety of government backing) or if you're not in a high federal tax bracket (less than or equal to 28 percent), but you *are* in a high state tax bracket (5 percent or higher). I don't recommend Treasuries for retirement accounts; they pay less interest than fully taxable bond funds.

Vanguard Intermediate-Term Treasury

Vanguard Admiral Intermediate-Term U.S. Treasury (higher yields if you have $50,000 to invest)

You should consider *federally* tax-free bond funds if you're in a high federal bracket (31 percent and up) but a relatively low state bracket (less than 5 percent). If you're in a high federal and state tax bracket, see the state and federally tax-free bonds later in this section.

Vanguard Municipal Intermediate-Term

State and federally tax-free bond funds may be appropriate when you're in high federal (31 percent and up) *and* state (5 percent or higher) tax brackets. (If one is not listed for your state or if you're only in a high federal tax bracket, remember to use the nationwide Vanguard municipal bond fund that I just listed in the last section.)

Some good state and federally tax-free intermediate-term bond funds are as follows:

Benham CA Tax-Free Intermediate-Term

Fidelity Spartan CA Intermediate Muni

Schwab CA Short-Intermediate Tax-Free

Vanguard CA Tax-Free Insured Intermediate Term

Fidelity Spartan NY Intermediate

Long-term bond funds

Long-term bond funds are the most aggressive and volatile bond funds around. If interest rates on long-term bonds increase substantially, you can easily see the principal value of your investment decline 10 percent or more. (See the discussion in Chapter 7 of how interest rate changes impact bond prices.)

Long-term bond funds generally are used for retirement investing in one of two situations: (1) where investors don't expect to tap their investment money for a decade or more, or (2) where investors want to maximize current dividend income and are willing to tolerate volatility. Definitely don't use these funds for investing money you plan to use within the next five years because a bond market drop can leave your portfolio with a bit of a hangover.

Taxable long-term bond funds to consider include

Vanguard Long-Term Corporate

Vanguard High Yield Corporate

U.S. Treasury bond funds are appropriate if you prefer a bond fund that invests in U.S. Treasuries (which have the safety of government backing) or if you're not in a high federal tax bracket (less than or equal to 28 percent), but you *are* in a high state tax bracket (5 percent or higher). I don't recommend Treasuries for retirement accounts; they pay less interest than fully taxable bond funds.

Vanguard Long-Term Treasury

Vanguard Admiral Long-Term U.S. Treasury (higher yields if you have $50,000 to invest)

Municipal (federally tax-free) long-term bond funds to consider include

Vanguard Municipal Long-Term

Vanguard Municipal Insured Long-Term

State and federally tax-free bond funds may be appropriate when you're in high federal (31 percent and up) *and* high state (5 percent or higher) tax brackets. (If a fund is not listed for your state or if you're only in a high federal tax bracket, remember to use the nationwide Vanguard Municipal bond funds.)

State and federally tax-free long-term bond funds to consider include

American Century-Benham CA Tax-Free Long-Term

Fidelity Spartan CA Muni Income

Vanguard CA Tax-Free Insured Long-Term

Fidelity Spartan CT Muni Income

Fidelity MA Muni Income

Fidelity MI Muni Income

Fidelity MN Muni Income

Vanguard NJ Tax-Free Insured Long-Term

Vanguard NY Insured Tax-Free

USAA NY Bond

Vanguard OH Tax-Free Insured Long-Term

Vanguard PA Tax-Free Insured Long-Term

USAA VA Bond

The Best Money Market Funds

As I explain in Chapter 7, money market funds are a safe, higher yielding alternative to bank accounts. (If you're in a higher tax bracket, you're especially in luck because money market funds come in tax-free versions.) Under Securities and Exchange Commission regulations, money market funds can invest only in the most creditworthy securities, and their investments must have an average maturity of less than 120 days. The short-term nature of these securities effectively eliminates the risk of money market funds being sensitive to changes in interest rates.

The securities that money market funds use are extremely safe. General-purpose money market funds invest in government-backed securities, bank certificates of deposits, and short-term corporate debt issued by the largest and most creditworthy companies and the U.S. government (although the latter may not be much comfort to you).

Of all the major types of mutual funds, a money market fund is usually the easiest type for investors to choose. In addition to high yields, good money market funds offer other useful services, such as free check writing, telephone exchange and redemptions, and automated, electronic exchange services with your bank account.

The main motivation for investing in a money market fund instead of a bank savings account is to earn a greater rate of return, or yield. Within a given category of money market funds (general, Treasury, municipal), money market fund managers are investing in the same basic securities. The market for these securities is pretty darn efficient, so "superstar" money market fund managers may eke out an extra 0.1 percent per year in yield but not much more.

Select a money market fund that does a good job with controlling its expenses. The operating expenses deducted before payment of dividends are the single biggest determinant of yield. All other things being equal (which they usually are with different money market funds), lower operating expenses translate into higher yields for you.

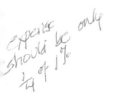

You have no need or reason to tolerate annual operating expenses of greater than 0.5 percent. Top quality funds charge a quarter of one percent or less annually. Remember, lower expenses don't mean that a fund company is cutting corners or providing poor service. Lower expenses are possible in most cases because a fund company has been successful in attracting money to invest.

Expenses are important, but so, too, are the consequences of taxes. What you actually get to keep on your investment returns (on non-retirement account investments) is what is left over after the federal and state governments take their cut of your investment income. If you're investing money held outside of a retirement account and you're in a high tax bracket (particularly the federal 31 percent or higher bracket), you should come out ahead by investing in *tax-free* money market funds. If you're in a high-tax state, a *state* money market fund, if good ones exist for your state, may be a sound move.

Tax-free refers to the taxability of the dividends paid by the fund. You don't get a tax deduction for money you put into the fund as you do with 401(k) or other retirement-type accounts.

Another factor that may be important to you is other investing you plan to do at the fund company where you establish a money market fund. For example, if you decide to do other mutual fund investing in stocks and bonds at T. Rowe Price, then keeping a money market fund at a different firm that offers a slightly higher yield may not be worth the time and administrative hassle, especially if you don't plan on keeping much cash in the money market fund.

Most mutual fund companies don't have many local branch offices. Generally, this fact helps fund companies keep their expenses low and pay you greater yields on their money market funds. As discussed previously, you may open and maintain your mutual fund account via the fund's toll-free 800 phone line and the mail. You don't really get much benefit, except psychological, if you select a fund company with an office in your area. But I don't want to diminish the importance of your emotional comfort level. (Fund providers Fidelity and Schwab have the largest branch networks.)

Using the criteria I just discussed, this section recommends the best money market funds: those that offer competitive yields, check writing, access to other excellent mutual funds, and other commonly needed money market services. Vanguard funds predominate the list because they offer rock-bottom expenses as well as most of the other goodies.

Money market funds that pay taxable dividends are appropriate for retirement account funds awaiting investment as well as non-retirement account money when you're not in a high federal tax bracket (less than or equal to 28 percent federal) *and* are not in a high state tax bracket (less than 5 percent). Here are the best taxable money market funds to consider:

Vanguard's Money Market Reserves Prime Portfolio

Fidelity Cash Reserves and Fidelity Daily Income Trust

Fidelity's Spartan Money Market (higher yields if you have $20,000 to invest)

Schwab Money Market

Schwab Value Advantage Money Market (higher yields if you have $25,000 to invest)

USAA Mutual Money Market

T. Rowe Price Summit Cash Reserves

U.S. Treasury money market funds are appropriate if you prefer a money market fund that invests in U.S. Treasuries, which have the safety of government backing, or if you're not in a high federal tax bracket (less than or equal to 28 percent) but *are* in a high state tax bracket (5 percent or higher).

Vanguard Money Market Reserves U.S. Treasury Portfolio

Vanguard's Admiral U.S. Treasury Money Market Portfolio (higher yields if you have $50,000 to invest)

Benham Capital Preservation & Government Agency funds

USAA's Treasury Money Market.

Fidelity's Spartan U.S. Treasury Money Market ($20,000 minimum)

Municipal (a.k.a. muni) money market funds invest in short-term debt issued by state and local governments. A municipal money market fund, which pays you federally tax-free dividends, invests in munis issued by state and local governments throughout the country. A state-specific municipal fund invests in state and local government-issued munis for one state, such as New York. So if you live in New York and buy a New York municipal fund, the dividends on that fund are federal and New York state tax-free.

So how do you decide whether to buy a nationwide or state-specific municipal money market fund? Federally-tax-free-only money market funds are appropriate when you're in a high federal (31 percent and up) but *not* a high state bracket (less than 5 percent).

If you're in a higher state tax bracket, your state may not have good (or any) state tax-free money market funds available. If you live in any of those states, you're likely best off with one of the following national money market funds:

Vanguard Municipal Money Market

Fidelity Spartan Municipal Money Market ($20,000 minimum)

USAA Tax-Exempt Money Market

The state tax-free money market funds in the following list are appropriate when you're in a high federal (31 percent and up) *and* a high state tax bracket (5 percent or higher). If none is listed for your state or you're only in a high federal tax bracket, remember that you need to use one of the nationwide muni money markets just described.

State and federally tax-free money market funds to examine include

Vanguard CA Tax-Free Money Market

American Century-Benham FL Municipal Money Market

Fidelity Spartan CA Muni Money Market

Fidelity Spartan FL Muni Money Market

USAA Tax-Exempt FL Money Market

American Century-Benham CA Tax-Free Money Market

Fidelity Spartan MA Muni Money Market

Vanguard NJ Tax-Free Money Market

Fidelity Spartan NY Muni Money Market

USAA Tax-Exempt NY Money Market

Vanguard OH Tax-Free Money Market

Vanguard PA Tax-Free Money Market

Fidelity Spartan PA Muni Money Market

USAA Tax-Exempt VA Money Market

How to Contact Fund Providers

The following list provides the phone numbers you can use to contact mutual fund companies and discount brokers that sell the mutual funds discussed in this chapter. To learn more about selecting and investing in mutual funds, pick up a copy of my book, *Mutual Funds For Dummies.*

American Century-Benham Funds: 800-345-2021

Brandywine Fund: 800-656-3017

Cohen & Steers Realty Shares, Inc.: 800-437-9912

Columbia Funds: 800-547-1707

Dodge & Cox Funds: 800-621-3979

Fidelity Funds: 800-544-8888

Fidelity Discount Brokerage: 800-544-8666

Lindner Funds: 314-727-5305

Neuberger & Berman Funds: 800-877-9700

PIMCO Funds: 800-927-4648

Schwab Funds: 800-435-4000

T. Rowe Price Funds: 800-638-5660

Tweedy Browne Funds: 800-432-4789

USAA Funds: 800-382-8722

The Vanguard Group: 800-662-7447

Warburg Pincus Funds: 800-927-2874

Jack White & Company: 800-323-3263

Part III
Real Estate

The 5th Wave   By Rich Tennant

"OF COURSE I COULD NEVER AFFORD A SHOE THIS SIZE IF I WEREN'T COLLECTING RENT FROM A TENNIS SHOE ACROSS TOWN AND TWO ESPADRILLES IN FLORIDA."

In this part . . .

Owning a home and investing in real estate are time-proven methods to building wealth. However, if you're not careful, you can easily fall prey to a number of pitfalls. In this part, you discover the right and wrong ways to purchase real estate and how to build your real estate empire. Even if you don't desire to be the next Leona Helmsley or Donald Trump, you'll also see how simply owning your own home can help you build your net worth over the years ahead.

Chapter 9

Buying Your Own Abode

In This Chapter

▶ Buying versus renting: Which is best for you?

▶ Figuring what amount to spend on a home

▶ Deciding when and what to buy

I hesitate somewhat to call a home in which you're living an investment. Homes suck up money the same way most politicians do. And most people don't plan on selling their homes to pay for their upcoming vacation or to finance their retirement.

Calling a home an investment is potentially problematic for another reason. Homes have decreased in value in many parts of the United States during the last five to ten years.

But all investments go through up and down periods. Over the very long-term, you see a lot more up than down in home values, so those who stay with it profit. Over the decades, the rate of return on investing in a home has been comparable to that achieved with stock market investments (see Chapter 2).

For most people, buying a home in which to live is their first, best, and only real estate investment. Homes may require a lot of financial feeding, but over the course of your life, owning a home versus renting should make and save you money. And while the pile of mortgage debt seems daunting in the years just after your purchase, someday when you're likely a little heavier, your hair's a little thinner and grayer, and your energy level a bit lower, your home may very well be your largest or second-largest asset.

Even though your home consumes a lot of dough while you own it, it can help you accomplish important financial goals, such as

✔ **Retiring.** By the time you hit your 50s and 60s, the size of your monthly mortgage payment should start to look small or nonexistent. Although other costs to owning a home exist — property taxes, maintenance, and insurance — the mortgage is the big one. Low housing costs can help you afford to retire or cut back from a full-time work week.

Increasingly, people are choosing to sell their homes and buy less-costly ones or even rent and use some or even all the cash to live on in retirement. Or some home owners are enhancing their retirement income by taking out a reverse mortgage to tap the *equity* (market value of home less outstanding mortgage debt) they have built up in their properties.

✔ **Telling your boss to shove it.** Actually, don't do that — it's not polite, and you never know when you may need her help. But have you dreamed of running your own business? It can be a source of great joy. Financial barriers prevent many people from pulling the plug on a regular job and taking the entrepreneurial plunge. You may be able to borrow against the equity you've built up in your home if you need cash to start up your business. Depending upon what type of business you have in mind, you may be able to have your office in your home.

✔ **Financing a few years at Super Overpriced State University.** When your kids are old enough to vote and head off to war, they also are ready for an expensive, four-year undertaking: college. Borrowing against the equity in your home is a viable way to help pay for educational costs for the kids.

Perhaps you won't make use of your home's equity for retirement, a small business, educational expenses, or another important financial goal. But even if you decide to pass your home on to your children, charity, or a long lost relative, it's still a valuable asset.

Besides providing solid rates of return, real estate is quite different from most other investments. In the following sections, I talk about what makes real estate an investment worthy of your dollars.

The Buying Decision

Most normal people approach property ownership with trepidation. As well they should. It's likely to be the largest financial transaction of your life — when was the last time you purchased something costing $100,000, $200,000, or more? And buying a home ranks high on the stress-o-meter. My anecdotal evidence suggests it's the most stressful personal financial deal you'll make.

Who wants stress? Why not keep renting and be happy? Actually, some people may be better off doing just that. More than a few couples have landed in divorce court thanks to squabbles over home ownership. Remodeling debates and arguments can drain your savings and your psyche.

I'm not trying to scare you off from buying a home — I believe that most people should buy and own a home. But home ownership is not for everybody and certainly not at every point in your life.

The decision about if and when to buy a home may be complex. Money matters, but so do personal and emotional issues. Buying a home is a big deal — you're settling down. Can you really see yourself coming home to this same place day after day, year after year? Of course you can always move, but now you've got a financial obligation to deal with.

Financially speaking, I advise waiting to buy a home until you can see yourself staying put for a minimum of three years. Ideally, I'd like you to think you have a solid chance of staying with the home for five or more years. Why? Buying and selling a home costs big bucks:

- **Inspection fees.** You shouldn't buy a property without checking it out, so you'll be paying some inspection expenses. Good inspectors can help you identify all sorts of problems with the plumbing, heating, and electrical systems, as well as the foundation, roof, termites, and so on.

- **Loan costs.** The costs of getting a mortgage include such items as the *points* (up-front interest that can run 1 to 2 percent of the loan amount), application and credit report fees, and appraisal fees.

- **Title insurance.** As I discuss in Chapter 11, when you buy a home, you and your bank need to be protected against the chance — albeit small — that the property seller doesn't actually legally own the home you're buying. That's where title insurance comes in — it protects you financially from unscrupulous sellers.

- **Moving costs.** You can lug all that furniture, clothing, and other personal belongings, but your time is worth something and your moving skills likely limited. Besides, do you want to end up in a hospital emergency room after being pinned by a runaway couch against the wall at the bottom of a stairwell?

- **Real estate agents' commissions.** These folks don't work for free — not even close. A commission of 5 to 7 percent of the purchase price of most homes gets siphoned off into the pockets of real estate salespeople and the companies they work for. This fee costs both buyers and sellers.

To cover all these costs plus the additional costs of home ownership, such as maintenance (for example, fixing leaky pipes and painting), the value of your home needs to appreciate about 15 percent over the years that you own it just for you to be as well off financially as if you had continued renting. Fifteen percent! If you may need or want to move elsewhere in a couple of years, it's risky to count on that kind of appreciation. If you happen to buy just before a sharp upturn in housing prices, you may get this much appreciation. But you can't count on this — you will probably lose money on such a short-term deal.

Some people are willing to invest in real estate even when they don't expect to live in it for long and would consider turning their home into a rental if they move within a few years. Doing so can work well financially in the long haul, but don't underestimate the responsibilities that come with rental property. (I talk about rental property in Chapter 10).

The pros and cons of renting

To hear some people — particularly enthusiastic salespeople in the real estate business — everybody should own a home. You may hear them say things like

"Renting is like throwing your money away."

"Buy a home for the tax breaks — you get no tax breaks as a renter."

As I discuss in the upcoming section, "Tax savings (yeah!)," it's true that the bulk of the costs of home ownership — namely mortgage interest and property taxes — are tax-deductible. But, and this is a very important but, these tax breaks are already largely factored into the higher cost of owning a home. You shouldn't buy a home just because of the tax breaks.

Renting is not throwing your money away, and you are not a failure if you do rent. Renting has its emotional and psychological rewards. First is the not-so-inconsequential fact that you have more flexibility to pack up and move on. You may have a lease to fulfill, but even those can be renegotiated if you want or need to move on. As a home owner, you've got a large monthly nut to take care of — to some people, this responsibility feels like a financial ball and chain. And you have no guarantee that you'll be able to sell your home in a timely fashion or at the price you desire.

Especially in some high-cost housing areas, you can get more for your money by renting. Another benefit of renting is that it may allow you to keep your housing expenses lower than if you did buy. Happy and successful renters I've seen include people who pay low rent, perhaps because they've made housing sacrifices. If you live in a shared rental home, you likely get more living space for your money than if you lived alone in a small property you purchased. If you're able to sock away 10 percent or more of your earnings, you're probably well on your way to accomplishing your future financial goals.

Another benefit of renting is that, as a renter, the money you are saving and investing hopefully is invested in financial assets, such as stocks, bonds, and mutual funds, which are likely quite accessible. Most home owners, by contrast, have a substantial portion of their wealth tied up in their homes. (Accessibility is a double-edged sword, as it may tempt you as a cash-rich renter to blow the money in the short term.)

Although renting has its benefits, renting has at least one big drawback: exposure to inflation. As the cost of living increases, your landlord can (unless you live in a rent-controlled unit) keep jacking up your rent. As a home owner, the big monthly expense of the mortgage payment does not increase, assuming that you buy your home with a fixed-rate mortgage. Your property taxes, home owner's insurance, and maintenance expenses are exposed to inflation. But these expenses are usually much smaller in comparison to your monthly mortgage payment or rent.

Here's a quick example to show you how inflation can work against you as a long-term renter. Suppose you are comparing the costs of owning a home that costs $160,000 to renting a similar property for $800 a month. Buying at $160,000 sounds a lot more expensive than renting, doesn't it? But this isn't a fair apples-to-apples comparison. You must compare the monthly cost of owning to the monthly cost of renting. You must also factor in the tax benefits of home ownership (mortgage interest and property taxes are tax-deductible), to the comparison so that you're comparing the after-tax monthly cost of owning versus renting. Figure 9-1 does just that for a 30-year example.

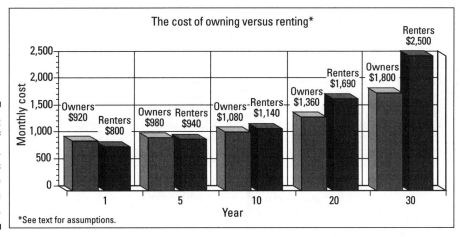

Figure 9-1: Because of inflation, renting is more expensive in the long run.

The cost of owning versus renting*

Monthly cost / Year

Year 1: Owners $920, Renters $800
Year 5: Owners $980, Renters $940
Year 10: Owners $1,080, Renters $1,140
Year 20: Owners $1,360, Renters $1,690
Year 30: Owners $1,800, Renters $2,500

*See text for assumptions.

The example in Figure 9-1 assumes that you purchase the property by making a 20 percent down payment and taking out a 7 percent fixed-rate mortgage. The rate of inflation of your home owner's insurance, property taxes, maintenance, and rent is assumed to be 4 percent per year.

As you can see in Figure 9-1, although it costs more in the early years to own, in the long run, owning is less expensive. This extra expense is because all your rental expenses increase with inflation. I haven't factored in the potential change in the value of your home over time. Over long periods of time, home prices tend to appreciate — this appreciation makes owning even more attractive.

If inflation is low or nonexistent, owning isn't necessarily more expensive in the long term. In the absence of inflation, your rent shouldn't escalate, but your home ownership expenses, which are subject to inflation — such as property taxes, maintenance, and insurance — shouldn't, either. And with low inflation, you can probably refinance your mortgage at a lower interest rate, which saves you on your monthly mortgage payments. With low or no inflation, owning should still cost less, but the savings versus renting aren't as dramatic as when inflation is greater.

I've witnessed some renters who do want to buy but can't, simply because they spend too much money on rent. Remember that in order to come up with the down payment to buy property, you must save money (unless you've got a benevolent relative). Saving a good chunk of money does require some sacrifice and living well beneath your means. In addition to shared housing, also consider smaller places and less popular, but safe, areas.

How much should you spend?

Buying a home is a long-term financial commitment. You will probably take out a 15- to 30-year mortgage to finance your purchase. The home you buy will need all sorts of maintenance over the years. So, before you make a commitment to buy, it's important to take stock of your overall financial health.

If you have good credit and a reliable source of employment, bankers eagerly offer to lend you money. They tell you how much you may borrow from them — the maximum that you are qualified to borrow. But that doesn't mean that you should borrow the maximum. What about your other financial options and goals? The most common mistake I see people make when buying a home is that they ignore their overall financial situation.

If you buy a home without considering your other monthly expenditures and long-term goals, you may end up with a home that dictates much of your future spending. Have you considered, for example, how much you should be saving monthly to reach your retirement goals? How about how much you want to be able to spend on recreation and entertainment, such as eating out, traveling, and collecting Pogs with your kids?

If you want to continue your current lifestyle, you have to be honest with yourself about how much you can really afford to spend as a home owner. First-time home buyers in particular run into financial trouble because they don't know their spending needs and priorities and how to budget for them. As much as buying a home can be a wise decision, it can also be a huge burden. Some people have trouble curtailing their spending despite the large amount of debt they just incurred and, in fact, spend even more because there are all sorts of nifty things to buy for a home. Many people prop up their spending habits with credit cards — a dangerous practice.

Don't let your home control your financial future. Take stock of your overall financial health, especially where you stand in terms of retirement planning (if you hope to someday retire), before you buy property or agree to a particular mortgage. Start by reading Chapter 3.

The banker's perspective on borrowing

All mortgage lenders want to know your ability to repay the money you borrow. So you have to pass a few tests. Mortgage lenders calculate the maximum amount you can borrow for buying a piece of real estate.

For a home in which you will reside, lenders total up your monthly housing expense. They define your housing costs as

Mortgage Payment + Property Taxes + Insurance

A lender does not consider maintenance and upkeep expenses in owning a home. (You shouldn't ignore this important issue in your budget, however.) Lenders typically loan you *up to* an amount so that no more than 33 percent of your monthly gross income (that's your income before taxes) goes toward housing expense. (If you're self-employed, lenders use the net income from the bottom line of your federal tax form Schedule C rather than gross monthly income.)

Although lenders may not care where you spend money outside your home, they do care about your other debt. A lot of other debt, such as credit cards or auto loans, diminishes the funds available to pay your housing expenses. Lenders know that having other debt increases the possibility that you may fall behind or actually default on your mortgage payments.

If you have consumer debt requiring monthly payments, lenders calculate another ratio to determine the maximum you can borrow. To your monthly housing expense, lenders add the amount you need to pay down your other consumer debt. These total costs typically cannot exceed 38 percent — anything higher and most lenders reject your loan application.

Consumer debt is bad news even without considering that it hurts your qualification for a mortgage. It's high cost and encourages you to live beyond your means. Unlike the interest on mortgage debt, consumer debt interest is not tax-deductible. Get rid of it now and forever! Rein in your spending and adjust to living within your means. If you can't live within your means as a renter, it's going to be even harder as a home owner.

Lending ratios vary slightly from lender to lender. Some lenders, for example, may allow your housing expense to reach up to 36 percent of your monthly income. Others may allow the ratio of housing expenses, plus other consumer debt payments, to reach up to 40 percent of your gross income.

An old rule of thumb says that you can afford to borrow three times (or two and one-half times) your annual income when buying a home. But this is a really rough estimate. The maximum that a mortgage lender loans you depends on interest rates. Lower interest rates make the monthly payment on a mortgage of a given size also drop. Table 9-1 gives you a ballpark idea of the maximum that you're probably eligible to borrow. Multiply your gross annual income by the number in the second column to determine the maximum size mortgage you can get.

Table 9-1	The Maximum Mortgage You'll Qualify For
When Mortgage Rates Are This:	*Multiply Your Gross Annual Income* (before Taxes) by This Figure to Determine the Maximum You May Be Able to Borrow:*
4%	4.6
5%	4.2
6%	3.8
7%	3.5
8%	3.2
9%	2.9
10%	2.7
11%	2.5

* If you're self-employed, this is your net income (after expenses but before taxes). The maximum amount that you can borrow depends on the property taxes you pay. These taxes vary from area to area, so the preceding table is based on average property tax rates. This table also assumes that you plan to take a 30-year mortgage.

For example, if you're getting a mortgage with a rate around 7 percent and your annual income is $50,000, multiply 3.5 × $50,000 to get $175,000, the approximate maximum mortgage allowed. So if you have a $45,000 down payment, then you can purchase a home costing about $220,000. As discussed in the preceding section, that estimate doesn't mean that you should borrow this much. This figure is the maximum, not the right amount for you and your financial goals. For example, the further behind you are in saving for retirement, the less able you will be to "afford" a large mortgage.

The only way to know what size mortgage you're eligible for is to talk to some lenders. Most are more than willing to prequalify you, which means that they take down some background data on you (income, debts, and so on) and run some numbers to tell you how much you can borrow. This preliminary meeting isn't a promise or guarantee — lenders won't commit to a loan until they have your documentation and property appraisal in hand.

When you're prequalified, the lender isn't committed to approving a loan for you. You're also under no obligation to work with a lender or mortgage broker who prequalifies you. Prequalification is a part of marketing. It benefits lenders by allowing them to learn, after a small investment of their time, whether they should spend their time trying to get you a loan.

A 20 percent down payment is a good target

Another factor to consider in deciding how much you should borrow is that most lenders require you to purchase *private mortgage insurance* (PMI) if your down payment is less than 20 percent. PMI protects the lender from getting stuck with a property that may be worth less than the mortgage you owe, in the event you default on your loan. On a moderate-size loan, PMI can add hundreds of dollars per year to your payments.

If you have to take PMI to buy a home with less than 20 percent down, keep an eye on your home's value and your loan balance. With luck, your property will appreciate over time and your loan balance will decrease as you make monthly payments. After the loan represents 80 percent or less of the market value of the home, you can, with an appraisal providing proof of the value of your property, get rid of the PMI.

What if you have so much money that you can afford to put down more than a 20 percent down payment? This problem doesn't usually arise — most buyers, especially first-time buyers, struggle to get a 20 percent down payment together. How much should you put down then? The answer depends on what else you can or want to do with the money. If you're considering other investment opportunities, determine whether you can expect to earn a higher rate of return on those other investments versus the interest rate you'll pay on the mortgage. Forget about the tax deduction for your mortgage interest. Yes, the interest is deductible, but don't forget that the earnings from your investments are taxable.

During this century, stock market and real estate investors have enjoyed average annual returns of around 10 percent per year. So if you borrow mortgage money at around 7 to 8 percent today, in the long term you should come out ahead by investing in such growth investments. Besides possibly generating a higher rate of return, other real estate and stock investing can help you diversify your investments, which is always a good thing.

You aren't guaranteed, of course, that you can earn 10 percent yearly (past returns don't guarantee the future). And don't forget that all investments come with risk. The advantage of putting more money down for a home and borrowing less is that it is essentially a risk-free investment (so long as you have proper insurance on your property).

If you prefer to put down just 20 percent and invest more elsewhere, that's fine. Just don't keep the extra money (beyond an emergency reserve) under the mattress, in a savings account, or in bonds that pay less interest than your mortgage costs you in interest. Go for growth by investing in stocks, real estate, or a small business. Otherwise, you don't have a chance at earning a higher return than the cost of the mortgage and thus you would be better off paying down your mortgage.

The price of owning

In order to figure out whether buying a particular home is going to ruin your personal finances or still allow you enough financial freedom, you must crunch at least a few numbers. Before you agree to buy, you should tally up what it's going to cost you per month to own, after factoring in all costs as well as the tax savings from home ownership.

The worksheet in Table 9-2 allows you to total up the estimated costs of owning.

Table 9-2	Monthly Expenses of Owning
Figure Out This	**Write It Here ($ per month)**
1. Monthly mortgage payment (see the following "Mortgage" section)	$ _____
2. Plus monthly property taxes (see the upcoming "Property taxes" section)	+ $ _____
3. Equals total monthly mortgage plus property taxes	= $ _____
4. Your income tax rate (see Table 9-4)	_____ %
5. Minus tax benefits (line 3 multiplied by line 4)	– $ _____
6. Equals after-tax cost of mortgage and property taxes (subtract line 5 from line 3)	= $ _____
7. Plus insurance ($30 – $100/mo., depending on property value)	+ $ _____
8. Plus maintenance (1% of property cost divided by 12 months)	+ $ _____
9. Equals total costs of owning (add lines 6, 7, and 8)	= $ _____

Mortgage

To determine the monthly payment on your mortgage, simply multiply the relevant number ("Multiplier") from Table 9-3 by the size of your mortgage expressed in (divided by) thousands of dollars. For example, if you will be taking out a $100,000, 30-year mortgage at 7 percent, then multiply 100 by 6.65 (from the table) for a $665 monthly payment.

Property taxes

Ask a real estate person, mortgage lender, or your local assessor's office what your annual property tax bill would be for a house of similar value to the one you are considering buying (the average around the country is about 1.5 percent of your property's value). Divide this annual amount by 12 to arrive at your monthly property tax bill.

Table 9-3	Your Monthly Mortgage Payment "Multiplier"	
Interest Rate	*15-Year Mortgage*	*30-Year Mortgage*
4.0%	7.40	4.77
4.5%	7.65	5.07
5.0%	7.91	5.37
5.5%	8.17	5.68
6.0%	8.44	6.00
6.5%	8.71	6.32
7.0%	8.99	6.65
7.5%	9.27	6.99
8.0%	9.56	7.34
8.5%	9.85	7.69
9.0%	10.14	8.05
9.5%	10.44	8.41
10.0%	10.75	8.78

Tax savings (yeah!)

Your mortgage interest and property taxes are tax-deductible on Form 1040, Schedule A of your personal tax return. When you calculate the costs of owning a home, the tax savings should be subtracted to provide you a more complete and accurate sense of what home ownership is going to cost you.

If you want to get a pretty specific estimate as to the tax savings from owning a given property, you can prepare your tax return with and without the home ownership deductions and calculate the difference. That process can take quite a while — here's a shortcut that gives you a pretty good answer:

Tax savings in home ownership = Your federal tax rate (see Table 9-4) multiplied by the total amount of your property taxes and mortgage.

Supposing that your mortgage payment and your property taxes come to about $800 per month and you're in the 28 percent tax bracket, your tax savings from home ownership write-offs would come to $224 per month ($0.28 \times \$800$).

Table 9-4 1997 Federal Income Tax Brackets and Rates		
Singles Taxable Income	*Married Filing Jointly Taxable Income*	*Federal Tax Rate*
Less than $24,650	Less than $41,200	15%
$24,650 to $59,750	$41,200 to $99,600	28%
$59,750 to $124,650	$99,600 to $151,750	31%
$124,650 to $271,050	$151,750 to $271,050	36%
More than $271,050	More than $271,050	39.6%

Technically speaking, not all of your mortgage payment is tax-deductible — only the portion of the mortgage payment that goes toward interest is tax-deductible. In the early years of your mortgage, however, the portion that goes toward interest is nearly all of it. Although your mortgage payment remains constant with a fixed-rate mortgage, over time your property taxes will probably rise. You may earn state tax benefits as well from your deductible mortgage interest and property taxes. On the other hand, you probably won't capture the full value of the state tax write-offs due to the intricacies of claiming itemized deductions in the income tax system.

When you buy a home, be sure to refigure how much you need to pay in income tax, because your mortgage interest and property tax deductions should help lower your tax bill. If you work for an employer, ask your payroll/benefits department for Form W-4. If you're self-employed, you can complete a worksheet that comes with Form 1040-ES (call 800-TAX-FORM for a copy). Many new home buyers don't bother with this step, and they end up getting a big tax refund the next year. Although getting money back from the IRS may feel good, it means that at a minimum, you made an interest-free loan to the IRS. In the worst case, the reduced cash flow during the year may cause you to accumulate debt or miss out on contributing to tax-deductible retirement accounts.

If you want a more precise estimate as to how home ownership may affect your tax situation, get out your tax return and try plugging in some reasonable numbers to "guesstimate" how your taxes will change. You can also speak with a tax advisor.

Is this a good or bad time to buy?

If you're thinking about buying a home, you may be worried about whether home prices are poised to rise or fall. No one wants to purchase a home that then plummets in value. And who wouldn't like to buy just before prices go on an upward trajectory?

Other home ownership tax breaks

Being able to deduct the mortgage interest and property taxes on your annual tax return is a valuable tax benefit you enjoy as a home owner. But you may, at various points in your life, be able to make use of other tax benefits as well.

If you buy a home in which you live (your *primary residence* in IRS-speak), you may roll over (defer) paying tax on your profit when you sell your home so long as within 24 months of the sale, you purchase and move into another home that costs at least as much. You can make use of this tax-free rollover once every two years unless you must relocate because you take a new job or are transferred to another location by your current employer.

While you're in your home, make sure to keep track of (and keep receipts for) money spent improving your property. For tax purposes, you can add the cost of these improvements to your original purchase price for the home. Improvements include expenses such as installing an alarm system, adding or remodeling a room, planting new trees and shrubs in your yard, and purchasing new appliances. These improvements increase the value of your home and lengthen its life. Maintenance and repair costs — such as the cost of hiring a plumber to fix a leaky pipe or recaulking around your bathtub — are not tax favored.

If you run your business out of your home, you may be able to take additional tax deductions beyond the mortgage interest and property taxes you already get to claim as a home owner. If you qualify for the so-called "home office" deduction, you may be able to write off some of your insurance, maintenance, and housecleaning expenses. The IRS is strict about who may take this deduction — pick up a copy of *Taxes For Dummies* to find out more.

Last but not least, thanks to the tax law changes passed in 1997, homeowners are allowed to exclude from taxable income a significant portion of their gain on the sale of a principal residence: up to $250,000 for single taxpayers and $500,000 for married couples filing jointly.

It's not easy to predict what's going to happen with real estate prices in a particular city, state, or country over the next one, two, or three or more years. Ultimately, the demand for homes and the prices for homes in an area are driven largely by the economic health and vitality of that area. With increased jobs, particularly ones that pay well, comes more demand for housing.

If you first buy a home when you're in your 20s, 30s, or even your 40s, you may end up being a home owner for several or more decades. That's a long time! Over such a long time, you'll experience lots of ups and downs, but likely more ups than downs, so I wouldn't be too concerned about trying to predict what's going to happen in the near term.

That said, you may be, at particular times in your life, ambivalent about buying a home. Perhaps you're not sure that you will stay put for more than three to five years. So part of your home-buying decision may hinge on whether current home prices in your local area offer you a good value.

Indicators of a bloated market

I live in the San Francisco Bay Area. Like many parts of the country, real estate prices in this area have gone through up and down periods. I've been amazed, however, at the heights of the speculative buying frenzy reached here as well as the depths of pessimism after a price drop.

I'll start with speculative excess. In the mid- to late-1980s, the Bay Area real estate market was booming. In 1989, prices seemed to be heading for the moon — median home prices (meaning that half the homes sold at prices above and half sold at prices below) had risen 137 percent from $110,000 in 1980 to $260,700 in 1989. Jobs were abundant — the Bay Area unemployment rate was less than 4 percent.

Despite the enormous increase in prices and high price levels in existence in the late 1980s, many people, including experts, were optimistic about continued price increases. In a survey of home prices around the nation, *Money* magazine in 1990 published projections prepared by the Wharton Econometrics Forecasting Associates (WEFA) economics firm projecting still more appreciation. WEFA predicted that home prices in the Bay Area would increase in value 11 percent faster than the rate of inflation between 1990 and 1995.

Neighbors and friends were talking about the stunning rise and increasing numbers of investors piled into the market. In a survey conducted by Case and Schiller in 1988 of San Francisco Bay Area home buyers, 37 percent said that they bought their property "strictly as an investment," motivated by the hope of future appreciation.

I knew more than a few people who had formally changed careers or took on a second career at that time with the new occupation being real estate investor. Many of these people were buying homes that needed renovation — sometimes known as fixer-uppers — and flipping them within a year or so after sprucing them up. While the tide was still rising fast, it seemed as if these folks were making shrewd investments. (These people didn't realize they were profiting from the rising tide until it receded.)

Another indicator that prices were reaching a speculative peak was that continually inflating housing prices were making front page news. In April 1989, the *San Jose Mercury News* ran an article on the front page of the first section entitled, "Why housing prices will keep going up." The *San Francisco Chronicle* ran a similar story months earlier that tracked the plight of Cathryn and Jim Reid, a couple who had been searching for a home for all of two months. The Reids were said to "wish they could turn back the clocks. If nothing else, it would save them a lot of money. . . ."

A real estate agent was cited in the *Chronicle* article as advising her clients at that time ". . . to act quickly if they see a house they like. If they do not, they will almost surely have to settle for something else." The real estate agent added that she counseled her clients, "If you see something you like, you can't go home and think about it for a week."

Heaven forbid that you think about what's likely the largest financial transaction of your life! Such was the mentality of those frothy times.

Fortunate potential buyers who did take the time to think about buying a home in this area in the late 1980s didn't jump blindly into the market. Only 11 percent of Bay Area residents could afford to buy the median-priced home in 1989, one of the lowest all-time readings of this indicator. (Note that affordability statistics can sometimes be misleading because potential buyers can simply buy less home.)

Besides the widespread euphoria and optimism, an even better indicator that the tide would change was that the high home prices caused many buyers to question what they were getting for their money as buyers versus what they had as renters. Comparing the cost of owning a home to the cost of renting that same property serves as a reality check on home prices.

Back in 1989, consider that $400,000, three-bedroom starter homes in the Menlo Park/Palo Alto area (a pleasant suburban area about a 40-minute drive outside of San Francisco) could be rented for $1,300 per month. Assuming a 20 percent down payment, the cost of owning such a home amounted to approximately $2,460 per month, even factoring in the tax benefits of home ownership (remember that mortgage interest and property taxes are deductible).

Why pay a near 90 percent premium to own a place ($2,460 per month versus $1,300)? Increasing numbers of renters did the smart thing — they continued to rent because it was a far better value. Guess what happened to home prices?

Signs that real estate is on sale

The time to buy real estate is when others don't want to and it's on sale. When the U.S. stock market crashed by dropping 35 percent in October 1987, people's sudden fascination with the profits to be made in the market came to a halt. Pessimism abounded, and many novice investors, fearing an even bigger drop, went so far as to sell their holdings.

Just as it was far safer and sensible to plunge head first into the U.S. stock market post-1987 crash, it makes more sense to get excited about home buying when prices are down.

In the next six years, home prices in the San Francisco Bay Area dropped about 13 percent from the market peak of 1989, 33 percent if you factor in inflation. So much for those predictions in *Money* magazine!

Over this same time period, interest rates dropped, thus making homes less costly to finance. A 30-year fixed-rate mortgage fell to about 7 percent, a substantial reduction from the 10 percent rates in 1989.

If you combine the beneficial drop in interest rates with the fact that those $400,000 homes were going for about $350,000 in 1995, it cost a home buyer in 1995 about $1,790 per month to own such a home versus rent of approximately $1,600 per month. In other words, you could own for just a slightly higher cost than the cost of renting. And with inflation, the cost of owning such a home would soon cost less than renting it. (Remember that the cost of renting normally increases more over the years than the cost of your home purchased with a fixed-rate mortgage.)

Not surprisingly, affordability is much improved. In 1995, approximately 33 percent of Bay Area residents could afford the median-priced home, triple that of 1989. In San Francisco, where the median-priced home sold fell from $289,000 in 1989 to $259,000 in 1995, the inventory of listings of homes for sale had also dropped. The supply of homes for sale naturally corrects markets out of balance. Over this time period, from a peak of 8,226, listings of homes for sale in San Francisco have plummeted about 25 percent to 6,203. Sellers who didn't need to sell were less eager to part with properties at 1995's lower prices.

Another source of future demand for housing can come from renters fleeing escalating rents. Since 1989, rents gradually increased and little new housing was built; the rental market was getting tight. In the Bay Area in 1995, apartment vacancy rates were down below 3.5 percent. Normal vacancy rates are in the 4 to 5 percent range. Also, few new apartments were being built.

Remember that jobs fuel the demand for housing. After peaking at 6.5 percent in 1992, Bay Area unemployment fell. In 1995, the unemployment rate fell to less than 6.0 percent.

Despite lower home prices and interest rates, an improved economy, and tightened rental and homes-for-sale inventory, people were showing far less interest in buying real estate in the Bay Area in 1995 than in 1989.

Once you purchase a home, you'll likely own it for many years, if not decades. Thus I wouldn't be concerned with the timing of your initial purchase. I know many people who avoided buying homes years ago because they thought prices were expensive. Investors have made the same mistake not investing in stocks. Examining the level of real estate prices compared to rents, the state of the job market, and the number of home listings for sale are useful indicators for the health of the housing market. But trying to time your purchase has more importance if you think you may be moving in less than five years. In that case, be careful to avoid buying in a frothy market.

Are You a House or Condo Kinda Person?

If you're ready to buy, you must make some decisions about what and where to buy. If you grew up in the suburbs, your image of a home may be the traditional single-family home with a lawn, a couple of kids, and a dog or cat. But single-family homes, of course, aren't the only or even the main types of residential housing in many areas. In some areas, particularly in some higher-cost, urban neighborhoods, nonsingle-family housing is more common. Other common types of higher-density housing include

- **Condominiums.** These are generally apartment-style units that are stacked on top of and side by side one another. Many condo buildings were originally apartments that were converted — by offering for sale the ownership of separate units — into condos. When you purchase a condominium, you're purchasing a specific unit as well as a share of the common areas (for example, pool, grass and other plantings, entry and hallways, laundry room, and so on).

- **Townhomes.** Townhomes are just a fancy way of saying attached or row homes. Think of these as being between a condominium and a single-family house. Townhomes are condolike in that they are attached (generally sharing walls and a roof) and are homelike in that they often are two-story buildings and come with a small yard.

- **Cooperatives.** These are buildings much like apartment and condominium buildings. When you buy a share in a cooperative, you own a share of the entire building, including some living space. In this respect, co-ops are a bit like a mutual fund. Unlike a condo, you generally need to get approval from the cooperative association for remodeling to your unit or renting your unit to a tenant. In some co-ops, you even must gain approval from the association for the sale of your unit to a proposed buyer.

Such shared housing offers two big potential advantages. First, this type of housing generally gives you more living space for your dollars. This makes sense because with a single-family home, a good chunk of the cost for the property is for the land the home sits upon. Land is good for decks, recreation, and playing children, but you don't live "in" it the way you do with your home. If you want to maximize living space for the housing dollars you spend, shared housing is the way to go.

Another benefit of shared housing is that in many situations, you're not personally responsible for general maintenance because the owners' association (which you pay for, directly or indirectly) takes care of it. If you don't have the time, energy, or desire to keep up a property, these types of shared housing can make sense. They may also provide you with better safety than a stand-alone home and access to shared recreation facilities, such as a pool, tennis courts, and exercise equipment.

So why doesn't everyone purchase this type of housing? First, as investments, single-family homes generally do better in the long run. In a good real estate market, single-family as well as other types of housing appreciate, although single-family homes tend to do better. Shared housing is easier to build (and to overbuild) — the greater supply tends to keep its prices depressed. Single-family homes tend to be more attractive to potential buyers, especially those who don't like listening to their neighbors argue. Most people, when they can afford it, prefer a stand-alone home.

If you can afford a smaller single-family home instead of a larger shared-housing unit, buy the single-family home. Shared housing makes more sense for people who don't want to deal at all with building maintenance and who value the security of being in a larger building with other people. Also know that shared-housing prices tend to hold up better in already developed urban environments. If possible, avoid them in suburban areas where the availability of developable land makes building a lot more units possible.

If you are interested in shared housing, be sure to have the property well inspected. Also examine the trend in maintenance fees over time to ensure these costs are under control (see Chapter 11 for more specifics on how to check out the property).

Finding the right property and location

Some people know where they want to live, look at a handful of properties, and then buy. Most people take much more time — finding the right house in the right area at the right price can take a lot of time. It can also entail much compromise when you're buying with other family members.

Be realistic about how long it will take you to get up to speed about the pros and cons of different areas and to find a home that will meet many needs and concerns. If you're a normal person with a full-time job and confined to occasional weekends and evenings of looking, three to six months is a short amount of time to settle on an area and actually find and negotiate successfully on a property. Six months to a year is not unusual or slow. Remember, you're talking about spending tens, if not hundreds, of thousands of dollars on a place you'll come home to every day until you move or sell it.

The biggest barrier to taking your time is real estate agents. Some of them are pushy and want to make a sale and get their commission. Don't work with such agents as a buyer — they can make you miserable, unhappy, and broke. If need be, begin your search without an agent to avoid this outside pressure.

Be open-minded

Before you start your search, you may have an idea about the type of property and location you are interested in or think you can afford. You may think, for example, that you can afford only a condominium in the neighborhood you want. But if you take the time to check out other communities, you may be surprised to find another area that meets most of your needs and has affordable single-family homes. You'd never know that, though, if you narrowed your search too quickly.

Even if you've lived in an area for a while and think that you know it well, look at different types of properties in a variety of locations before you start to narrow your search. Be open-minded and be sure to know which of your many criteria for a home you *really* care about. You may have to be flexible on some of your preferences.

Suppose that the following items are on your wish list for a property:

- ✔ Good natural lighting
- ✔ Spacious rooms
- ✔ Historic, detailed architecture
- ✔ Walking distance to public transit
- ✔ Close to tennis courts and other fitness facilities
- ✔ An extra bedroom for guests

If you're like most people, your desires outstrip your budget. Ask yourself which of the items on your wish list are you most willing to give in on. For example, how often do you have guests? If the answer is not often, treat having a guest room as a luxury. On the other hand, if you have lots of relatives visit, perhaps because you recently had a baby, you may prefer the guest room to living near fitness facilities. Maybe you can keep some exercise equipment in that guest room!

After you focus on a particular area or neighborhood, make sure you're seeing the full range of properties available. If you want to spend $200,000 on a home, look at properties that are more expensive. Most real estate sells for less than its listing price and you may feel comfortable spending a little bit more if you see what you can get by stretching a little bit. Also, if you're working with an agent, make sure you don't overlook homes that are for sale by owner (that is, not listed with real estate agents). Otherwise, you may miss out on some good properties.

Research, research, research

It's a mistake to assume what an area is like from anecdotes or from a small number of personal experiences. You may have read or heard that someone was mugged or shot in a particular area. That doesn't make that area dangerous or more dangerous than others. *Get the facts.* Anecdotes and people's perceptions are often not accurate reflections of the facts. Here are some key items worth checking out:

✔ **Amenities.** Hopefully, you won't be spending all your time at work, slaving away to make your monthly mortgage payment. I hope you have time to use parks, sports and recreation facilities, and so on. You can get a sense of these attractions by driving around. Most real estate agents just love to show off their favorite neighborhoods. Cities and towns can also mail you information booklets detailing what their town has to offer and where to find it. Check the government white page listings in the appropriate phone directories.

✔ **Schools.** If you have kids, you'll care about this issue a lot. Unfortunately, many people make snap judgments about school quality without doing their homework. Visit the schools and don't blindly rely on test score statistics. Talk to parents and teachers and discover what's going on at the school.

If you don't have (or want!) school-age children, you may be tempted to say, "What the heck do I care about the quality of the schools?" You should care because parents care and there are lots of them out there. Even if you don't have kids, the quality of the local schools has direct bearing on the value of your property. Consider these issues even if they are not important to you, because they can affect the resale value of your property.

✔ **Property taxes.** What will your property taxes be? Property tax rates vary from community to community. Check with the town's assessor's office or with a good real estate broker.

✔ **Crime.** Call the local police department or visit your public library to get the facts on crime. Cities and towns keep all sorts of crime statistics for neighborhoods. Your tax dollars are paying for this stuff — make use of it!

✔ **Future development.** Check with the planning department in towns you're considering living in as to what types of new development and major renovations are in the works for neighborhoods you're interested in. Planning people may also be aware of problems in particular areas.

✔ **Catastrophic risks.** Are the neighborhoods you're considering buying a home in susceptible to major risks, such as floods, mud slides, fires, or earthquakes? Proper home owner's insurance can protect you financially from these vagaries. You should also consider how you deal with such a catastrophe emotionally — insurance eases only the financial pain of a home loss.

All areas have some risk, and a home in the safest of areas can burn to the ground. Just getting out of bed entails risks, so you can't eliminate all risks — but you can at least educate yourself and be aware of what they are.

If you're new to an area or don't have a handle on an area's risks, try a number of different sources. Knowledgeable and honest real estate agents may help, but you may also do some digging for primary information. For example, the U.S. Geologic Survey puts together maps that help you to see the difference in potential earthquake risks by area. The USGS has offices all around the country — check your local phone directory in the government white pages section. The Federal Emergency Management Agency (FEMA) has maps showing flood risk areas (800-358-9616). Insurance companies and agencies also can tell you what they know of risks in particular areas as well.

Developing an appraiser's mind-set

You'll look at lots of properties for sale, perhaps dozens or even hundreds over many months. Use these viewings as an opportunity to find out what places are worth. The listing price is not what a house is worth — it may be, but odds are it's not. Property that is priced to sell usually does just that — sell. What's left on the market is often overpriced. The listing price on such properties may be what an otherwise greedy or uninformed seller and his or her agent are hoping some fool will pay.

Of the properties you see, keep track of the price at which it ends up selling for (good agents can help). Properties often sell for less than the listed price. Doing so gives you a better sense of what you can afford as well as gives you a good handle on what properties are really worth.

Spend time in the 'hood

After you set your sights on that special home, you better thoroughly check out the surroundings you will be living near, should you decide to buy. You want to know what you're getting yourself into.

Go back to the neighborhood in which it is located at different times of the day and on different days of the week. Knock on a few doors and meet your potential neighbors. Ask questions. Talk to property owners as well as renters. Because they don't have a financial stake in the area, renters are often more forthcoming with negative information about an area.

Once you decide where and what to buy, you're ready to try and put a deal together. Issues common to both home as well as investment property purchases — such as mortgages, negotiations, inspections, and so on — are covered in Chapter 11.

Chapter 10

Investing in Real Estate
for Challenge and Profit

· ·

· ·

*1*f you've bought your own home already (and even if you haven't), you may be interested in real estate as an investment. Over the years, decades, and centuries, real estate investing, like the stock market and small business investments, has generated vast wealth for some participants. As discussed in Chapters 2 and 9, the rate of return from good real estate investments is comparable to that available from investing in the stock market.

Real estate is like other types of ownership investments, such as stocks, where you have an ownership position in an asset. That ownership means greater potential for profit, but don't forget that it also means greater risk. Real estate is not a gravy train or a simple way to get wealthy. Like stocks, real estate goes through good and bad performance periods. Most people who make money investing in real estate do so because they invest and hold property over many years. The vast majority of people who don't make money in real estate make easily avoidable mistakes, which I discuss in this chapter.

Simple, Profitable Ways
to Invest in Real Estate

Investing in real estate that you are responsible for renting can be a lot of work. You have all the headaches of maintaining a property, including finding and dealing with tenants, without the benefits of living in and enjoying the property.

Unless you're extraordinarily interested in and motivated to own investment real estate, start with, and perhaps limit your real estate investing to, a couple of much simpler yet still profitable methods.

A place to call home

During your adult life, you need to provide a roof over your head. You may be able to sponge off your folks or some other relative for a number of years, and if you're content with this, good for you! By minimizing your housing costs, you can save more money for a down payment. Go for it, if your relatives will!

In the long term, because you need a place to live, why not own real estate instead of renting it? Real estate is the only investment that you can live in or rent to produce income. You can't live in a stock, bond, or mutual fund! Unless you're expecting to move within the next few years, buying a place makes good long-term financial sense. In the long term, owning usually costs less than renting and allows you to build equity in an asset. Read Chapter 9 to learn about buying a home.

Real estate investment trusts

Real estate investment trusts (REITs) are entities that generally invest in different types of property, such as shopping centers, apartments, and other rental buildings. REIT managers, for a fee, identify and negotiate the purchase of properties they believe to be good investments and manage these properties, including all tenant relations. Thus, REITs are a good way to invest in real estate for people who don't want the hassles and headaches that come with directly owning and managing rental property.

Surprisingly, most books that focus on real estate investing neglect REITs. Why? I have come to the conclusion they do so for three major reasons. First, if you invest in real estate through REITs, you don't need to read a long, complicated book on real estate investment. Second, real estate brokers write many of these books. Not surprisingly, the real estate investment strategies touted in these books include and advocate the use of brokers. You can buy REITs without real estate brokers. Finally, a certain snobbishness prevails among people who consider themselves to be "serious" real estate investors. One real estate writer/investor went so far as to say that REITs aren't "real" real estate investments.

Please. No, you can't drive your friends by a REIT and show it off. But those who put ego aside when making real estate investments are happy they considered REITs and have enjoyed double-digit annual gains over the past decade.

You can research and purchase shares in individual REITs, which trade as securities on the major stock exchanges (see Chapter 6 for how to do this). Even better is to buy a mutual fund that invests in a diversified mixture of REITs (see Chapter 8 for real estate fund recommendations). Unlike direct real estate investments, investments in REITs are easy to sell.

In addition to providing you with a diversified, low-hassle real estate investment, REITs offer an additional advantage that traditional rental real estate does not. You can easily invest in REITs through a retirement account (for example, IRA or Keogh). As with traditional real estate investments, you can even buy REITs and mutual fund REITs with borrowed money. You can buy with 50 percent down when you purchase such investments through a brokerage account. (This latter practice, called buying on margin, can only be done through a non-retirement account.)

Are You Cut Out to Be the Next Donald Trump?

Every year *Forbes* magazine publishes a special issue profiling the 400 wealthiest Americans, known as the Forbes 400. Mobsters and drug kingpins are left out — to get on the list, you must make the money through seemingly legitimate and legal channels. Twenty people made the most recent list primarily because of their real estate investing. For another ten people, real estate was an important secondary contributing factor in their wealth-building.

Consider the case of Thomas Flatley. An Irish immigrant, he was practically broke when he came to America at age 18. After dabbling at his own small business, he got into real estate development. Today he owns more than 5,000 apartments, 14 hotels, and more than 6 million square feet of office and retail space, and his net worth is estimated at more than $400 million.

Should you form a real estate corporation?

When you invest in and manage real estate with at least one other partner, you can set up a company through which you collectively own the property.

The main reason you may want to consider this action is liability protection. A corporation can reduce the chances of lenders or tenants suing you.

To find out more about the pros and cons of incorporating and the different entities under which you may do business, see Chapter 13.

Then you have the case of Donald Trump. He made big bucks on real estate and once was a billionaire. He got overextended with debt, thanks to some careless bankers. When the East Coast real estate market turned tail, Trump got clobbered and nearly ended up in bankruptcy. Only through extracting big concessions from lenders was Trump, the unfaithful borrower, spared from financial ruin. Trump, along with other real estate tycoons who took on too much debt as the real estate market was peaking, ultimately was responsible for the big losses, and in some cases failure, of banks. Today Trump's net worth is a fraction of its former self, and he no longer holds a place on the Forbes 400 list.

The Trump example also highlights that financially successful people take their lumps. Not only did Trump's real estate investments almost bring down his empire, but his stock market investing skills are suspect as well. After the U.S. stock market crashed in October 1987, quickly losing about 35 percent, Trump boasted that he had sold all his stock the month prior to the crash. (No one has found a way to verify this assertion.) In late October, Trump told the *Wall Street Journal,* "I think the market is going to go down further because there are just too many things wrong with the country." This period was actually a fantastic time to buy, and those who did, or simply held tight, reaped big rewards. The U.S. stock market, as measured by the Dow Jones Industrial Average, was trading around 1,700 at that time and has spent most of the time since going up, subsequently trading over 5,000!

Why real estate investing is attractive

Scores of other Americans who built their wealth through companies they started or by other avenues also diversify into real estate investments. What do these wealthy folks know, and why do they choose to invest in real estate? Following are some of the many reasons:

- **Limited land.** Short of using landfill to build over water, the supply of land on planet Earth is fixed, thanks in part to water covering about 70 percent of our globe. And because people are prone to reproduce (I must confess to being party to this as well), demand for land and housing continues to grow.

  Land, and what you can do with it, is what makes real estate valuable. Cities and islands, such as Hawaii, Tokyo, San Francisco, Los Angeles, and New York City, have the highest housing costs around.

- **Leverage.** Real estate is different from most other investments in that you can borrow up to 80 to 90 percent or more of the value of the property. Thus, your small investment of 10 to 20 percent down can be used to purchase, own, and control a much larger investment. Of course, you hope that the value of your real estate goes up — if it does, you make money on your investment as well as on all the money that you borrowed.

Here's a quick example to illustrate. Suppose you purchase a property for $100,000 and make a $20,000 down payment. Over the next three years, imagine that the property appreciates to $120,000. Thus, you've made a profit of $20,000 on an investment of just $20,000. In other words, you've made a 100 percent return on your investment. (Note that this scenario is a simplified example because you have expenses from the property that may exceed the rental income you collect. If the property's income just covers the expenses, then your return is 100 percent.)

WARNING!

Leverage is good for you if property prices appreciate, but leverage can work against you. If your $100,000 property decreases in value to $80,000, even though it's only dropped 20 percent in value, you actually lose 100 percent of your original $20,000 investment. If you have an outstanding mortgage on this property of $80,000 and need or want to sell, you actually need to pay money into the sale to cover selling costs, in addition to losing your entire original investment. Ouch!

✔ **Growth and income.** Another reason real estate is a popular investment is that you can make money in two major ways from it. First, you hope and expect over the years that your real estate investments appreciate in value. The appreciation of your properties compounds tax-deferred during your years of ownership. You don't pay tax on this profit until you sell your property — even then you can roll over your gain into another investment property and avoid paying tax. (See the sidebar, "Roll over those rental property profits," for details on tax-free exchanges of investment properties.)

In addition to making money from your properties increasing in value, you can also make money from the ongoing business you're running. You rent out investment property to make a profit based on the property's rental income exceeding your expenses (mortgage, property taxes, insurance, maintenance, and so on). Unless you make a large down payment, in the early years of rental property ownership, your monthly operating profit is small or nonexistent. Over time, your operating profit, which is subject to ordinary income tax, should rise as you increase your rental prices faster than your expenses. During soft periods in the local economy, however, rents may rise slower than your expenses (or the rents may even fall).

✔ **Diversification.** An advantage of holding some investment real estate is that its value doesn't necessarily move in tandem with other investments, such as stocks or small business investments, you hold.

✔ **Ability to "add value."** Unlike investing in the stock market, you may have some good ideas about how to improve a property and make it more valuable. Perhaps you can fix up a property or develop it further and raise the rental income accordingly. Perhaps through legwork, persistence, and good negotiating skills, you're able to purchase a property below its fair market value.

Roll over those rental property profits

Unlike when you sell a stock or mutual fund investment that you hold outside a retirement account, you can avoid paying tax on your profit (similar to deferring tax from the sale of your residence at a profit) when you sell a rental property. You may roll over your gain into another "like kind" investment real estate property.

Under current tax laws, the IRS continues to take a broad definition of what like kind property is. They allow you, for example, to exchange undeveloped land for a multiunit rental building.

The rules for properly doing one of these 1031 exchanges or Starker exchanges are complex. Third parties are usually involved. You may not receive the proceeds — they must go into an escrow account. You also have less time to complete the rollover — 6 months versus the 24 months for rolling over the profit from the sale of your primary residence. You must also have identified a replacement property within 45 days of the sale of the first property. Make sure that you find an attorney and/or tax advisor who is an expert at these transactions to ensure that you do it right.

If you don't roll over your gain, you'll owe even more tax than on a gain on your home or primary residence because of how the IRS defines your gain. If you bought the property for $200,000 and sell it for $250,000, you not only owe tax on that difference, but you also owe tax on an additional amount, depending on the property's depreciation. The amount of depreciation that you deducted on your tax returns reduces the original $200,000 purchase price, making the taxable difference that much larger. For example, if you deducted $25,000 for depreciation over the years that you owned the property, you owe tax on the difference between the sale price of $250,000 and $175,000 (= $200,000 purchase price minus $25,000 depreciation).

Relative to investing in the stock market, it is easier for persistent and savvy real estate investors to buy property below its fair market value. You can do the same in the stock market, but the scores of professional, full-time money managers analyzing stocks make it harder to find bargains.

✔ **Ego gratification.** Face it, real estate investing appeals to some investors because it's one of the few investments that's tangible. Although few admit it, some real estate investors get an ego rush from a tangible display of their wealth. You can drive by investment real estate and show it off to others. In a piece appropriately written for the *New York Times,* "What My Ego Wants, My Ego Gets," Donald Trump publicly admitted what most everyone else long ago knew: He holds his real estate investments for his ego. Trump confessed of his purchase of the famed Plaza Hotel in the Big Apple, ". . . I realized it was 100 percent true — ego did play a large role in the Plaza purchase and is, in fact, a significant factor in all of my deals."

You're less likely to make emotionally based decisions with real estate investing

One of the problems with investing in the securities markets, such as the stock market, is that prices are constantly changing. Every day, newspapers, television news programs, and online computer services dutifully report the latest price quotes. From my observations and work with individual investors, the constant changes in the financial markets and reporting on those changes cause some investors to lose sight of the long-term and big picture.

In the worst cases, large short-term drops lead investors to panic and sell at what end up being bargain prices. Or headlines about big increases pull investors in lemminglike fashion into an overheated and peaking market. Because all you need to do is pick up a telephone and place your sell or buy order, some stock market investors fall prey to snap, irrational judgments.

Like the stock market, the real estate market is constantly changing. However, to a real estate investor, short-term, day-to-day, and week-to-week changes are transparent. Publications don't report the value of your real estate holdings daily, weekly, or even monthly, which is good because it focuses you on the longer term. If prices do decline over the months and years, you're much less likely with real estate to sell in a panic. Preparing a property for sale and eventually getting it sold takes a good deal of time, and this added time helps keep your vision in focus.

How to tell whether real estate investing is not for you

Real estate investing is not for everyone, not even close. Most people are better off doing their ownership investing in a diversified portfolio of stocks, such as through stock mutual funds. From my experience working with and teaching clients and students, you should shy away from real estate investing that involves managing property that you own if any of the following describe you:

✔ **Time starved.** Buying and owning investment real estate and being a landlord is a time sink. If you're not willing to do your homework when evaluating properties to purchase, you can end up overpaying for a property or buying a heap of trouble. As for managing a property, you can hire a property manager to help with screening and finding good tenants and troubleshooting problems with the building, but this step costs money and still requires some time involvement.

Also, remember that most tenants don't care for a property the same way as property owners do. If every little scratch or carpet stain sends your blood pressure skyward, avoid distressing yourself as a landlord.

✔ **Not funding your retirement accounts.** If you haven't exhausted contributing to retirement accounts such as 401(k)s, SEP-IRAs, Keoghs, and so on (see Chapter 3), do that first before doing serious real estate investing. Why? Funding retirement accounts gives you an immediate tax deduction as you contribute money to them. And after the money is inside a retirement account, all the growth and income from your investments is not taxed until you withdraw money from the accounts. You derive no tax benefits while you're accumulating your down payment for an investment real estate purchase. Furthermore, the operating profit or income from your real estate investment is subject to tax as you earn it.

✔ **Real estate doesn't interest you.** Some people simply don't feel comfortable and informed when it comes to investing in real estate. If you've had experience and success with stock market investing, that's a good reason to stick with it and avoid real estate. Over long periods of time, both stocks and real estate have provided comparable returns.

Direct Real Estate Investment Options

If you think you're cut out to be a landlord and to be responsible for buying, owning, and managing rental real estate, you have literally millions of direct real estate investment options from which to choose.

Before you begin this potentially treacherous journey, I strongly recommend that you read Chapter 9. Many concepts that you need to know to be a successful real estate investor are similar to those needed when buying a home. The rest of this chapter focuses on issues that are more unique to real estate investing.

Realistic expectations

If you've attempted to read or have read some of the many real estate investing books that have been published over the years, some deprogramming may be in order. Too often, authors attempt to make real estate investing sound like the one and only sure way to become a multimillionaire and with little effort. Consider the following statements made by real estate book authors, which are accompanied by my rebuttals:

> **"Rather than yielding only a small interest payment or dividend, real estate in prime locations can appreciate 20 percent a year or more."**

It's true that bank accounts, bonds, and stocks pay interest or dividends that typically amount to 3 to 6 percent per year. But bank accounts and bonds are not comparable investments — they are far more conservative and liquid and, as such, don't offer the potential for double-digit returns. Stock market investing is comparable to investing in real estate, but you shouldn't go into real estate investments expecting 20 percent per year or more. Those who purchased good Los Angeles real estate in the 1950s and held onto it for the next three decades earned handsome returns as the population of this area boomed. Finding areas like Los Angeles and knowing how long to hold onto investments in these areas is easier said than done. Expect to earn 8 to 12 percent per year, not 20 percent or more.

"A good piece of property can't do anything but go up."

Any city, town, or community has good pieces of real estate. But that doesn't mean that it can't and won't have its slow or down years. Real estate in some parts of the Midwest and South, for example, has appreciated quite slowly — at or just above the rate of inflation — for periods as long as a generation or more.

"Real estate is the best way of preserving and enhancing wealth. . . . [it] stands head and shoulders above any other form of investment."

Hogwash and balderdash! Investing in stocks or in a small business is every bit as profitable. In fact, more great fortunes have been built in small business investing than in any other form of investment. Over the long term, stock market investors have enjoyed, with far less hassle, average annual rates of return on par with real estate investors.

Real estate, like all investments, has its pros and cons. Investing in real estate is time intensive and carries investment risks and, as you can see later in this chapter, comes with other risks. Invest in real estate because you enjoy the challenge and for the diversification, not as a get-rich-quick outlet.

Evaluating your options

As I discuss in Chapter 9, it doesn't make a whole lot of sense to purchase real estate if you don't intend to hold it over a number of years — preferably at least five. Even if you're lucky enough to buy right before big price increases, you'll likely not make a profit. All the costs associated with buying and then selling a property can easily gobble up all of your profit, and sometimes cause you to lose money. And if prices hold steady or decline during your short period of ownership, you'll lose money. Ideally, you should plan to make real estate investments that you hold until, and perhaps through, your retirement years.

But what to buy? Choices abound, and most people have so little time and money. Here's my take on the good and not-so-good real estate investments.

Greed will separate you from your money

Working hard for money, saving some, and watching it grow slowly over the years and decades is boring. It's very American to want to make a lot of money in a hurry. Real estate investors with lofty expectations for high returns become bait for various hucksters and operators who promise great riches but ensure that people stay in rags.

You should know by now to stay away from the infomercial pitches, but hundreds of thousands of viewers fall prey annually. Among the more infamous real estate infomercial promoters is Tom Vu. At his seminars, according to the *Los Angeles Times*, he says, "Well, if you make no money with me, you a loser." Vu, who came to the U.S. from Vietnam in the mid-1970s, claims to have made a fortune investing in real estate using a fairly simple system. He says he searches for property owners who are in debt up to their eyeballs and offers to buy their properties with no money down. By finding desperate buyers, he says, you can buy real estate at a big discount to its fair market value.

Vu makes his money from running high-priced seminars to teach basic techniques, which you can read about in a book for about $20. Vu charges up to $15,000 for a five-day seminar! If overpaying this much isn't enough, Vu's former "students," who have filed a number of lawsuits, including a class action suit, say that his methods don't work and that he reneged on his promises to go into partnership on properties they identified. A number of states have and are investigating Vu's practices, have barred further Vu seminars in their state, and are seeking compensation for victims. Unfortunately, Vu appears to have moved much of his money overseas. Other real estate seminar hucksters such as Robert Allen and Ed Buckley saw their seminar enterprises end up in bankruptcy, sunk by the claims of their unhappy students.

Other scams abound. Stephen Murphy was a real estate investor who claimed to make a fortune buying foreclosed commercial real estate and wrote and self-published a book to share his techniques with the public. Murphy's organization called the people who bought his book and pitched them on going in on property purchases with him that supposedly would return upwards of 100 percent or more per year. Murphy had other ideas and siphoned off nearly two-thirds of the money for himself and for promotion of his books! He even hoodwinked Donald Trump to write praise for his book and work saying, "I really admire Steve Murphy. . . . Steve commands some very wise, intelligent . . . and unique purchasing strategies." I'll say!

New York attorney Alan Harris also defrauded real estate investors out of millions of dollars (including actress Shirley Jones) when he pocketed money that was to be invested in property. The lure: As interest rates plummeted during the 1980s, Harris promised investors higher yields.

If an investment "opportunity" sounds too good to be true, it is. If you're going to invest in real estate, avoid the hucksters and either invest directly in properties that you control or invest through reputable REITs.

Residential housing

Your best bet for real estate investing is to purchase residential property. People always need a place to live. Residential housing is easier to understand, purchase, and manage than most other types of property, such as office and retail property. If you're a home owner, you already have experience with locating, purchasing, and keeping up residential property.

Start by reviewing the material in Chapter 9. The common residential housing options are single-family homes, condominiums, and townhouses. There are also multiunit buildings that you can purchase. In addition to the considerations addressed in Chapter 9, from an investment and rental perspective, consider these additional points when deciding what type of property to buy:

- ✔ **Tenants.** Single-family homes, where you need to find just one tenant, are simpler to deal with than a multiunit apartment building where you must find and manage multiple renters, as well as maintain multiple rental units.

- ✔ **Maintenance.** Condominiums are generally the lowest maintenance properties around for individual owners because most condominium associations already deal with issues for the whole building, such as roofing, gardening, and so on. Note that you're still on the hook for maintenance that is needed inside your unit, such as servicing appliances, interior painting, and so on, as well as paying for the cost of the external maintenance. With a single-family home or apartment building, you're responsible for it all. That doesn't mean you have to perform all the work yourself. As a condominium complex typically does, you can hire someone to do the work. But you still have to find the contractors and coordinate and oversee the work.

- ✔ **Appreciation potential.** Although condos may be somewhat easier to keep up, they tend to appreciate less than homes or apartment buildings, unless the condos are located in a desirable urban area.

One way to add value to some larger properties is to "condo-ize" them. In some areas, if zoning allows, you may be able to convert a single-family home or multiunit apartment building into condominiums. Doing so requires significant research, both on the zoning front as well as with estimating remodeling and construction costs.

Also look for property where simple cosmetic and other fixes may allow you to increase rents. Such improvements should increase the market value of the property.

- ✔ **Cash flow.** As I discuss later in the chapter, your rental property brings in rental income that you hope covers and exceeds your expenses. The difference between the rental income you collect and the expenses you pay out is known as your *cash flow*.

What about converting your current home into a rental when you move?

If you're moving into another home, turning your current home into a rental property can make good sense. After all, it saves you the time and cost of finding a separate rental property.

Unfortunately, many people make the mistake of holding onto their current home for the wrong reasons when they buy another. This mistake often happens when home owners are confronted with the prospect of selling their home in a depressed market. Nobody likes to lose money and sell their home for less than they paid for it. Thus, some are tempted to hold onto their home until prices recover.

If you're planning on moving and are motivated to keep your current home as a long-term investment property, by all means do so. But turning your home into a short-term rental is usually a bad move. First, you may not want to be a landlord, yet you're forcing yourself into the landlord business when you convert your home into a rental. Second, if the home does eventually rebound in value, you'll owe tax on the profit if the property is a rental when you sell and don't buy another rental property. (You can defer tax on your profit by purchasing another rental property through a 1031 exchange — see the discussion earlier in this chapter.)

Unless you can afford a large down payment (25 percent or more), the early years of rental property ownership may be financially challenging. It's generally hardest to make a profit in the early years from the monthly cash flow with a single-family home because such properties usually sell at a premium price relative to the rent they can command (you're paying extra for the land, which isn't rentable). Apartment buildings, particularly those with more units, generally can produce a small positive cash flow even in the early years.

With all properties, as time goes on it's easier to generate a positive cash flow as your mortgage debt is paid down and you hopefully can increase your rents.

Unless you really want to minimize maintenance responsibilities, I would avoid condominium investing. Single-family home investing is generally more straightforward for most people. Just make sure you run the numbers (I show you how in the "Cash flow" section later in this chapter) on your rental income and expenses to see if you can afford the negative cash flow that often occurs in the early years of ownership. Apartment building investing is best left to more-sophisticated investors who like a challenge and can manage more-complex properties. As I discuss in the next chapter, make sure that you do thorough inspections before you buy.

Tax credits for low-income housing and old buildings

If you invest in low-income housing or particularly old commercial buildings, you can gain special tax credits. The credits represent a direct reduction in your tax bill because you're spending to rehabilitate and improve such properties. The credits exist to encourage investors to consider investing in and fixing up old or run-down buildings that likely would continue to deteriorate otherwise.

The credits range from as little as 10 percent of the expenditures to as much as 90 percent, depending on the property type. The IRS has strict rules governing what types of properties qualify. Tax credits may be earned for rehabilitating nonresidential buildings built in 1935 or before. *Certified historic structures,* both residential and nonresidential, also qualify for tax credits. See IRS Form 3468 to find out more about these credits.

Land

If tenants are a hassle and maintaining a building a never-ending pain, why not invest in pure, unadulterated land? Simply buy land in an area that will soon experience a building boom. Hold onto it until prices soar and then cash in.

Such an investment idea sounds good in theory. In practice, it's not easy to make the big bucks by investing in land. Although land doesn't require upkeep and tenants, it does require financial feeding. Investing in land is a cash drain. Because it costs money to purchase land, you have a mortgage payment to make. Mortgage lenders charge higher interest rates on loans to purchase land because they see it as a more speculative investment. You also don't get depreciation tax write-offs because land is not depreciable.

If you pay cash, you'll have money tied up in the investment. You'll also have property tax payments to meet as well as other expenses. But you'll have no income from the property to offset these expenses.

If you do someday want to develop the property, that will cost a hefty chunk of money. Obtaining a loan for development is challenging and more expensive than on a developed property.

Identifying, many years in advance, which communities will experience rapid population and job growth is not easy. Land prices in those areas believed to be the next hot spot already sell at a premium price. If growth doesn't meet expectations, appreciation will be low or nonexistent.

If you're going to invest in land, be sure that you

- ✔ **Can afford it.** Tally up what your annual carrying costs will be so that you can see what the annual cash drain will be. What will be the financial consequences of this outflow — for example, will you be able to fully fund your tax-deductible retirement accounts? If you can't, the lost tax benefits are another cost of owning land.

- ✔ **Understand what further improvements the land needs.** Running utility lines, building roads, landscaping, and so on, all cost money. Especially if you're planning on developing and building on the land, research what these things will likely cost. Don't make these estimates with your rose-tinted sunglasses on — improvements almost always cost more than people expect.

- ✔ **Know its zoning status.** The value of land is heavily dependent upon what you can develop on it. Never, ever purchase land without thoroughly understanding how it is zoned and what can and cannot be built on it. Also research what the disposition is of the planning department and communities nearby. Areas that are antigrowth and development are less likely to be good places for you to invest in land.

- ✔ **Are familiar with the local economic and housing situation.** In the best of all worlds, you want to buy land in an area that is home to rapidly expanding companies and that has a shortage of housing and developable land.

Commercial real estate

Ever thought about owning and renting out a small office building or strip mall? If you're really motivated and willing to roll up your sleeves, you might consider such a real estate investment. Generally, you're better off not investing in commercial real estate; it is much more complicated than investing in residential real estate. It's also riskier from an investment and tenant turnover perspective. When tenants move out, new tenants sometimes require extensive and expensive improvements, which you'll likely need to provide to compete with other building owners.

If you are a knowledgeable real estate investor and like a challenge, I think that there are two good reasons to invest in commercial real estate. The first reason is if your analysis of your local market suggests that it's a good time to buy.

Another reason to consider buying commercial real estate is if your own small business might use some of the space. Just as it's generally more cost-effective to own your home rather than rent over the years, so it should be with commercial real estate if — and this is a big if — you buy at a reasonably good time and hold for many years.

So how do you evaluate the state of your local commercial real estate market? You must check out, over a number of years, the supply and demand statistics.

How much space is available for rent, and how has that changed in recent years? What is the vacancy rate, and how has that changed over the years as well? Also, examine the rental rates, usually quoted as a price per square foot.

Warning signs are a market where the supply of available space has increased faster than demand, leading to falling rental rates and higher vacancies. A slowing local economy and higher unemployment rates also spell trouble for commercial real estate prices. Each market is different, so be sure to check out the details of your area. I explain in the next section where to find such information.

Deciding where and what to buy

If you're going to invest in real estate, you can do tons of research to decide where and what to buy. A good real estate broker may be able to help you get your hands on some of the information and data you need. But you must remember that brokers aren't in the education and information provider business — they make their living by selling. (In Chapter 11, I explain how to find a good real estate agent.)

In the sections that follow, I explain what to look for in a community and area to invest in. Keep in mind, though, that as in other aspects of life, you can spend the rest of your life looking for the perfect real estate investment, never find it, never invest, and miss out on lots of opportunities, profit, and even fun.

Economic issues

People need a place to live, but an area doesn't attract people to buy homes if no jobs exist. Ideally, look to invest in real estate in communities that have diverse job bases. If the local economy is heavily reliant on jobs in a small number of industries, that dependence increases the risk of your real estate investments. The U.S. Bureau of Labor Statistics compiles this data for metropolitan areas and counties. A good local library should have this data.

Also, consider which industries are more heavily represented in the local economy. If most of the jobs come from slow-growing or shrinking employment sectors, such as farming, small retail, shoe and apparel manufacturing, and government, real estate prices are unlikely to rise quickly in the years ahead. On the other hand, areas with a greater preponderance of high-growth industries, such as technology, stand a greater chance of faster price appreciation.

Also, check out the unemployment situation and examine how the jobless rate has changed in recent years. Good signs are declining unemployment and increasing job growth. Again, the Bureau of Labor Statistics tracks such data.

I'm not suggesting that you conduct a nationwide search for the best areas. It's best to invest in real estate close to home because you're more familiar with the local area and you'll have an easier time managing local property. If you live in or near a major metropolitan area, you should find some areas that fit the bill.

Real estate market

The price of real estate, like the price of anything else, is driven by supply and demand. The smaller the supply and the greater the demand, the higher prices should spiral. When the supply of housing can easily expand at a very fast rate, prices struggle to rise.

John Reed, a real estate investor and writer, learned this the hard way: "I personally lost all the money I had made in fifteen years of apartment investing as a result of owning apartments in Texas when the overbuilding occurred in the mid-eighties," Reed says.

Ouch! Imagine investing for 15 years and then losing it all! For sure, credit was loose in some areas during the 1980s, which fueled a building boom. But in many parts of Texas, as in some other parts of the country, a ton of buildable land existed. This abundance inevitably leads to overbuilding. When the supply of anything expands at a much faster rate than demand, prices usually fall.

Upward pressure on real estate prices has the potential to be greatest in areas with little buildable land. This characteristic was one of the things that attracted me to real estate in the San Francisco Bay Area when I moved there in the mid-1980s. If you look at a map of this area, you can see that the city of San Francisco and the communities to the south are on a peninsula. The rest of the Bay Area is bounded by ocean and bay inlets and mountains. Eighty-two percent of the land in the greater Bay Area is not even available for development because of state and federal government parks, preserves, and other areas protected from development or impossible to develop. Of the land available for development, about 98 percent of it in San Francisco, and two-thirds of the land in nearby counties, has already been developed.

In the long term, the lack of buildable land in an area can prove to be a problem. Too-high real estate prices may cause employers and employees to relocate to less-expensive areas. If you're looking to invest in real estate in an area with little buildable land and sky-high prices, run the numbers to see if the deal makes economic sense. (I explain how to do this later in this section.)

In addition to buildable land, here are some other important real estate market indicators to give you a sense of the health, or lack thereof, of a particular market:

✔ **Building permits.** The trend in the number of building permits tells you how the supply of real estate properties will soon be changing. A long and sustained rise in permits over several years can indicate that the supply of new property will dampen future price appreciation. Many areas experienced enormous increases in new building during the mid- to late-1980s, right before prices peaked due to excess inventory. Conversely, new building dried up in many areas in the late 1970s and early 1980s as builders and developers were strangled by onerous interest rates.

✔ **Vacancy rates.** As with building permits, low vacancy rates generally bode well for future real estate price appreciation. If few rentals are vacant, that means more competition and demand for existing units. That's a good sign for investors. Conversely, high vacancy rates indicate an excess supply of real estate, which will put downward pressure on rental rates as many landlords compete to attract tenants.

✔ **Listings of property for sale and number of sales.** Just as lots of new buildings being built is bad for future real estate price increases, increasing numbers of listings of properties for sale is generally a problem in the making. As property prices reach high levels, some investors decide it's worth cashing in and investing elsewhere. When the market is flooded with listings, prospective buyers can be choosier, exerting downward pressure on prices. At high prices (relative to the cost of renting), more prospective buyers elect to rent and the number of sales relative to listing drops.

A good sign is a decreasing and low level of listings of property for sale. This lack of listings indicates that the demand from buyers meets or exceeds the supply of property for sale from sellers. When the cost of buying is relatively low compared with the cost of renting, more renters elect and can afford to purchase, thus increasing the number of sales.

✔ **Rents.** The trend in rental rates that renters are willing and able to pay over the years gives a good indication as to the demand for housing. When the demand for housing keeps up with the supply of housing and the local economy continues to grow, rents generally increase. This increase is a positive sign for continued real estate price appreciation.

Property valuation and financial projections

How do you know what a property is really worth? Some say it's worth what a ready, willing, and financially able buyer is willing to pay. But some buyers pay more than what a property is truly worth. And sometimes buyers who are patient, do their homework, and bargain hard are able to buy property for less than its fair market value.

Crunching some numbers to figure what revenue and expenses a rental property will likely bring is one of the most important exercises you can go through when deciding if you should buy a property and how much it's worth. In the sections that follow, I walk you through these important calculations.

Cash flow

Cash flow is the difference between the money that a property brings in minus what you have to pay out for expenses. You should care about this a whole lot! If you pay so much for a property that its expenses (including the mortgage payment and property taxes) consistently exceed its income, you'll have a money drain on your hands. Maybe for the first few years that's okay with you, and you have the financial reserves to withstand the temporary drain. But you should know what you're getting yourself into up front.

One of the biggest mistakes novice rental property investors make is not realizing all the costs associated with investment property. In the worst cases, some investors end up in personal bankruptcy from the drain of *negative cash flow* (expenses exceeding income). In other cases, I've seen the negative cash flow hamper people's ability to accomplish important financial goals.

The second biggest mistake rental property investors make is believing the financial statements that sellers and their brokers prepare. Like an employer views a resumé, you should always view such financial statements as advertisements rather than sources of objective information. In some cases, sellers and agents lie. In most cases, these statements contain lots of projections and best-case scenarios.

Ask for a copy of Schedule E (Supplemental Income and Losses) from the property seller's federal income tax return. Most people, when they complete their tax return, try to minimize their revenue and maximize their expenses — the opposite of what they and their agents normally do on the statements they sometimes compile to hype the property sale. Confidentiality and privacy shouldn't be an issue in your asking for Schedule E because you're just asking for this one schedule and not the person's entire income tax return. (If the seller owns more than one rental property for which financial data is compiled on Schedule E, he can simply black out this other information if he doesn't want you to see it.)

You should and must prepare your own financial statements based on facts and a realistic assessment of a property (see Table 10-1). There's a time and a place for unbridled optimism and positive thinking, such as when you're lost in a major snowstorm. If you think pessimistically, you may not make it out alive! But deciding whether to buy a rental property is not a life or death situation. Take your time and do it with your eyes and ears open and with a healthy degree of skepticism.

The monthly rental property financial statement that you just prepared is for the here and now. Over time, you hope and expect that your rental income will increase faster than the property's expenses, thus increasing the cash flow. If you want, you can use Table 10-1 for future years' projections as well.

Table 10-1	Monthly Rental Property Financial Statement

(Note: If you're purchasing a simple residential rental property, such as a single-family home, some of the following will not apply.)

	$ per month
Rents: Ask for copies of current lease agreements and also check comparable unit rental rates in the local market. Ask if any concessions were made (such as a month or two of free rent), which may make rental rates appear inflated. Make your offer contingent on the rents being accurate.	$ _____
Garage rentals: Some properties come with parking spaces that are rented. As with unit rental income, make sure that you know what the spaces are really renting for.	+$ _____
Laundry income: Dirty laundry isn't just on the evening news — it can make you wealthier! Don't underestimate or neglect to include the cost of maintenance of machines when you figure the expenses of your rental building.	+$ _____
Other income:	$ _____
Vacancy allowance: It's difficult to keep any rental occupied all the time. It may take some time to find a good tenant who is looking for the type of unit(s) you have to offer. Occasional maintenance and refurbishing work may be done in between tenants. Allow for a vacancy rate of 2 to 10 percent of the time (multiply 2 to 10 percent by the rents figured in the first line).	−$ _____
Total income:	=$ _____
Mortgage: See Chapter 9, including Table 9-3, for how to calculate the size of your mortgage payment.	$ _____
Property taxes: Ask a real estate person, mortgage lender, or your local assessor's office what your annual property tax bill would be for a rental property of comparable value to the one you are considering buying. Divide this annual amount by 12 to arrive at your monthly property tax bill.	+$ _____
Utilities: Get copies of utility bills from the current owner. Get bills over the previous 12-month period — a few months won't cut it because utility usage may vary greatly during different times of the year. (In a multiunit building, it's a plus for each unit to have a separate utility meter so that each tenant can be billed for what he/she uses.)	+$ _____
Insurance: Ask for a copy of the current insurance coverage and billing statement from the current owner. If you're considering buying a building in an area that has floods, earthquakes, and so on, make sure that the cost of the policy includes these coverages. Although most catastrophes can be insured against, I would avoid buying in a flood-prone area. Flood insurance does not cover lost rental income.	+$ _____

(continued)

Table 10-1 *(continued)*

Water: Again, ask the current owner for statements documenting the water bills over the past 12 months. + $_____

Garbage: Get the bills from the owner. + $_____

Repairs/maintenance/cleaning: You can ask the current owner what to expect here and check the tax return, but even doing this may provide an inaccurate answer. Some building owners defer maintenance. (A good property inspector can help to ferret out problem areas before you commit to buy a property.) To be on the safe side, estimate that you'll spend about 1 percent of the purchase price per year on maintenance, repairs, and cleaning. Remember to divide by 12! + $_____

Rental advertising/management expenses: Finding good tenants takes time and promotion. If you list your rental through rental brokers, they normally take one month's rent as their cut. Owners of larger buildings sometimes have an on-site manager to show vacant units and deal with maintenance and repairs. Put the monthly pay for that person on this line or the preceding line. If you provide a below-market rental rate for an on-site manager, make sure you factor this into the rental income section. + $_____

Extermination/pest control: Once a year or every few years, you likely need to take care of pest control. Spraying/inspections generally range from $200 for small buildings. + $_____

Legal/accounting and other professional services: Especially with larger rental properties, you'll likely need to consult with lawyers and tax advisors from time to time. + $_____

Total expenses	= $_____
Total income (from preceding page)	$_____
Total expenses (from above)	– $_____
Pretax profit or loss	= $_____

Depreciation: The tax law allows you to claim a yearly tax deduction for depreciation. You can't depreciate land. You break down the purchase of your rental property between the building and land. You can make this allocation based on the assessed value for the land and the building or on a real estate appraisal. Residential property is depreciated over 27½ years (3.64 percent of the building value per year) and nonresidential property is depreciated over 39 years (2.56 percent of the building value per year). For example, if you buy a residential rental property for $300,000 and $200,000 of that is allocated to the building, that means that you can take $7,273 per year as a depreciation tax deduction ($200,000 × .0364). – $_____

Net income	= $_____

Important note: Though depreciation is a deduction that helps you reduce your profit for tax purposes, it doesn't actually cost you money. Your cash flow from a rental property is the revenue minus out-of-pocket expenses.

Deductible rental losses

If your rental property shows a loss for the year (when you figure your property's income and expenses on Schedule E), you may be able to deduct this loss on your tax return. If your modified adjusted gross income (AGI) is less than $100,000 and you actively participate in managing the property, you are allowed to deduct your losses on operating rental real estate — up to $25,000 per year. Limited partnerships and properties in which you own less than 10 percent are excluded. (If you really *must* know, your modified AGI is your AGI from line 31 of Form 1040 minus the taxable portion of Social Security [line 20b] and passive activity income [line 17] plus your IRA deductions [lines 23a and b], one-half of self-employment tax [line 25], passive activity losses [line 17], and interest on Form 8815.)

In order to deduct a rental property operating loss on your tax return, you must actively participate in the management of the property. This rule doesn't necessarily mean that you have to perform the day-to-day management of the property. In fact, you can hire a property manager and still actively participate by doing such simple things as approving the terms of the lease contracts, tenants, and expenditures for maintenance and improvements on the building.

If you make more than $100,000 per year (single or married), you start to lose these write-offs. If your income exceeds $100,000, the $25,000 limit is reduced by 50 cents for every dollar of income over $100,000. When your income reaches $150,000, the $25,000 allowance is completely phased out. People in the real estate business (for example, agents and developers) who work more than 750 hours per year in the industry may not be subject to these rules.

Valuing property

Examining and estimating a property's cash flow is an important first step to deciding what a property is ultimately worth. But on its own, that step does not provide enough information to decide intelligently whether to buy a particular real estate rental property. Just because a property has a positive cash flow doesn't mean that you should buy it. Real estate generally sells for less, and therefore has better cash flow, in areas that investors expect to earn lower rates of appreciation.

In the stock market, you have more clues as to what a specific security is worth. Most companies' stocks trade on a daily basis, so you at least have a recent sales price to start with. Of course, just because a stock recently traded at $20 per share doesn't mean that it's worth $20 per share. Investors may be overly optimistic or pessimistic.

Just as you should compare a stock to other comparable stocks, so too should you compare the value of real estate with other comparable real estate. But what if all real estate is overvalued — such a comparison doesn't necessarily reveal the state of inflated prices. In addition to comparing a real estate investment property to comparable properties, you should also do some global evaluation of whether prices from a historic perspective appear too high, too low, or just right. To answer this last question, see "Is this a good or bad time to buy?," in Chapter 9.

To value a piece of property, you can try one of three approaches. You can hire an appraiser, enlist the help of a real estate agent, or crunch the numbers yourself. These approaches are not mutually exclusive — you probably want to at least review the numbers and analysis that an appraiser or real estate agent puts together. Here are the pros and cons of the different approaches:

✓ **Appraisers.** The biggest advantage of hiring an appraiser is that he or she values property for a living. An appraisal also gives you some hard numbers to use for negotiating with a seller. Make sure that you hire an appraiser who works at it full-time and has experience valuing the type of property you're considering. Ask for examples of a dozen similar properties that he/she has appraised in the past three months in the area.

The drawback of appraisers is that they cost money. A small home may cost a couple hundred dollars to appraise and a larger multiunit building $1,000 or more. The danger is that you spend money on an appraisal for a building you don't end up buying.

✓ **Real estate agents.** If you're working with a good real estate agent (I discuss how to find one in the next chapter), he or she should be able to draw up a list of comparable properties and help you estimate the value of a property you're considering buying. The advantage of having your agent help with this analysis is that you don't pay extra for this service.

The drawback of asking an agent what to pay for a property is that his/her commission depends on your buying a property and the amount you pay. The more you're willing to pay for a property, the more likely the deal will fly and the more the agent will make. Beware of pushy agents who impatiently advocate quickly buying or offering a high price for a property.

✓ **Do-it-yourself.** If you're comfortable with numbers and analysis, you can try to estimate the value of the property yourself. The hard part is identifying comparable properties. It's usually impossible to find identical properties, so you'll need to find similar properties and then make adjustments to their selling price so that you can do an apples-to-apples comparison.

Among the factors that should influence your analysis of comparable properties are the date they sold; the quality of their location; lot size; building age and condition; the number of units; the number of rooms, bedrooms, and bathrooms; garages; fireplaces; and yard. A real estate agent should be able to provide this information, or you can track it down for properties that you've seen or that you know have recently sold.

For example, if a similar property sold six months ago for $250,000 but prices overall have declined 5 percent in the last six months, subtract 5 percent from the sales price. Ultimately, you have to attach a value or price to differences between comparable properties and the one you're considering buying. Through a series of adjustments, you can compare the value of your target property to others that have recently sold.

Information sources

When you're trying to evaluate properties, you need to put on your detective hat. If you're creative and inquisitive, you'll soon realize that this isn't a hard game to play. You can collect useful information about a property and the area in which it is located in lots of ways.

The first place to begin your inquiries is with the real estate agent listing the property for sale. One thing that most agents love to do is talk and schmooze. Try to understand why the seller is selling. This knowledge helps you to structure an offer that's appealing to the seller and makes the best use of your dollars and other bargaining chips.

As for specifics on the property's financial situation, as I explain earlier in this chapter, ask the sellers for specific independent documents, including Schedule E from their tax return. Hire inspectors (explained in Chapter 11) to investigate the property's physical condition.

Local government organizations have treasure troves of details about their communities. See also the other recommended sources in Chapter 9, as well as some other sources I recommend earlier in this chapter.

The wisdom of buying in the "best" areas

Some people, particularly those in the real estate business, say, "Buy real estate in the best school districts." Or, "Buy the worst home in the best neighborhood." Conventional wisdom is often wrong, and this is yet another case.

Remember that as a real estate investor, you hope to profit from being able to sell your properties, many years in the future, for a much higher price than you purchased them. If you buy into the "best," there's not much upside.

Take school districts. Conventional wisdom says that you should look at the test scores of different districts and buy real estate in the best (that is, highest score) districts. But odds are that real estate in those areas is probably already priced at a premium level. If things deteriorate, such an area might experience more downside than an area where property buyers haven't bid prices up into the stratosphere.

The biggest appreciation often comes from those areas and properties that benefit the most from improvement. Identifying these in advance isn't easy, but look for communities where the trend in recent years has been positive. Even many average areas do better in terms of property value appreciation than today's best areas.

Getting a good buy

Everyone likes to get a deal or feel like they bought something at a really good price. How else can you explain the American retail practice of sales? Merchandise is overpriced so that it can then be marked down to create the illusion that you're getting a bargain. Some real estate sellers and agents do the same thing. They list property for sale at an inflated price and then mark it down after they realize that no one will pay the freight. "$30,000 price reduction!" the new listing screams. Of course, this reduction isn't a deal.

It is possible to purchase a piece of real estate at a discount to what it's really worth. Without doing a lick of work, that means you've made money — one of the ultimate thrills of being a capitalist!

Scores of books claim to have the real estate investing strategy to beat the system. Often these promoters claim that you can become a millionaire or multimillionaire through investing in some sort of distressed property. A common strategy is to purchase property that a seller has defaulted on or is about to default on. Or how about buying a property in someone's estate through probate court? Maybe you'd like to try your hand at investing in a property that has been condemned or has toxic waste contamination!

It is possible to get a good buy and purchase a problem property at a discount larger than the cost of fixing the property. However, these opportunities are hard to find, and sellers of such properties are often unwilling to sell at a big enough discount to leave you much room to profit. If you don't know how to thoroughly and correctly evaluate the problems of the property, you can end up overpaying.

In some cases, the strategies these real estate gurus advocate involve taking advantage of people's lack of knowledge. For example, some people don't know that they can protect the equity in their home through filing personal bankruptcy. If you can find a seller in such dire financial straits, and desperate for cash, you may be able to get a bargain buy on the home. (You may or may not struggle with the moral issues of buying property on the cheap this way, but that's one of the not-so-ultimate thrills of being a capitalist.)

Other methods take lots of time and digging. Some involve cold-calling property owners to see if they are interested in selling. This method is a little bit like trying to fill a job opening by interviewing people you run into on a street corner. Although you may eventually find a good candidate this way, if you factor in the value of your time, deals turn from bargains to a pig in a poke.

Without making things complicated or too risky, you can use some of the following time-tested and proven ways to buy real estate at a discount to its fair market value:

✔ **Find a motivated seller.** Be patient and look at lots of properties, and sooner or later you'll come across one that a seller needs to sell. Perhaps the seller has bought another property and needs the money out of the other one to close on the recent purchase. Having access to sufficient financing lined up can help secure such deals.

✔ **Buy unwanted properties with fixable flaws.** The easiest problems to correct are cosmetic. Some sellers and their agents are lazy and don't even bother to clean a property. One single-family home that I bought had probably three years' worth of cobwebs and dust accumulated. It seemed like a dungeon at night because half the light bulbs were burned out.

Painting, tearing up old, ugly carpeting, refinishing hardwood floors, and putting in new plantings in a yard are relatively easy-to-fix problems. It makes the property worth more and makes renters willing to pay higher rents. Of course, these things take money and time, but many buyers aren't interested in dealing with it. If you have an eye for improving property and are willing to invest the time required to coordinate the fix-up work, go for it! Just make sure to hire someone to conduct a thorough property inspection (see the next chapter for more details).

Be sure to factor in the loss in rental income if you can't rent a portion of the property during the period of fix-up. Many investors have gone belly-up from the double cash drain of fix-up expenses and lost rents.

✔ **Buy when the real estate market (and other investors) are depressed.** When the economy has taken a few knocks and investors have rushed for the exits, it's time to wheel out your shopping cart of cash. Buy when prices and investor interest are down. During depressed markets, it's easier to obtain properties that produce a positive cash flow even in the early years. In Chapter 9, I explain how to spot a depressed market.

✔ **Check for zoning opportunities.** Sometimes, you may be able to make more productive use of a property. For example, some multiunit apartment buildings may legally be converted into condominiums. Some single-family residences may have a rental unit if local zoning allows for it. A good real estate agent, contractor, and the local planning office in the town or city where you're looking at property should be able to help you identify properties that you can change how they're being used. If you're not a proponent of development, then you're probably not going to like this strategy.

If you buy good real estate and hold it for the long term, you should earn a decent return from your investment. Over the long haul, having bought a property at a discount becomes an insignificant issue. You make money from your real estate investments as the market appreciates and your ability to manage your property well.

Crummy Real Estate "Investments"

You can invest in real estate in a number of different ways. Some rarely make sense because they're near-certain money losers. Others may work for you depending on what you're looking for.

Second/vacation homes are not investments

A sometimes idyllic notion and expanded part of the American dream is the weekend cottage or condo — a place you can retreat to when crowded urban or suburban living conditions get on your nerves. When it's not in use, you may be able to rent out your vacation home and earn some income to help defray part of the expenses of keeping it up.

If you can realistically afford the additional costs of a second, or vacation, home, I'm not going to tell you how to spend your extra cash. Investment real estate is property that you rent out 90 percent or more of the time. Most second-home owners I know rent their property out very little — 10 percent or less of the time. As a result, second homes are usually money drains. Even if you do rent it most of the time, lots of tenant turnover decreases your net rental income.

Part of the allure of a second home is the supposed tax benefits. Even when you qualify for some or all of them, tax benefits only partially reduce the cost of owning a property. I've seen more than a few cases in which the second home is such a cash drain that it prevents its owners from contributing to and taking advantage of tax-deductible retirement savings plans.

If you don't rent out a second home property most of the time, ask yourself whether you can afford such a luxury. Can you accomplish your other financial goals — saving for retirement, paying for the home in which you live, and so on — with this added expense? Keeping a second home is more of a consumption than an investment decision.

Time shares

Time shares are a near-certain money loser. With a time share, you buy a week or two of ownership, or usage, of a particular unit, usually a condominium, in a resort location. If you pay $8,000 for a week of "ownership" (in addition to ongoing maintenance fees, which can easily run $200 per year or more), you're paying the equivalent of more than $400,000 for the whole unit ($8,000/week × 52 weeks), but a comparable unit nearby may sell for only $150,000. All the extra markup pays the salespeople's commissions, administrative expenses, and profits for the time share development company.

People usually get hoodwinked into buying a time share when they're enjoying a vacation someplace. They're easy prey for salespeople who, often using high pressure sales tactics, want to sell them a souvenir of the trip. The cheese in the mousetrap is an offer of something free (for example, a free night's stay in a unit) for going through the sales presentation.

The time share concept, unfortunately, was imported into the U.S. in the early 1970s and has stuck ever since. Even large and otherwise reputable companies, such as Disney, Marriott, and Hilton, have gotten into this business in recent years. It's a good business for them — selling lousy time share investments to the public — but now you won't be one more of their victims!

If you can't live without a time share, consider buying a used one. Many previous buyers, who almost always have lost a lot of their original investment, are trying to dump their time shares. This fact should tell you something. You may be able to buy a time share from an existing owner at a fair price. But why commit yourself to taking a vacation in the same location and building at the same time each year? Many time shares let you trade your weeks; however, doing so is a hassle, and you're limited by what you can trade for, which are typically time slots that other people don't want. Most of these are undesirable — that's why they're trading them!

Limited partnerships

In Chapter 1, I give good reasons to avoid limited partnerships. Limited partnerships sold through stockbrokers and financial planners who work on commission are burdened by high sales commissions and ongoing management fees. Good real estate investment trusts, discussed earlier in this chapter, are infinitely better alternatives. REITs, unlike limited partnerships, also have the virtue of being completely liquid.

More scams

It's bad enough to invest in investments where the deck is stacked against you. Even worse is to put your money into such an investment that's a scam. First Pension was an outfit run by loan broker William Cooper that bilked investors out of more than $100 million. First Pension was sold as a limited partnership that invested in mortgages. Using a Ponzi-type (pyramid) scheme, Cooper used the money from new investors to pay dividends to earlier investors.

Another way that some investors invest in real estate is to invest in second mortgages. The allure of lending your money to a property buyer is the double-digit returns. As I discuss in Chapter 7, the only way to charge interest rates of 10 percent or higher is to lend your money to higher-risk borrowers.

Even worse than the high risk that comes with higher interest rates is the problem that some second mortgage investments are hypes and scams. Liz Pulliam reported in the *Orange County Register* that Irvine Mortgage Corporation promised second mortgage investors 14 percent returns by investing in properties with at least 30 percent equity. It also boasted no investor losses over 25 years.

When the real estate market softened in California in the early 1990s, some of these second mortgages defaulted. Investors, many of whom placed their retirement dollars with the Irvine mortgage company, later discovered that some of the properties that they had lent money on never had their mortgage recorded against it. These properties ended up in default.

Time shares, a truly terrible investment discussed in this section, also have been subject to bankruptcy and problems of fraud as well.

Chapter 11

Real Estate Dilemmas and Decisions

· ·

· ·

*I*n Chapter 9, I cover what you need to know to purchase a home, and in Chapter 10, I review the fundamentals of investing in real estate. In this chapter, I discuss issues such as understanding and selecting mortgages, working with real estate agents, negotiating, and other important details, that help you actually put a real estate deal together. And I provide some words of wisdom about taxes and selling that may come in handy down the road.

Financing 101

Unless you're affluent or buying a low-cost property, you likely need to borrow some money to finance your property acquisition. *Mortgages,* which are the loans to finance the purchase of real estate, are important. If you can't line up financing, your deal may fall apart. If you don't shop correctly for a good loan, it can end up costing you thousands, perhaps even tens of thousands, of dollars in extra interest and fees. Even worse, you can be saddled with a loan that you someday can't afford, and you may end up in bankruptcy.

There are two major types of mortgages: those with a fixed interest rate and those with an adjustable rate (known as ARMs for adjustable-rate mortgages). When you buy real estate, you have to choose the one that best fits your needs. Your choice depends on your financial situation, how much risk you're willing to accept, and what type of property you're purchasing. It's harder, for example, to obtain fixed-rate loans on properties that lenders perceive to be riskier investments.

Fixed-rate mortgages

Fixed-rate mortgages, which are typically for a 15- or 30-year term, have interest rates that stay fixed or level. With a fixed-rate mortgage, you lock in an interest rate that doesn't change over the life of your loan. Because the interest rate stays the same, your monthly mortgage payment stays the same. You have nothing complicated to track and no uncertainty. Fixed-rate loans give people peace of mind and payment stability.

Fixed-rate loans are not without risks, however. If interest rates fall significantly after you obtain your mortgage, you face the danger of being stuck with your higher-cost mortgage if you're unable to refinance. This scenario may happen, for example, if your financial situation worsens (for example, you lose your job) or the value of your property decreases. Even if you are able to refinance, you'll probably have to spend a good amount of time and money to complete it.

Adjustable-rate mortgages (ARMs)

In contrast to a fixed-rate mortgage, an adjustable-rate mortgage (ARM) carries an interest rate that varies. You can start with one interest rate this year and have different ones for every year, possibly even every month, during a 30-year mortgage. Thus the size of your monthly payment fluctuates. Because a mortgage payment makes an unusually large dent in most property owners' checkbooks, signing up for an adjustable without understanding its risks is crazy, if not dangerous.

The advantage of an adjustable-rate mortgage is that if you purchase your property during a period of relatively high interest rates, you can start paying your mortgage with an artificially depressed initial interest rate. And if interest rates decline, you can capture much of the benefits of lower rates, without the cost and hassle of refinancing. (A decline in interest rates may make it desirable to refinance an adjustable-rate loan too, as I discuss later in the chapter.)

Choosing between a fixed-rate or adjustable-rate mortgage

Choosing between a fixed-rate or adjustable-rate loan is an important decision in the real estate buying process. You should weigh the pros and cons of each mortgage type and decide what's best for your situation *before* you go out to purchase real estate (or refinance).

In the real world, most people ignore this advice. The excitement of purchasing a home or other piece of real estate tends to cloud judgment. My experience has been that few people look at their entire financial picture before making major real estate decisions.

Balloon loans

Balloon loans generally start the way traditional fixed-rate mortgages start. You make level payments based on a long-term payment schedule, over 15 or 30 years, for example. But at a predetermined time, usually three to ten years from the loan's inception, the remaining loan balance becomes fully due.

Balloon loans may save you money because they have a lower interest rate than a longer-term fixed-rate mortgage. Sometimes, balloon loans may be the only option for the buyer (or so the buyer thinks). Buyers are more commonly backed into these loans during periods of high interest rates. When a buyer can't afford the payments on a conventional mortgage and really wants a particular property, a seller may offer a balloon loan.

Balloon loans are dangerous and can literally blow up on you, financially speaking, that is. Your financial situation can change, and you may not

be able to refinance when your balloon loan comes due. What if you lose your job, or your income drops? What if the value of your property drops, and the appraisal comes in too low to qualify you for a new loan? What if interest rates rise, and you can't qualify at the higher rate on a new loan?

I recommend avoiding balloon loans. You should take such a loan if, and only if, such a loan is your only financing option, you've really done your homework to exhaust other financing options, and you're certain that you'll be able to refinance when the balloon comes due. If you take a balloon loan, get one with as much time as possible, preferably seven to ten years, before it becomes due. Don't get suckered into a balloon loan because you fall in love with a place and you just have to buy it. Remember: You can buy other properties at other times.

Unfortunately, too many real estate buyers try to let their interest rate crystal ball dictate whether they should take an adjustable- or fixed-rate mortgage. For example, people who think interest rates have nowhere to go but up are attracted to a fixed-rate mortgage.

You can't predict the future course of interest rates. It's not that I don't think you're smart, it's simply that even the professional financial market soothsayers and investors can't predict where rates are heading. If you could, you could make a fortune investing in bonds and interest-rate futures and options.

So cast aside your crystal ball and ask yourself these two vital questions to help decide whether a fixed or adjustable mortgage will work best for you.

How comfortable are you with taking risk?

How much of a gamble can you take with the size of your monthly mortgage payment? For example, if your job and income are unstable and you need to borrow an amount that stretches your monthly budget, you can't afford much risk. If you're in this situation, stick with fixed-rate mortgages.

Too many people take adjustables when they can't really afford them. Those who can afford adjustables can save money. But sooner or later, interest rates go up, and sometimes they go up a lot. When they do, property owners who can't really afford much higher payments face a financial crisis. If you don't have emergency savings that you can tap into to make the higher payments, how can you afford the monthly payments — much less all the other expenses of real estate ownership?

If you can't afford the highest allowed payment on an adjustable-rate mortgage, you have no business taking one. You shouldn't take the chance that the rate may not rise that high — it can, and you could lose the property. Ask your lender to calculate the highest possible monthly payment allowed on your loan. That's the payment you would face if the interest rate on your loan went to the highest level allowed, or the *lifetime cap*.

An adjustable-rate mortgage places most of the risk of fluctuating interest rates on you. Almost all adjustables limit, or *cap,* the rise in the interest rate allowed on your loan. Typical caps are 2 percent per year and 6 percent over the life of the loan.

In addition to being financially able to afford an adjustable loan, what about dealing with it psychologically? If you feel the need to be constantly checking interest rates, it's probably not worth gambling on rates. Another potential risk factor is your personal life. Are you planning to start a family soon? Your income may fall when you or your spouse take a leave from, or reduce your work at, your job(s). With children, your expenses will surely rise. An adjustable may not work for you in this case.

If you are in a position to take the financial risks that come with an adjustable-rate mortgage, you have a better chance of saving money with an adjustable than with a fixed-rate loan. Your interest rate starts lower and stays lower if the overall level of interest rates stays unchanged. Even if rates go up, they will probably come back down over the life of your loan. So if you can stick with your adjustable for better and for worse, you probably will come out ahead in the long run.

Adjustables make more sense if you borrow less than you're qualified for. Or perhaps you're able to save a sizable chunk — more than 10 percent — of your monthly income. Maybe you're certain that your income is destined to soar to the moon. If your income significantly exceeds your spending patterns, you'll feel less anxiety about fluctuating interest rates. If you do choose an adjustable loan, you may feel more financially secure if you have a hefty financial cushion (at least six months' to as much as a year's worth of expenses reserved) that is accessible if rates go up.

Consider an adjustable-rate mortgage only if you're financially secure enough to handle the maximum possible payments over an extended period of time. You must also be emotionally secure to handle volatile rates. Don't take an adjustable mortgage because the initially lower interest rates allow you to afford the property you want to buy (unless you're absolutely certain that your income will rise to meet future payment increases). Try setting your sights on a property that you can afford to buy with a fixed-rate mortgage.

How many years do you expect to stay put?

Saving interest on most adjustables is usually a certainty in the first two or three years. An adjustable-rate mortgage starts at a lower interest rate than a fixed one. If rates rise, you can end up giving back or losing the savings you achieve in the early years of the mortgage. (When the adjustable mortgage does adjust, it should be limited or capped in the amount of each interest rate change.)

If you aren't going to keep your mortgage more than five to seven years, you'll probably end up paying more interest to carry a fixed-rate mortgage. A mortgage lender takes extra risk in committing to a fixed-interest rate for 15 to 30 years. Lenders often don't know any better than you about what may happen in the intervening years, so they charge you a premium in case interest rates move much higher in future years. If you're pretty sure that you'll hang onto a property or need to refinance in less than five years, you should come out ahead with an adjustable.

Short- versus long-term mortgages

Most mortgage lenders offer you the option of 15-year or 30-year mortgages. You can also have 20-year and 40-year options, but these are unusual. No matter, these choices raise another important question: Should you opt for a shorter- or longer-term mortgage?

To afford the monthly payments, many first-time property buyers need to spread their mortgage loan payments over a longer period of time, and a 30-year mortgage is the way to do it. Investment property buyers who can't handle negative cash flow (see Chapter 10) also are attracted to the lower payments on a 30-year mortgage.

A 15-year mortgage has higher monthly payments because you pay it off quicker. At a fixed-rate mortgage interest rate of 7 percent, for example, a 15-year mortgage comes with payments that are about 35 percent higher than those for a 30-year mortgage.

Don't consider a 15-year mortgage unless you can afford the higher payments that come with it. But even if you can afford these higher payments, it's not necessarily better to take the 15-year option. The money for making extra payments doesn't come out of thin air. You may have better uses for your excess funds.

If you choose a 30-year mortgage, you maintain the flexibility to pay it off faster if you want (except in those rare cases where there is a prepayment penalty). If you choose to make larger-than-necessary payments, you can create your own 15-year mortgage. However, you can fall back to making only the payments required on your 30-year schedule when the need arises.

You may be at risk if you lock yourself into higher monthly payments with a 15-year mortgage. If money gets too tight in the future, you can fall behind in your mortgage payments. You *may* be able to refinance your way out of the predicament, but you can't count on it. If your finances worsen or your property declines in value, odds are you'll have trouble qualifying for a refinance.

Suppose that you can qualify for a 15-year mortgage, and you're financially comfortable with the higher payments. The appeal of paying off your mortgage 15 years sooner is enticing. Besides, the interest rate is lower on a 15-year mortgage. So if you can afford the higher payments on the 15-year mortgage, you'd be a dummy not to take it, right?

It's not that simple.

Whether a shorter-term mortgage with its faster payback works for you depends on your situation and other financial options. First, think about what other productive uses you may have for the extra money you're considering throwing into the mortgage payments. If you would end up blowing the extra money, take the shorter-term mortgage. That's a no-brainer.

The penalties of paying off your mortgage faster if you have kids

If you have children who will someday go off to college, you have an even greater reason to fund your retirement accounts before you consider paying down your mortgage quickly. Under current rules for determining financial aid for college expenses, money in your retirement accounts is not counted as an asset.

Equity in your home (the difference between its market value and your loan balance) is still counted by many schools as an asset. When you pay down your mortgage balance faster, you're building more equity in your home. On paper, you appear wealthier to the financial aid folks than when you save the money in a retirement account. In other words, your reward for paying down your mortgage balance will likely be less financial aid!

Paying down your mortgage faster, especially when you have children, is rarely a good financial decision when you haven't exhausted contributions to retirement accounts. Save first in retirement accounts and get the tax benefits.

But suppose that you did something more mature with the money and contributed it to a retirement account. That step may make better financial sense because money you funnel into 401(k)s, SEP-IRAs, Keoghs, and other types of retirement accounts (see Chapter 3) is tax-deductible.

Suppose that you have an extra $300 per month. If you put that $300 into a retirement account, you get to subtract that $300 from the income on which you pay taxes. If you're paying a moderate 35 percent in federal and state income taxes, you shave $105 per month (that's $300 multiplied by 35 percent) off your tax bill. (You're going to pay taxes when you withdraw the money from the retirement account someday. In the meantime, you've got the money that would have gone to taxes growing on your behalf.) If instead you add $300 to your mortgage payment to pay off your mortgage faster, you get zero tax benefits.

If the investments in your retirement account plummet in value, then the impact of the tax-deferred compounding of your capital may be negated. Paying down the mortgage, on the other hand, is like investing your money in a sure thing — but with a modest rate of return.

It's true that in most cases you get to deduct your mortgage interest on your tax return. So if you're paying 7.5 percent interest, it really may only cost you around 5 percent after you factor in the tax benefits. If you think you can do better by investing elsewhere, go for it. As I discuss in Chapter 2, investments such as stocks and real estate have generated better returns over the long haul. These investments carry risk, though, and are not guaranteed to produce such returns.

If you're uncomfortable investing and would otherwise leave the extra money sitting in a money market fund or savings account, you're better off paying down the mortgage. If you have extra cash and have contributed the maximum allowed for retirement accounts, you may want to invest in real estate or a business. You have to decide whether it is worth the extra risk to make that particular investment instead of paying less interest on your mortgage.

Prepayment penalties

Avoid loans with prepayment penalties. You pay this charge, usually 2 to 3 percent of the loan amount, when you pay off your loan before you're supposed to. Normally, prepayment penalties don't apply if you pay off a loan because you sell the property. But when you refinance a loan with prepayment penalties, you have to pay the penalty. If interest rates drop, your hands will be tied financially to take advantage of the lower rates.

The only way to know whether a loan has a prepayment penalty is to ask.

Getting a great fixed-rate mortgage

If you think a fixed-rate mortgage suits your needs, you'll be relieved to hear that comparing them is much easier than shopping for an adjustable loan. However, the many different lenders in a given market try to differentiate themselves (and confuse borrowers) with myriad fees and other terms on their fixed-rate mortgage offerings.

The all-important interest rate

The interest rate on a fixed-rate loan is the rate that you're paying month in and month out, year in and year out, for borrowing the money. As of this writing, fixed-rate loans can be found for around 7 percent. You may think that comparing one fixed-rate loan to another, then, is quite simple. As with your golf score and the number of times your boss catches you showing up late for work, a lower number (interest rate) is better, right?

Unfortunately, banks generally charge an up-front chunk of interest, known as *points,* in addition to the ongoing interest over the life of the loan. The interest rate on a fixed-rate loan must always be quoted with the points on the loan. If one lender offers 30-year mortgages at 6.75 percent and another lender offers them at 7 percent, the 6.75-percent loan is not necessarily better. You also need to know how many points each lender charges.

Points are up-front fees paid by you to the lender when you close on the mortgage loan. Points are actually percentages: One point is equal to 1 percent of the loan amount. So when a lender tells you a quoted loan has 1.5 points, you pay 1.5 percent of the amount you borrow as points. On a $100,000 loan, for example, 1.5 points cost you $1,500.

If you are willing to pay more points on a given loan, the lender should reduce the interest rate. If you want to pay fewer points, your interest rate increases.

You may want to take a higher interest rate on your mortgage if you don't have enough cash to pay a lot of points, which are paid up front when you close the loan. On the other hand, if you're willing and able to pay more points, you can lower your interest rate. You may want to do so because the interest rate on your loan determines your payments over a long, long time — 15 to 30 years.

Suppose one lender quotes you a rate of 6.75 percent on a 30-year fixed-rate loan and charges one point (1 percent). Another lender, which quotes 7 percent, doesn't charge any points. Which is better? The answer depends on how long you plan to keep the loan.

The 6.75-percent loan is 0.25 percent less than the 7-percent loan. But because you have to pay 1 percent (one point) up front on the 6.75-percent loan, it takes you about four years to earn back the savings to cover the cost of that point. So if you expect to keep the loan more than four years, go with the 6.75 percent option.

No-point loans are no free lunch

Never, ever forget that if a loan has no points, it's sure to have a higher interest rate. That's not to say that it's better or worse than comparable loans from other lenders. But don't get sucked in by a no-points sales pitch. Many lenders who spend big bucks on advertising these types of loans rarely have the best mortgage terms.

All things being equal, no-point loans make more sense for refinances because points aren't immediately tax-deductible as they are on

purchases (you can deduct the points you pay on a refinance *only* over the life of the mortgage). On a mortgage for a property that you're purchasing, a no-point loan may help if you are cash poor at closing.

Consider a no-point loan if you can't afford more out-of-pocket expenditures now or if you think that you'll only keep the loan a few years. Make sure to shop around and compare different lenders' no-point loans.

To make it easier to perform an apples-to-apples comparison of mortgages from different lenders, get interest rate quotes at the same point level. For example, ask each lender for the interest rate on a loan for which you pay one point.

Hooking the Hoover Deluxe to your wallet — other fees

In addition to points and the ongoing interest rate, lenders tack on all sorts of other up-front charges in processing your loan. Get an itemization of these other fees and charges in writing from all lenders you are seriously considering. You need to know the total of all lender fees so that you can accurately compare different lenders' loans and so that you can determine how much closing on your loan will cost you.

These other fees can pile up in a hurry. Here are the common ones you'll see:

- **Application and processing fees.** Most lenders charge a couple hundred dollars to work with you to complete your paperwork and funnel it through their loan evaluation process. The justification for this fee is that if your loan is rejected, or if it is approved and you decide not to take it, the lender needs to cover its costs. Some lenders return this fee to you upon closing when you go with their loan.

- **Credit report.** Most lenders charge a fee to pay for the cost of obtaining a copy of your credit report. This report tells the lender whether you've been naughty or nice to other lenders in the past. If you have problems on your credit report, get them cleaned up before you apply for a mortgage. Your credit report fee should cost no more than $50.

✔ **Appraisal.** The property for which you are borrowing money needs to be valued. If you default on your mortgage, a lender doesn't want to get stuck with a property worth less than you owe. The cost is typically several hundred dollars for most residential properties to as much as $1,000 or more for larger investment properties.

Some lenders offer loans without points or other lender charges. Remember: Lenders aren't charities. If they don't charge points or other fees, they have to make up the difference by charging a higher interest rate on your loan. Such loans may make sense for you when you lack the cash to close a loan or when you're planning to hold onto the loan for just a few years.

To minimize your chances of throwing money away on a loan for which you may not qualify, ask the lender whether you may not be approved for some reason. Be sure to disclose any problems on your credit report or problems with the property that you are aware of. Don't expect them to run through a list of qualities on which they don't like taking risks. Lenders may not take the time to ask about these sorts of things in their haste to get you to complete their loan applications.

Finding a great adjustable-rate mortgage

If you're comfortable with the ups and downs that come with an adjustable-rate mortgage, you've got to understand more to compare them with one another than with a fixed-rate loan. Adjustables come with many more features and options that I'll soon explain — *caps, indexes, margins,* and *adjustment periods* — that aren't issues with fixed-rate loans.

Selecting an adjustable-rate mortgage has a lot in common with selecting a home to buy. You have to make trade-offs and compromises. And you can't make them until you prioritize what's important to you.

The start (teaser) rate

Just as the name implies, this interest rate is the one that your mortgage begins with. Don't judge a loan by this rate alone. You won't be paying this attractively low rate for long. You can be absolutely certain that the interest rate rises as soon as the terms of the mortgage allow.

Think of the start rate as a teaser or seducing rate. This term implies that the initial rate on your loan is set artificially low to entice you. In other words, even if the market level of interest rates doesn't change, your adjustable is destined to increase. An increase of one or two percentage points is common.

Start rates are probably one of the least important items to focus on when comparing adjustables. You'd never know this from the way lenders advertise adjustables — you see ads with the start rate in gargantuan bold type and everything else in microscopic footnotes! The formula for determining the future interest rates on an adjustable and rate caps are far more important in determining what a mortgage is going to cost you in the long run.

Future interest rates

The formula for determining the future interest rates on an adjustable should be the first thing that a mortgage lender or broker tells you about. More likely, though, he or she teases you with a low initial interest rate. You want to know exactly how a lender figures how much your interest rate increases. All adjustables are based on the following formula, which specifies how the interest rate is set on your loan in the future:

$$Index + Margin = Interest Rate$$

The *index* measures the overall level of interest rates that the lender chooses to calculate the specific interest rate on your loan. Indexes are generally (but not always) widely quoted in the financial press. For example, the six-month treasury bill rate is an index used on some mortgages. As of this writing, the going rate on six-month treasuries is approximately 5 percent. The *margin* is the amount added to the index to determine the interest rate you pay on your mortgage. Most loans have margins of around 2.5 percent. For example, the rate of a mortgage, driven by the following formula,

$$Six-month treasury bill rate + 2.5 percent$$

Common indexes for adjustable-rate mortgages

The number of different indexes varies mainly in how rapidly they respond to changes in interest rates. *Treasury bills (T-bills)* are issued by the U.S. government. Because they are government IOUs, a whole lot of them are out there. Most adjustables are tied to the interest rate on 6-month or 12-month T-bills.

Certificates of deposit (CDs) are interest-bearing bank investments that lock you in for a specific period of time. Adjustable-rate mortgages are usually tied to the average interest rate banks are paying on six-month CDs. Like T-bills, CDs tend to respond quickly to changes in the market level of interest rates. Unlike T-bills, CD rates tend to move up a bit more slowly when rates rise and come down faster when rates decline.

The *11th district cost of funds (cost of funds)* index tends to be among the slower-moving indexes. (Although you probably don't want to know what or where the 11th district is — and you definitely don't *need* to know — it's in the Western region of the U.S.) Adjustable-rate mortgages tied to 11th district cost of funds tend to start out at a higher interest rate. A slower-moving index has the advantage of moving up less quickly when rates are on the rise. On the other hand, you have to be patient to benefit from falling interest rates.

is set at the going rate for six-month treasuries plus 2.5 percent. So when six-month treasuries are yielding 5 percent, the interest rate on your loan should be 7.5 percent. This figure is known as the *fully indexed rate*. If this loan starts out at 5 percent, you know that if the rate on six-month treasuries stays the same, your loan should eventually increase to 7.5 percent.

Mortgage lenders and brokers often push the wrong index at the wrong time (for you)

"Beware! Your mortgage payment is going up!"

So go some of the many solicitations that will surely fill your mailbox during a period of rising interest rates if you hold an adjustable-rate mortgage, especially one that has an interest rate tied to one of the faster-moving indexes, such as CDs or treasury bills. Such solicitations advise you to refinance into a loan that's tied to a slower-moving index, such as the 11th district cost of funds (COFI). One pitch letter I received during a period of rising rates: "You can lower your rate by almost 3 percent merely by switching to a loan based on the 11th district cost of funds index!"

As with other things that sound too good to be true, it ain't that simple. Remember that the terms of an adjustable-rate mortgage are composed of several factors. If you select an adjustable-rate mortgage tied to one of the faster-moving indexes, you're taking on more of the risk of interest rate increases being reflected at the next adjustment. Because you're taking on more of the risk of interest rate increases, lenders cut you breaks in other ways, such as through lower caps or points.

If you want the security of an ARM tied to a slower-moving index, you're going to pay for that security in one form or another, such as a higher start rate, caps, margin, or points. You may also pay in other less obvious ways. A benefit of staying put with your faster-moving adjustable index is that you benefit after interest rates fall. A slower-moving index, such as the 11th district cost of funds index (COFI), lags behind general changes in market interest rates, so it continues rising after interest rates peak and goes down more slowly after rates have turned tail, which they seemed to have done early in 1995. Ray Brown, co-author with me of *Home Buying For Dummies* (IDG Books Worldwide), says, "Loans tied to COFI are like holding onto a helium balloon when rates fall." And while the 11th district cost of funds index moves more slowly, it ultimately goes up by about the same amount as market changes in interest rates.

Interestingly, when interest rates were at rock bottom levels in late 1993, more lenders seemed to be pushing adjustables tied to the fast-moving indexes. Did they know interest rates were going to increase? Given the fact that short-term interest rates at the time approximated the 3.5 percent rate of inflation, short-term rates were likely to hold steady or increase.

With the benefit of hindsight, you may think that the slower-moving index was the one to choose at the interest rate bottom. This conclusion is not necessarily so if you end up holding your mortgage through the cycles of both increasing and decreasing interest rates.

Trying to predict interest rates and the wisdom of banks is a dangerous game. When you choose a mortgage, it's far more important to keep sight of your own financial situation.

Compare the fully indexed rate to the current rate of fixed-rate loans. You may be surprised to learn that the fixed-rate loan is at about the same interest rate or even a hair lower. This insight may cause you to reconsider your choice of an adjustable, which can, of course, rise to an even higher rate in the future.

Adjustment period or frequency

Every so many months, the mortgage-rate formula discussed in the preceding section is used to recalculate the interest rate on an adjustable-rate loan. Most adjustables adjust every 6 or 12 months, but some may adjust as frequently as monthly.

In advance of each adjustment, the lender should send you a notice telling you your new rate. (Check these adjustments as lenders sometimes make mistakes!) All things being equal, the less frequently your loan adjusts, the less financial uncertainty you have in your life. Less-frequent adjustments usually mean that your loan starts at a higher interest rate, though.

You might also consider a hybrid loan, which combines features of fixed- and adjustable-rate mortgages. For example, the initial rate may hold constant for three to five years and then adjust once a year or every six months thereafter. Such loans may make sense for you if you foresee a high probability of keeping your loan seven years or less but want some stability in your monthly payments. The longer the initial rate stays locked in, the higher the rate.

Rate caps

After the initial interest rate expires, the interest rate on an ARM fluctuates based on the loan formula. Almost all adjustables come with a rate cap, which limits the maximum rate change (up or down) allowed at each adjustment. This limit is usually referred to as the adjustment cap. On most loans that adjust every six months, the adjustment cap is 1 percent. In other words, the interest rate charged on the loan can move up or down no more than one percentage point in a given adjustment period.

Loans that adjust more than once per year usually limit the maximum rate change allowed over the entire year as well. On the vast majority of such loans, 2 percent is the annual rate cap. Finally, almost all adjustables come with lifetime caps. These caps limit the highest rate allowed over the entire life of the loan. It's common for adjustable loans to have lifetime caps of 5 to 6 percent higher than the initial start rate.

I can't stress this point enough: Never, ever take out an adjustable-rate mortgage that lacks rate caps! It's worse than giving a credit card with an unlimited line of credit to your 16-year-old for the weekend — at least you can close the credit card account on Monday!

When you want to take an adjustable-rate mortgage, you must identify the maximum payment you can handle. If you can't handle the payment that comes with a 10 or 11 percent interest rate, for example, then you shouldn't look at adjustables that may go that high.

Avoid ARMs with negative amortization

As you make mortgage payments over time, the loan balance you still owe is gradually reduced or amortized. The reverse of this process — increasing your loan balance — is called *negative amortization*.

Negative amortization is allowed by some adjustable-rate mortgages. How can your outstanding loan balance grow when you're continuing to make mortgage payments? When your mortgage payment is less than it really should be.

Some loans cap the increase of your monthly payment but not that of the interest rate. Thus, the size of your mortgage payment may not reflect all the interest that you owe on your loan. So, rather than paying the interest that is owed and paying off some of your loan balance (or *principal*) every month, you end up paying off some but not all of the interest you owe. Thus the extra unpaid interest you still owe is added to your outstanding debt.

This negative amortization is like paying only the minimum payment required on a credit card bill. You keep racking up finance charges (in this case, greater interest) on the balance as long as you make only the artificially low payment. Taking a loan with negative amortization defeats the whole purpose of borrowing an amount that fits your overall financial goals.

My advice: Avoid adjustables with negative amortization. The only way to know whether a loan includes it is to explicitly ask. Most lenders and mortgage brokers aren't forthcoming about telling you. You'll find it more frequently on loans that lenders consider risky. If you're having trouble finding lenders willing to deal with your financial situation, be especially careful.

Finding low-cost lenders

You can easily save thousands of dollars in interest charges and other fees by shopping around for a good mortgage deal. It doesn't matter whether you do so on your own or hire someone to help you. Shop till you drop because you have lotsa money at stake!

Doing it yourself

Many mortgage lenders are competing for your business. Although having a large number to choose from is good for keeping interest rates lower, it also makes shopping around a chore. The major lenders are banks, savings and loans, and mortgage bankers. Unlike banks, which are in many different businesses, mortgage bankers only do mortgages. The better ones offer some of the most competitive rates.

Large banks whose names you recognize from their advertising usually don't offer the best rates. Make sure that you check out some of the smaller savings and loans and credit unions in your area as well.

Real estate agents can also refer you to lenders with whom they've done business. Those lenders don't necessarily offer the most competitive rates — the agent simply may have done business with them in the past or gotten client referrals from them.

Look in the real estate section of one of the larger Sunday newspapers in your area for charts of selected lender interest rates. These tables are by no means comprehensive or reflective of the best rates available. In fact, many of them are sent to newspapers for free by firms that distribute mortgage information to mortgage brokers. Use them as a starting point by calling the lenders that list the best rates.

HSH Associates (800-873-2837) publishes mortgage information for most metropolitan areas. For $20, you can receive a list of dozens of lenders' rate quotes. You need to be a real data junkie to wade through all the numbers on the multipage report of abbreviations in small type.

Safety loans — it may pay not to put all your eggs in one basket

It can take several weeks for a lender to complete your property appraisal and evaluation of your loan package. When you're under contract to buy a property, having your loan denied after waiting several weeks can mean that you lose the property as well as the money you spent applying for the loan and having the property inspected. Some property sellers may give you an extension to apply for a loan at another lender, but others don't.

When job hunting or applying to college, people rarely set their sights on just one position or school. They may have a first choice, but they also have safety choices as well. So why put your financial assets, time, and energy spent on a real estate deal at stake by applying for a single loan? I've applied for a loan on a property at two lenders with some real estate I've purchased, and in at least one case I'm glad I did because a mortgage broker I once used didn't deliver what he promised.

Applying for a second loan means additional application fees. Completing two lenders' applications also involves more time and work. It's not a lot of additional time, however, because lenders require many of the same types of documentation and forms.

You want the best deal you can get. If a lender knows that you have no other options, he or she may be less willing to work hard to get you the best deal. You should consider getting a backup loan for this reason as well.

It's best to alert each lender you apply with that you're applying elsewhere. The second lender to pull your credit report will see the other lender's recent inquiry on your report. You should tell both lenders that you are sincerely interested — just as you would all prospective employers.

Mortgage brokers

A competent mortgage broker can be a big help in getting you a good loan and getting it closed. A good mortgage broker keeps abreast of many different mortgages being offered in the marketplace. He or she can shop among lots of lenders to get you the best deal available.

An organized and detail-oriented mortgage broker can also help you through the process of completing all those tedious and voluminous documents required by lenders. Like a good resumé writer, mortgage brokers can help polish your loan package so that the information is presented in its most favorable, yet still truthful, light. Brokers can also help educate you about various loan options and the pros and cons of available features.

Mortgage brokers are of greatest value to those who don't bother shopping around for a good deal or who may be shunned by most lenders. If you're too busy or disinterested to shop around for a good deal on a mortgage, a competent mortgage broker can probably save you money.

Brokers can also help if you anticipate that lenders may be skittish about offering you a loan. Problems on your credit report make lenders uncomfortable. If you're borrowing a large amount (90 percent or more) of the value of a property, many lenders aren't interested. Certain types of properties, such as co-ops and tenancies-in-common, give many lenders cold feet because these buildings tend to give them more problems.

Be careful, because some brokers are lazy and don't shop the market for the current best rates. Worse, some brokers may direct their business to lenders from which they can take a bigger cut or commission.

A mortgage broker typically gets paid a percentage, usually 0.5 to 1 percent, of the loan amount. This commission is completely negotiable, especially on larger loans that are more lucrative.

You should ask what the commission is on loans a broker is pitching. Some brokers may be indignant that you ask — that's their problem. You have every right to ask — it's your money.

Even if you plan to shop on your own, it may be worthwhile to talk to a mortgage broker. At the very least, you can compare what you find with what brokers say they can get for you. Again, be careful. Some brokers tell you what you want to hear — that is, that they can beat your best find — and then aren't able to deliver when the time comes.

If your loan broker quotes you a really good deal, make sure to ask who the lender is. (Most brokers refuse to reveal this information until you pay the necessary fee to cover the appraisal and credit report.) You can check with the actual lender to verify the interest rate and points the broker quotes you and make sure that you're eligible for the loan.

Dealing with loan problems

Even if you are a perfect or near-perfect credit risk, you may have financing problems with some properties. And, of course, not all real estate buyers have a perfect credit history, tons of available cash, and no debt. If you're one of those borrowers who ends up having to jump through more hoops than others to get a loan, don't give up hope. Few borrowers are perfect from a lender's perspective, and many problems aren't that difficult to fix.

The best defense against loan rejection is to avoid it in the first place. You can sometimes head off potential rejection by disclosing to your lender anything that may cause a problem before you apply for the loan. For example, if you already know that your credit report indicates some late payments from when you were out of the country for several weeks five years ago, write a letter explaining this situation.

Lack of down payment money

Most people, especially when they're making their first real-estate purchase, may be strapped for cash. In order to qualify for the most attractive financing, most lenders require that your down payment be at least 20 percent of the property's purchase price. The best investment property loans sometimes require 25 to 30 percent down for the best terms. In addition, you need reserve money to pay for other closing costs such as title insurance and loan fees.

If you don't have 20-plus percent of the purchase price available, don't panic and don't get depressed — you can still own real estate. Some lenders may offer you a mortgage even though you may be able to put down only 5 to 10 percent of the purchase price. These lenders will likely require you to purchase private mortgage insurance (PMI) with your loan. This insurance generally costs a few hundred dollars per year and protects the lender if you default on your loan. (When you do have at least 20 percent equity in the property, you can generally eliminate the PMI.)

Another way to raise the level of your down payment funds is to dip into your retirement savings. Some employers allow you to borrow against your retirement account balance, under the condition that you repay the loan within a set number of years. Also, thanks to the 1997 tax bill, first time home buyers can make penalty-free withdrawals of up to $10,000 from IRA accounts.

If you don't want the cost and strain of extra fees and bad mortgage terms, another option is to postpone your purchase. Go on a financial austerity program and boost your savings rate. You may also consider lower-priced properties. Smaller properties and ones that need some work can help keep down the purchase price and, therefore, the required down payment.

If lower-priced properties don't meet your needs, you may be able to have your cake and eat it too by finding partners. Make sure to write up a legal contract to specify what happens if a partner wants out. Family members sometimes make for good partners. Your parents, grandparents, maybe even your siblings may have some extra cash they'd like to loan, invest, or even gift you!

Finally, some property owners or developers may be willing to finance your purchase with as little as 5 to 10 percent down. You can't be as picky about such seller-financed properties because a limited supply is available and many that are need work or haven't yet sold for other reasons.

Credit history blemishes

Late payments, missed payments, or debts that you never bothered to pay can tarnish your credit report and squelch a lender's desire to make you a mortgage loan. If you are turned down for a loan because of your less-than-stellar credit history, request (at no charge to you) a copy of your credit report from the lender that turned down your loan.

If problems are accurately documented on your credit report, start by trying to explain them to your lender. If the lender is unsympathetic, try calling other lenders. Tell them your credit problems up front and see whether you can find one willing to offer you a loan. Mortgage brokers may also be able to help you shop for lenders in these cases.

TIP

Credit problems you can fix yourself

Sometimes it may feel that you're not in control when you're applying for a loan. In reality, you can fix a number of credit problems yourself. And those that can't be fixed can often be explained. Remember that some lenders are more lenient and flexible than others. Just because one mortgage lender rejects your loan application doesn't mean that all the others will as well.

As for erroneous information listed on your credit report, get on the phone to the credit bureaus and start squawking. If specific creditors are the culprits, call them, too. Keep notes from your conversations and make sure to put your case in writing and add your comments to your credit report. If the customer service representatives you talk with are no help, dash off a copy of your letter to the president of each company. Let the

head honcho know that his or her organization caused you problems in obtaining credit. Send a copy to the Better Business Bureau and the state organization that oversees such lenders.

Another common credit problem is having too much consumer debt at the time you apply for a mortgage. The more credit card, auto loan, and other consumer debt you rack up, the less mortgage you qualify for. If you're turned down for the mortgage, consider it a wake-up call and a blessing. In addition to the high interest rate on consumer debt and the loans encouraging you to live beyond your means, you now have a third reason to get rid of debt. Hang onto the dream of buying real estate and plug away at paying off your debts before you make another foray into real estate.

Low appraisals

Even if you have sufficient income, a clean credit report, and an adequate down payment, your loan may be turned down if the appraisal of the property you're seeking to buy comes in too low. If this happens, don't be upset, be grateful. Odds are your lender may have saved you from paying too much for a property. It's unusual for a property not to appraise for what a buyer agrees to pay. If the appraisal came in low, the odds are quite high you overpaid — in other words, the real market value of the property is less than you agreed to pay.

Assuming that you still like the property, renegotiate a lower price with the seller using the appraisal as ammunition.

With a property you already own and are refinancing, if the appraisal is too low, obviously a different tack is in order. If you have the cash available, you can simply put more money down to get the loan balance to a level for which you qualify. If you don't have the cash, you may have to forgo the refinance until you save more money or until the property value rises.

In rare cases, lenders sometimes lowball an appraisal on refinances to sabotage a loan. A lender may do so, for example, if it has your current mortgage under better terms. If you suspect that this may be the case, make sure to ask for a copy of your appraisal, which you are entitled to. You're paying for it! If you have comparable sale prices from your area that support your case, go back to the lender and see what it has to say. If you're still not satisfied, you can take your beef to a state regulator of mortgage lenders. It may be a lot less hassle, though, to apply for a new mortgage through another lender.

Not enough income

If you're self-employed or have been changing jobs, your income may not be what it used to be or, more important, what a mortgage lender likes to see given the amount you want to borrow. A simple (but often not possible) way around this problem is to make a larger down payment. For example, when purchasing a primary residence, if you put down 30 percent or more, you may be able to get a no-income verification loan. If you can make that large a down payment, lenders probably don't care what your income is — they'll simply repossess and then sell your property if you default on the loan.

Most people don't have tons of extra cash burning a hole in their wallet. If you can't make a large down payment, another option is to get a cosigner for the loan. Your relatives may be willing cosigners. As long as they aren't borrowed out themselves, they may be able to help you qualify for a larger loan than you can get on your own. As with partnerships, be sure to put your agreement in writing so that you have no misunderstandings.

When to refinance

When you buy a property, you take out a mortgage based on your circumstances and available loan options at that time. But things change. Maybe interest rates have dropped or you have access to better loan options now than when you purchased. Or perhaps you want to tap into some of the real estate equity for other investments.

Everybody likes to save money

If interest rates drop and you're able to refinance, you can lock in interest rate savings. But just because interest rates have dropped since you took out your original mortgage isn't reason enough to refinance your mortgage. Remember when you refinance a mortgage, you have to spend money and time to save money. So you need to crunch a few numbers to determine whether refinancing makes sense for you.

If your loan has a higher rate of interest than comparable new loans, you may save money by refinancing. Because refinancing costs money, it's a bit of a gamble whether you can save enough to justify the cost.

Your chances of saving money by refinancing are good if your current loan's interest rate is more than 1 percent higher and you're planning to keep the property for at least five years.

Not all refinances cost tons of money — you can find *no-cost* refinances or *no-point* loans. These loans may not be your best long-term options, however. As I explain earlier in the chapter, you get no free lunches. No-cost or no-point loans come with higher interest rates.

Calculate how many months it will take you to recoup the costs of refinancing, such as appraisal, loan fees and points, title insurance, and so on. For example, if the refinance costs you $2,000 to complete and reduces your monthly payment by $100, it may appear that you'll make the cost of the refinance back in 20 months. (Note that this method is how most mortgage lenders and brokers do the calculation because it makes the refinance appear more attractive than it actually is.) But because you lose some tax write-offs if your mortgage interest rate and payment are reduced, you can't simply look at the reduced amount of your monthly payment.

If you want a better estimate but don't want to spend hours crunching numbers, take your tax rate as specified in Chapter 3 (for example, 28 percent) and reduce your monthly payment savings on the refinance by this amount. That means, continuing with the example in the preceding paragraph, that if your monthly payment drops by $100, you're actually only saving around $72 a month after factoring in the lost tax benefits. So it takes 28 months ($2,000 divided by $72), not 20 months, to recoup the refinance costs.

If you can recover the costs of the refinance within a few years or less and aren't planning to move in that time frame, do the refinance. If it takes longer to recoup the refinance costs, refinancing may still make sense if you anticipate keeping the property and mortgage that long. If you estimate it taking more than five to seven years to break even, refinancing is probably too risky to justify the costs and hassles.

Money for other investments

Refinancing to pull out cash for some other purpose from a piece of real estate you own can make good financial sense because, under most circumstances, mortgage interest is tax-deductible. Perhaps you want to purchase another piece of real estate, or start or purchase a business. Maybe you'd like to be rid of some high-cost consumer debt on credit cards or an auto loan. The interest on consumer debt is not tax-deductible and is usually at a much higher interest rate than what mortgage loans charge you.

The most important question is whether a lender is willing to lend you more money against the equity in your property (which is the difference between the market value of your property and the loan balance). You can "guesstimate" whether you can afford larger payments by using Table 9-1 in Chapter 9 to find the maximum loan for which you may qualify as long as the value of your property allows.

Be careful not to borrow more than you need to accomplish your financial goals. For example, just because you can borrow more against the equity in your real estate doesn't mean that you should do so to buy an expensive new car or put in a splashy new kitchen or bathroom in your home.

When to consider a home equity loan

Home equity loans, also known as second mortgages, allow you to borrow against the equity in your home in addition to the mortgage you already have (a first mortgage).

A home equity loan may be beneficial if you need more money for just a few years, or if your first mortgage is at such a low interest rate that refinancing to get more cash would be as costly. Otherwise, I would avoid home equity loans.

If you need a larger mortgage, why not refinance the first one and wrap it all together? Home equity loans have higher interest rates than comparable first mortgages. They are riskier from a lender's perspective because the first mortgage lender gets first claim against your property if you file bankruptcy or you default on the mortgage.

Interest on home mortgage loans of up to $1 million (first or second residences) is tax deductible for loans taken out after October 13, 1987. (Loans taken before that date have no limit.) Interest deduction on home equity loans is limited to the first $100,000 of such debt.

Working with Real Estate Agents

When you purchase real estate, if you're like most people, you enlist the services of a real estate agent. A good agent can help screen property so that you don't spend all your free time looking at potential properties to buy, negotiate a deal, and help coordinate inspections and other preclosing items.

But all agents, good, mediocre, and awful, are subject to a conflict of interest because of how they are compensated — on commission. I must say that I respect real estate agents for calling themselves what they are. Real estate agents don't hide behind an obscure job title, such as "shelter consultant." (Many financial "planners," "advisors," or "consultants," for example, actually work on commission and sell investments and life insurance and are, therefore, stockbrokers and insurance brokers and not planners, advisors, or consultants.)

Real estate agents are not in the business of providing objective financial counsel either. They don't tell you to spend less money on a home because you aren't saving enough for retirement. They won't tell you to rent because of your current personal circumstances and the state of the real estate market. Just as car dealers make their living selling cars, real estate agents make their living selling real estate. Never forget this fact as a buyer.

So don't expect an agent to give you objective advice about what you should do given your overall financial situation. Speak with a tax or financial advisor who works on a fee-for-service (hourly) basis and provides advice after examining your overall financial situation. Even better, educate yourself so that you can make more-informed decisions.

You may not realize the myriad problems and conflicts that are created from agents deriving a commission from a real estate purchase. The pursuit of a commission and a larger commission may encourage an agent to get you to do things that aren't in your best interests, such as the following:

- ✔ **Buy, and buy sooner rather than later.** If you don't buy, your agent doesn't get paid for all the hours he or she spends working with you. The worst agents fib and use tricks to motivate you to buy. They may say that other offers are coming in on a property you're interested in. Or they show you a bunch of dumps and then one good listing they think you'll like to get you motivated to buy that one.

- ✔ **Spend more than you should.** Because real estate agents get a percentage of the sales price of a property, they have a built-in incentive to encourage you to buy more than fits comfortably with your other financial objectives and goals. An agent doesn't have to consider or care about your other financial needs.

- ✔ **Buy their company's listings.** Agents also have a built-in incentive (higher commission) to sell their own listings.

- ✔ **Buy in their territory.** Real estate agents typically work a specific territory. As a result, they usually can't objectively tell you the pros and cons of the surrounding region.

- ✔ **Use people that scratch their backs.** Some agents refer you to lenders, inspectors, and title insurance companies that have referred them business. Some agents also solicit and receive referral fees (or bribes) from mortgage lenders, inspectors, and contractors to whom they refer business.

Unfair and restrained competition?

A number of independent, non-profit agencies have reviewed the residential real estate brokerage industry and have reported troubling and concerning findings. One such significant report was prepared by the Federal Trade Commission during Ronald Reagan's presidency.

The FTC report expressed concern that real estate brokerage firms are interdependent in their listing and selling of homes, through the Multiple Listing Service, and that this discourages price competition. "... the MLSs... link competitors in such a way that price competition and the free flow of information to consumers are both impeded."

The Consumer Federation of America, a nonprofit consumer advocacy group, said of agents in its report, "... Commissions are overpriced, quality of service bears no relation to commission levels, agents face serious conflicts of interest, most buyers are inadequately represented by agents, and agents dominate most state regulatory bodies. The residential real estate industry functions as a cartel that overcharges home buyers and sellers over $10 billion a year."

When a real estate agent lists a home for sale in the MLS, the commission, to be paid to a broker who successfully sells that listing to a buyer, is posted in the listing. Commissions generally are 6 percent in most areas and 7 percent in some lower-cost areas. Although higher-priced homes may occasionally be listed at a 5 percent commission, it is amazing that, despite huge increases in real estate prices (far in excess of the rate of inflation) in many areas over the past decades, commissions are still the same percentage of an ever larger sales price. It's interesting to note that in other countries, such as Australia, Great Britain, Canada, and New Zealand, commission rates are about half — in the 3 percent range — of what they are in the United States.

Real estate industry literature dating as far back as the 1920s openly proclaims the value of the MLS "... as a means of raising and stabilizing commission rates." If a property seller wants to list a home with an agent at a lower commission, the consumer is free to attempt to negotiate a lower rate with the listing agent. Many consumers, however, believe that commissions are fixed, set, or somehow regulated. A listing in the MLS at a low commission runs the risk of other agents not showing the property.

Real estate agents do predominate many state regulatory boards, and most local agent associations prohibit comparative price advertising as "disparaging." Interestingly, traditional agents openly disparage discount brokers that generally charge a flat fee for their service rather than a percentage of the listing price and also often refuse to show discount broker listings (as well as homes for sale by owner).

Competition is further restrained by the prohibition of agents from soliciting clients who have a listing with another agent. Real estate agents have also successfully fought and prevented public access to the MLS. Traditional agents have also been attacked for the practice of receiving and giving kickbacks from real estate service providers that steer them business and vice versa.

How to find a good agent

A mediocre, incompetent, or greedy agent can be a real liability. Whether you're hiring an agent to work with you as a buyer or seller, you want someone who is competent and with whom you can get along. Working with an agent costs you a lot of money, so make sure that you get your money's worth.

Interview several agents. Check references. Ask agents for the names and phone numbers of at least three clients with whom they've worked in the past six months in the geographical area in which you are looking. By narrowing to six months the period during which they worked with references, you maximize the chances of speaking with clients other than the agent's all-time favorites.

You should look for these traits in any agent you work with (ask the agent's references), whether as a buyer or seller:

- **Full-time employment.** Some agents work in real estate as a second or even third job. Information in this field changes constantly — keeping track of it is hard enough on a full-time basis. It's hard to imagine a good agent being able to stay on top of the market and moonlight elsewhere.

- **Experience.** When you're establishing a new checking account, working with an employee straight out of school, first week on the job, isn't going to harm you financially — it may just take a little longer. With a real estate deal, you've got a lot at stake financially and emotionally. You want to do the best that you can. Hiring someone with experience doesn't necessarily mean looking for an agent who's been kicking around for decades. Many of the best agents come into the field from other occupations, such as business and teaching. Some sales, marketing, negotiation, and communication skills can certainly be acquired in other fields, but experience in this field does count.

- **Honesty and integrity.** You're trusting your agent with a lot. If the agent doesn't level with you about what a neighborhood or particular property is really like, you suffer the consequences.

- **Interpersonal skills.** An agent has to be able to get along not only with you but also with a whole host of other people involved in a typical real estate deal: other agents, property sellers, inspectors, mortgage lenders, and so on. An agent doesn't have to be Mr. or Ms. Congeniality, but he or she should know how to put your interests first without upsetting others.

- **Negotiation skills.** Putting a real estate deal together involves negotiation. Is your agent going to exhaust all avenues to get you the best deal possible? Most people don't like the sometimes aggravating process of negotiation, so they hire someone else to do it for them. Be sure to ask the agent's references how the agent negotiated for them.

✔ **High quality standards.** Sloppy work can lead to big legal or logistical problems down the road. If an agent neglects to recommend an inspection, for example, you may be stuck with undiscovered problems after the deal is done.

Some agents who pitch themselves as buyer's brokers claim that they work in your interests. This claim is pure bunk. Agents representing you as buyer's brokers still get paid only when you buy. And they still get paid on commission as a percentage of the purchase price. So they still have an incentive to sell you a piece of real estate, and the more expensive it is, the more commission they make.

Buying and selling require somewhat different skills. Some rare agents can do both outstandingly well. You're not bound by a rule or moral obligation to use the same agent when you sell a property as when you buy. Don't feel indebted to sell through the agent who worked with you as a buyer just because he sends you holiday cards every year asking how the garden is growing. Remember, he works on commission.

Buyers can negotiate commissions, too!

Not only do many consumers not realize that commissions are negotiable, but even more people don't know that as real estate buyers, they can negotiate agent commissions. Conventional wisdom says that the seller pays the agent's commission, so it doesn't concern or cost you as a buyer. Wrong! If the agents involved in your real estate deal are amenable to reducing their commissions, all things being equal, the seller should be willing to accept less money for the property.

Remember that both buyer *and* seller pay commissions. If agents weren't involved in the deal, the seller could afford to sell for less and still come out ahead. Selling for less, of course, saves the buyer money. So home buyers as well as sellers should care about the commission the agents involved in the deal get.

It's often easier to negotiate an agent's commission when an offer is on the table and the agent wants to get a deal done. Don't let them try to snow you by saying that, because the seller signed a contract that included the commission percentage, it can't be changed. Everything is negotiable when an offer is in play, including the commission.

If you, as the buyer, and the property seller aren't that far apart on price, as a buyer, you can suggest that the agents lower their commissions. To get a deal done, you may be surprised at what agents are willing to do. Be forewarned that some agents, particularly those who work for larger companies, try "the car dealer trick." They say that they must get approval from their office manager to cut their commission, and guess what? They come back to say their request was denied or that they aren't allowed to reduce their commission. Commissions are negotiable, so don't fall for this trick. Later in this chapter, I explain how to negotiate real estate agents' commissions when selling a home.

Agents sometimes market themselves as *top producers,* which means that they sell a relatively larger volume of real estate. This title doesn't count for much for you, the buyer. It may be a red flag of an agent who focuses on completing as many deals as possible.

When you're buying a home, you need an agent who is patient. The last thing you need or want is an agent who tries to push you into making a deal. You need an agent who is willing to allow you the necessary time to get educated and help you make the best decision for you.

You also need an agent who is knowledgeable about the local market and community. If you're looking to buy a home in an area in which you're not currently living, an informed agent can have a big impact on your decision.

As a buyer, especially a first-time buyer or someone with credit problems, finding an agent with financing knowledge is also a plus. Such an agent may be able to refer you to lenders that can handle your type of situation, which can save you a lot of legwork.

Buying without a real estate agent

You can purchase property without an agent if you're willing to do some additional legwork. You need to do the things that a good real estate agent does, such as searching for properties, scheduling appointments to see them, negotiating the deal, and coordinating inspections.

If you don't work with an agent, you should consider having an attorney review the contracts, unless you're a legal expert yourself. It helps to have someone else not vested in the transaction look out for your interests. In almost all cases, real estate agents are not legal experts, so getting legal advice from an attorney is generally better. (In some states, you need to hire an attorney in addition to the real estate agent.)

One possible drawback to working without an agent is that you have to do the negotiations yourself. If you're a good negotiator, doing so can work to your advantage. But if you get too caught up emotionally in the situation, negotiating for yourself can backfire. If you're not sure whether you can handle the negotiations involved in purchasing your real estate investment, take a look at the next section for tips on what you need to know to close the deal yourself. If you're *still* not sure, I recommend that you follow my earlier tips for choosing a good real estate agent.

If you're experienced or savvy about real estate and have found a property on your own, there's no reason you can't put a deal together yourself. Go ahead; I know people who have done it successfully and who have come out ahead financially.

Closing the Perfect Deal

After you locate a property you want to buy and understand financing options, the real fun begins. Now you've got to put the deal together. Here are some key things to keep in mind.

Negotiating 101

When you work with an agent, the agent usually carries the burden of the negotiation process. Even if you delegate responsibility for negotiating with the selling agent or seller to the agent, you should still have a plan and strategy in mind. Otherwise, you may overpay for real estate.

 My first word of advice is to leave your emotions out of any property purchase. This feat is easier said than done and hardest to do when purchasing a home in which you'll live. Try, as best you can, not to fall in love with a property. Keep an open mind and keep searching for other properties even when you make an offer because you may be negotiating against an unmotivated seller. Other good properties are out there. Having a backup in mind is good psychologically.

You should also try to learn about the property and owner before you make your offer. How long has the property been on the market? What are its flaws? Why is the owner selling it? For example, if the seller is moving because he got a job in another town where he's about to close on a home purchase, he may be eager to get his money out of the property and may be willing to reduce the price. Or if the house has been on the market for a while, the seller may be more willing to negotiate than after just a week on the market. The more you understand about the property you want to buy and the seller's motivations, the better you will be able to draft an offer that meets both parties' needs.

 Many listing agents just love to blab and tell you the life history of the seller — be all ears! Either you or your agent may be able to get them to spew forth lots of good information about the seller. That said, please take my next words of advice seriously: Never tell your agent *anything* you yourself wouldn't tell the seller. I don't want to sound cynical, but if you tell your agent something like, "Let's offer $200,000, but I'm willing to go to $215,000," your agent may not keep this as confidential as you'd like. Even if your agent can keep this information private, the knowledge can influence how he or she negotiates — you'll make your agent a better negotiator by keeping things closer to your own vest.

 Also, bring facts to the bargaining table. Get comparable sales data to support your price. Too often, home buyers and their agents pick a number out of the air when making an offer. If you were the seller, would you be persuaded to lower your asking price? Pointing to recent and comparable home sales to justify your offer price strengthens your case.

Remember that price is only one of several negotiable items. Sometimes sellers get fixated on selling their homes for a certain amount. Perhaps they want to get at least what they paid for it themselves several years ago. You may be able to get a seller to pay for certain repairs or improvements or to offer you an attractive loan without all the extra fees that a bank charges. Also be aware that the time needed for you to close on your purchase is a bargaining chip. Some sellers may need cash soon and are willing to concede other points if you can close quickly. Likewise, the real estate agent's commission is negotiable, too.

Insist on inspections

When you buy a property, you're probably making one of the biggest financial purchases and commitments of your life. Unless you've built homes and other properties and done contracting work yourself, you probably have no idea what you're getting yourself into when it comes to furnaces and termites.

Spend the money and time to hire inspectors and other experts to evaluate the major systems and potential problem areas of the home. Because you can't be certain of the seller's commitment to selling, I recommend doing the inspections *after* you have successfully negotiated and have a signed sales contract. Although you won't have the feedback from the inspections to help with this round of negotiating, you can always go back to the seller with the new information. Make your purchase offer contingent on a satisfactory inspection.

Areas that you want to hire people to help you inspect include

- Overall condition of the property — for example, is the paint peeling, are the floors level, are appliances present and working well, and so on?
- Electrical, heating, and plumbing systems
- Foundation
- Roof
- Pest control and dry rot
- Seismic/slide risk

(With multiunit rental property, be sure to read Chapter 10 for other specifics on what to check out, such as parking.)

Inspection fees often pay for themselves. If you uncover problems that you weren't aware of when you negotiated the original purchase price, the inspection reports give you the information you need to go back and ask the property seller to fix the problems or reduce the purchase price of the property.

Never accept a seller's inspection report as your only source of information. When a seller hires an inspector, he or she may hire someone who isn't as diligent and critical of the property. For example, what if the inspector is buddies with the seller or agent selling the property? By all means, review the seller's inspection reports if available, but get your own as well.

Also, beware of inspectors who are popular with real estate agents. They may be popular because they are soft touches and don't rock the boat by bothering to document all the property's problems.

As with other professionals whose services you retain, interview a few inspection companies. Ask which systems they inspect and how detailed a report they will prepare for you. Consider asking the company you're thinking of hiring for customer references. Ask it for names and phone numbers of three people who used its services within the past six months. Also, request from the inspection company a sample of one of its reports.

The day before you close on the purchase of your home, do a brief walk-through of the property to make sure that everything is still in the condition it was before and that all the fixtures, appliances, curtains, and other items that were to be left as per the contract are still there. Sometimes, sellers don't recall or ignore these things, and consequently don't leave what they agreed to in the sales contract.

Title insurance and escrow fees

Mortgage lenders require title insurance to protect against someone else claiming legal title to your property. This can happen, for example, when a husband and wife split up, and the one who remains in the home decides to sell and take off with the money. If both spouses are listed as owners on the title, the spouse who sells the property (possibly by forging the other's signature) has no legal right to do so. The other spouse can come back and reclaim rights to the home even after it has been sold. In this event, both you and the lender can get stuck holding the bag. (If you're in the enviable position of paying cash for a property, you should still buy title insurance even though a mortgage lender won't prod you to do so. You need to protect your investment.)

Many people don't seem to know that title insurance and escrow fees vary from company to company. As a result, they don't bother to shop around and simply use the company that their real estate agent or mortgage lender suggests. This ignorance can cost you money. Shop around.

Escrow charges pay for neutral third-party services to ensure that the instructions of the purchase contract or refinance are fulfilled and that everyone gets paid.

When you call around for title insurance and escrow fee quotes, make sure that you understand all the fees. Many companies tack on all sorts of charges for things such as courier fees and express mail. If you find a company with lower prices and want to use it, it doesn't hurt to ask for an itemization in writing so that you don't have any surprises.

An insurance company's ability to pay claims is always important. Most state insurance departments monitor and regulate title insurance companies. Title insurers rarely fail, and most state departments of insurance do a good job in shutting down financially unstable ones. You can check with your state's department if you're concerned. You can also ask the insurer for copies of its ratings from insurance-rating agencies.

Real estate agents and mortgage lenders can be a good starting point for referrals, as they usually have a broader perspective on cost and service quality of different companies. Call other companies as well. Again, agents and lenders may be biased toward certain companies simply because they are in the habit of using them or they refer business to each other.

Selling

When you purchase and own real estate, the day will come when you'll need or want to sell. In the previous two chapters, I explain how to evaluate whether your reasons for selling are sound and if the real estate market is at a high level. I also explain how to roll over your capital gains when you sell. Before you're ready to sell, be sure that you understand the tax ramifications of your decision as well as how to sell your property. If desired, work with a real estate agent.

Deciding when to sell

You should buy and hold real estate for the long term. If you do your homework and buy in a good area and work hard to find a fairly priced or underpriced property, why sell it in a few years and incur all the selling costs and time and hassle to locate and negotiate another property to purchase?

Some real estate investors like to buy properties in need of improvement, fix them up, and then sell them and move on to another. Unless you're a contractor and have a real eye for this type of work, don't expect to make a killing. In fact, it's more likely that your profit will be eroded through the myriad costs of frequent buying and selling. In the long run, the vast majority of your profits comes from the appreciation of the overall real estate market in the communities you own property in rather than from improving the value of your properties so that you get more out of them than the cost of the improvements you make to them.

You should use the reasons you bought in an area as a guide if you're considering selling. Go back to the criteria I discuss in Chapter 10. For example, if the schools are deteriorating in the community and the planning department is allowing development that will hurt the price of your property longer-term and the rents you can charge, that's a good reason to sell. Unless you see significant problems like these in the works, holding good properties over many years is a great way to build your profits and minimize transaction costs.

Negotiating real estate agents' contracts

Most people use an agent to sell real estate. As I discuss in "How to find a good agent," earlier in this chapter, selling and buying a home demand agents with different strengths. When you're selling a property, you want an agent who can get the job done efficiently and for as high a price as possible.

As a seller, you should seek agents who have marketing and sales expertise and who are willing to put in the time and money necessary to get your home sold. Don't necessarily be impressed by an agent who works for a large company. What matters more is what the agent is going to do to market your property.

When you list your home for sale, the contract that you sign with the listing agent includes specification of the commission to be paid if the agent succeeds in selling your home. In most areas of the country, agents usually ask for a 6 percent commission. In an area that has lower-cost housing, they may ask for 7 percent.

Regardless of the commission an agent says is "typical," "standard," or "what my manager requires," always remember that commissions are negotiable. Because the commission is a percentage, you have much greater ability to get a lower commission on a higher-priced home. If an agent makes 6 percent selling both a $200,000 home and a $100,000 home, the agent makes twice as much on the $200,000 home. Yet selling the higher-priced home does not take twice as much work. (And selling a $400,000 home certainly doesn't take four times the effort of a $100,000 home sale.)

If you live in an area with higher-priced homes (above $200,000), 5 percent commissions can be negotiated. For expensive properties ($400,000 and up), a 4 percent commission is reasonable. You may find, however, that your ability to negotiate a lower commission is greatest when an offer is on the table. In fact, as I explain earlier in the chapter, because of the cooperation of agents working together through the MLS, if you list your home for sale at a lower commission than most other properties, some agents aren't interested in showing it to prospective buyers.

Agents argue that they do a lot of work to sell property. And they sometimes put many hours into deals that never come to fruition. Agents who work for a company say that they share a good portion of the commission with the owners of their real estate company. I've even heard agents argue that they need the higher commission because of all the income taxes they have to pay on their earnings! To all this I say, sorry guys and gals — your compensation should depend on the time you put in on a deal and your expertise.

In terms of the length of the listing agreement, three months is reasonable. If you give an agent too long a listing (6 to 12 months), the agent may simply toss your listing into the multiple listing book and not expend much effort to get your property sold. Practically speaking, you can fire your agent whenever you want, regardless of the length of the listing agreement. But a shorter listing (for example, three months) may be more motivating for your agent.

Selling without a real estate agent

The temptation to sell real estate without an agent is usually to save the commission that an agent deducts from your home's sale price. If you have the time, energy, and marketing experience, you can sell your home and possibly save some money.

The major problem with attempting to sell your home on your own is that you can't list it in the multiple listing service (MLS), which only real estate agents can access. As discussed earlier in the chapter, the MLS functions as an effective near monopoly over the selling of homes. And if you're not listed in the MLS, many potential buyers never know that your home is for sale. Agents working with buyers don't generally look for or show their clients homes that are for sale by owner or listed with a discount broker.

Besides saving you time, a good agent can help ensure that you're not sued for failing to disclose known defects of your property. If you decide to sell your home yourself, make sure that you have access to a legal advisor who can review the contracts.

An intermediate step between selling property yourself and using an agent is listing with a discount broker who charges less than traditional real estate agents to help you sell your property. A discount broker may help you develop advertisements, prepare contracts, and negotiate with potential buyers. You may be responsible for showing the home to prospective buyers.

Discounters usually charge a fixed fee or a percentage of the sales price. The cost should be much less than a traditional agent charges. For selling traditional residential property, try contacting Help-U-Sell (800-366-1177), a discounter that has 350 offices nationwide. Alternatively, try negotiating a better commission from a regular agent.

Part IV
Small Business

"WHAT'LL WE DO WITH ALL THIS INVENTORY?"

In this part . . .

Although the businesses may be small, the potential for earning healthy profits and finding a fulfilling career isn't. Here you discover such things as how to develop a business plan, identify marketable products or services, find customers, and wallop the competition! If starting your own shop seems either too overwhelming or too uninspiring, you also find out how to buy an existing business.

Chapter 12

Preparing to Start Your Own Business

*A*t the corner of Telegraph and Durant Avenues in Berkeley, Alex Popov was selling shoes as fast as he could. He wasn't particularly interested in shoes. Yet he spent 12 months to find and lease this costly retail location a stone's throw away from the teeming University of California at Berkeley campus.

Selling the 5,000 pairs of shoes that came with the location and securing the lease were just two of the many obstacles on Popov's road to pursuing his dream: starting and building his own business. The business, which he opened at the end of 1995, is Smart Alec's Intelligent Fast Food. His restaurant sells healthy, gourmet fast food. "I wanted a business that could grow, but I also wanted psychic income — I want to raise people's awareness about health and nutrition."

But by the time the business opened, few people saw or appreciated all the little and big steps Popov had taken to achieve his dream. While working as a sales engineer in late 1992, Popov started seriously contemplating an entrepreneurial path. "The desire to start my own business came before the idea," Popov says. "I eventually saw that even with a college education, I didn't know what made for good nutrition and the connection between diet and health." Popov soon learned. He spent hundreds of hours researching the deleterious health effects of the standard American diet.

Like many entrepreneurs, Popov transitioned gradually into running his own business. After six months of research, which came after regular work hours, he quit his job as an engineer and started an export business. Even though the export business had nothing to do with what he was still aiming to do — open a healthy fast-food restaurant — it did pay the bills. More important, unlike his job as an engineer, his new job wasn't full-time, so Popov had more time to develop his business ideas.

Scaling back time working for others can help keep a minimal but stable income flowing. Sometimes, relying on savings, which most entrepreneurs do, or on family members is the key. Lana Greer, a former college administrator, started her own consulting business with the backing of her husband, who was working full-time in a stable position. Although Greer had several small consulting projects lined up before she left her full-time job, the Greers did not depend on her income in the beginning. "We reduced our living expenses and kept tabs on our spending," Greer says. "I spent very little money up front to start my business. Some people go out right away to rent office space and buy computers and copiers. I preferred to 'bootstrap' my business — I think it gives me more flexibility." Because she gave up her benefits package, Greer needed to secure personal insurance coverage and establish her own retirement savings plan.

Psychologically, leaving the security of company employment is difficult. "When you leave a job, you leave security and the benefit of being able to quickly explain what you do at a cocktail party," Greer says. "It was hard to leave the stability that comes from having a place to go, a network of people, and a paycheck with benefits."

Before transitioning into new ventures, most entrepreneurs develop some type of business plan to serve as a tentative road map for their efforts. The plans' formality varies as much as the businesses themselves. In Popov's case, his plan was quite detailed and structured. After speaking with lots of other business people and gathering information about his industry, Popov wrote a business plan for Smart Alec's Intelligent Fast Food. The business plan then became the sales document he used to raise $250,000 of capital from investors (primarily from one wealthy individual) to fund the leasing and development of a high-visibility retail location.

All entrepreneurial plans change over time, sometimes dramatically. Some people who start their own businesses evolve into avenues they never imagined when they started their journey. After consulting for seven years on software development, Marcy Swenson was introduced socially to the guitar player in a pop rock band, St. Surreal. Over time, her friendship and interaction with band members enabled her to see that the band was working really hard on its music and seemed talented, but no one was taking care of the business side. "They didn't know how to market themselves," says Swenson.

Working without pay, Swenson initially helped the band by booking performances and creating flyers to attract bigger audiences to its shows. After thinking about the band's lack of success in pitching demo tapes to local radio stations, Swenson hit on an even better idea: a CD, which would sound better and look professional. "When I explored the costs of making a CD ourselves, I was energized to see that it didn't cost much . . . about $2,000 to press 1,000

CDs," says Swenson. The band's CD is now played on local radio stations and sold in independent record stores.

Eventually, Swenson received a nominal salary for managing the band, which takes up about 90 percent of her work time. She earns royalties on CD sales as well as the band's future projects. Swenson's next goals are to distribute the CD to major music stores and to interest a studio in producing CDs for the band.

Looking back, Swenson's metamorphosis is quite extraordinary for a former computer consultant. She says, "I never had a plan with a checklist." But like Popov, Swenson had an interest and love for what she pursued: In her case, it was music. This venture has also changed her future work interests. "It may position me to get involved in blending the arts and the computer world — possibly in multimedia," says Swenson.

Looking only at the accomplishments of small business owners can fool you into forgetting what happens behind the scenes as a business is born. Any honest entrepreneur can quickly reel off a list of problems and mistakes. You have to be willing to experiment and fail sometimes. James Collins, a business consultant and author of the national best-seller, *Built to Last*, recommends within reason and financial constraint, "Try a lot of stuff and keep what works."

Among other struggles, Popov had to persuade the Berkeley City Council to issue a zoning variance to permit his restaurant to operate and had to deal with difficult lease negotiations. After the elation of producing the CD, Swenson was disappointed to discover that a local club's band scheduler wouldn't listen to the band's CD, which she had just given him, for six weeks. Realizing that this answer could just be a slow, polite way to say no, Swenson asked the bartender to play the CD on the club's stereo. She called the scheduler by phone while it was playing, and he liked the music. The result: The band landed the club.

To succeed as an entrepreneur, being thick-skinned doesn't hurt. Naysayers and rejections abound. Neither Popov nor Swenson had formal work experience in the industry they chose. Many people saw this lack of experience as a negative. The reality is that lack of experience may actually be a huge advantage. "Entrepreneurs from outside an industry bring a fresh pair of eyes and insights to established and sometimes entrenched industries . . . this can lead to breakthrough thinking," Collins says.

Have You Got the Right Stuff?

Many people dream about running their own company. Tales of entrepreneurs becoming multimillionaires focus attention on the financial rewards without revealing the business and personal challenges and costs associated with being in charge.

Business owners know the good and the bad. Consider all the activities that your company has to do well in order to survive and succeed in the competitive business world. You have to develop products and services that the market-place purchases. And you have to price your offerings properly and promote them. What good are your products and services if others don't know about them? After you've been successful in developing offerings that meet a need, new worries begin: competitors. Your success will likely spur imitators.

Even though you may never desire a career in accounting, you'll be confronted with tracking revenue and expenses, making tax payments, and perhaps handling a payroll. You may find yourself poring over lease contracts and evaluating office space. You'll likely need to read trade and professional journals to keep current with changes in your field. Although you may never want to be a human resource manager, you need to know about the right ways to hire, train, and retain good employees. You may soon become an expert on insurance and other employee benefits.

And then business owners face personal and emotional challenges, which rarely get airtime among all the glory of the rags-to-riches tales of multimillionaire entrepreneurs. Major health problems, divorces, fights and lawsuits among family members in business together, the loss of friends, and even suicides have been attributed to the passions of business owners consumed with winning or overwhelmed by their failures.

Had enough, already? I'm not trying to *scare* you, but I do want you to be *realistic* about starting your own business. Maybe you do have the right stuff to run your own company, but most people don't.

Ten questions to see if you have the right stuff

The keys to success and enjoyment as an entrepreneur vary as much as the businesses do. But if you can answer yes to most of the following questions, you've got the qualities and perspective needed to be a small business owner. Don't be deterred by those questions that you can't answer in the affirmative. A perfect entrepreneur doesn't exist. Part of succeeding in business is knowing what you can't do as well as what you can and finding creative ways (or people) to help you.

1. Are you a self-starter? Do you like challenges? Are you persistent? Are you willing to do research to solve problems?

Running your own business is not glamorous most of the time, especially in the early years. You have lots of details to mind and things to do. Success in business is the result of doing lots of little things well. If you're accustomed to working for larger organizations where much of the day is spent in meetings, on office politics and gossip, and with little accountability, you probably won't like or succeed at running your own business.

2. Do you value independence and self-control?

Particularly in the early days of your business, you have to enjoy working on your own. If you're a people person, however, many businesses offer lots of contact. But recognize the difference between socializing with coworkers and networking with business contacts and customers. When you leave a company environment and work on your own, you're giving up a lot of the socializing. Of course, if you work in an uptight environment or with people you don't really value socializing with, venturing out on your own may be a plus.

3. Can you develop a commitment to an idea, product, or principle?

Most entrepreneurs work 50 hours per week, 50 or so weeks a year — that's about 2,500 hours per year. If your product, service, or cause that you're pursuing doesn't excite you, and you can't motivate others to work hard for you, it's going to be a long year!

One of the worst reasons to start your own business is for the pursuit of great financial riches. Don't get me wrong. If you're good at what you do and know how to market your services or products, you may be able to make more money working for yourself. But for most people, money is not enough of a motivation. And many people make the same or less money on their own than they did or could working for a company.

4. Are you willing to make financial sacrifices and live a reduced lifestyle before and during your early entrepreneurial years?

"Live like a student, before and during start-up of your small business" was the advice given to me by my best business school professor, James Collins, when I started my business. With most businesses, you're going to expend money during the start-up years and likely have a reduced income versus working for a company.

In order to make your entrepreneurial dream a reality, you're going to have to do a good job living well within your means both before and after your start-up. But if you really are happier running your own business, sacrificing expensive vacations, overpriced luxury cars, the latest designer clothing, and $2.50 lattes at the corner cafe shouldn't be too painful.

5. Do you recognize that, when running your own business, you will still have bosses?

Besides the allure of huge profits, the other reason some people mistakenly go into business for themselves is that they say they are tired of working for other people. Obnoxious, evil bosses are enough to make anyone want to be an entrepreneur. I understand — I've been there. When I worked at a consulting firm, I

Don't start a business for tax write-offs

"Start a small business for fun, profit, and huge tax deductions," a financial advice book declares, adding that "the tax benefits alone are worth starting a small business." A seminar company offers a course entitled "How to Have Zero Taxes Deducted from Your Paycheck." This tax seminar tells you how to solve your tax problems: "If you have a sideline business, or would like to start one, you're eligible to have little or no taxes taken from your pay."

All this sounds too good to be true — and of course it is. Not only are the strategies sure to lead to IRS audit purgatory, but you're also likely to be seduced by such books and seminars to pony up $100 or more for audiotapes or notebooks of "inside information."

Unfortunately, many self-proclaimed self-help gurus claim that you can slash your taxes simply by finding a product or service that you can sell on the side. The problem, they argue, is that as a regular wage earner who receives a paycheck from an employer, you can't write off many of your other (personal) expenses. Open a sideline business, they say, and you can deduct your personal expenses as a business expense.

The pitch is enticing, but the reality is something quite different. You have to spend money to get tax deductions, and the spending must be for legitimate purposes of your business in its efforts to generate income. If you're thinking that it's worth the risk of taking tax deductions for your hobby because you won't get caught

unless you're audited, the odds are stacked against you. The IRS audits an extraordinarily large portion of small businesses that show regular losses. And in the early 1990s, the IRS greatly tightened the rules for writing off business meals, entertainment, and travel.

The bottom line is that you need to operate a real business for the purpose of generating income and profits, not tax deductions. An activity is considered a hobby (and not a business) by the IRS if it shows a loss for three or more of the preceding five tax years. (Horse racing and breeding is considered a hobby if it shows a loss for five or more of the preceding seven tax years.) Some years, a certain number of businesses lose money. But a real business can't afford to do so year after year and remain in operation. Even if your sideline business passes this hobby test, as well as other IRS requirements, it's illegal to deduct any expenses not directly applicable to your business.

If these hobby loss rules indicate that you're engaging in a hobby and you still want to claim your losses, you must convince the IRS that you are seriously trying to make a profit and run a legitimate business. The IRS will want to see that you are actively marketing your services, building your skills, and accounting for income and expenses. The IRS also wants to see that you're not deriving too much pleasure from an activity. If you are, the IRS says what you're doing must be a hobby and not a business. Business isn't supposed to be too pleasurable!

had a boss — I'll call him Goofus — whom I positively detested. Although the team that I led had many weeks to prepare client presentations, Goofus wouldn't really focus on the material until a couple of days before the presentation. Then he made massive changes, causing the entire team as well as the production department, which produced the presentation, to work 16-hour days and into the wee hours of the morning. Goofus also made himself inaccessible for input and advice and even ignored voice mails, until he got into crisis mode. He never apologized for his behavior and couldn't have cared less about people's personal lives. Because of people like Goofus, people who wanted some semblance of control in their lives, as well as a personal life, left the consulting business.

When you run your own business, you will have customers and other bosses just like Goofus who are miserable to deal with. If you have enough customers, you can simply decide not to deal with such jerks. Don't worry, though; the worst customers usually can't make your life anywhere near as miserable as bosses like Goofus.

6. Can you withstand rejection, naysayers, and negative feedback?

"I thought every no that I got when trying to raise my funding brought me one step closer to a yes," says Alex Popov, the entrepreneur I introduced earlier in this chapter. Unless you come from an entrepreneurial family, don't expect your parents to endorse your "risky, crazy" behavior. Most of the time, parents simply think that you're safer and more secure working for a giant company (which, of course, is a myth, because corporations can lay you off in a snap). It's also easier for them to say to their friends and neighbors that you're a big manager for IBM or Microsoft rather than explain that you're working on some kooky business idea out of a spare bedroom.

Even other entrepreneurs can be wet blankets on your good ideas. Two of my entrepreneurial friends were each critical to me of each other's idea, yet both have succeeded!

7. Are you able to identify your shortcomings and hire or align yourself with people and organizations that complement your skills and expertise?

To be a successful entrepreneur, you do need to be a bit of a jack-of-all-trades: marketer, accountant, customer service representative, administrative assistant, and so on. Unless you get lots of investor capital, which is rare for a true start-up, you're not going to be able to afford to hire help in the early months, and perhaps even years, of your business.

It may make sense for you, however, to partner with or buy certain services or products rather than trying to do everything yourself. And over time, if your business grows and succeeds, you should be able to afford hiring more help. If you can be honest with yourself and surround and partner with people whose skills and expertise complement yours, you'll have a winning team!

8. Do you deal well with ambiguity? Do you believe in yourself?

When you're on your own, determining when and if you're on the right track is difficult. Some days, things won't go well. If you are the company, bad days are much harder to take. So being confident, optimistic, and able to work around obstacles are necessary skills.

Wet blankets through history

"This 'telephone' has too many shortcomings to be seriously considered as a means of communication. The device is inherently of no value to us." — Western Union internal memo in response to Alexander Graham Bell's telephone, 1876.

"The concept is interesting and well formed, but in order to earn better than a C, the idea must be feasible." — a Yale University management professor in response to Fred Smith's paper proposing reliable overnight delivery service. Smith went on to found Federal Express Corporation.

"We don't tell you how to coach, so don't tell us how to make shoes." — a large sporting shoe manufacturer to Bill Bowerman, inventor of the waffle shoe and cofounder of NIKE, Inc.

"So we went to Atari and said, 'Hey, we've got this amazing thing, even built with some of your parts, and what do you think about funding us? Or we'll give it to you. We just want to do it. Pay our salary, we'll come work for you.' And they said, 'No.' So then we went to Hewlett-Packard, and they said, 'Hey, we don't need you. You haven't got through college yet.'" — Steve Jobs, speaking about attempts to get Atari and HP interested in his and Steve Wozniak's personal computer. Jobs and Wozniak founded Apple Computer.

"'You should franchise them,' I told them. 'I'll be your guinea pig.' Well, they just went straight up in the air! They couldn't see the philosophy.

. . . When they turned us down, that left Bud and me to swim on our own." — Sam Walton, describing his efforts to get the Ben Franklin chain interested in his discount retailing concept in 1962. Walton went on to found Wal-Mart.

"We don't like their sound, and guitar music is on the way out." — Decca Recording Company in rejecting The Beatles, 1962.

In 1884, John Henry Patterson was ridiculed by his business friends for paying $6,500 for the rights to the cash register — a product with "limited" or no potential. Patterson went on to found National Cash Register (NCR) Corporation.

"What's all this computer nonsense you're trying to bring into medicine? I've got no confidence at all in computers and I want nothing whatsoever to do with them." — a medical professor in England to Dr. John Alfred Powell, about the CT scanner.

"That is good sport. But for the military, the airplane is useless." — Ferdinand Foch, Commander in Chief, Allied Forces on the Western Front, World War I.

"The television will never achieve popularity; it takes place in a semi-darkened room and demands continuous attention." — Harvard Professor Chester L. Dawes, 1940.

Reprinted with permission from *Beyond Entrepreneurship, Turning Your Business into an Enduring Great Company*, James C. Collins and William C. Lazier, Prentice Hall.

9. Do you understand why you started the business and how you personally define "success"?

Many business entrepreneurs define success by such measures as sales revenue, profits, number of branch offices and employees, and so on. These are fine measures. Other organizations, particularly non-profits, have other measures. Handgun Control, a non-profit organization, defines success by the passage of laws restricting and banning guns and by educating the American public about the dangers of guns. In order to accomplish such goals, money is necessary, but such a cause-focused organization has a very different bottom line than a for-profit organization.

10. Can you accept lack of success in the early years of building your business?

A few, rare businesses are instant hits, but most businesses take time — years, perhaps even decades — to build momentum. Some successful corporate people suffer from anxiety when they go out on their own and encounter the inevitable struggles and lack of tangible success in building their company.

Myths of being an entrepreneur

Many myths persist about what it takes to be an entrepreneur, partly because those who aren't entrepreneurs tend to hang out with others who aren't. The "successful" entrepreneurs who are popularized by the mass media — such as Donald Trump, Ted Turner, and Michael Jackson — lead to misperceptions and misconceptions.

One myth is that you have to be well connected or know people to be successful as an entrepreneur. This is pure bunk. Much more important is being a decent human being. Enough rude, inconsiderate, and self-centered people are in the business world, and if you're not that way, you'll be able to meet people who can help you in one way or another. Besides, if you look in the mirror, you'll see your best and most trusted resource.

Another myth is that you need to be really smart and have an M.B.A. or some other fancy degree. Again, pure bunk. Many successful entrepreneurs — Bill Gates, Steve Jobs, and so on — don't even have college degrees, for goodness sakes. Perusing *Forbes* magazine's list of the 200 best small companies shows that 36 of the CEOs didn't earn a college degree and 128 don't have advanced degrees! These statistics are all the more amazing when you consider the relatively large number of entrepreneurs with humble backgrounds who leave or are forced out of the successful enterprises they've started.

I'm not saying that a good education isn't worthwhile in general and for helping you succeed in your own business. (For example, about 5 percent of the 200 best small businesses are run by Ivy Leaguers, yet Ivy League college grads make up less than 1 percent of all graduates.) But a formal education isn't necessary.

As for intelligence, which is admittedly a difficult thing to measure, the majority of entrepreneurs have IQs under 120 and a surprising percentage under the average of 100 — more entrepreneurs, in fact, have IQs under 100 than have IQs greater than 130.

Another commonly held belief is that to be an entrepreneur, you must be a gregarious big-egoed extrovert. Although some studies have shown that more entrepreneurs are extroverted, many entrepreneurs are not.

A final myth to dispel is the notion that starting your own business is risky. Some people focus on the potential for failure. Consider the worst case — if your venture doesn't work out, you can always go back to a job similar to the one you left behind. Also, recognize that risk is a matter of perception, and as with investments, people completely overlook some risks. What about the risk to your happiness and career in staying in a boring, claw-your-way-up-the-corporate-ladder kind of job? You always risk a layoff when working for a company. An even greater risk is that you'll wake up when in your 50s and 60s and think that it's too late to do something on your own and wish you had tried to sooner.

Alternatives to starting your own company

Sometimes, entrepreneurial advocates imply that running your own business is just the greatest thing in the world and everyone would be happy doing it if they just set their mind to it. The reality is that some people aren't going to be happy as entrepreneurs. If you're one of those people who didn't score highly on the ten-question entrepreneur quiz I gave you in the last section, don't despair. You could very well be happier and more successful doing something other than starting your own business.

Some people are happier working for a company, either for-profit or non-profit. Others do well buying an existing small business rather than trying to start one from scratch. Following are some options to consider.

Being an entrepreneur inside a company

A happy medium is available for people who want the challenge of running their own show without giving up the comforts and security that come with a company environment — for example, you can manage an entrepreneurial venture at a company. That's what John Kilcullen, president and chief executive officer of IDG Books Worldwide (this book's publisher), did when he helped launch the book publishing division of IDG in 1990.

Kilcullen had solid publishing industry experience and wanted to take on the responsibility for growing a successful publishing company. But he also knew that it took a lot of money and resources to be a player in book publishing. By being a member of the founding team of four in the new IDG Books division, Kilcullen had the best of both worlds.

Kilcullen had always had a passion to start his own business but found that most traditional publishers were not interested in giving autonomy and money to a division and letting it run with the ball. "I wanted the ability to build a business on my own instincts . . . the appeal of IDG was that it was decentralized. IDG was willing to invest and provide the freedom to spend as we saw fit."

If you're able to secure an entrepreneurial position inside a larger company, in addition to significant managerial and operational responsibility, you can also negotiate sharing in the financial success that you help create. The parent company's senior management wants you to have the incentive that comes from sharing in the financial success of your endeavors. Granting of bonuses, stock options, and the like often are tied to the performance of a division.

Investing in your career

Some people are happy or content with being employees. Companies need and want lots of good employees, so you'll *always* be able to find a job if you have skills, a work ethic, and the ability to get along with others.

You can improve your income-earning ability and invest in your career a variety of different ways:

- **Work, work, work.** Be willing to work extra hours and take on more responsibility. Don't bite off more than you can chew — otherwise your supervisors won't have faith that they can count on you to deliver. Those who take extra initiative and deliver really stand out in a company where many people working on a salary have a time-clock, 9-to-5 mentality.

- **Read, read, read.** One of the reasons that you don't need a Ph.D., master's degree, or even an undergraduate college degree to succeed in business is that you can learn a lot on your own. You can learn by doing, but you can also learn a lot by reading. A good bookstore has no entrance requirements, such as an elevated high school grade point average or SAT scores. You just walk through the doors. A good book isn't free, but it costs a heck of lot less than taking more college or graduate courses!

- **Study, study, study.** If you haven't completed your college or graduate degree and the industry you're in values those who do, it may be worth investing the time and money to finish your education. Talk to others who have taken that path and see what they have to say, allowing for the human tendency to justify the path one has previously chosen.

Small business investment options

The ways to make money with small businesses are only limited by your imagination. Choosing the option that best meets your needs is not unlike choosing other investments, such as in real estate or in the securities markets. Following are the major ways to invest in small business and what's attractive and ugly about each.

Starting your own business

Of all your small business options, starting your own business involves the greatest amount of work. Although you can do this work on a part-time basis in the beginning, most people end up in their business full-time — it's your new job, career, or whatever you want to call it.

For most of my working years, I've run my own business and, overall, I really like it. That's not to say that running my own business doesn't have its drawbacks and down moments. In my experience counseling small business owners, I've seen many people of varied backgrounds, interests, and skills succeed and be happy with running their own business.

Most people perceive starting their own business as the riskiest of all small business investment options. But if you're going into a business that utilizes your skills and expertise, the risk is not nearly as great as you may think.

Suppose that you're a teacher and making $30,000 per year working for a school district. Maybe you'd like to set up your own tutoring service and would be happy making a comparable amount of money. If you find through your research that others performing these services are charging $30 per hour, you need to actually tutor about 20 or so hours per week, assuming that you work 50 weeks per year. Because you can run this business from your home (which can possibly generate small tax breaks) without purchasing new equipment, your expenses should be nil.

Rather than leaving your job cold turkey and trying to build the business from scratch, maybe you can start moonlighting as a tutor. Over a couple of years, if you can get up to ten hours per week on average, you're halfway to your goal. If you leave your job and focus all your energies on your tutoring business, getting to 20 hours per week of billable work shouldn't be a problem. Still think starting a business is risky?

Many businesses can be started with low start-up costs, by leveraging your existing skills and expertise. You can build a valuable company and job if you have the time to devote to building "sweat equity." As long as you check out the competition and offer a valued service at a reasonable cost, the principal risk with your business is that you won't do a good job marketing what you have to offer. If you can market your skills, you're home free.

Wearing two hats at once

Starting a business of your own outside your full-time job can be done. Some businesses as well as jobs, of course, have greater time demands than others. And the combination of your current job and personal life may not afford you the time and energy to get your own business going on the side. If you're single or childless, wearing two work hats is much more doable.

Chris, who worked at a management consulting firm, started a computer consulting and repair firm. Although management consulting jobs are demanding — it's not a 9-to-5 kind of job — Chris, who was single, made his venture work by his willingness to work extra hours. He typically worked 10-15 hours per week at the computer business, often squeezing in calls during the day at his consulting job. Some work environments don't offer as much autonomy as a consulting firm to allow someone this flexibility.

Chris also was able to pull off starting and running his company by finding a partner to work full-time in the business. His partner was more interested in and experienced with the day-to-day operations of such a company. Chris was better at setting up the corporate framework. Chris also spent one summer between his first and second years at business school setting up accounting and other management systems for the company.

After three years, Chris's business was grossing $2.2 million and had 14 employees and decent profitability with about 10 percent net profit on sales. Not bad for a part-time investment of Chris's time.

Buying an existing business

If you don't have a specific idea for a business you want to start but have business management skills and an ability to improve existing businesses, buying an established business may be for you. Although you don't have to go through the riskier start-up period if you take this route, you will likely need more capital to buy a going enterprise.

You also need to be able to deal with stickier personnel and management issues. The history of the organization and the way things work will predate your ownership of the business. If you don't like making hard decisions, firing people who don't fit with your plans, and coercing people into changing the way they did things before you arrived on the scene, buying an existing business likely isn't for you. Or the good employees may have been loyal to the old owner, and they split when you arrive.

Some people perceive buying an existing business as safer than starting one. Buying someone else's business can actually be riskier. You're likely to have to shell out far more money, in the form of a down payment, up front to buy a business. If you don't have the ability to run the business and it does poorly, you have a lot more to lose financially. Another risk is that the business is for sale for a reason — it's not very profitable, it's in decline, or it's generally a pain in the neck to operate.

Good businesses for sale don't come cheaply. If the business is a success, the current owner has removed the start-up risk from the business, so the price of the business should be at a premium to reflect this lack of risk. If you have the capital to buy an established business and you have the skills to run it, consider going this route. Chapter 14 goes into detail about how to buy a good business.

Investing in someone else's business

If you like the idea of profiting from successful small businesses but don't want the day-to-day headaches of being responsible for managing the enterprise, investing in someone else's small business may be for you. Although this route may seem easier, fewer people are actually cut out to be investors in other people's businesses.

Consider investing in someone else's business if you meet the following criteria:

✔ You have sufficient assets so that what you are investing in small, privately held companies is a small portion (20 percent or less) of your total financial assets.

✔ You can afford to lose what you're investing. Unlike investing in a diversified stock mutual fund (Chapter 8), you can lose all your investment when investing in a small, privately held company.

 ✔ You're astute at evaluating corporate financial statements and business
 strategy. Investing in a small, privately held company has much in common with investing in a publicly traded firm. The difference is that private
 firms aren't required to produce comprehensive, audited financial statements that adhere to certain accounting principles the way that public
 companies are. Thus, you have a greater risk of not having sufficient or
 accurate information when evaluating a small private firm.

See Chapter 14 for more information on investing in small businesses.

Blueprinting a Business Plan

If you've gotten yourself psyched up to consider starting your own business,
the next step is to figure out what you want to do and how you're going to do it.
You don't have to have a perfectly detailed plan that spells out all the minutiae.
Doing such an involved plan is a waste of your time because things change and
evolve over time.

But you do need a general plan to help define what it is that you think you want
to do and what you need to do to accomplish it. If you don't like planning and
writing, don't break out in hives. This business plan shouldn't be a waste of
your time and energies to put together; it should become a working document
or blueprint for the early days, months, and years of your business.

How detailed a plan you need depends upon your goals and the specifics of
your business. A simple, more short-term focused plan (ten pages or so) is fine
if you don't aspire to build an empire. However, if your goal is to grow, hire
employees, and open multiple locations, then your plan needs to cover longer-
term issues and be longer in length (20 to 50 pages). If you want outside
investor money, a longer business plan is a necessity.

As you put together your plan and evaluate your opportunities, open your ears
and eyes. Expect to do research and to speak with other entrepreneurs and
people in the industry. Many people are willing to spend time talking with you
as long as they realize that you're not interested in competing with what
they do.

Your business concept

What is your business going to do? What product or service is it going to offer?
Maybe your business goal is to perform tax preparation services for small
business owners. Perhaps you want to start a consulting firm, open a restaurant
that sells healthy fast food, run a plumbing service, or manufacture widgets.

Alan Tripp started a company called Score Advantage Learning Centers. He describes his concept as follows: "Score is a storefront center for computer-assisted learning, where kids use computers to improve their reading, writing, math, and science skills."

To be viable, your concept need not be unique. Tons of self-employed consultants, plumbers, tax preparers, and restaurant owners are out there. The existence of lots of other people already doing what you want to do validates the potential for what you're setting out to do. I know lots of wage slaves who say they would love to run their own business if they could only come up with "the idea." Most of these people will still be waiting when they're ready to start drawing their Social Security checks. It's more important to be committed to the idea of running your own business. In the beginning, the business opportunities you pursue can be quite general to your field of expertise or interest. What you do over time will evolve.

I'm not saying a new, innovative idea doesn't have any merit. An innovative idea gives you the chance to hit a big home run. The first people to successfully develop a new idea can achieve big success.

Even if you aspire to build the next billion-dollar company, you can put a twist on older concepts. Suppose you're a veterinarian but you don't want a traditional office where people must bring their cats and dogs for treatment. You believe that because many people are starved for free time, they want a vet who makes house calls. Thus, Vet on Wheels may be born. You may want to franchise the business and have locations around the country. But if you want to run your own veterinary business, you also can succeed doing what thousands of other vets are now doing and have done over the years with a traditional office.

Outlining your objectives

The reasons for starting and running your own small business are as varied as the entrepreneurs behind their companies. Before you start your firm, it's useful to think about what you're seeking to achieve. These objectives need not be cast in concrete and will surely change over time. If you like, you can write up your objectives into a short and motivating mission statement.

When you ask an M.B.A., especially one from a big-name school, to think about objectives, he or she usually says something like, "My goal is to be running a $20 million company in seven years." Financial objectives are fine, but your objectives likely shouldn't be just financial, unless money is the only reason for running your own business.

In introductory economics courses, students are taught that the objective of every for-profit firm is to maximize profits. As with many things taught in economics courses, this theory has one problem — it doesn't hold up in the real world. Most small business owners I know don't manage their businesses maniacally in the pursuit of maximum profits. Following are some other possible objectives to consider:

✔ **Working with people you like and respect.** Some customers may be willing to buy your products and services, and some employees and suppliers may offer you their services for a good price, but what if you can't stand working with them? If you have sufficient business or just have your own standards, you can choose whom you do business with.

✔ **Educating others.** Maybe part of your goal in starting your business is to educate the public about something you're an expert in. Alex Popov, the entrepreneur you met earlier in this chapter who started a healthy fast-food restaurant, saw education as an important part of his company's purpose.

✔ **Improving an industry/setting a higher standard.** Perhaps part of your goal in starting your business is to be outspoken about your industry and to show how it can better serve its customers. John Bogle, who founded the Vanguard Group of mutual funds, is a good example of someone who wanted to improve an industry. When he started Vanguard in the early 1970s, Bogle structured the company so that it would be owned by the shareholders (customers) of the company's individual mutual funds. Because he relinquished ownership of his company, Bogle gave up the opportunity to build a personal net worth that would easily be several billion dollars today. But Bogle wanted to build a mutual fund company that kept operating costs to a minimum and returned profits to the customers in the form of lower operating fees, which are deducted from a mutual fund's returns. He's also been outspoken about how owners of many mutual fund companies operate their funds out of self-interest rather than with their customers in mind.

Of course, you can't accomplish these objectives without profits, and doing these things is not inconsistent with making greater profits. But if your objectives are more than financial or your financial objectives are not your number-one concern, don't worry — it's usually a good sign.

Analyze the marketplace

The single most important area to understand is the marketplace your business competes in. To be successful, your business must not only produce a good product or service, but it must also reach and convince customers to buy. You should also discern what the competition has to offer, as well as its strengths and vulnerabilities. In most industries, you also need to understand government regulations that affect the type of business you're considering.

Research model companies

If your business provides products or services similar to those offered by other companies, identify one, two, or three of your competitors that do a good job or seem most similar. Which of these companies' practices do you want to emulate? In what areas can you improve upon or differentiate your offerings?

Even if you have an innovative and apparently unique concept, examine companies in related and even dissimilar fields to identify those you want to mimic. You may identify traits and characteristics from several, which you can build into the composite of your own firm.

For the model companies you examine, find out about the following:

✔ Why they chose their location

✔ How they promote their services and products

✔ How they provide or manufacture their products and services

✔ What types of customers they attract

✔ What their revenues, expenses, and profitability are

✔ How they've expanded their locations over time (if this is your goal)

Meeting customer needs

If the market analysis is the most important part of the business plan, then understanding your customers is the most important part of your market analysis. If you don't understand your target customers and their needs, you're dead. Actually, you're still alive — just don't expect to have a successful business.

If you're in a business that sells to consumers, consider the gender, age, income, geographic location, marital status, number of children, education, living situation (rent or own), and the reasons they want your product or service. Who are your target customers? Where do they live, what do they care about? If you sell to businesses, understand similar issues. What types of businesses will buy your product or services? Why?

The best way to get to know your potential customers is to get out and talk to them. In-person interviews or a paper-based survey both have their benefits. Although more time-consuming, live interviews provide the most accurate and useful information. These interviews allow you to go with the flow of the conversation, improvise questions, and probe more interesting areas. Although paper-based surveys can be mailed or faxed to many people with a minimal investment of your time, the response rate is usually quite low and the answers are usually not as illuminating. Offer a product or service sample or some other promotional item to those who help you with your research. Doing so attracts people who are interested in your product or service, which helps you define your target customers.

Also, try to get a sense of what customers are paying and are willing to pay for the products or services you offer. Analyzing the competition's offerings helps, too. Some products or services also require follow-up or additional servicing. Understand what customers need and what they are willing to pay for it.

If you're trying to raise money from investors, you should also include some estimates as to the size of the market for your product or services. Of course, such numbers are ballpark estimates. But sizing the market for your product helps you estimate profitability, the share of the market needed to be profitable, and so on.

Beating the competition

In war or sports, it pays to size up the competition. Examining competitor strategies is a must for any business owner. Otherwise, you're going on blind faith that what you're offering stacks up well versus the other alternatives in the industry. Always examine the products and services that competitors offer, as well as their benefits and pricing.

First, you need to decide if you have a realistic chance of winning the battle. It is crazy, I think you'll agree, to go into the same discount warehouse retailing business and compete head-to-head with Wal-Mart, Price-Costco, or Home Depot. Even if you can find some wealthy investor foolish enough to fund your venture, you'll likely get clobbered.

Second, you want to discover your competitors' weaknesses so that you can exploit them. Rather than trying to beat Price-Costco on its terms, maybe you've identified a need for a neighborhood pet supply store that offers a much broader and specialized range of pet supplies than just the big-selling brands of dog and cat food that Price-Costco sells. Knowledgeable customer sales representatives to answer customer questions and make product suggestions can also be in your competitive arsenal.

Thus, you can beat Price-Costco on three counts: convenience of location for people in your neighborhood, breadth of product offerings, and customer assistance. Trying to compete with Price-Costco on its terms by offering only economy sizes of the best-selling brands of pet food would be foolish. Your prices would have to be higher, because you won't be able to negotiate the volume purchases that Price-Costco can. You would also have greater overhead (not in absolute dollars but as a percentage of your revenue) running a small business.

That's not to say that your neighborhood pet supply store can't offer some best-selling pet food. As I'm sure you know, some convenience store customers are willing to pay top dollar for smaller bags of supplies close to home. Many people don't shop at Price-Costco despite its low prices.

If you want to open a neighborhood pet supply store, evaluate a number of different locales to see where other similar stores are located. Visit those stores and observe their strengths and weaknesses. If you're discreet, you may be able to interview some customers outside the stores to see what they like and don't like about them.

Don't make the mistake of thinking that even if you have a completely innovative product or service that no other business is currently offering, you don't have competitors. All businesses have competitors. For example, suppose you start a business that sells classified advertising space online on a World Wide Web site. If you're the first to offer this service, you may think that you don't have competitors, but of course you do. While not online, lots of newspapers and magazines offer classified ads. A competitor is an alternative company a customer can use to meet a similar need. Remember, customers *don't* think, "I want to place this ad on the Internet." They *do* think, "What are the costs and benefits of the different places where I can place this ad?"

Knowing the regulation

Most businesses are subject to some sort of regulation. If you're considering a retail business, for example, few communities permit you to run it out of your home. If you lease or purchase a private location, you are subject to and restricted by the zoning placed on that location. So you had better check what you can and cannot sell through that location. Check with the zoning department of your city or town — don't go on the word of a real estate broker or property owner who has a sales interest in saying, "No problem!"

If you were going to start a veterinary practice, you would quickly discover that special zoning is required to use a piece of real estate for a vet's office. Getting a local zoning board to allow for a new location to get such special zoning is quite difficult, if not impossible, in some areas.

With some businesses, other licenses and filings with local, state, or even the federal government are required. For example, financial advisors who provide investment advice are required to be registered with the U.S. Securities and Exchange Commission as well as with a state agency (in most states) where advisors are monitored.

If you're entering an industry you're relatively new to, start by asking questions and opening your ears. Speak to people who are currently in the field and your local Chamber of Commerce to see what, if any, licenses or filings you must complete. Also, check out your local bookstore. If you're interested in running a veterinary practice, read books on the subject. Look in a bookstore with a good business section. Also, check at the newsstand and a local library for trade magazines that may deal with your questions. Libraries have books and online services that can help you locate specific articles on topics of interest to you.

Service or product delivery

Every business has a product or service to sell. How are you going to provide this product or service? Suppose you want to start a business that delivers groceries and runs errands for busy people or people who are older or disabled and can't easily do everything for themselves.

You should map out the steps of how you will provide the service. When potential customers call you to inquire about your business, what kinds of information do you want to record about their situation? You should have a pricing sheet and other marketing literature (discussed later in this chapter) that you can mail them.

After someone calls and says, "I want to hire you!," you need to collect more details. Try drawing up an information sheet that prompts you for the information you need (for example, address, delivery time promised, items desired, and so on).

If you want to be a tax preparer, you'll probably need forms or a filing system to give to your customers to help them organize the information they give to you. The point is to map out in advance a system to work with. The system will evolve over time — you can be guaranteed of that — but a tentative game plan has great value.

If you're manufacturing a product, you definitely want to map out the process you're going to use. Otherwise, you'll have no idea how much time the manufacturing process is going to take or what it's going to cost.

As you grow and hire employees to provide the services or make the products, the more you codify what you do, the better they can replicate your good work.

Marketing

After you have a good idea about what your company's services or products are all about, you need to get more specific about the following:

- ✔ **How much are you going to charge for your services and products?** Start by looking at what competing products and services cost. Also, estimate your costs, which helps you figure what you need to charge to cover your costs and make a reasonable profit.

- ✔ **How are you going to promote and advertise?** It's not enough to have a great product or service if you keep it a secret. You gotta get the word out. It's doubtful you have the budget or want to reach the same region that television and radio reach.

   Start with people you know. Develop a punchy, informational one-page letter announcing your company's inception and what you have to offer and mail it to your contacts. Include an envelope with a reply form that allows recipients to provide the addresses of others who may be interested in what you have to offer. Send these folks a mailing as well, referencing who passed their name along to you.

Finding and retaining customers is vital to any business that wants to grow and keep its costs in line. One simple, inexpensive way to stay in touch with customers you've dealt with or others who have made inquiries and expressed interest in your company's offerings is via a mailing list. Once a quarter, once a year, or whatever makes sense for your business, send out a simple, professional-looking postcard or newsletter announcing new information about your business and what customer needs you may be able to fulfill. Such mailings also allow you to remind people that you're still in business and that you provide a wonderful product or service. Computer software gives you a fast, efficient way to keep a customer mailing list up-to-date and to print mailing labels.

✔ **How will you position your product and services versus the competition?** Remember the local pet supply store — it positions itself as being convenient and having a broad, comprehensive selection and knowledgeable customer assistance.

Books are similarly positioned in the book marketplace. I hope, in your mind, my financial books are down-to-earth, practical and answer-oriented, and educational.

✔ **Where are you going to sell your product or service?** Business consultants label this decision the distribution channel question. For example, if you're going to go into the hula-hoop manufacturing business, you may consider selling via mail order, through toy stores, or through discount warehouse stores. Selling through each of these different distribution channels requires unique marketing and advertising programs.

If you're marketing a product or service to companies, you should also give thought to who the key decision-makers are at the company.

Organization and people

Many small businesses are one-person operations. So much the better for you — you have none of the headaches of hiring, payroll, and so on. You only have to worry about you — and that may be a handful in itself!

But if you desire to manage the work being done rather than doing it all yourself and if you hope to grow your business, you'll eventually want to hire people. (I explain the best way to fill your personnel needs in the next chapter.) If hiring is your goal, give some thought now to the skills and functional areas of expertise these people will need. If you want to raise money, this section of your business plan is essential to show your investors that you're a long-term planner and thinker.

Maybe you'll want an administrative assistant, researcher, marketing person, or sales representative. What about a training specialist, finance person, or real estate person if you need to expand to many sites? Consider what background you desire in those you hire and look at what types of people similar companies have selected and hired. (Look at those model companies that you read about earlier in this chapter.)

You should also give some thought as to what legal form of organization — for example, sole proprietorship, partnership, S corporation, limited liability company — your business will adopt. This topic is also addressed in the next chapter.

Protecting your ideas

One valid concern entrepreneurs have in circulating copies of their business plan is that they may be giving away all their hard work and ideas to someone or some company that can end up being a competitor. In addition to exercising common sense regarding whom you share your plan with, keep highly proprietary information, such as product design specifications, out of your plan. Share such information with serious investors only if it's a necessity to gain the investment. If your work and ideas are proprietary and protectable, speak with an attorney concerning (or learn more about) copyrights, trademarks, and patents.

Also place a nondisclosure statement in the front of your business plan. Following is a sample nondisclosure:

This confidential Business Plan has been prepared in order to raise financing for XYZ Inc. This material is being delivered to a select number of potential investors, each of whom agrees to the following terms and conditions:

Each recipient of this Business Plan agrees that, by accepting this material, he or she will not copy, reproduce, distribute, or discuss with others any part of this plan without prior written consent of XYZ Inc.

The recipient agrees to keep confidential all information contained herein and not use it for any purpose whatsoever other than to evaluate and determine interest in providing financing described herein.

This material contains proprietary and confidential information regarding XYZ Inc. and is based upon information provided to XYZ by sources deemed to be reliable. Although the information contained herein is believed to be accurate, XYZ Inc. expressly disclaims all liability for any information, projections, or representations (expressed or implied) contained herein from omissions from this material or for any written or oral communication transmitted to any part in the course of its evaluation for this financing. The recipient acknowledges this material shall remain the property of XYZ Inc., and XYZ Inc. reserves the right to request the return of the material at any time and in any respect, to amend or terminate solicitation procedures, to terminate discussions with any and all prospective financing sources, to reject any and all proposals, or to negotiate with any party with respect to the financing of XYZ Inc.

The projections contained in the pro-forma Financial Section are based upon numerous assumptions. Although XYZ Inc. believes these assumptions are reasonable, no assurance can be given as to the accuracy of these projections because they are dependent in large part upon unforeseeable factors and events. As a result, the actual results achieved may vary from the projections, and such variation can be material and adverse.

Run the numbers: financial projections 101

An idea often becomes a bad idea or a business failure if you neglect to look at or be realistic about the financial side of the business you want to start. If you're a creative or people-person type who hates numbers, the financial side may be the part of the business plan you'll most want to blow off. Don't — doing so will cost you perhaps tens of thousands of dollars in avoidable mistakes. Ignoring the financial side can even lead to the bankruptcy of a business founded with a good idea.

Before you launch your business, you should do enough research so that you can come up with some decent financial estimates to address these issues. Financial projections are mandatory and will likely be closely scrutinized by knowledgeable investors if you're seeking outside money. You will also need to think through how and when investors can cash out.

Start-up and development costs

You need to spend money to get your business from the idea stage to an operating enterprise. Before the revenue begins to flow in, you need to spend money to develop and market your products and services. Understand what you need to spend money on and the likely timing of the needed purchases.

If you were going to build a house, you would develop a list of all the costs of doing so. How much is the land, construction, carpeting, landscaping, and so on, going to cost? You can try to develop all these cost estimates yourself or you can speak with local builders and have them help you. Likewise, with your business, you can hire a business consultant who knows something about your type of business. I think you're best served by doing the homework yourself — you learn a lot more and it's far cheaper.

If you're going to be working in an office setting, either at home or in outside space, you need furniture, such as a desk, chair, filing cabinets, computer, printer, and office supplies. Read the sections on equipping an office, finding office space, and working from home in the next chapter. If you need to obtain licenses or register with any government bodies, don't forget to factor in those costs, too.

If you're running a retailing operation, you need to also estimate your initial inventory costs. Remember, it takes time to sell your inventory, especially when you first start up. And as a new business, suppliers won't give you months on end to pay for your initial inventory. Be realistic — otherwise money tied up in inventory can pinch you and can possibly send you to financial ruin.

Income statement

Preparing an estimated *income statement,* which summarizes your revenue and expenses, is a challenging and important part of your business plan. Preparing an income statement is difficult because of all the estimates and assumptions that go into it. If you're honest, this step is where you may discover that it's tougher to make a decent profit than you thought. This section of your plan helps you with your pricing decisions.

Consider the Vet on Wheels business idea I discuss in "Business concept," earlier in this chapter. What range of veterinary services are you able to provide by making house calls? You can't do everything that you can in a larger office setting. What equipment do you need to perform the services? How much do you charge for the services? You need to estimate all these things to develop a worthwhile income statement. You should be able to answer these questions from all the insights and information you pulled together regarding what customers want and what your competitors are offering.

With service businesses, in which you or your employees are selling your time, be realistic about how many hours you can bill. A third to half of your time may end up being billable given the other overhead activities you need to perform.

Because it takes a business several years to build up a customer base, try to prepare estimated income statements for the first three years. In the earlier years, you have more start-up costs. In later years, you reap more profits as your customer rolls expand. Doing income statements over several years is also essential if you're seeking investor money.

Chapter 6 explains the elements of an income statement.

Balance sheet

An income statement measures the profitability of a business over a span of time, such as a year. But it tells you nothing of a business's resources and obligations. That's what a balance sheet does. Just as your personal balance sheet itemizes your personal assets (for example, investments) and liabilities (loans and debts you owe), a business balance sheet details a company's assets and liabilities.

If you operate a cash business — you provide a service and are paid for that service and don't hold inventory, and so on — a balance sheet has limited use. An exception is if you're trying to get a bank loan for your service business, in which case you will need a balance sheet. (But you'll have a hard time getting a bank loan on such a business, even with your balance sheet.)

A complete balance sheet is not as important as tracking the available cash, which will be under pressure in the early years of a business as expenses can continue to exceed revenue for quite some time.

A complete balance sheet is useful for a business that owns significant equipment, furniture, inventory, and so on. The asset side of the balance sheet provides insight into the financial staying power of the company. For example, how much cash is on hand to meet expected short-term bills? Conversely, the liability side of the ledger indicates the obligations, bills, and debts the company has coming due in the short- and long-term.

See Chapter 6 for an explanation of all the elements of a balance sheet.

Executive summary

It may seem odd to list this last, but you're not going to be able to write an intelligent, thoughtful two- to three-page summary of your entire business plan until the body of the business plan is fleshed out. This summary should go in the front of the plan and provide the highlights of your entire plan. Such a summary has more use if you're sharing your plan with an interested investor who may not want to wade through a 40- to 50-page plan. The executive summary provides a "Reader's Digest" summary to whet the prospective investor's appetite.

Chapter 13
Running Your Small Business

*A*fter doing your research and evaluation, at some point you need to decide whether to actually start your business. In reference to his business plan, Alex Popov (introduced in Chapter 12), founder of Smart Alec's, a healthy fast food restaurant, says, ". . . something just clicked one day, and I said to myself, 'Yes, this is a business that is viable and appropriate now.'"

This sudden realization is how it happens with most would-be entrepreneurs and how it's worked with every business I've ever started. If you really want to, you can conduct and analyze market research and crunch numbers until the cows come home. Even if you're a linear, logical, analytic, quantitative kind of person, in the final analysis you need to make a gut-level decision: Are you going to jump in the water and start swimming, or are you going to stay on the sidelines and remain a spectator? Watching isn't nearly as fun as doing. If you feel ready but have some trepidation, you're normal. Just go for it!

Business Start-Up: Your Preflight Check List

As you decide to start your own business, you also need to ponder and make some other decisions about a number of important issues. Just like a pilot before he launches an airplane into flight, you need to make sure that all systems are in order and ready to do the job. If your fuel tanks aren't adequately filled, your engines cleaned and working, and your wing flaps properly positioned, you may never have the chance of getting your business off the ground.

Preparing to leave your job

The number one reason that wannabe entrepreneurs remain wannabe entrepreneurs is the psychological and financial aspects. You may never discover that you have tons of talent to run your own business, and perhaps a good idea to boot, unless you prepare yourself fiscally and emotionally to leave your job. Money and mind issues cause many aspiring entrepreneurs to be indentured servants of their employers and cause those who do break their bondage to soon return to being employees.

The money side is easier to deal with than your mind, so I'll start with that. It's a foregone conclusion that the vast majority of small business opportunities you're going to pursue will lead to a net reduction in the income you bring home from your work — at least in the early years of your business. Accept this fact and plan accordingly.

You should do all you can to reduce your expenses and lifestyle to a level that fits with the entrepreneurial life that you want to lead. If you haven't examined your monthly spending patterns, you must! Now is the time to make your budget lean, mean, and entrepreneurially friendly. Determine what you spend each month on rent, mortgage, groceries, eating out, telephone calls, insurance, and so on. Unless you're one of those organized computer geeks who others love to hate who keeps all this data detailed on a software package like Quicken or Microsoft Money, you'll need to whip out your checkbook register, credit card statement, and anything else that documents your spending. Don't forget to estimate your cash purchases that don't leave a trail, such as when you eat lunch out or drop a $20 bill on gas and a Ring Ding.

Don't tell me that everything you spend your money on is a necessity and that you can't cut anywhere. Question every expenditure! If you don't, working as an employee will be a necessity, and you'll never be able to pursue your dream.

Beyond the bare essentials of food, shelter, health care, and clothing, most of what you spend money on is discretionary. In other words, you spend money on luxuries. Even what you spend on the necessities, such as food and shelter, is part necessity and a fair amount of luxury and waste. If you need a helping hand and an analyst's eye in preparing and developing strategies for reducing your spending, pick up a copy of my first book, *Personal Finance For Dummies*.

So reduce your expenses to the level they were when you lived at home or were a college student — remember those enjoyable days. Spending more doesn't make you happy; you'll be miserable over the years if your excess spending makes you feel chained to a job you don't like. Life is too short to spend most of it working at a full-time job that doesn't make you happy.

If reducing your spending is the most important financial move you can take before and during the period you want to start your business, the second good thing you should do is to spend some time figuring how you'll manage the income side of your personal finances. Following are some good strategies to ensure that you'll earn enough to live on:

- **Transition gradually.** One way to pursue your entrepreneurial dreams, and not starve while doing so, is to continue working part-time in a regular job while working part-time in your own business. If you have a job that allows you to work half-time, seize the opportunity. Some employers even allow you to maintain your benefits.

  In addition to the money, splitting your time allows you to adjust to a completely new way of making a living. Some people have a hard time adjusting if they quit their job cold turkey and confront themselves with working full-time as an entrepreneur.

  Another option is to completely leave your job but line up a chunk of work that provides a decent income for at least some of your weekly work hours. Consulting for your old employer is a time-tested first "entrepreneurial" option with low risk.

- **Get/stay married.** Actually, as long as you're attached to someone who has a regular job and you manage your spending so that you can live on that person's income alone, you're golden! Just make sure to talk things through with the love of your life to ensure no misunderstandings and resentments. Maybe someday you can return the favor — that's what my wife and I did. She was working in education (no big bucks here!) when I started an entrepreneurial venture after business school. We lived a spartan lifestyle and made do just fine on her income. Several years later, when things were going swimmingly for me, she left her job to work on her own.

Replacing and valuing your benefits

Part of the money side of things are the benefits that your employer provides. Walking away from these for many people is both financially and psychologically challenging. Benefits can be valuable, but you may be surprised how quickly you can replicate them in your own business.

Health insurance

Some prospective entrepreneurs fret over giving up existing and finding new health insurance. Unless you have a significant existing medical problem (known in the insurance business as a *pre-existing condition*), getting health insurance as an individual is not difficult.

The first option to explore is whether your existing coverage through your employer's group plan can be converted into individual coverage. If it can be, great, just don't act on this option until you've explored other health plans on your own, which may offer similar benefits at lower cost. Also get proposals for individual coverage from Blue Cross/Blue Shield, Kaiser, and other major health plans in your area. Take a high deductible, if available, to keep costs down.

Under government regulations called "COBRA," an employer with 20 or more employees is generally required to continue your health insurance coverage (at your own expense) for up to 18 months after you terminate employment. Moreover, thanks to a health care reform bill passed in 1996, if you have or develop a health problem while covered under COBRA, the law enables you to purchase an individual policy at the same price that a healthy individual can. These laws create a nice buffer zone for the budding entrepreneur, but don't get lazy and wait until the last minute of the 18th month to start shopping for your individual plan. COBRA plans are usually not the low-cost leaders. You'll probably save money and prevent headaches by shopping for and locking up your individual plan as soon as possible.

Long-term disability insurance

Equally if not more important than health insurance is long-term disability insurance. Most people's greatest asset is their ability to earn money. If you suffer a disability and can't work, how would you manage financially? Long-term disability insurance protects your income in the event of a disability.

Before you leave your job, make sure that you attempt to secure an individual long-term disability policy. After you leave your job and are no longer earning steady income, you won't be able to qualify for a policy. Most insurers then want to see at least six months of self-employment income before they're willing to write you a policy. The risk is, if you become disabled during this time, you're uninsured and out of luck.

Check with any professional associations you belong to or could join to see if they offer long-term disability plans. As with employer-based programs, association plans are sometimes less expensive because of the purchasing power of the group.

Life insurance

If you have dependents who are counting on your income, you need life insurance. If you have coverage through your employer, odds are you can replicate it on your own. And unlike disability insurance, in the vast majority of cases, on your own you can purchase a life insurance policy at a lower cost than you can generally purchase additional life insurance through your employer.

Retirement plans

If your employer offers retirement savings programs, such as a 401(k) plan or a pension plan, don't despair about not having these in the future. (Of course, what you've already earned and accumulated is yours.) One of the best benefits of self-employment are retirement savings plans — SEP-IRAs (Simplified Employee Pension Individual Retirement Accounts) and Keoghs — that allow you to sock away a hefty chunk of your earnings on a tax-deductible basis.

Retirement plans are a terrific way for you, as a business owner, and your employees to tax-shelter a healthy portion of earnings. If you don't have employees, regularly contributing to one of these plans is usually a no-brainer. With employees, the decision is a bit more complicated but still often a great idea. Small businesses with a number of employees should also consider 401(k) plans. I explain how these plans work in Chapter 3.

You can't take advantage of these plans until your business attracts customers and is producing profits. So get to work on your business expansion!

Other benefits

Yes, employers offer other benefits that you may value. For example, you *seem* to get paid holidays and vacations. In reality, your employer is simply paying you for working the other 47 weeks or so out of the year and spreading your salary over 52 weeks. You can do the same when you price your products and services and decide when you'll work.

Another "benefit" of working for an employer is that the employer pays for half (7.65 percent) of your Social Security and Medicare taxes. Although it's true that you must pay the entire tax (15.3 percent) when you're self-employed, the IRS allows you to take half of this amount as a tax deduction on your Form 1040. So it's not as painful as you think. As with vacation and holidays, you can build the cost of this tax into your product and service pricing. Just think: Your employer could pay you a higher salary if it wasn't paying half these taxes as a benefit.

Some employers offer other insurance plans, such as dental or vision care plans. Ultimately, these plans cover small out-of-pocket expenditures that aren't worth insuring for. Don't waste your money purchasing such policies, especially when you're self-employed.

Financing your business

When you do your business plan (which I explain how to in Chapter 12), you should estimate your start-up and development costs. Many worthwhile small businesses can be started with little capital. And most businesses that require healthy investments of cash can be successfully launched without gobs of money.

Bootstrapping

Whether you want to maintain a small shop that just employs yourself, hire a few employees, or dream about building the next Wal-Mart or Apple Computer, you need capital. However, misconceptions abound about how much money a company needs to achieve its goals and sources of funding.

"There's an illusion that most companies need tons of money to get established and grow," says James Collins, former lecturer at the Stanford Graduate School of Business and co-author of the best-seller, *Built to Last.* "The Silicon Valley success stories of companies that raise gobs of venture capital and grow 4,000 percent are very rare. They are statistically insignificant but catch all sorts of attention," he adds.

Studies show that the vast majority of small businesses obtain their initial capital from personal savings and family and friends rather than outside sources such as banks and venture capital firms. A Harvard Business School study of 100 of the Inc. 500 (500 large, fast-growing private companies) found that more than 80 percent of the successful companies were started through the founder's personal savings. The median start-up capital — a modest $10,000. And these are successful, fast-growing companies! Slower-growing companies tend to need even less capital.

Even among high-technology firms, which tend to be more capital intensive, 79 percent are initially funded through the founder's personal savings and family and friends, according to a study by Edward B. Roberts, author of *Entrepreneurs in High Technology* (Oxford Press).

Making do with a small amount of capital and spending it as you can afford to is known as *bootstrapping.* Bootstrapping is just a fancy way of saying that a business is living within its means. Bootstrapping forces a business to be resourceful and less wasteful. It's great training for producing cost-effective products and services that the marketplace will find offer good value. Bootstrapping also offers the advantage of not devastating and draining your personal finances and preventing you from getting into business in the first place because of a lack of or an inability to raise capital.

Millions of successful small companies were bootstrapped. And like small redwood saplings that grow into towering trees, small companies that were bootstrapped can eventually grow into hundred-million and even multibillion dollar companies. Ross Perot started EDS not only with his big ears but also with a mere $1,000. Hewlett Packard was started out of a garage in Palo Alto, California. Motorola, Sony, and Disney were all bootstrapped.

With the initial infusion of capital, many small businesses can propel themselves for years after they develop a service or product that can bring in more cash flow. Jim Gentes, the founder of Giro, the bike helmet manufacturer, raised just $35,000 from personal savings and loans from family and friends to make and distribute his first product and then used the cash flow for future products.

Eventually, a successful growing company may want outside financing to expand even faster. Raising money from outside investors or lenders is much easier after you've demonstrated that you know what you're doing and that a demonstrated market exists for your product or service.

Sources of funding

As I explain earlier in the chapter, aspiring entrepreneurs must examine their personal finances for opportunities to reduce their own spending. If you want to start a company, the best time to examine your finances is years before you want to hit the entrepreneurial path. As with other financial goals, advance preparation can go a long way toward achieving the goal of starting a business. The best funding source and easiest investor to please is yourself.

Alan Tripp, founder and CEO of Score Advantage Learning Centers, a chain of storefront interactive learning centers, had planned for seven years before taking the entrepreneurial plunge. He funded his first retail center fully from personal savings. He and his wife lived frugally to save the necessary money — they were caretakers for two years in order to save more money. Tripp's first center, opened in 1992, proved the success of his business concept: retail learning centers where kids can use computers to improve their reading, math, and science skills. With a business plan crafted over time and hard numbers to demonstrate the financial viability of his operation, Tripp then successfully raised the funds from outside investors to open his next four centers.

Some small business founders put the cart before the horse and don't plan and save for starting their business the way Tripp did. And in many cases, small business owners want capital but don't have a clear plan or need for it.

If you're starting a new business or have been in business just a few years, borrowing, particularly from banks, may be difficult. Borrowing money is easier when you don't really need to do so. No one knows this fact better than small business owners.

Small business owners who successfully obtain bank loans do their homework. A business plan together with three years of financials and tax returns for the business and its owner, as well as projections for the business, are generally needed. Be sure to hunt around for banks that are committed to and understand the small business marketplace.

The Small Business Administration (SBA) guarantees some small business loans that banks originate. Many of these loans would not otherwise be made by banks because of the business's lack of collateral and risk. In addition to guaranteeing loans for existing businesses, about 20 percent of SBA-backed loans go to start-ups, which must have founders who put up at least a third of the funds needed and demonstrate a thorough understanding of the business, ideally through prior related industry experience. Effective in 1995, the SBA no longer does direct lending (except for disaster loans).

Getting money from family and friends

Because they know you and hopefully like and trust you, your family and friends may seem like a good source of investment money for your small business. They also have the added advantage of offering you better terms than a banker, wealthy investor, or a venture capitalist.

Before you solicit and accept money from those you love, consider the pitfalls. First, it's one thing to default on a loan made by a large, anonymous impersonal lender if your business hits the skids but quite another if it's one of your dear relatives. It can make future Thanksgiving meals mighty uncomfortable!

Second, most entrepreneurs receive surprisingly little encouragement from those they are close to. Most parents, for example, think you've snapped a few of your cerebral synapses if you announce your intention to quit your corporate job with lofty job title, decent pay, and benefits. The lack of emotional support can be far more discouraging, though, than the lack of financial support.

From entrepreneurs I've observed, it seems that family investment in a small business works best under the following conditions:

- ✔ A letter of agreement, spelling out the terms of the investment or loan, is prepared and signed as if you're doing business with a banker or some other investor you know for business purposes only. As time goes on, people have selective recall. Putting things in writing reminds everyone what you agreed to.

- ✔ Safe loans. Borrowing from family works best in cases where you're quite certain that the loan can be repaid and you can probably qualify for a loan through other channels.

- ✔ Equity investment, where a person is willing and able to lose all the money invested but is hoping to hit a home run and enjoys helping you with your dream.

The SBA offers a number of workshops and counseling services for small business owners. Its SCORE (Service Corps of Retired Executives) consulting services provide advice and critique of business plans and advice on raising money for your business for free — actually your tax dollars are at work. The SBA charges a nominal fee for seminars. To get more information on SBA's services and how to contact a local office, call 800-827-5722.

In addition to SBA-backed loans available through banks, credit unions are often more willing to make personal loans to individuals. Borrowing against equity in your home or other real estate is also advantageous because real estate loans generally entail lower and tax-deductible interest.

Retirement savings plans are another potential source of capital. These loans allow you to borrow against your investment balance and are usually available at competitive rates, today around 8 percent. Just make sure that you're not taking on too much debt and jeopardizing a large portion of your retirement savings.

If you've got the itch to get your business going and can't wait to save the money and lack other ways to borrow, the plastic in your wallet may be your ticket to operation. Many credit cards can be acquired at interest rates of 10 percent or less. Because credit cards are unsecured loans, if your business fails and you can't pay back your debt, your home equity and assets in retirement accounts aren't at risk.

No matter what type of business you have in mind and how much money you think is needed to make your dream come true, remember to be patient. Start small enough to not need outside capital (unless you're in an unusual situation where the window of opportunity is now, and it will go away if you don't get funding soon). Doing so instills the discipline required for building a business piece by piece over time. The longer you can wait to get a loan or equity investment, the better the terms are for you because the risk is lower for the lender or investor.

Courting investors and selling equity

Beyond family members and friends, your next best source of capital if you want an equity investor (and not a loan from a lender) are private individuals with sufficient money — also known as wealthy individuals. Although you want such investors to care about their investment, it's best if their investment in your business is no more than 5 to 10 percent of their total portfolio. No one wants to lose money, but doing so is less painful if you're well diversified. A $10,000 loan from a millionaire is 1 percent of his portfolio.

Before you approach wealthy people, you need to have a good business plan, which I explain how to prepare in Chapter 12. If you have a plan already, be sure that it includes a nondisclosure statement like the sample I provide in Chapter 12.

Finding people who may be interested in investing is not difficult, but you need to be persistent and creative. Accountants and attorneys you know may have contacts. Networking with successful entrepreneurs in similar fields may produce an investor or two. Also, consider customers or suppliers of your business who like what you do and believe in its potential.

Finding your way to wealthy individuals who don't know you may prove fruitful as well. Alex Popov, whom you met in Chapter 12 and earlier in this one, sent hundreds of letters to people who lived in upscale neighborhoods. The letter, a one-page summary of the opportunity, got an astounding 5 percent response for interest in receiving a business plan. Ultimately through this search method, Popov found one wealthy investor who funded his entire deal.

Determining how much of the business you're selling for the amount invested is not easy. Basically, the equity percentage should hinge upon what the whole business is worth (see Chapter 14 for how to value a business). If your whole business is worth $500,000, and you're seeking $100,000 from investors, that $100,000 should buy 20 percent of the business.

New businesses are hardest to value, which is another reason you're best off trying to raise money after you've demonstrated some success. The further along you are, the lower the risk to an investor and the lower the cost to you (in terms of how much equity you must give up) to raise money.

The incorporation decision

Most businesses operate as sole proprietorships. A sole proprietorship doesn't mean that just one person is in the business but rather that, for legal and tax purposes, your business is not a corporation. If you run a sole proprietorship, your business income and costs are reported on your tax return on Schedule C (Profit or Loss From Business), which is attached to your personal income tax return, Form 1040.

Incorporating, which establishes a distinct legal entity under which you do business, takes time and costs money. So incorporation must offer some benefits. A major reason to consider incorporating is for liability protection. Incorporating effectively separates your business from your personal finances, which protects your personal assets from lawsuits arising from your business.

Before you incorporate, ask yourself and perhaps others in your line of business, or advisors (legal, tax, and so on) who work with businesses like yours what can cause you to be sued. Then see if you can purchase insurance to protect against these potential liabilities. Insurance is superior to incorporation because it pays claims. You can still be sued even if you're incorporated. If you're incorporated and someone successfully sues you, your company has to cough up the money. This situation not only costs a lot of money but can also sink your business. Only insurance can cover such financially destructive claims.

You can also be sued if someone slips and breaks a bone or two while on your property. To cover these types of claims, you can purchase a property or premises liability policy from an insurer.

Accountants, doctors, and a number of other professionals can buy liability insurance. A good place to start searching for liability insurance is through the associations that exist for your profession. Even if you're not a current member, check out the associations anyway — you may be able to access the insurance without membership, or you can join the association long enough to get signed up. (Associations also sometimes offer competitive rates on disability insurance.)

Because corporations are legal entities distinct from their owners, they offer other features that a proprietorship or partnership doesn't. For example, corporations can have shareholders who own a piece or percentage of the company. These shares can be sold or transferred to other owners, subject to any restrictions in the shareholder's agreement.

Corporations also offer *continuity of life,* which simply means that they can continue to exist despite an owner's death or the owner's transfer of his or her share (stock) in the company.

Don't waste your money incorporating if you simply want to have a corporate-sounding name. If you operate as a sole proprietor, you can choose to operate under a different business name ("doing business as," or d.b.a.) without the cost and hassles of incorporating.

Tax-deductible insurance and other benefits

A variety of insurance and related benefits are tax-deductible to corporations for all employees. These benefits include the full cost of health and disability insurance as well as up to $50,000 in term life insurance benefits per employee.

In addition to insurance, companies can also have dependent care plans where up to $5,000 per employee may be put away on a tax-deductible basis for child care and/or care for elderly parents. Corporations can also offer cafeteria or flexible spending plans, which allow employees to pick and choose which benefits they spend their benefit dollars on.

If your business is not incorporated, you and the other business owner(s) cannot deduct the cost of the preceding insurance plans for yourselves, but you can deduct these costs for employees as well as 30 percent of your health insurance costs for yourself and covered family members.

Corporate taxes

Aside from the tax treatment of insurance and other benefits, another difference between operating as a sole proprietor and as a corporation is that a corporation's profits are taxed differently than those realized in a sole proprietorship. Which is better for your business depends on your situation.

Suppose that your business is doing really well and making lots of money. If your business is not incorporated, all profits from your business are taxed on your personal tax return in the year that those profits are earned. If you intend to use these profits to reinvest in your business and expand, incorporating can potentially save you some tax dollars. If your business is incorporated (as a regular or so-called C corporation), the first $75,000 of profits in the business are generally taxed at a lower rate in the corporation than on your personal tax return if you operated as a sole proprietorship. One exception to this rule is personal service corporations, such as accounting, legal, and medical firms, which pay a higher rate up to $335,000 in profits.

Resist the short-term temptation to incorporate just so that you can have money left in the corporation taxed at a lower rate. If you want to pay yourself the profits in the future, you can end up paying more taxes. Why? Because first you pay taxes at the corporate tax rate in the year your company earns the money. Then you pay taxes again on your personal income tax return when the corporation pays you.

Another reason not to incorporate, especially in the early months of a business, is that you cannot immediately claim the losses for an incorporated business on your personal tax return. Because most businesses produce little revenue in their early years and have all sorts of start-up expenditures, losses are common.

S corporations and limited liability companies: the best of both worlds?

Wouldn't it be nice to get the liability protection and other benefits that come with incorporating without the tax complications and hassles that come with incorporation? Well, S corporations or limited liability companies may be for you.

Subchapter S corporations provide the liability protection that comes with incorporation. And the business profit or loss passes through to the owner's personal tax return. So if the business shows a loss in some years, the owner may claim those losses in the current year of the loss on his or her personal tax return. If you plan to take all the profits out of the company, an S corporation may make sense for you.

The IRS allows most small businesses to be S corporations, but not all. In order to be an S corporation, a company must be a U.S. company, have just one class of stock, and have no more than 35 shareholders, who are all U.S. residents or citizens and are not partnerships, corporations, or, with certain exceptions, trusts.

Limited liability companies (LLCs) offer business owners benefits similar to those of S corporations but are even better in some cases. Like an S corporation, an LLC offers liability protection for the owners. LLCs also pass the business's profits and losses through to the owner's personal income tax returns.

But limited liability companies have fewer restrictions regarding shareholders. For example, LLCs have no limits on the number of shareholders. The shareholders in an LLC can be foreigners, corporations, and partnerships.

Compared with S corporations, the only additional restriction LLCs carry is that sole proprietors and professionals cannot always form an LLC (although they can in Texas). Most state laws require you to have at least two partners and not be a professional firm. (Also, note that LLCs are not available in Hawaii, Massachusetts, or Vermont.)

Making the decision

If you're totally confused about whether to incorporate because your business is undergoing major financial changes, it's worth getting competent professional help. The hard part is knowing where to turn because it's a challenge to find one advisor who can put all the pieces of the puzzle (financial, legal, and taxes) together. And be aware that you may get wrong or biased advice.

Attorneys who specialize in advising small businesses can help explain the legal issues. Tax advisors who do a lot of work with business owners can help explain the tax considerations. Most attorneys and tax advisors don't understand the business side of business. Try to find those who do, or you'll also need a business advisor.

If you've weighed the factors and you're on the fence, my advice is to keep it simple — don't incorporate. Why? Because, once you incorporate, it takes time and money to unincorporate. Start off as a sole proprietorship and then take it from there. Wait until the benefits of incorporating in your case clearly outweigh the costs and drawbacks of incorporating.

Finding and keeping customers

You should have given a lot of thought already to the customers of your business when you wrote the plan for your business (see Chapter 12). Just as the sun is the center of our solar system, everything in your business should revolve around your customers. If you take care of your customers, they'll take care of you and your business for many years after.

The first thing I recommend doing is putting together a mailing list of people you know who may be interested in what you're offering. Draft and mail an upbeat, one-page letter providing an overview of what you're offering. As you have new news — successes to report, new products and services, and so on — do another mailing. Your letter doesn't have to be a color, multipage newsletter-type thing, although you can do those if your budget and desire allow. Short letters get read more than something that looks like another glossy, advertorial, multipage newsletter. Most people are busy and don't care about your business enough to read something lengthy.

In addition to mailings, other successful ways to get the word out and attract customers are limited only to your imagination and resourcefulness. Consider the following ideas:

- ✔ If your business idea is indeed innovative or somehow different, or if you have grand expansion plans, add some local media people to your mailing list and send them the one-page updates on your business, too. Newspaper, radio, and even television business reporters are always looking for story ideas. Just remember to make your press releases more informational and less of an advertisement.

- ✔ If your business seeks customers in a specific geographic area, blanket the area with your one-page letter by going door to door. Perhaps include a coupon that offers your products or services at a reduced cost (perhaps at your cost) to get people to try it. Make sure that people know that this is a special opening-for-business bargain.

After you attract customers, don't treat them as if business is a one-night stand. Treat your customers as you would like to be treated by a business. If customers like your products and services, they not only come back to buy more when the need arises, but they also probably tell others. Satisfied customers are every business's lowest-cost marketers.

Although good customer service is just good common sense, I never cease to be amazed by how many businesses have mediocre or poor customer service. One of the reasons for poor service is that as your business grows, your employees are on the customer service front lines. If you don't hire good people and give them the proper incentives to service customers, many of them won't do it. If most people are on a salary, the day-to-day servicing of customers may just be an annoyance. One way to make your employees care about customer service is to base part of their pay on the satisfaction of the customers they work with. Tie bonuses and increases at review time to this issue. You can easily measure customer satisfaction with a simple survey form, such as the one shown in Figure 13-1.

Think about your own experiences with poor customer service. Most people have them monthly. Not having a green thumb, I hired a gardening company to install a garden. The company did a decent job in the early days of the project and expressed interest in providing ongoing maintenance. Within days of the garden installation, some problems, minor from my perspective, surfaced. A large jasmine vine that had survived for more than a year started to die. One worker thought the vine could be dying because some roots were inadvertently cut during installation, but no one ever came out to look at the vine or suggest what to do. A number of plants were poorly placed and quickly encroached onto the lawn. Again, I asked someone to come out and take a look, and no one did.

Unfortunately, I figured out that because I had paid for the job, the company wasn't very interested in addressing the problems. Even though the company's workers did a good job with the project overall, the lack of follow-up left me with a bad taste in my mouth and will cause me to think twice when someone asks me to recommend a good gardening company.

Treating the customer right starts the moment the selling process begins. Honesty is an often underused business tool. More than a few salespeople mislead and lie in order to close a sale. Many customers discover after the purchase that this deception has occurred, and then they get angry. Not only has the unethical business likely lost future business from this customer, but it will surely lose referrals.

Finding and equipping an office

You can easily go overboard spending money when it comes to office space and outfitting that space. The most common reason small business owners spend more than they should is to attempt to project a professional, upscale image.

You can have an office or retail location that works for you and your customers without spending a fortune if you observe some simple rules.

If you would like to comment on other topics or occasions, please feel free to do so on a separate piece of paper and return in the envelope provided. PLEASE CHECK THE SINGLE MOST APPROPRIATE RESPONSE.

1. **Overall, how satisfied are you with the quality of service you receive from Schwab?**

Very Satisfied	Satisfied	Somewhat Satisfied	Neutral	Somewhat Dissatisfied	Dissatisfied	Very Dissatisfied
☐	☐	☐	☐	☐	☐	☐
7	6	5	3		2	1

2. **How satisfied were you with the following aspects of the service you received *on this occasion*?**

	Very Satisfied	Satisfied	Somewhat Satisfied	Neutral	Somewhat Dissatisfied	Dissatisfied	Very Dissatisfied	N/A
A. Courtesy and friendliness	☐	☐	☐	☐	☐	☐	☐	☐
B. Gave you confidence in our ability to serve you	☐	☐	☐	☐	☐	☐	☐	☐
C. Ability to answer your questions clearly or obtain an answer in a timely manner	☐	☐	☐	☐	☐	☐	☐	☐
D. Overall service provided	☐	☐	☐	☐	☐	☐	☐	☐
	7	6	5	4	3	2	1	0

3. **Based on the service received *on this occasion*, how likely is it that you will continue to use Schwab for your investment services?**

Definitely	Probably	Might or Might Not	Probably Not	Definitely Not
☐	☐	☐	☐	☐
5	4	3	2	1

4. **Based on the service received *on this occasion*, would you recommend Schwab to a friend or business associate?**

Definitely	Probably	Might or Might Not	Probably Not	Definitely Not
☐	☐	☐	☐	☐
5	4	3	2	1

5. **Was there anything this employee did that particularly pleased you? If yes, what was it?**

_____

_____

6. **Schwab is committed to providing the guidance investors need to make their own investment decisions. If applicable, please tell us how you would rate the following *on this occasion*.**

	Very Satisfied	Satisfied	Somewhat Satisfied	Neutral	Somewhat Dissatisfied	Dissatisfied	Very Dissatisfied	N/A
A. Effort made to understand your needs	☐	☐	☐	☐	☐	☐	☐	☐
B. Information offered to address your needs	☐	☐	☐	☐	☐	☐	☐	☐
C. Guidance offered to assist you in using Schwab's products and services.	☐	☐	☐	☐	☐	☐	☐	☐
	7	6	5	4	3	2	1	0

7. **If you contacted us by phone or came into one of our branches, how satisfied were you with how quickly you were able to speak with the Schwab representative that helped you *on this occasion*?**

Very Satisfied	Satisfied	Somewhat Satisfied	Neutral	Somewhat Dissatisfied	Dissatisfied	Very Dissatisfied
☐	☐	☐	☐	☐	☐	☐
7	6	5	4	3	2	1

8. **How did you contact Schwab *on this occasion*? (choose one)**

By Telephone :

1 ☐ Called Schwab's main number (800-435-4000)
2 ☐ Called a Schwab specialized service 800 number
3 ☐ Called TeleBroker and transferred to a representative

4 ☐ Called my local branch
5 ☐ Transferred back to my local branch

In Person:

6 ☐ Came into the branch

7 ☐ Other: _____

If we could change one thing to serve you better, what would that be?

_____

_____

THANK YOU.

CS 296-1 (9-95)

Figure 13-1:
This is the customer service questionnaire that an investment company sends out to customers. The form is coded to match the specific representative who worked with the customer.

Source: Charles Schwab & Co., Inc.

✔ **Buy, don't lease or finance, equipment.** Unless you're running a manufacturing outfit where the cost of equipment is prohibitive to buy outright, try to avoid borrowing and leasing. If you can't buy office furniture, computers, cash registers, and so on, with cash, then you probably can't "afford" them! Buying such things on credit or by leasing — leasing is invariably the most expensive way to go — encourages you to spend beyond your means.

Consider buying used equipment, especially furniture, which takes longer to become obsolete. The more a piece of equipment is used in other businesses, the more beneficial it should be for you to purchase rather than lease. Many other businesses using the equipment should make it easier for you to unload it if you want to sell it down the road. Leasing may make more sense with oddball-type equipment that is more of a hassle and costly for you to unload after a short usage period.

✔ **Don't get carried away with technological and marketing gadgets and devices.** I know it's hard to imagine, but the business world worked just fine (and in some respects better) before faxes, E-mail, and the growth of the World Wide Web. Many small business owners I speak with spend all sorts of money on such things because they feel the need to be "competitive" and "current." Think of a Web site as buying an expensive online Yellow Pages ad, because that's what it basically is. As for E-mail and faxes, the mail works just fine. So does picking up the phone or meeting in person — these are much more personal ways of doing business.

Voice mail is one device many small business owners find worth spending money on. Voice mail sounds more professional than an answering machine and can handle simultaneous calls with ease. Best of all, voice mail can save you money on administrative help.

Dealing with unhappy and difficult customers

Some people say, "The customer is always right." In other words, even if a customer is being a jerk and trying to take advantage of you or is just being all-around difficult, you should bend over backward to please that customer.

I don't buy this way of thinking. You should give the benefit of doubt to customers because they can do lots of good for your business if you keep them happy and lots of harm if you don't. But some customers are a major pain in the posterior and impossible to please. Trying to keep them happy can be a time-consuming, costly process.

Difficult people often don't have many friends, so you probably won't get referrals anyway, and those who they do refer to you may be as difficult as they are.

If your business didn't do right by a customer, apologize and bend over backward to make the customer happy. Offer a discount on the problem purchase or, if possible, a refund on product purchases. Also, be sure that you have a clear return and refund policy. Be willing to bend that policy if doing so helps you satisfy an unhappy customer or rids you of a difficult customer.

Bootstrap-equipping your office makes sense within certain limits. If customers come to you, of course, you don't want a ratty-looking store or office. But on the other hand, you don't have to purchase the Rolls Royce equivalent of everything you need for your office. For example, in my office I have multiple computers, and the oldest, bought in 1988, still runs DOS. It works great and looks fine. I didn't buy my fax machine for several years until after the start of my business, and I wish I had waited even longer because its presence encourages people I work with to procrastinate sending me things!

The working-from-home decision

You may be able to run a relatively simple small business from your home. If you have the choice of running your business out of your home versus securing outside office space, consider the following issues:

- ✔ **Cost control.** As I discuss earlier in the chapter, bootstrapping your business can make a whole lot of financial and business sense. If you have space in your home that you can use, then you've found yourself a rent-free business space. (If in your consideration of a home to buy you opt for a larger place, then you can't really say that your home office is rent free.)

- ✔ **Business issues.** What are your business's and customers' needs? If you don't need fancy office space to impress others or in which to meet with clients, work at home. If you operate a retail business that requires lots of customers coming to you, getting outside space is probably the best (and legally correct) choice. Check with the governing authorities of your town or city to learn what regulations exist for home-based businesses.

- ✔ **Discipline.** At home, are you going to have the discipline to work the number of hours you need and desire, or will you be tempted to make half a dozen snack trips to the kitchen and turn on the television for late-breaking news? The hardest time to discipline yourself is usually in the early days when you don't have enough work to fully occupy your time. The sometimes amorphous challenge of figuring out how to grow the business may cause you to focus your energies elsewhere.

- ✔ **Family matters.** Last, but not least, your home life should factor into where you decide to work. If you're single and living alone, home life is less of an issue. One advantage to working at home when you're a parent is that you can be a more involved parent. If nothing else, the one to two hours per day many people spend commuting can be spent with your kids! Just be sure to try and set aside work hours, during which time you're off limits for child-care stuff.

Talk to other family members about how they feel about your working at home. Get specific about what you plan to do, where, when, and how. Will you have clients come over? What time of day and where in the home will you meet with them? You may not think it's an imposition, but your spouse may. Home business problems have come between many a couple.

Finding space and negotiating a lease

You may be in the market for office or retail space unless your business can be run from your home. Finding good space, and buying or leasing it, takes tons of time if you do it right.

In the early months and years of your business, buying an office or a retail building generally doesn't make sense. The down payment consumes important capital, and you may end up spending lots of time and money on a real estate transaction for a location you may not be interested in the long term. Buying this type of real estate rarely makes sense unless you see staying put five or more years.

It's far more likely that you'll lease space. Renting office space is simpler than renting retail space because a building owner is less concerned about your business and its financial health. Your business needs more credibility to rent retail because a business affects the nature of the strip mall or shopping center where you lease. Owners of such properties don't want quick failures, or someone who will do a poor job of running the business.

Because renting retail is harder, if you and your business don't have a track record with renting space, it's useful to get references. If you seek well-located retail space, you're competing with national chains like Starbucks, so you better have an A+ credit rating and track record. Consider subletting and circulating flyers to businesses in the area where you want to be. Also prepare financial statements to show that you're creditworthy (personally and in business). Most property owners want a personal guarantee — try to avoid doing so, but that's hard to do.

Most space for lease is listed with brokers. Working with a broker can be useful, but the same conflicts exist as with residential brokers. Also examine space for lease without a broker, where you deal with the landlord directly.

Such landlords may be in a position to give a better deal and are not worried about recouping a brokerage commission.

The biggest headaches with leasing space are understanding and negotiating the lease contract. Odds are good that you're presented a standard, preprinted lease contract that is said to be fair and the same one that everyone else signs. **Don't sign it!** This contract is the lessor's first offer. You need to have an expert review it and help you modify it. Find yourself an attorney who regularly deals with such contracts.

Office leases are simpler — they can be full service, which includes janitorial. Retail leases are triple net, which means that you as the tenant pay for maintenance (for example, resurfacing the parking lot, cleaning, and gardening), utilities, and property taxes. If you're worried about such a lease because you don't control many of these expenses, you're correct. If the property is sold, the property taxes can also jump. Your lease contract should include a cap for the triple net costs at a specified limit per square foot. Also compare your site's costs to other sites to compare the deal you're being offered.

Try to exclude from the lease contract removal costs, if toxic waste is discovered. Also exclude increased property taxes caused by sale of the property. If feasible, get your landlord to pay for remodeling — it's cheaper for the landlord to do it and less hassle for you. With retail leases get an option for renewal — this is critical in retail, where location is important. The option should specify the cost — for example, something like 5 percent below market as determined by arbitration. Also get an option that the lease can be transferred to a new owner if you sell the business.

If you really think you want to purchase rather than lease because you see holding it for at least five years, be sure to read Chapter 10 first.

Dealing with Dreary — and Critical—Stuff

As a small business owner, you wear many hats. Following are some other things you should know about managing your business.

Small business accounting (groan!)

One of the less glamorous aspects of running your own business is dealing with accounting. Unlike when you work for an employer, you are on the line and responsible for tracking your business's income, expenses, and taxes (for you *and* your employees). Although you may be able to afford to hire others to help with these tasks, you still must be knowledgeable to keep control of your business, to stay out of trouble with the tax authorities, and to minimize your taxes. The following sections show you how you can handle the accounting aspect of your business.

Home office and outside space both offer tax benefits

One mistake some small business owners make is to set up a home office thinking they'll get all sorts of extra tax breaks. This idea is usually ill conceived. The cost of office space you rent or purchase outside your home is an expense that can be deducted on your business tax return. With a home-based office, if you own your home, you already get to claim the mortgage interest and property taxes as tax deductions (as itemized deductions on Schedule A) on your personal tax return.

You can qualify for some minor tax breaks, such as deductions for utilities, repairs, and insurance, for the portion of a home devoted to business. Another home-based office expense that you can take if you are a home owner is depreciation (see Chapter 10 for an explanation). Be warned, however, that when you sell your home at a later date, you can't roll over a capital gain on the portion of your home that was depreciated for your business. Currently, you can get around this problem by simply using the home office space for some additional personal purpose during the year that you sell your home. Then you can roll over the entire gain.

Not only are home office write-offs for your business not substantially better than if you use outside space, qualifying for home office deductions is much more difficult. In recent years, the IRS has greatly restricted who qualifies for home office deductions. To claim the home office deduction on your tax return, your home office must be used on a regular and exclusive basis as either a place where you meet with customers or the principal place where you carry on your business. In tax year 1993, the IRS added further requirements regarding the relative importance of the work performed and the time spent in your home office. If you think you want to try to claim a home office deduction, educate yourself by picking up a copy of *Taxes For Dummies*.

Tax recordkeeping and payments

With revenue hopefully flowing into your business, and expenses surely flowing out, you must keep records to help satisfy your tax obligations and also so that you have a handle as to the financial status and success of your business. As a small business owner, you are responsible for properly tracking your income and expenses. If you don't, when it comes time to file the necessary tax forms for your business, you won't be able to complete them accurately. And if the IRS audits you — and the probability of being audited as a small business owner is about 400 percent higher than when you're an employee at a company — you'll need to prove some or even all of your expenses and income.

In order to keep your sanity, and keep the IRS at bay, make sure that you do the following:

- **Pay your taxes each quarter and on time.** When you're self-employed, you're responsible for the accurate and timely filing of all taxes owed on your income on a quarterly basis. Taxes are due by the 15th of January, April, June, and September (unless the 15th falls on the weekend, in which case the payment is due the Monday following the 15th). To pay correctly, call the IRS at 800-TAX-FORM and ask for Form 1040-ES (Estimated Tax for Individuals). This form comes complete with an easy-to-use estimated tax worksheet and four payment coupons to send in with your quarterly tax payments. Mark the due dates for your quarterly taxes on your calendar so that you don't forget!

  If you have employees, you also need to withhold taxes from each pay-check they receive. And you then must make timely payments to the IRS and to the appropriate state authorities. In addition to federal and state income tax, you also need to withhold and send in Social Security and any other state- or locally-mandated payroll taxes. Pay these taxes immediately and *never* use them to fund your business needs.

  If you want to learn about the myriad rules and regulations of withholding and submitting taxes from employees' paychecks, ask the IRS for Forms 940 and 941. I recommend using a payroll service to ensure that your payments are made on time, correctly, and to all the different places that tax filings need to go.

- **Keep your business accounts separate from your personal accounts.** The IRS knows that small business owners, as a group, cheat more on their tax returns than do employees of companies. One way dishonest entrepreneurs do so is by hiding business income and inflating business expenses. Thus, the IRS looks with a jaundiced eye at business owners who use and commingle funds in personal-checking and credit-card accounts for business transactions.

  Although you'll find it a bit more troublesome to open and maintain separate business accounts, do so. And only pay for legitimate business expenses through your business account. You'll be thankful come tax preparation time to have separate records, which will make the IRS easier to deal with if and when you're audited.

✔ **Keep good records of your business income and expenses.** You can use file folders, software, or a shoe box to collate your business income and expenses, but just do it! When you need to file your annual return, you want to be able to find the documentation that allows you to figure your business income and expenses. For most people, the file folder system works best. If your business is small, one folder for income and one for your expenses will do. Computer software may help you with this drudgery as well. Because you must go through the hassle of entering the data, software is more useful in larger small businesses and in those businesses that process lots of checks or expenses.

Documentation is made easier for most businesses if you charge expenses on a credit card or write a check. These methods of payment leave a paper trail, which simplifies tallying up your expenses come tax time and makes the IRS auditor less grumpy in the event you're audited. (Just be careful to not overspend, as many people do with credit cards!)

In addition to keeping good records, you also need to decide on what basis, cash or accrual, your business will keep its books. Most small business owners use the cash method. Sole proprietorships, partnerships, S and personal service corporations generally can use the cash method. C corporations and partnerships that have C corporations as partners may not use the cash accounting method. *Cash accounting* simply means that for tax purposes you recognize or report income in the year received and expenses in the year paid.

The advantage of operating on a cash basis is that you can control the amount of your business income and expenses that your business reports for tax purposes year to year. Doing so can lower your tax bill. Suppose that, looking ahead to the next tax year, you have good reason to believe that your business will make more money and thus push you into a higher tax bracket. Therefore, you can likely reduce your tax bill by paying more of your expenses in the next year. For example, rather than buying a new computer late this year, wait until early next year. (***Note:*** Credit card expenses are recognized as of the date when you made the charges, not when you pay the bill.)

Likewise, you can control somewhat when your customers pay you. If you expect to make less money next year, simply don't invoice customers in December of this year. Wait until January so that you receive more of your income next year.

How to (legally) pay less to the IRS

Every small business has to spend money. And spending money in your business holds the allure of lowering your tax bill. But don't spend money on your business just for the sake of generating tax deductions. Spend your money to make the most of tax breaks that are legally yours for the taking. Following are some ways to pay less to the IRS:

✔ **Take it all off now or spread it around for later.** As a small business owner, you can deduct up to $18,000 (for tax year 1997) per year for purchases of equipment (for example, espresso machines, computers, desks, chairs) for use in your business. By deducting via a section 179 deduction, you can immediately deduct the entire amount spent on equipment for your business. Normally, equipment for your business is depreciated over a number of years. With depreciation, you claim a tax deduction yearly for a portion of the total purchase price of the equipment. For example, if you drop two grand on a new computer, you can take a $400 deduction annually for depreciation of this computer (if you elect straight-line depreciation). If you elect the special 179 deduction, you can claim all of the $2,000 outlay at once (so long as you haven't exceeded the $18,000 annual cap).

It's enticing to take all the deduction in one year using the section 179 deduction method, but you may pay more taxes in the long run that way. Consider that in the early years of most businesses, profits are low. When you're in a low tax bracket, the value of your deductions is low. If your business is growing, you would likely be better off depreciating your early year deductions, thereby postponing to higher tax bracket years your taking of some of the deductions.

✔ **Make the most of your auto deductions.** If you use your car for business, you can claim a deduction. But don't waste a lot of money on a car thinking that the IRS helps pay for all of it — because they don't. The IRS limits how large an annual auto expense you can claim for depreciation. For example, if you buy a car in 1997, the maximum amount of depreciation that you can take is $3,160 in the first year, $5,000 in the second year, $3,050 in the third year, and $1,775 in the fourth and following years until the car is depreciated down to nothing. The way the math works, you are effectively limited by these depreciation caps if you spent more than about $15,800 on a car in 1997. Another advantage of purchasing a more reasonably priced car: You won't be burdened with documenting your actual auto expenses and calculating depreciation. You can use the auto expense method of just claiming a flat 31.5 cents per mile (tax year 1997).

✔ **Deduct travel, meal, and entertainment expenses.** To be deductible, travel must be for a bona fide business purpose. For example, if you live in Chicago and fly to Honolulu for a week, spend one day at a seminar for business purposes, and then the other six days snorkeling and getting skin cancer on Waikiki Beach, only the expenses for the one day of your trip devoted to business are deductible. (An exception to this rule to get more of your trip written off does exist: If you extend a business trip to stay over a Saturday night to qualify for a lower airfare, and you save money in total travel costs by extending your stay, you can claim the extra costs incurred to stay over through Sunday!)

With meal and entertainment expenses, don't waste your money. Only 50 percent of your business expenses are deductible; by all means, take that 50 percent deduction when it's legally available to you, but don't spend frivolously on these things thinking that you can deduct it all. No business deductions are allowed for club dues, such as for health, business, airport, social clubs, or entertainment facilities, like executive boxes at sports stadiums.

Hiring employees

As your business grows, you'll likely be able to hire help. Finding qualified, loyal, hard-working employees may seem like a challenge, but doing so is not actually that hard.

Finding and retaining good employees

A perfect way to find employees to fill an open position doesn't exist, but the first and most important step for you to take is to make a list of the attributes you're looking for and to write as specific an advertisement as possible. Your time is valuable, and if you aren't specific enough in listing your open positions, you'll be buried in resumés from people who aren't good fits for the skills you're looking for. Items to consider in your job listing include the following:

✔ **Skills and background.** Do they need specific degrees, training, work experience, or credentials? Do you want someone who is detail oriented, organized, creative, skilled at selling, or all of the above?

✔ **Compensation and benefits.** You should list the pay and major benefits. Listing a pay range is fine, just say that it's a pay *range,* or something along the lines of "compensation package commensurate with experience."

No-no's for ads and interviews — asking about age, ethnicity, plans to have children or get pregnant, personal issues, and so on.

Even if you prepare a fairly detailed job listing, you will still need to sift through many resumés to find those worthy of an interview. One strategy I like to use to cut down on the number of time-consuming, in-person interviews is to do your first-round interviews by phone. Develop a short list of focused questions to help you weed out those who don't fit the bill from those who do.

For example, when I once advertised for a part-time administrative position, I wanted to hire someone who wasn't using the job as filler until he or she found a full-time job. After I whittled down the pile of résumés to those candidates who looked the most promising, I simply asked each person on the phone why he or she was looking for a part-time position and how it would fit with other work plans. Although it's possible that some people chose not to answer questions completely honestly, I was able to screen out a lot of people who were not really interested in a permanent part-time position.

Interviewing in-person is more art than science. The hard part is predicting what the person will be like to work with from an in-person interview. To determine the skills of those you're considering, try the following:

- ✔ **Get them to relax.** People give more honest answers that way.

- ✔ **Dig for clarification and elucidation.** If someone says he reduced the costs of a division by 20 percent, ask how he did it. Who came up with the ideas, who implemented them? What were the challenges and drawbacks?

- ✔ **Get college transcripts and SAT scores for recent grads.** This information can indicate intelligence, willingness to work, and interests.

- ✔ **Speak with your prime candidates at multiple points in time and pool input from numerous people.** A marginal candidate can fool you in one interview but usually not over several.

- ✔ **Check references.** This is the last step for those you are seriously interested in. Yes, it takes time, but it can pay big dividends. Skip this important step at your own peril — it could cause you to hire a smooth talker who turns out to be a lousy employee.

Dealing with employee tax issues

When you hire employees, you definitely make your tax life more difficult. I highly recommend using a payroll company, as explained in "Tax recordkeeping and payments," earlier in this chapter, to handle making the payments to all the different government entities.

Some small business owners are tempted to classify everyone they hire as independent contractors. Doing so puts the burden for tax payments onto the workers. Business owners perceive that such an arrangement saves them money because the employer isn't paying for half of the Social Security and Medicare tax and other taxes that employers are required to pay for employees.

The IRS prefers that people you hire be classified as employees because independent contractors are tempted to cheat more than employees on their taxes by underreporting their income and inflating their business expenses. If a business hires independent contractors to perform work, the contractors are responsible for paying all their taxes. Business owners are now required to file Form 1099 with the IRS and some states. On Form 1099, business owners report the amount of money paid to contractors who receive $600 or more from the business. This form allows the IRS to keep better tabs on contractors who may not be reporting all their income.

Unless a company offers employee benefits (insurance, retirement savings plans, and so on), a person your business hires should prefer to be an independent contractor. Contractors have more leeway to deduct business expenses, including the deduction for a home office. Contractors can also tax-shelter a healthy percentage of their employment income in a retirement savings plan (Keogh or SEP-IRA), as discussed earlier in the chapter. But one additional expense for contractors is their obligation to pay the full share of Social Security taxes (although they can then deduct half as a tax deduction). An employer would pay half the Social Security taxes.

So how do you, as the business owner, decide if someone is a contractor or an employee? Some cases are hard to determine, but the IRS has a 20-point set of guidelines to make most cases pretty clear cut.

Independent contractors are people, such as legal, tax, and financial advisors. These people are considered contractors because they generally train themselves and figure out how they can accomplish a job with little direction or instruction from an employer. Contractors usually perform work for a number of companies and people, and they sometimes hire others to work with them.

On the other hand, employees usually work for one employer and have set hours of work. For example, a full-time secretary hired by a business is considered an employee because he or she takes instructions from the employer regarding when, where, and how to do the desired work. Another indication of employee status is if being at the work site is important to the secretary completing the desired work.

What do you do if your situation falls in between these two types, and you're perplexed about whether the person you're hiring is a contractor or employee? Ask a tax advisor or call the IRS at 800-829-3676 and ask for Form SS-8, Determination of Employee Work Status. Complete the form, mail it, and the IRS will tell you whether the situation you outline is an employee or contractor. You may not like their answer, but this way they have less latitude to blame you.

Keeping a life

David Packard, cofounder of Hewlett Packard, said, "You are likely to die not of starvation for opportunities, but of indigestion of opportunities."

Most small businesses succeed in keeping their owners more than busy — in some cases, too busy. If you provide needed products or services at a fair price, customers will beat a path to your door. You'll grow and be busier than what you can personally handle. You'll need to start hiring people. I know small business owners who work themselves into a frenzy and put in 80 or more hours a week and don't make enough to show for it.

If you enjoy your work so that it's not really work and end up putting in long hours because you enjoy it, terrific! But success in your company can cause you to put less energy into other important aspects of your life that perhaps don't come easily or as easily.

Although careers and business success are important, if you really think about it, at best these things should be no higher than fourth on your overall priority list. Your health, family, and friends can't be replaced — but a job or business can.

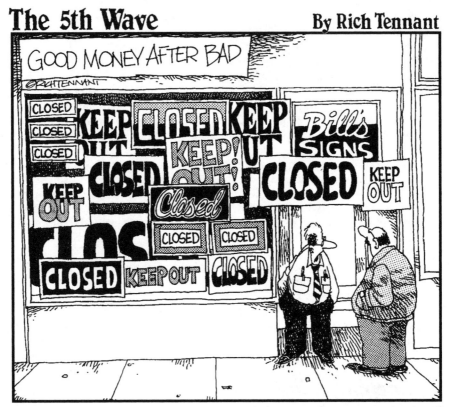

" I opened with a big sale on 'CLOSED' signs, and no one came in. I decided to add some 'KEEP OUT' signs but still no one came in. But now I'm gonna invest in some 'BIO-HAZARD' signs — throw 'em in the window and see what happens."

Chapter 14
Buying Businesses

● ●

In This Chapter

▶ The pros and cons of buying a small business

▶ The right stuff — the skills you need to be successful when buying a small business

▶ Eeny, meeny, miny, mo, choosing the business you can make go

▶ Franchises and multilevel marketing companies

▶ The art of checking out and negotiating a successful purchase

● ●

*Y*ou might think from the title of this chapter that I'm going to teach you about being an investment banker and how to buy, sell, merge, and split up businesses like they do. I'm not. Plenty of investment bankers are in the world and because they are reasonably bright people willing to work 80-plus hours a week and run their lives into the ground (I never said they are really bright!), you'll have a tough time competing with them on their terms.

This chapter is for those people who want to run or invest in an existing small business but don't want to start that business themselves. And, of course, make good money and have fun along the way!

Why Buy?

Each year, hundreds of thousands of small businesses change hands. Buying an existing business has its pros, cons, and pitfalls. Buying an existing business is definitely not for everyone who is interested in participating in small business, but it does work for some people.

Advantages to buying a business rather than creating it

When you decide to purchase a home, you can choose between buying an existing one (that more than likely has been lived in) or building one from scratch. The vast majority of people are happy to purchase an already-built home. Why? Because building a home is a lot of work, takes a lot of time, and has a lot of potential for screwups.

I don't want to scare you off if you want to start a business. For most people, starting and building a business isn't as difficult as building a home. However, as with buying an existing home, buying someone else's business works better for some people. The main advantages to buying a business are as follows:

- ✔ **You avoid start-up hassles and headaches.** Starting a business from scratch requires dealing with a lot of stuff — just take a look at Chapters 12 and 13 for starters. Beyond formulating a plan, in the early years you have to deal with a variety of issues, such as developing a marketing plan, finding customers, locating space, hiring employees, and incorporating. Although you still need a game plan for a business that you buy and you need to fix any problems it has, if you buy a good business, part of what you're buying is a more finished entity.

Consider the learning curve for the type of business you're considering purchasing. Buying an existing business makes more sense if the business is complicated. For example, purchasing a business that manufactures a musical instrument makes more sense than purchasing a plumbing business, which doesn't need much more than a little plumbing know-how and a few tools to start up. Unless you've built musical instruments before and understand the intricacies of the production process, starting such a business from scratch is quite risky and perhaps foolhardy. (However, purchasing an existing plumbing business may still make sense if you don't want to build a stable of customers from scratch.)

- ✔ **You lack an idea for a business you want to start.** Starting a business is hard if you lack an idea for a product or service to sell. If nothing new strikes your fancy, you have a good reason to buy an existing business.

- ✔ **You reduce risk.** After a business has an operating history and offers a product or service with a demonstrated market, some of the risk in the company is removed. Although investing in something that is proven is far from a sure thing, the risk should be significantly lower than the risk involved in a start-up. Looking at historic financial statements also helps you make more-accurate financial forecasts than with a start-up venture.

- ✔ **You enhance your ability to attract investor or lender money.** You should have less difficulty raising money from investors and lenders to catalyze your business than with a start-up. Why? For the reasons just discussed. Attracting most investors to something that's more than an idea is easier. And for the amount they invest, investors demand a smaller piece of an existing business than they would with an investment in an idea.

- ✔ **It's your only ticket into some businesses.** Some businesses in some geographic territories — such as bottlers or car dealerships — can only be entered through buying an existing business.

- ✔ **You can find businesses where you can add value.** Some entrepreneurs who start businesses don't see the potential for growth or don't want to grow their business. They may be burned out, content with their current profit, or simply ready to retire. Finding businesses where the potential exists to improve operating efficiency and to expand into new markets is not too hard. Relative to investing in stocks or real estate, it's easier for a business-minded person to find small companies that are undervalued relative to the potential they have to offer.

However, just because you think you see potential to improve a business, never, ever pay a high price based on your high expectations. You can be wrong — you may be looking at the business through rose-colored glasses. Even if you are correct about the potential, you shouldn't pay the current owner for the hard work and ingenuity you will bring to the business if you successfully purchase it. Offer a fair price based on the value of the business *now* (I explain how to figure this later in the chapter) and realize the rewards of your improvements *after* you make them.

Disadvantages of buying a business

Just as everyone doesn't enjoy running or cooking, some people do not enjoy the negatives that come with buying an existing business. If these issues don't turn you off, maybe you have what it takes to successfully purchase and run an existing business:

✔ **You buy the baggage.** When you buy an existing business, the bad comes with the good. All businesses have their share of the bad. The business may have problem employees, for example, or it may have a less-than-stellar reputation in the marketplace. Even if the employees are good, they and the culture of the company may not mesh with where you'd like to take the company in the future.

Do you have the disposition and desire to motivate people to change or to fire them? Do you have the patience to work at improving the company's products and reputation? All these issues are barriers to running and adding value to a company. Some people enjoy and thrive on such challenges, while others toss and turn in their sleep at night with such pressures. Think back on your other work experiences for clues as to what challenges you have tackled and how you felt about them.

✔ **You need to do a lot of inspection.** If you think buying a company is easier than starting one, think again. You must know what you're buying *before* you buy. So you need to do a thorough inspection, perform due diligence, kick the tires, whatever you want to call it. For example, you need to rip apart financial statements to ascertain if the company really is as profitable as it appears and to determine its financial health.

After you close the deal and the checks and/or money have been transferred, you can't turn back. Unless a seller has committed fraud or lied (which is difficult and costly for a buyer to prove in a court of law), it's buyer beware about the quality of the business you're buying. In "Evaluating and Buying a Small Business," later in this chapter, I cover all the homework you need to do before you buy.

✔ **You need more capital.** Existing businesses have value, which is why you generally need more money to buy a business than to start one. If you're short of cash, starting a company is a lower-cost path to small business.

✔ **Lower risk means lower returns.** If you purchase a good business and run it well, you can make decent money. In some cases, you can make a lot of money. But you generally have less upside and potential for hitting it really big than with a business you start. Those who have built the greatest wealth from small business are those who have started them rather than those who buy existing ones. If you buy one, you'll still have plenty of potential profits and wealth to be made, just not as much.

✔ **You don't get the satisfaction of creating a business.** Whether for your ego or your psyche, entrepreneurs who build their own businesses get a different experience than those who buy someone else's enterprise. You can make your mark on a business you buy, but doing so takes a number of years. Even then, the business is never completely your own creation.

Prerequisites to buying a business

Not everyone is cut out to succeed with buying an existing business. Having the money to buy a business, unfortunately, is not your ticket to success. Even if you've got sufficient funds to buy an existing business, you may be blind to a whole host of problems and pitfalls and end up losing your entire investment. You'll meet some small business buyers later in this chapter who did just that.

Conversely, some people with little money to invest in buying a business succeed wildly. You can purchase a good small business with little and, in rare cases, with no money down. So what, then, are the traits common to people who successfully buy and operate an existing small business?

Non-financial stuff

First, you should have business experience and background. If you were an economics or business major in college and took accounting and other quanti-tatively oriented courses, you're off to a good start.

Even better than academic, ivory-tower learning is work experience in the type of business you want to buy. If you're a veterinarian and want to purchase an existing practice, go work in one. If you want to run a restaurant, go work in one. Consider the experience as paid on-the-job training for running a business.

If you have worked on business management issues with a variety of industries, you also have the right background. Consultants get such training. The danger in having done only consulting is that you're usually not on the front lines where most of the serious business operational battles take place.

If none of the above apply to you, I'm not going to say that you're going to fail if you buy a business, but I will say that the deck is stacked against you. If you don't have a business background and work experience, you may still succeed. More likely is that you may simply survive.

You will likely do far better with some remedial work. Get some hands-on experience, which is more valuable than any degree or credential you can earn through course work. There's no substitute for real live experience marketing to and interacting with customers, grappling with financial statements, dealing with competitive threats, and doing the business of business. I'm not saying don't do *any* academic course work. You may, in fact, be required to get a credential to be able to do the work that you want to do — such as an M.D., if you want to practice medicine. If you don't need a specific credential, selected courses, as well as reading good business books (I recommend some in Chapter 15), can boost your knowledge base.

Financial background

To purchase a business, as with real estate, you need to make a down payment on the purchase price. In most cases, you need to put down 25 to 30 percent. Bankers and business sellers who make loans to business buyers normally require such down payments in order to protect their loan. Small business buyers who make a small down payment are more likely to walk away from a loan obligation if the business gets into financial trouble.

If you lack significant capital for a down payment, you can try asking family or friends to invest. You can also set your sights on a less-expensive business or seek business owners willing to accept a small down payment. If you can find a business for sale where the owner wants less than 20 percent down, you may be on to something good. Be careful, though, because an owner willing to accept such a small down payment may be having a difficult time selling because of problems inherent in the business or because it's overpriced.

Many existing small businesses for sale can be purchased with a loan from the selling owner. Also check for loans with banks in your area that specialize in small business loans. (See "Sources of funding" in Chapter 13 for other financing ideas.)

How to Find Good Businesses to Buy

Unless you're extraordinarily lucky, finding a good business to buy takes a great deal of time. If you're spending time outside of working hours, finding a business to buy can easily take a year or two. If you have the money to afford the luxury of looking full-time and not working, many months still will likely pass before you find, analyze, negotiate, and close on the purchase of a business.

Buying with less money down

I'm hesitant to tell stories of people who, with small down payments, bought solid companies and ended up becoming multimillionaires. But this feat can be done — I just don't want to mislead you into believing that it's easy or that just anyone can do it.

I know two people who were able to hit home runs with businesses they bought with small down payments. Ken and his business partner purchased an off-site file storage company from an older owner who wanted to retire. The business was doing about half a million a year in sales and had allowed the owner to earn a decent living. After working for a year at a low salary, Ken gained the trust of the owner, who sold Ken and his partner the business for just $20,000 down — which represented less than 5 percent of the $550,000 purchase price. Ken and his partner had lots of great ideas about how to grow and build the business and did just that. Within seven years, after acquiring another area business and starting another location, sales and profits mushroomed, and the partners' stake in the business was worth about $7 million.

If you think Ken's story is extraordinary, check out Kyle's. He worked as an investment banker and learned the techniques of companies borrowing lots of money through selling high yield (junk) bonds. Kyle and a business partner pulled off the purchase of a company that manufactures musical instruments. With $250,000 down, Kyle and his partner bought the business for $95 million! In case you don't have your calculator handy, that's a down payment of less than one-half of 1 percent! Kyle's stake in the company is now worth tens of millions of dollars.

Despite pulling off these smashing successes in their early 30s, both Ken and Kyle had excellent backgrounds to prepare them. Kyle, a Stanford M.B.A., had worked as a management consultant and investment banker. He also had a love of musical instruments and knew how to structure deals with little money down. Ken, also a Stanford M.B.A., had a background as a financial analyst and had done lots of research into the off-site file storage industry.

Above all else, it pays to be persistent, patient, and willing to spend some time on things that don't lead immediately to results. You need to be willing to sort through some rubbish to find the keepers. If you're the sort who requires immediate gratification in terms of completing a deal, you'll either make yourself miserable in your search or end up rushing into a bad deal. Following are the best techniques for identifying good businesses for sale that meet your needs.

Define what you're looking for

Just as you can't purchase a home or other piece of real estate without defining some search or screening criteria, you're going to end up spinning your wheels in your business search unless you set some boundaries. You don't have to be rigid or precisely define every detail of the business you want to purchase. However, the better you set some parameters, the sooner you can start laying the groundwork to purchase.

Each person has a different set of shopping criteria. Following are some good ones to help narrow your field of search:

- ✔ **Size/purchase price.** Unless you're already wealthy, the money you have to invest in a business will constrain the size of business you can afford. As a rough rule of thumb, figure that you can afford to pay a purchase price of about three times the amount you have earmarked for the business. For example, if you have $50,000 in the till, you should look at buying a business for $150,000 or less. Because many business sellers overprice their businesses, you can probably look at businesses listed at a price above $150,000, perhaps as high as $200,000.

- ✔ **Location.** If you're rooted already and don't want to move or have a long commute, the business's location further narrows the field. Although you may be willing to look at a broader territory, maybe even nationally if you're willing to relocate, evaluating businesses long distance is difficult and expensive. Unless you're looking at a highly specialized type of company, try to keep your search local.

- ✔ **Industry.** Industry-specific expertise that you want to use in the business you buy can help whittle the pool of businesses down further. If not, I highly recommend focusing on some specific niches in industries that interest you or that you know something about. Focusing helps you conduct a more thorough search and turns up higher-quality companies. The industry knowledge you accumulate in your search process can pay big dividends during your years of ownership in the business.

If you're having a hard time brainstorming about specific industries, here's a trick to jump start your cerebral synapses. Take a walk through the Yellow Pages. Listed alphabetically are all the businesses known to exist in your area. Remember that a separate yellow page directory exists for businesses that sell mainly to consumers, while a "business-to-business" yellow book lists businesses whose customers primarily are other businesses. Look at either or both, depending upon what types of business you think you may be interested in.

You also may want to buy a business in a sector that is experiencing fast growth so that you, too, can ride the wave. Check out *Inc.* magazine's annual Inc. 500 list of the fastest-growing smaller companies in America.

- ✔ **Opportunity to add value.** Some buyers want to purchase a business with problems that need fixing or with untapped opportunities. For most people, managing a business is enough of a challenge. As with real estate, most people are happier leaving the fixer-uppers to the contractors. However, some businesses without major problems can offer significant untapped potential.

After you've defined your shopping criteria, you're ready to go to the marketplace of businesses for sale. I recommend typing up your criteria on a single page so that you can hand it to others who may put you in touch with businesses for sale. Shopping for a small business is like a challenging Easter egg hunt: You never know what'll turn up in the bushes. You'll likely shop using several of the following methods to turn up businesses that meet your needs.

Look at publications

If you're focused on specific industry sectors, you may be surprised to learn that there are all sorts of specialty newsletters and magazines. Just think of the fun you'll have reading publications such as the *Alternative Energy Retailer, Specialty Foods Merchandising, Coal Mining Newsletter, Advanced Battery Technology,* or *Gas Turbine World!* Specialty publications get you into the thick of an industry and also contain ads for businesses for sale or business brokers who work in the industry.

A useful reference publication that can be found in public libraries with decent business sections is a two-volume set entitled *Small Business Sourcebook* (Gale). Organized alphabetically, this reference contains listings of publications, trade associations, and other information sources by industry.

Conducting literature searches of general interest business publications can help identify articles on your industry of interest. The *Reader's Guide to Periodicals* and online computer searches at your local library can help find the articles. Larger local newspapers in your area also contain classified ads of businesses for sale.

Network with advisors

Speak with accountants, attorneys, bankers, and business consultants who specialize in working with small businesses. These advisors sometimes are the first to learn of a small business owner's desire to sell. Advisors may also be able to suggest good businesses not for sale whose owners may be worth approaching anyway (see the next section).

Knock on some doors

If you're a home owner and someone came to your door and said they were interested in buying your home, you'd probably say that you're not interested in selling. If the interested buyer said they really liked the type of property you had and were willing to pay a good price, the person may get a little more of your attention, but you'd still likely turn him away. If you, as the home owner, were considering selling anyway, you might be all ears, especially if you think you can sell directly and save paying a broker's selling commission.

Some business owners who haven't listed their business for sale are right now thinking about selling. So if you approach enough businesses that you're interested in, you'll find some of these not-yet-on-the-market businesses with owners interested in selling.

Why would you want to go to this trouble and bother business owners? Simple. You increase your possibility of finding the right business for you. You may also be able to get a good deal on such a business. You can negotiate with such a seller from the beneficial position of not having to compete with other potential buyers.

Instead of calling on the phone or literally knocking on the business's door, start your communications by mail. Sending a concise letter of introduction explaining what kind of business you're looking for and what a wonderful person you are demonstrates that you're investing some time into this endeavor. By all means, follow up by phone a week or so after you send the letter.

Work with business brokers

A decent number of small businesses for sale are listed through business brokers. Just as a real estate agent makes a living selling real estate, a business broker makes a living selling businesses.

Business brokers generally sell smaller small businesses — those with less than $1 million in sales annually. These businesses tend to be family-owned or sole proprietorships, such as restaurants, dry cleaners, other retailers, and service firms. Approximately half of such small businesses are sold through brokers.

If you don't have your heart set on buying a particular type of business, a doughnut shop for example, one advantage of working with brokers to buy a business is that they can expose you to other businesses you may not have considered. Brokers can also share their knowledge about some of your ideas — like the fact that you need to get up at 2 a.m. to make doughnuts if you succeed in buying a doughnut shop. Still want to buy one?

Most business brokerage firms sell different types of businesses. Some firms, however, specialize in one industry or a few industries.

The pitfalls with working with brokers are numerous:

✔ **Commission.** Brokers are not your business advisors, they are salespeople. That fact doesn't make them corrupt or dishonest, but it does mean that their interests are not aligned with yours. Their incentive is to do a deal and do the deal soon — and the more you pay, the more they make.

Business brokers typically get paid 10 to 12 percent of the sales price of the business. Technically, this fee is paid by the seller, but as with real estate deals done through brokers, the buyer often pays too. Remember, if a broker isn't involved, the seller can sell for a lower price and still clear more money, and the buyer is better off, too.

- ✔ **Undesirable businesses.** Problem businesses are everywhere, but a fair number end up with brokers. The reason: The owners had trouble selling on their own.

- ✔ **Packaging.** This problem relates to the last two. Brokers help not-so-hot businesses look better than they really are. Doing so may involve lying but more typically involves stretching the truth, omitting negatives, and hyping potential. (Owners who are selling themselves may do these things as well).

You (and your advisors) need to do the due diligence on a business you may buy. Never, ever trust or use the selling package a broker prepares for a business as your sole source of information. Brokers, as well as sellers, can stretch the truth, lie, and commit fraud.

- ✔ **Access to limited inventory.** Unlike real estate brokers who can access all homes listed with brokers for sale in an area through a shared listing service, a business broker can only tell you about his office's listings. (Confidentiality is an issue, as a shared listing service increases the number of people who can find out that a business is for sale and the particulars of the sale.)

If you're going to work with a business broker, use more than one. Working with a larger business brokerage firm or one that specializes in listing the type of business you're looking for can maximize the number of possible prospects you see. In some areas, brokerages pool listings to allow access. Florida, for example, has a state association of business brokers that shares listings. However, even in areas like Florida, some of the larger brokerages opt not to be included because they benefit less by sharing their listings.

- ✔ **Few licensing requirements.** Unlike real estate agents in most states, the business brokerage field is not regulated and no licensing is required at the federal level. Approximately 20 states require real estate licenses of business brokers who operate in their state. This licensing requirement may seem odd, and it is. States don't know which existing departments should monitor business brokers. Real estate seems logical to some state governments, because some of the selling process (getting listings and working on commission) is similar. Real estate or leases are also parts of many business deals. Some states allow those with securities brokerage licenses to operate as business brokers. The majority of states have no requirements — anyone can hang out a shingle and work as a business broker.

You can find business brokers in the Yellow Pages under "Business Brokers." Ads for businesses for sale may lead you to a broker as well. You can also ask tax, legal, and business consultants for good brokers they may know. If you've found a broker you think you'd like to work with, check references from other buyers who have worked with the broker. Be sure that the broker works full-time and has solid experience. Some business brokers dabble in it part-time and make a living other ways.

Ask the broker you're interested in for the names of several buyers of similar businesses they've worked with in the past six months to narrow down the field so that they can't just refer you to the three best deals of their career. Also, check whether complaints have been filed against the brokerage with the local Better Business Bureau and any state regulatory department (for example, real estate, attorney general, department of corporations) that oversees business brokers.

Consider a franchise

Among the businesses that you can purchase are those that are clones of one another. Some companies expand their locations through selling replicas, or *franchises*, of their business. When you purchase a franchise, you're buying the local rights to a specified geographic territory to sell the company's products or services under the company's name and to use the company's system of operation. In addition to an up-front franchisee fee, franchisers also typically charge an ongoing royalty.

As a consumer, you likely have done business with franchises. Franchising is a huge part of the business world. Companies that franchise — such as McDonald's, Pizza Hut, H&R Block, Midas Muffler, 7-11 stores, Gymboree, Century 21 Real Estate, Holiday Inn, Avis, Subway, and FootLocker — account for approximately $1 trillion in sales annually. Purchasing a good franchise can be your ticket into the world of small business ownership.

Franchise advantages

When you purchase a franchise, unlike buying other businesses, you are not buying an operating enterprise. Although the parent company should have a track record and multiple locations with customers, you will be starting from scratch if you purchase a new franchise. (Existing franchises can be purchased from owners interested in selling.) As the proud owner of a new franchise, you do not have customers. As with starting a business, you must find them.

So why would you want to pay a good chunk of money to buy a business without customers? Actually, you should consider purchasing a good franchise for the same reasons that you would purchase other good, established businesses. A company that has been in business for a number of years and has successful franchisees proves the demand for the company's products and services and that its system for providing those products and services works. The company has worked the bugs out and hopefully solved common problems. As a franchise owner, you benefit from and share in the experience that the parent company has gained over the years.

Franchises offer two additional advantages that most other freestanding businesses don't. A larger and successful franchise company should have brand name recognition. In other words, some consumers recognize the company name and may be more inclined to purchase its products and services. Some consumers feel more comfortable getting a muffler job done by franchiser Midas Muffler rather than hunting around and calling Discount Muffler World or Manny's Muffler Bazaar from a yellow page listing. The comfort from dealing with Midas may stem from the influence of seeing its advertisements (Midas boasts 1,800 locations and sales of more than 100 million mufflers), recommendations of friends, or your own familiarity with Midas's services, perhaps in another part of the country.

Another advantage of owning a franchise is the centralized purchasing that it offers. You would hope and expect that as a corporation made up of 1,800 locations, Midas buys mufflers at a low price. Volume purchasing generally leads to bigger discounts. In addition to possibly saving franchisees money on supplies, the parent company can also take the hassle out of the logistics of figuring where and how to purchase supplies.

Franchise pitfalls

As with purchasing other small businesses, pitfalls abound in buying a franchise. And franchises are not for everyone. Some of the more common problems that you should be on guard for include the following:

- ✔ **You're not the franchise type.** When you buy a franchise, you're buying into a system that has been created for you. People who like structure and following established rules and systems more easily adapt to the franchise life. But if you're the creative sort who likes to experiment and change things to keep life interesting, you'll probably be an unhappy franchisee.

  Unlike starting your own business where you may get into the game without investing lots of your time and money, buying a business that ends up not being what you want can be a more expensive learning experience. For example, you may find you don't like being on the phone and dealing with the public after shelling out good money to purchase a travel agency franchise.

- ✔ **You're required to buy overpriced supplies.** Centralized, bulk purchasing through the corporate headquarters is supposed to save franchisees time and money on supplies and other expenditures. Some franchisers, however, attempt to make big bucks through large markups on proprietary items franchisees are contractually obligated to buy from them.

- ✔ **The franchise is unproven.** One of the problems with buying a franchise is that you are not buying an ongoing, established business with customers. If the concept has not stood the test of time and other franchisees, you don't want to be a guinea pig as the first franchisee. And some franchisers are more interested in simply selling franchises to collect the up-front franchise money. Reputable franchisers want to help their franchisees succeed so that they can collect an ongoing royalty from the franchisees' sales.

- ✔ **The franchise is a pyramid scheme.** Unscrupulous, short-term focused business owners sometimes attempt to franchise their business and sell as many franchises as quickly as possible. Some even have their franchisees sell franchises and share the loot with them. Everything becomes focused on selling franchises rather than operating a business that sells a product or service well. In rare cases, franchisers engage in fraud and sell next to nothing, except the hopes of getting rich quick.

Evaluating a franchise

No matter what type of franchise you're buying, do lots of homework before you agree to buy. Following is my top ten list of issues to examine for a franchise you're noodling about buying. Get solid answers to all these questions and issues and then make your decision about whether to buy.

1. **Request and read the Uniform Franchise Offering Circular (UFOC).**

   The Federal Trade Commission (FTC) requires all franchisers to issue this document at least 10 days before a prospective franchise buyer writes a check or signs a document to purchase. If you think you're interested in a particular franchise, ask for this important document. Don't be put off by its size. Read the document cover to cover. The UFOC contains a treasure trove of valuable information, such as the names and addresses of the ten closest franchisees, as well as a list of franchises that were terminated, not renewed, or bought back by the company. Pending or settled litigation is disclosed and should indicate potential or actual troubles between franchisers and franchisees. The UFOC also gives you the employment background of the senior management of the franchiser and the costs to the franchisee of purchasing a franchise as well as required inventory, leases, and other costs.

2. Are the franchisers looking for a partner or a sale?

In your first interactions with the franchising company, observe the demeanor and approach of those you speak with. Although all such companies should have enthusiastic people, some of whom are full-time salespeople, the best franchising companies want to check you out almost as much as you should want to check them out. Smart franchisers don't want to sell a franchise to someone who is likely to crash and burn or tarnish the good reputation they've worked so hard to build. These companies know that their interests are aligned with yours — they make more money from ongoing royalties if they sell franchises to good franchisees who are successful.

Run as fast as you can, in the opposite direction, if the franchisers tell tales of great riches from just a small investment of your time and money. Some franchisers are more interested in selling franchises than in finding and helping the most-qualified franchisees succeed. Such franchisers may also attempt to pressure you into making a quick decision to buy and be evasive about providing detailed information about their business. If they don't want to give you the UFOC, run extra fast.

3. Speak with franchisees.

Talk with franchisees both currently part of the company, as well as those who quit or were terminated. Start with the lists of franchisees provided in the UFOC — not with the references of the company's happiest franchises in the country eagerly provided by the franchisers. Ask the franchisees what their experiences, both good and bad, have been with the parent company. Those franchisees for whom things didn't work out generally are more forthcoming about the warts of the system, but also try to identify if some of these people were poor fits. Conversely, active franchisees will be more likely to see things through rose-colored glasses, if, for no other reason, than to reinforce their decision to buy a franchise. Observe which franchisees are happiest and most successful and see if you share their business perspectives and traits.

4. Understand what you're buying.

Good franchises cost a reasonable chunk of change up front. On the low end, service businesses, which can be run from home, go for around a

$25,000 up-front franchise fee; compare that to the several hundred thousand to a million dollars required for the brick-and-mortar locations of established franchisers, such as McDonald's. Additionally, ongoing franchise royalties run about 3 to 10 percent of gross revenue. The UFOC should detail all the up-front costs. What are you getting for this payment? Is the system and name brand really worth this fee? What kind of training will you receive?

5. **Look at comparables.**

Few franchises are unique. Compare the cost of what a franchise is offering you to the cost of purchasing franchises from different companies in the same business. For example, if you're considering purchasing a tax-preparation franchise from a newer company, compare the terms and offerings to H&R Block's and Jackson Hewitt's, two large and successful tax preparation franchise firms.

6. **Consider the start-up alternative.**

If you look at the "best" franchises in a particular business and think, "Hey, I can do this as well or better and at less cost on my own," then consider starting from scratch. Be careful to be realistic, though, because many hidden costs — both out-of-pocket financial costs and costs in the form of tons of time — are involved in starting a business.

7. **Check with the regulators.**

Franchises are generally regulated at both the federal and state level. The FTC regulates nationally, and the state level regulatory agency is usually called something like the department of corporations or the attorney general's office. Check with these regulators to see whether complaints are on file. (As I mention at the start of this list, the UFOC should also detail pending litigation against the company by disgruntled franchisees.) You may also want to check with the Better Business Bureau in the city where the franchising company is headquartered to discover whether anything is on file.

8. **Run a credit report on the company.**

Another indicator of what kind of business relationships the franchiser maintains is to examine its credit report. Just as you have a personal credit report on file, business credit reports show how a company has dealt with payments and debts owed to suppliers and creditors.

9. **Review the franchise contract.**

If your digging has made you feel more, rather than less, comfortable with the franchise purchase, you now need to get down to the nitty-gritty of the contract. Franchise contracts are usually long and tedious. Read the contract completely to get a sense of what you're getting yourself into. Have an attorney experienced with franchising agreements review the contract as well. In addition to the financial terms, the contract should specify how disputes are handled, what rights you have to sell the franchise in the future, and under what conditions the parent company has to terminate the franchise. Make sure that you can live with and be happy with the non-financial parts of the contract.

10. Negotiate.

Different companies have different negotiating styles. Some offer their best deal up front and don't engage in haggling. Others don't put their best foot forward in the hopes that you'll simply sign and accept the inferior terms and conditions. Some naive franchise buyers see the contract as cast in stone and don't think to negotiate. Remember that almost everything is negotiable.

Don't skip these ten points when you're evaluating a franchise. You may be most tempted to cut corners in reviewing a franchise from a long-established company. Don't. You may not be right for the specific franchise or perhaps the "successful" company has been good at keeping problems under wraps.

In "Evaluating and Buying a Small Business," later in this chapter, I explain the homework you should complete prior to buying an existing business. Read that section as well, especially if you're considering the purchase of an existing franchise from another franchisee.

Multilevel marketing companies

A twist, and in most cases a bad one, on the franchising idea is multilevel marketing (MLM) companies. Sometimes known as network companies, MLMs can be thought of as a poor-person's franchise. I know dozens of people, from clients I've worked with to students I've taught in my courses, who have been sorely disappointed with the money and time they've spent on MLMs.

Some people are enthusiastic about MLMs. One book on the subject says,

> . . . like an elemental force of nature, network marketing has risen from the soil and roots of America's heartland, boldly promising wealth, freedom, and limitless horizons to those with the courage to seek them out.

One day I received a letter from a client of mine describing an MLM opportunity. "It is the best thing I've ever seen," gushed the letter, ". . . I have friends who are making $10,000, $25,000, $70,000, and $125,000 per month! $195 starter fee gets you literally a national distributorship."

The company, which I'll call "Superhype Telemarketing," sells long-distance phone service and claims to offer rates far lower than AT&T's, Sprint's, and MCI's. You pay for your starter kit, go through a short training seminar, and — voilà — you're in business for yourself. Work when you want, get a share of every dollar your customers spend on long-distance, and best of all, recruit others as representatives and make money off of business they bring in as well.

For those weary of traditional jobs, the appeal is obvious. Work at home, part-time, no employees, no experience necessary, and make big bucks. If your parents raised you right, however, you should be skeptical. If you can make $10,000, $25,000, $70,000, and $125,000 per month, wouldn't everyone be doing it?

Superhype Telemarketing is one of many companies that use multilevel marketing. Representatives who work as independent contractors solicit customers as well as recruit new representatives, known in the industry as your "down line."

A big problem to watch out for is the business equivalent of the pyramid scheme — businesses that exist to sign up other people. A little bit of digging on my part revealed the following about Superhype Telemarketing. Its marketing director advocates that you ". . . sell directly to those that you have direct influence over. The system works great because you don't need to resell month after month. It's an opportunity for anybody — it's up to them how much work they want to put into it."

Quality multilevel marketing companies are the exception

A number of network companies have achieved success over the years. Amway, HerbaLife, and Mary Kay have stood the test of time and achieved significant size. Amway founders Richard De Vos and Jay Van Andel achieved multibillionaire status.

Not all multilevel companies are created equal, and a few are worth a look. Mary Kay is an example of a successful network company with a 30-plus year history. Mary Kay has 375,000 sales representatives and does business in 23 countries. Although not shy about the decent money its more successful salespeople are making, Mary Kay doesn't hype the income potential. Local sales directors typically earn $50,000 to $100,000 per year, but this income comes after many years of hard work. Top sellers are rewarded with gifts, such as the infamous pink Cadillac.

The ingredients for Mary Kay's success include competitive pricing, personal attention and social interaction, which many stores don't or can't offer their customers. "We make shopping and life fun . . . we make people look and feel good," says Mary Gentry, one of Mary Kay's sales directors.

Prospective Mary Kay reps are encouraged to try the products first and host a group before they sign up and fork over the $100 to purchase a showcase of items to sell. To maximize sales, Mary Kay representatives are encouraged to keep a ready inventory because customers tend to buy more when it's immediately available. If reps want out of the business, they can sell the inventory back to the company at 90 cents on the dollar originally paid, a good sign that the company stands behind its product.

Quality multilevel marketing companies make sense for people who really believe in and want to sell a particular product or service and don't want to or can't tie up a lot of money buying a franchise or other business. Just remember to check out the MLM company, and remember, you won't get rich in a hurry, or probably ever.

Any MLM examination should start with the product or service. In Superhype Telemarketing's case, hundreds of companies offer telephone service, so the service is hardly unique. Superhype Telemarketing claims to be much cheaper than AT&T, Sprint, and MCI, as well as local toll-call providers. Some of the company's marketing materials claim savings of as much as 50 percent to 75 percent. The reality: Comparing Superhype Telemarketing's cost to AT&T, which certainly isn't the lowest cost, shows little difference. If you make more than $10 in long-distance calls per month, AT&T charges about $0.13 per minute for a call clear across the country during weekday evenings versus $0.12 for Superhype Telemarketing. If you place more than $50 per month in calls, AT&T rates drop to the same level as Superhype's.

A call to the Better Business Bureau in the city where Superhype Telemarketing is headquartered revealed that the company has been the subject of dozens of filed complaints of unauthorized switching of consumers' long-distance phone service by Superhype sales representatives and misrepresentation of savings.

So what about the big money — can you make tens of thousands to a hundred thousand dollars per month or more working for Superhype? For starters, you have to pay to become a Superhype representative. The fee of $195 gets you a kit that provides advice, 12 months of a corporate newsletter, and a small amount of training. If you want to get paid a $40 fee for training others who sign up, you pay $395 to be a trainer and have the ability to train others.

The company put me in touch with one of its most successful salespeople, Big Al. Big Al told me he had been a representative with the company since 1990. "I used to be in real estate and got tired of the headaches of dealing with tenants. . . the idea of earning residual payments for everyone signed up to use a phone service appealed to me," Big Al said. Working part-time in 1991, he said, without my asking, he made $17,000 in his first year and then, working full-time, earned $60,000 in 1992, $670,000 in 1993, and $1.4 million in 1994.

Being a skeptic, I asked for proof from Big Al. He said he'd be happy to fax me a copy of a big check that he was presented with in 1993. What he sent was marketing materials that showed photos of "top leaders" being presented with oversized checks, similar to the props that companies use for P.R. opportunities when making a big contribution to charity. Big Al's check, which was supposedly for one month in 1993, was for $57,000.

Not satisfied with this copy as proof, I asked Big Al for his monthly sales report from Superhype, which I know the company provides to all its representatives. He said he didn't have this information because his tax preparer was working on his return. When I pointed out that the month in question was in 1993, not 1994, he said that all his financial statements were in storage and because he was soon heading out of town for ten days, he wouldn't have a chance to retrieve them until he got back. I then suggested that his tax preparer send me proof of income for 1994 or other proof. I'm still waiting.

As for the company's other top producers, the company never provided proof of the hyped income claims. All this hype reminds me of the movie *Quiz Show* (if you haven't yet, I recommend you see it), an eye-opening account of how television quiz shows in the 1950s were rigged to dupe the public.

Big Al, who is also one of the company's most successful recruiters, also claimed that the company is contractually obligated to pay residuals and can't cut sales reps out of the picture financially after they've signed up others. However, according to Superhype's marketing director, "There is no guarantee of future payments. The company has the ability to change its program at any time." So if Superhype's management or a future buyer of the company decides to cut commissions, reps will be left holding an empty bag.

Also cause for pause: Superhype's marketing packages contain a feature article, which is from a supposed business periodical, that praises the company. Buried in the fine print on the back page of the reprint of the "article," which is sandwiched around a two full-page ad for the company, is the following: "Information contained in feature articles is provided by the company." Turns out when a company like Superhype buys the space for the ad, the "story" comes with it as well! The sticker price is in excess of $10,000. Rather than an independent appraisal of the company, this article is basically an ad bought by Superhype.

Work-from-home "opportunities"

"We made $18,269.56 in just 2 ½ weeks! Remarkable, home-based business! We do over 90 percent of the work for you! Free info: 800-555-8975."

"Earn $4,000 per month on the new instant information superhighway."

"You can be earning $4,000 to $10,000 each month in less than 30 days! We'll even help you hire agents to do the work for you ... FREE!"

"Work from home. Company needs help. Earn $500-$900 per week. Anyone can do this — will train. Full time or part time. Call 555-8974. Only for the serious — please!"

Especially in magazines read by small business owners and wannabe small business owners, you find lots of ad copy like the preceding ones. In most cases, these ads are from grossly overhyped multilevel marketing companies. In other ads, no legitimate company exists but simply a person or two or three tries to sell you some "information" that explains the business opportunity. This information may cost several hundred dollars or more. Such packages end up being worthless marketing propaganda and rarely provide useful information that couldn't be had at a far lower cost or no cost.

Never buy into anything like these ads pitched to you through the mail or over the phone.

The bottom line on any network marketing "opportunity" is to remember that it's a job. No company is going to pay you a lot of money for little work. As with any other small business venture, if you hope to earn a decent income, it will take at least three to five years of low income to build up your business. Most people who buy into networks such as Superhype's make little money, and many quit and move on. According to a Superhype company document, more than 60 percent of its representatives make less than $100 per month and fewer than 5 percent make more than $1,000 monthly. You'd never know this information from its advertising or sales hype.

Also think twice before signing up relatives, friends, and coworkers, the first people network marketers encourage you to sell to. A danger in doing business with those people whom you have influence over is that your reputation and integrity are on the line. So, too, could be your friendships and family relations.

Do your homework and remember that due diligence requires digging for facts and talking to people who don't have a bias or reason to sell to you. Do the same homework that I recommended for franchises in "Evaluating a franchise." Be skeptical of multilevel marketing systems, unless the company has a long track record and many people who are happy. Assume that an MLM company is not worth pursuing until your immense due diligence proves otherwise.

Evaluating and Buying a Small Business

If you put in many hours, eventually you'll come across a business that interests and intrigues you enough to consider actually purchasing it. As with purchasing a piece of real estate, two important hurdles stand between you and becoming the new owner. First, you need to inspect what you're buying, and second, you need to negotiate a deal and finalize a contract. Expect to spend lots of time on both of these activities.

Due diligence — check this out

In the American legal system, a person is presumed innocent until proven guilty beyond a reasonable doubt. When you're purchasing a business, however, you should assume that the selling business owner is guilty of making the business appear better than what it is (and possibly lying) until you prove otherwise.

I don't want to sound cynical, but an owner can use more than a few ways to make a business look more profitable, financially healthier, and more desirable than it really is. You cannot decide how much inspection or due diligence to conduct on a business based on your gut-level feeling.

Mary made the mistake of following her gut-level feeling when she purchased a restaurant. The previous owner, henceforth referred to as the Shrewd Gourmet, was a charming, well-dressed older gentleman who was well educated, well traveled, and well informed about his wines. He dazzled Mary with his organization and attention to detail and flattered her with sweet nothings about how successfully she could run his restaurant.

The "fact sheet" that the Shrewd Gourmet prepared showed, over a period of several years, steadily increasing revenue and even more rapidly increasing profits for the restaurant. In the 12 months before the negotiations, the restaurant grossed in excess of $500,000 and had profits of about $150,000.

Mary had received an inheritance two years earlier and was eager to pursue her dream of owning a restaurant. She collected wine and enjoyed eating at good restaurants. But she hated the details of business and wanted nothing of finding a location, hiring help, developing a menu, and all the other details of starting a business from ground zero.

After just a couple of offers and counteroffers, Mary agreed to purchase the restaurant lock, stock, and barrel and paid all cash. The Shrewd Gourmet tossed Mary the keys and rode off into the sunset to enjoy his retirement, financed in part by Mary.

The first few months, business seemed a little slower than Mary had anticipated, but overall things seemed to be going relatively fine. But by the end of the first year, Mary found that she had a number of significant problems.

First, the business revenue and profits appeared to have sunk. For the first full year under Mary's ownership, Mary grossed around $300,000, and after expenses, she broke even. Expenses ran higher and revenue lower than the Shrewd Gourmet's historic financial statements had indicated. For the most part, Mary couldn't figure out why.

Second, Mary ended up in lease hell. In her tenth month of ownership, a rather unpleasant and ugly surprise confronted Mary. The owner of the building that housed Mary's restaurant wanted to jack up the rent 300 percent when the restaurant lease expired. Mary couldn't believe the building owner could be so greedy or think that she was foolish enough to pay such a hefty increase.

To make a long story short and to spare you the agonizing details of what Mary discovered in the ensuing months and years, Mary's restaurant eventually sucked her into bankruptcy. Turns out that the Shrewd Gourmet used a lot of American advertising license in preparing the financial statements for Mary — in other words, he lied big-time. Also, the building lease had been at a rate well below market rents because the Shrewd Gourmet had negotiated a favorable lease long ago.

What to check out when buying a business

When you find a business that you think you're interested in purchasing, you absolutely, positively must do your homework before you buy. However, just as with purchasing a home, you don't want to expend buckets of money and time on detailed inspections until you are able to reach an agreement with the seller. What if you're dealing with a seller who is unrealistic about what the business is worth? The serious, time-consuming, and costly due diligence should be done after you have an accepted offer to purchase a business. Such inspections should be a contingency in your purchase contract (see "Contingencies," later in the chapter).

Ultimately, if you're going to buy a business, you should have a plan similar to but likely shorter than the one I presented in Chapter 12. Addressing the issues in a plan goes a long way toward helping you do your due diligence.

Following are some additional questions to answer about a business you're contemplating purchasing (address as many of the easier questions as possible before you make your offer):

1. Why is the owner selling? Ask the owner or the owner's advisors why they are selling and selling now. You may not get a straight or honest answer, but the answer may shed some light on the owner's motivations and need to sell. Some owners want to bail when they see things getting worse.

2. What is the value of the assets you're buying? This value includes not only equipment but also "soft" assets, such as the firm's name and reputation with customers and suppliers, customer lists, patents, and so on. Asking key customers if they would still buy from the business if you took it over is smart. Ask the same question of key employees, if possible. You've got to get out and interview key employees, customers, suppliers, advisors, and competitors.

3. What do the financial statements reveal? Search for the same things that you would look for in a company whose stock you're considering purchasing (see Chapter 6 for how to read financial statements and what to look for). Don't take the financial statements at face value simply because they are audited. The accountant who did the audit could be incompetent or chummy with the seller. One way to check for shenanigans is to ask for a copy of the business's tax returns from the seller. Owners are more likely to try to minimize reported revenue and maximize expenses on their tax return to keep from paying more tax. After you have an accepted purchase offer, have a tax advisor experienced in such matters do an audit.

4. If the company is leasing the space, what do the lease contracts say? Mary the restaurateur got into trouble because she overlooked this important step. A soon-to-expire lease at a low rate can ruin a business's profit margins. With a retail location, the ability to maintain a good location is critical as well. Check comparables — that is, what other similar locations lease for — to see if the current lease rate is fair and talk to the building owner to discover his plans. Ask for and review (possibly with the help of a legal advisor) the current owner's lease contract.

5. What liabilities, including those that may be hidden "off" the balance sheet, are you buying with a business? Limit liabilities, such as environmental contaminations, through a contract. Conduct legal searches for liens, litigation, and tax problems.

6. What does a background check turn up on the owners and key employees? Do they have good business experience, or do they have criminal records and a trail of unpaid debts?

The Shrewd Gourmet retired out of state, perhaps out of the country. Mary may never know because efforts to locate him have failed. Either he was the kind of fellow who didn't like leaving a forwarding address, or he knew there was a good reason to disappear without leaving tracks to find him. If Mary had found him, she could have tried to sue him for lying about the business's profitability.

Although somewhat extreme, problems of the magnitude left hidden in Mary's restaurant are not that unusual among businesses for sale. Because you can't guess what hidden surprises exist in a business, you've got to dig for them. Until you prove to yourself beyond a reasonable doubt that these surprises don't exist, you should not go through with a business purchase.

Negotiating a good deal

After you've found what you think is a good business and done some home-work, you're ready to make an offer. Negotiating takes time and patience. Unless you're legally savvy, find an attorney who focuses his or her practice on small business dealings to help with the contract.

Have an attorney review and work with your contract. Also consider obtaining input from a qualified tax person. Good advisors can help you inspect what you're buying and look for red flags in the company's financial statements. Advisors can also help structure the purchase to protect what you're buying and to gain maximum tax benefits. If you're working with a business broker, be sure to use an attorney and accountant as well.

To get a good deal, a number of things need to fall into place.

What's the business worth?

How can you buy a business if you don't know its worth? The price that a business is listed for sale for is often in excess of — and sometimes grossly so — what the business is really worth.

A starting point for valuing a business you're considering buying is to look at comparables — that is, what other similar businesses have sold for. A smart home buyer or real estate investor looks at comparables when ready to make an offer on a property.

The challenging part is to find the specific sales price and other information on businesses that have sold. Small businesses are privately held, and the terms of sales are not a matter of public record. Following are some good sources:

  ✔ **Business brokers.** If you're already working with a business broker or looking at businesses listed with a business broker, the broker should be able to provide a comparable market analysis of similar businesses that the broker's office has sold. It should go without saying that you should use this analysis as a starting point. Remember that brokers, particularly those who have a business listed for sale that you're interested in, make more money the more you pay for a business. Brokers also generally have access to sales data only on the small number of similar businesses their office has sold.

✔ **Businesses you've looked at that have sold.** If your search lasts months or perhaps years, keep track of similar businesses you've considered that eventually sell. These sales are extra valuable comparables because you may have been able to see the business and obtain more details about the company's financial position.

✔ **Advisors who work with comparable companies.** Attorneys, tax advisors, and business consultants you work with can help provide you with comparables. If an advisor doesn't have memories of or experience with similar deals, then you're speaking with the wrong advisor. You need advisors who can bring applicable experience to the negotiating table.

✔ **Business appraisers.** If you really want to buy a business and your initial investigation suggests that the seller is committed to and serious about selling, you should consider hiring a business appraiser. The Institute of Business Appraisers (561-732-3202) can provide you with a list of association members in your area. Also check the business-to-business Yellow Pages in your area under Appraisers — Business.

✔ **Research firms and publications.** A small number of companies publish comparable sales information or do searches for a fee:

  • Bizcomps is an annual publication that provides sales price, revenue, and other financial details for businesses sold. This compendium of sales information is available for different major regions of the U.S. (Western, Central, and Eastern editions). A national edition provides sales information for larger manufacturing, wholesale, and service businesses. Call 619-457-0366 for a sample of this publication. Each directory sells for $98.

  • Financial Research Associates (FRA) provides balance sheet and income statement comparisons for small companies through its annual *Financial Studies of the Small Business* directory. Call 941-299-3969 to receive a background package on this directory, which sells for $97.

✔ **Read trade publications.** As I've already recommended earlier in the chapter, trade publications can help you get smarter about a particular industry and how to value companies within the industry. Many publications are willing, for a small fee, to send you past articles on the topic.

When you look at comparables, you'll find that figuring what multiple of earnings these businesses sold for is valuable to your search. What a business sold for — its price — divided by its annual earnings or profits is like the price-earnings ratio for stocks. I discussed in Chapter 5 how the price-earnings ratio works for evaluating the value of larger, publicly traded companies. Because they are less well established and riskier from an investing standpoint, small privately held businesses sell for a lower multiple of earnings than comparable but larger companies.

Taking profits for granted

You cannot and should not blindly take the profit from the bottom line of a business's financial statement as the gospel. As part of your due diligence, you should have a tax advisor do an audit after you negotiate a deal.

Even if the financial statements of a business are accurate, you (and your tax advisor) still must look for more-subtle problems, which may make the profits of the business appear better or worse than they truly are. Many of the same issues that I explain to look for in Chapter 6 when analyzing the financial statements of public companies that have issued stock apply to evaluating the financial statements of small companies.

If necessary, factor out one-time events from the profit analysis. For example, if the business

last year got an unusually large order that is unlikely to be repeated and hasn't been the norm in the past, you should subtract this amount from the profitability analysis. Also examine the owner's salary to see whether it's too high or low for the field. Owners can pump up the profitability of their company in the years before they sell by reducing or keeping their draw to a minimum or by paying family members in the business less than fair market salaries.

You should also consider whether the rent or mortgage expense will be different when you buy the business. This change clearly affects the profitability of the business. Also, consider in what will happen to profits when you factor in the financing costs from borrowing money to buy the business.

Some advisors and business brokers advocate using a multiple of revenue to determine the value of a business. Revenue is a poor proxy for profitability. Two businesses in the same field can have identical revenue yet quite different profitability because of how well they are run, the pricing of their products and services, and the types of customers they attract.

In addition to looking at the sales price of other businesses relative to earnings, you can also consider the value of a company's assets. The so-called *book value* of a company's assets is what the assets are worth per the company's balance sheet. These figures should be checked to ensure that the asset values are correct. Another, more conservative way to value such assets is to consider the liquidation/replacement cost (see Chapter 6).

Contingencies

When you purchase a home, you should make your offer contingent upon satisfactory inspections, mortgage loan approval, and the property seller legally holding title to the home. When you make a purchase offer for a business, you want to make your offer contingent upon a number of similar issues:

> ✔ **Due diligence.** Your purchase offer should be contingent upon a thorough review of the company's financial statements and interviews of key employees, customers, suppliers, and so on. You should be allowed to employ whomever you like in helping with these evaluations. You may also

want to defer paying a portion of the purchase price for 6 to 12 months to make sure that everything is as the owner/seller claimed.

✔ **Financing.** Unless you're making an all-cash offer, finding financing at an acceptable interest rate should be another condition of your purchase offer. By the time you make an offer, you should know whether the seller is willing to loan you money for the purchase. Sellers can be the best financing sources. Be sure to check with your area's banks that specialize in small business loans (some of which are backed by the Small Business Administration) and compare their terms to what, if any, loan the seller is offering. Specify the acceptable loan terms, including the maximum interest rate at which you will go ahead with the purchase.

✔ **Limited liability.** Make sure that the seller is liable for environmental cleanup and undisclosed existing liabilities (debts).

✔ **Non compete**. The last thing you would want is to buy the business and then have the former owner set up an identical business down the road. Insist that a non compete clause be in your purchase offer, which specifies for, say, two years that the seller can't establish a similar business. Also consider asking the owner to consult with you for 6 to 12 months to make sure that you tap all his or her valuable experience, as well as to transition relationships with key customers, employees, and suppliers. You can even make the total purchase price dependent on the future success of the company.

Allocation of the purchase price

Unlike when you purchase a home and offer, say, $200,000 for the home, if you offer $200,000 for a business, the purchase price should be broken down, or allocated, among the assets of the business and other categories. Although this stuff makes accountants giddy and likely causes your eyes to glaze over, snap to attention because how you structure the purchase can save you tens of thousands of dollars in taxes.

As a buyer, you're generally better off allocating as much of the purchase price to the assets of the business. Why? Because such assets can generally be depreciated (written off for tax purposes) faster than, say, land, which is not depreciable, or goodwill, which is depreciated over 15 years. For tax reasons, the seller's interests will likely oppose yours. The purchase of the business and allocation of the purchase price among business assets must be reported on IRS Form 8594. Make sure that you do so because if you don't, the penalty is up to 10 percent of the amount not reported.

Final steps

Usually with the help of an attorney, you should take these additional steps prior to closing the purchase of the business:

✔ Notify creditors of the transfer of ownership. In counties where the company does business, a transfer of ownership notice should be published in a general circulation newspaper. If you omit this step, unsecured creditors can come after your business if the previous owner had outstanding debts.

✔ Check to make sure no liens are filed against assets of the business and, if you're buying real estate, that the property title is clear.

✔ Get the seller to provide proof certifying that federal and state employment, sales, and use taxes are all paid up.

Investing in Someone Else's Business

Buying and running a company involves a mountain of work, especially if you want to do it right. Through investing in someone else's business, if you structure things right, you can avoid the hassle of the day-to-day operations yet participate in the growth of a potentially lucrative business.

It's easier to be careless with other people's money

Although some people are extra careful when investing other people's money, many small business owners seeking investors need money for the wrong reasons. Some business owners are impatient and perhaps don't understand the feasibility of bootstrapping.

Other businesses need money because they are in trouble. One small furniture retailer in my area conducted a stock offering to raise money. On the surface, everything seemed fine, and the company had made it onto the Inc. 500 list of fast-growing small companies. Turns out the company wanted to issue stock because it had expanded too quickly and wasn't selling enough merchandise to cover its high overhead. The company ended up in a bankruptcy.

Another problem with small businesses seeking investors is that many small business owners are willing to take more risk and do less up-front planning and homework with other people's money. Many well-intentioned people fail at their businesses. An M.B.A. whom I know from a top business school — I'll call him Jacob — convinced an investor to put up about $300,000 to purchase a small manufacturing company. Jacob put a small amount of his own money into the business and immediately blew about $100,000 on a fancy-schmancy computer scheduling and order-entry system.

Jacob also wasn't much interested in sales, which the previous owner headed up. Jacob hired a sales manager, who turned out to be a disaster to work with. Many of the front-line salespeople fled to competitors, taking key customers with them. By the time Jacob came to his senses, it was too late — the disaster had unfolded. He tried to cut costs, but this hurt the quality and timeliness of the company's products. The business dissolved, and the investor lost everything.

A provision enacted with the 1993 tax law changes allows investors to exclude half their capital gains from small business investments held for five or more years in small businesses (*small* being defined as businesses with gross assets at less than $50 million). With the maximum federal capital gains rate at 28 percent, this new provision lowers the capital gains tax to 14 percent. So if you have a knack for identfying up-and-coming entrepreneurs, you may be able to make rewarding investments that aren't too taxing. This special tax break cannot be used for businesses in the fields of health, law, engineering, architecture, hospitality, farming, insurance, financing, or the mineral extraction industries.

Putting money into your own business (or someone else's) can be a high-risk but potentially high-return investment. The best options are those you understand well. If you hear about a great business idea or company from someone you know and trust, do your research and make your best judgment. That company or idea may well be a terrific investment.

Before investing in a project, ask to see a copy of the business plan and compare it with the suggested business plan model in Chapter 12. Thoroughly check out the people running the business. Talk to others who don't have a stake in the investment about the idea and learn from their comments and concerns. But don't forget that many a wise person has rained on the parade of what turned out to be a terrific business idea.

Avoid limited partnerships and other small-company investments pitched by brokers, financial planners, and the like. These people want you to buy limited partnerships because they earn a hefty commission from them. If you want a convenient way to invest in businesses and earn tax breaks, buy some stock mutual funds inside a retirement account.

Part V
The Part of Tens

The 5th Wave — By Rich Tennant

"IT HASN'T HELPED ME SELL MORE HOT DOGS, BUT I'VE HAD SEVERAL INQUIRIES FOR INVESTMENT ADVICE."

In this part . . .

The Part of Tens contains shorter chapters, each including about ten items on important investing topics that didn't quite fit elsewhere in the book. The topics in this part cover the risky stuff and the good stuff among other investment reading you can do, collectible investing, what you need to know when you're considering selling an investment, and how your computer can help (or hinder) your investing potential.

Chapter 15

Ten Warnings and Recommendations about Investing Resources

*O*ver the years, I've read several hundred financial books. I hope you haven't subjected yourself to this task! Let me first say that most books contain at least a few things to teach us.

The problem, however, is that too many investing books are burdened with wrongheaded advice and misinformation. As a nonexpert, you may have a hard time sifting through the dung heap for the tidbits of treasure. More likely is that the "bad stuff" will pollute your otherwise clear thinking and quick mind and cause you to make investing mistakes that millions before you have made.

I hope that I'm not the first person to tell you to not believe everything you read. Publishing is no different than any other business — companies are in it to make money. As with other industries, but even more pronounced with most publishing companies, is the sometimes shortsighted desire to reap quick profits, which causes some companies to produce things that appear attractive in the short-term but are toxic long-term.

Books as bait to lure you to buy something overpriced

In some cases, the worst books may end up steering you toward purchasing a crummy investment product that the author has a vested interest in selling you. Unfortunately, most publishers don't do their homework to check out a prospective author. Some publishers don't care what the author is up to, as long as he or she is willing and able to write a salable book. Authors who run around the country conducting seminars are a plus to the publisher.

That's one reason why Charles Givens's financial advice books attracted publishing giant Simon & Schuster. Givens was a master at self-promotion and conducting hundreds of seminars around the country. Chapter 1 (see the last section, "Don't believe everything you read or hear") recounts the myriad problems and conflicts of interest with the advice of Givens's books.

The worst books also tend to confuse more than they convey. Such authors have an incentive to make things complicated and mysterious. Their agenda may be to sell you a high-priced newsletter or convince you to turn your money over to them to manage.

One book author said to me, "Royalties, schmoyalties . . . I write books to hook people into my monthly newsletter. I can make $185 per year off of a $195 newsletter sale. You can't do that with a book." You sure can't, but this author's books were short on information and advice and said that you needed to keep up with the latest developments to make the right investments. When you subscribe to his newsletter, you're told that the financial markets are so complicated and rapidly changing that the newsletter is really no substitute for using his money management service!

In other cases, particularly when a book is written with a larger firm, the book's objective may be to function as an advertising tool, not to help the reader make informed decisions. For example, the best-selling book *Discipline of Market Leaders* was supposedly written for entrepreneurs and corporate leaders to learn about growing and managing their businesses. As *Business Week* said in its review of this book, ". . . reading the entire book leaves one with the feeling that the authors are trolling for clients, saving their best insights for those who will pay for more — much more — than a hardcover book."

Don't believe unaudited performance claims

Particularly in the newsletter business, prognosticators fill your mailbox with promotional material making outrageous claims about their returns. Private money managers, not subject to the same scrutiny and auditing requirements as mutual funds, can do the same.

When considering hiring a money manager, you should be especially wary of any making claims of high returns. "Millions of people are out there saying they've done great with their investments," Kenneth L. Fisher, an investment manager and *Forbes'* columnist says. "There are many ways to calculate returns. Never believe in a track record that hasn't been audited by a major accounting firm with experience in doing these sorts of audits in the investment business."

And so, too, can book authors avoid careful scrutiny of claims of especially high returns. Some book publishers are happy to look the other way or even to solicit and encourage great boasts that they use in the packaging to sell books.

Consider these two recent books: *The Beardstown Ladies' Common-Sense Investment Guide: How We Beat the Market — and How You Can, Too* and *The Whiz Kid of Wall Street's Investment Guide* by Matt Seto.

The Beardstown investment club claims a whopping 23.4 percent annual return since the club's inception in 1983. In the book, the authors advocate forming an investment club, pooling your money, and using a simple stock selection method to beat the pants off the market and the suspendered managers of mutual funds. The bulk of this book walks the reader through how this invest-ment club evaluated and selected individual stocks using the *Value Line Investment Survey,* a publication I've used and recommended for many years. Harmless enough.

Seto's book boasts, "Matt Seto manages a portfolio that consistently outper-forms 99% of all mutual fund managers . . . and returns an annual average of 34 percent." In his book, this 17-year-old investing genius says to forget bonds, real estate, and mutual funds and grow rich by investing entirely in individual stocks.

Each of these books makes prominently displayed and marketed performance claims. The Beardstown club's returns and Seto's returns, versus the market averages, place them shoulder to shoulder with the legendary Peter Lynch, of the now famous Fidelity Magellan fund, and Warren Buffett, an investor who Peter Lynch described as "the Greatest Investor of them all." Problem is, neither of the books contain information as to how these investment gurus calculate their returns nor are the authors able to substantiate them when asked to.

When I first wrote about the Beardstown book for the *San Francisco Examiner* in April 1995, I offered to work with an accounting firm to calculate the club's returns if the club supplied the necessary information. I asked the same of Seto when I read his book in late 1995. Neither of these authors could supply the documentation to prove their claims and backpedaled when pressed.

Initially, the Beardstown club said they would send the information, but months passed, and it never arrived. When pressed, the club's media spokesperson told me that the club has ". . . chosen not to make our return an issue. . . . we're not out to be bragging." Kind of surprising, given the claims plastered all over their book. If their returns were this good, this club could be making hundreds of thousands of dollars per year managing the Value Line mutual fund, which, like the club, invests in stocks highly rated by Value Line. While the club was supposedly making more than 23 percent per year, Value Line was only getting 15 percent! Seto only supplied partial documentation that could not prove his claim of an astounding 34 percent return. Meanwhile, the printing presses crank away.

Other dangers in narrowly focused advice guides written by novices

Although I disagree with the Beardstown guide's premise — that an investment club can pick individual stocks and beat the market and the best professional money managers — the book has even bigger problems that are common to many narrowly focused investment books pitching one investment. The book does not address the importance of choosing investments that fit an investor's overall financial strategies and goals, which, as you've read throughout this book, is something that is essential to smart investing. Making sound investing decisions, of course, involves more than picking "good" investments. The book completely ignores the rest of your financial situation, such as your tax bracket and your ability to contribute money into retirement accounts. Pooling money through investment clubs doesn't work well because different club members have different investing and tax needs.

"Our individual needs were not a factor in the selection of the stocks. We didn't consider taxes," says the club's spokesperson. A number of the stocks that the club invested in paid healthy dividends. Although appropriate for retired members of the club, such stocks unnecessarily add to the tax burden of younger club members, who are still in their working years.

Also surprisingly absent in the book was advice to take advantage of funding tax-deductible retirement accounts. The club spokesperson, for example, says, "I don't put the maximum possible in my 401(k). I put up to the amount that my employer matches." She believes that she can earn higher returns investing in individual stocks outside of a tax-sheltered account than she can investing in the funds provided by her employer in its 401(k) plan. Even if she could earn higher returns picking her own stocks, she might rethink whether she'll end up with higher returns. The lost tax benefits from not using her 401(k) plan are huge (see Chapter 3).

Fearmongers prey on investors' insecurities

Every year, heck, every month — come to think of it, every week — books and newsletters are published saying that dramatic changes are on the horizon. Fear not, these writers say, they'll show you the way.

A classic example of such Chicken Little, the sky-is-falling mentality can be found in Douglas Casey's book, ominously entitled *Crisis Investing,* which rocketed to the number one position on the best-seller lists in 1979 and 1980. The opening to this book says

> This book is based upon the premise that the United States will soon experience a massive depression, and that the effects of that depression will persist well into and even beyond the 1980s. . . .

Casey didn't give investors much credit, saying, ". . . most investors in America are generally no more rational than their precursors in defunct Rome." Casey's book made numerous dire predictions, which would cause even the most level-headed person to run for cover. Table 15-1 shows what Casey predicted in this book would happen by the mid-1980s and what actually did happen:

Table 15-1   The Tale of the Tape: One Prognosticator's Accuracy

Casey's Prediction	What Actually Happened
"Inflation of well over 20% — at first — then *accelerating* rapidly thereafter."	Inflation, which was at 14 percent at the time Casey's book was published, plummeted to less than 3 percent in the next three years and today is at about the same low level.
"Unemployment rates in excess of those experienced during the Great Depression of the 1930's"	In case your history book isn't handy, unemployment during the Great Depression soared above 25 percent. In 1980, unemployment was running about 7 percent, eventually got up to almost 11 percent in 1982, and then dropped to near 5 percent in the late 1980s.
"The complete collapse of the Social Security System, as well as most, if not all pension funds."	Never happened.
"Many stocks will become worthless, along with bonds, and it will prove impossible to float new stocks or bonds. Brokerage firms will collapse. . . . the Dow Jones Average will fall to at least 300 in the not-too-distant future."	Never happened. The Dow Jones average, which was trading between 800 and 1,000 at the time, went on an upward rampage, breaking 2,000 by 1986 and 5,000 by 1995.
"The Federal Government will nationalize large bankrupt industries to get them back in production . . ."	Entire industries never went bankrupt, and the government never got into the business of nationalizing (taking over) businesses.
"Strict controls on wages, prices *and* profits . . . chaotic shortages resulting in rationing . . . bankruptcy on a massive scale of local and state governments . . . confiscation of gold from individuals . . . the true price of gold should be at least $3,300 an ounce."	None of these things ever came close to happening. Gold prices, which broke $800 an ounce around the time Casey's book was published, collapsed to less than $350 by 1982 and have traded between $300 and $500 an ounce ever since.

So how can a book that was filled with such horrendously wrong advice and predictions make it to the top of the best-seller lists? In 1979 and 1980, the U.S. economy was coming off a difficult period during which interest rates, inflation, and unemployment had already greatly increased. The time was ripe for the doom-and-gloomers to come out of the woodwork and claim that they knew what was going to happen next. This scenario would be like me traveling to a site where a hurricane had just been and predicting that the rain and wind damage would be five times worse from the next soon-to-arrive storms.

In order for you to make sound investing choices, you don't need predictions and soothsayers. If you choose to follow these prognosticators, and you're lucky, little harm will be done. But more often than not, you can lose lots of money following their predictions. Stay far away from publications that purport to be able to tell what's going to happen next. No one has a crystal ball.

You're no Warren Buffett (and he didn't make $14 billion picking stocks)

In recent years, Warren Buffett has received lots of attention for his investing prowess. Numerous books have been published about him (none by Buffett himself), most of which were written and promoted from the philosophy embodied in the marketing slogan, "He did it his way; now you can, too," for the book, *The Warren Buffett Way.*

You can read every book ever written about Buffett, and the odds are about 10 million to 1 that you're going to be able to invest like he does. It's not that you're not an intelligent, willing-to-learn kind of person. But consider that you can't invest like Buffett for the same reason that you can't learn to be a professional basketball player by reading books about basketball greats Larry Bird and Michael Jordan, even if they themselves wrote the books.

One financial market commentator said of Buffett and the financial markets, "If making money in the market is so easy, why has only Warren Buffett made $14 billion picking stocks?"

However, Buffett did not make $14 billion picking individual stocks. It's true that Berkshire Hathaway, the firm that Buffett purchased in 1965 and still runs today, makes substantial investments in the stocks of individual companies. However, Buffett built much of his great wealth through his buying and managing a variety of businesses, particularly insurance companies.

Buffett's interest in investing, companies, and insurance began at a young age. At the age of 21, he wrote the article "The Security I Like Best," about the insurance company GEICO, for a small New York paper. In addition to 13 insurance companies, Berkshire Hathaway owns divisions such as See's (candy manufacturer), the *Buffalo News* (newspaper), Nebraska Furniture Mart (home furnishings retailer), Borsheim's (jewelry), *World Book* (encyclopedias), Kirby's (home cleaning products manufacturer), Fechheimer Brothers (uniforms), and H.H. Brown and Dexter (shoe manufacturers).

The property and casualty insurance businesses that Buffett's firm, Berkshire Hathaway, ultimately bought, most of which are located in Nebraska, afforded Buffett lots of low-cost money, which his firm could invest in a tax-favored way. Specifically, insurance companies collect premiums from policyholders and invest the money, called "float," until insurance claims need to be paid. Unlike almost all other insurers, Berkshire Hathaway, which is in Nebraska, a state with loose insurance company regulations, can invest much of its float in riskier investments like stocks.

While most other insurers invest no more than 20 percent in stocks, with the remainder in conservative, boring, low-return bonds, Buffett has taken full advantage of Nebraska's loose regulations, investing at times more than 95 percent of the float in stocks. Buffett likes to buy name-brand company stock and is attracted to almost anything that hooks consumers. Witness his investment in tobacco companies of which he said, "I'll tell you why I like the economics of the cigarette business. It costs a penny to make. Sell it for a dollar. It's habit-forming. And there's fantastic brand loyalty."

The float is also invested in a tax-favored way as these reserves compound tax-free and the final capital gains are taxed at a reduced rate thanks to the protection afforded insurance companies. Buffett's insurance operations have also shrewdly kept their float reserved from claims at higher-than-needed levels to take full advantage of these tax benefits.

As Berkshire Hathaway grew over the years, acquired more businesses, and squirreled away more money to invest, Buffett's wealth also ballooned, thanks to his 41 percent ownership stake in the outstanding stock of the company. So to say that Buffett built his entire $14 billion wealth through stock picking and that you can replicate what he did simply by reading books about him is flat-out, downright erroneous!

You don't need to follow your investments like a hawk

If you aren't reading books about how to become the next billionaire, predict the next depression, or form an investment club and make as much as Warren Buffett, just about everywhere you turn these days — on radio, on television, and in the online world — gives you near up-to-the-minute updates on the state of various financial markets around the globe. Although most investors have a natural curiosity about how their investments are doing, the constant barrage of updates, from my experience working with individuals, causes a loss of focus on the big picture.

In many cases, publishing and media companies report what I call the "noise" rather than the news of the day. Some companies are far worse about doing so than others. Over the next week, take a close look at how you spend your time keeping up with financial and other news and information. Do the programs and publications you use most heavily really help you better understand and map out sound investing strategies? Or do they end up confusing, overwhelming, and paralyzing you with bits and pieces of contradictory and often hyped noise? I'm not saying tune out completely, but I am saying to devote less time to the noise of the day and more time to self-education. How can you do that? Read good books.

Books worth reading

Exceptional investing books — ones that are readable, educational, and insightful — are rare. Some of the better investment books are technical in nature and are written by career investment folks, so even the better-written books may require reading through more than once. Make the investment of time; it'll pay big dividends (and capital gains!). Following are my picks for books that are worth the trouble of tracking down and reading.

A Random Walk Down Wall Street

Now in its sixth edition, *A Random Walk Down Wall Street* (Norton), by Burton Malkiel, is a classic that was first published in 1973. Malkiel is an entertaining and intelligent writer. Drawing from examples from this century and others, Malkiel teaches how speculative bubbles and fear and greed, as well as economic and corporate fundamentals, can move the financial markets.

One of the fundamental premises of his book is that the financial markets cannot be predicted, especially in the short term. Common sense confirms this premise: If someone could figure out a system to predict the markets and make a fortune, then that person wouldn't waste time writing a book, publishing a newsletter, and so on. Malkiel, in fact, is one of the pioneers and proponents of index mutual funds, which simply invest in a relatively fixed basket of securities in order to track the overall market performance rather than to attempt to beat it. See Chapter 8 to find out about index funds and how to use them.

Needless to say, many Wall Street types weren't and still aren't excited about this book. As Malkiel says, the very term *random walk* is an "obscenity." But Malkiel presents a mountain of compelling arguments and data to support his case that most Wall Street firms and their investment research aren't worthy of an investor's hard-earned money. He also convincingly and thoroughly trashes the whole field of technical analysis, which purports to be able to predict security prices based on charting and following past price movements.

Malkiel explains how to look at some common-sense indicators, such as whether the stock and bond markets are fairly valued and your own personal goals and desire to take risk, to develop a thoughtful and successful investment plan. Rather than try to predict the future, Malkiel explains how the level of risk an investor accepts with investments will ultimately determine future returns.

Bogle on Mutual Funds: New Perspective for the Intelligent Investor

Investors who want to evaluate and select mutual funds should pick up a copy of *Bogle on Mutual Funds: New Perspectives for the Intelligent Investor* (Irwin) by John C. Bogle. The book's greatest strength is that it educates investors about how to get the most for their mutual fund investment dollars. Bogle does a masterful job explaining the pitfalls of investing in mutual funds and the dangers inherent in chasing after yesterday's star performers.

Although Bogle is the founder and former chairman of the Vanguard Group of mutual funds, the nation's largest completely no-load (commission-free) mutual fund company, he does not plug any of Vanguard's funds (or other fund company funds for that matter). As he says in the preface, ". . . much of the philosophy that I express in this book is a reflection of the Vanguard philosophy."

Bogle is the Ralph Nader of the mutual fund industry. In his book, he criticizes the traditional ownership structure in the fund industry in which the fund parent company owns and operates the funds to maximize its profits rather than the profits of the shareholders. Some may find this criticism distracting, but Bogle's insights highlight some weaknesses in this large and rapidly growing industry. Vanguard has a unique operating structure among fund companies in that it charges rock-bottom fees to manage funds because the funds are operated on an at-cost basis. This practice simply means that there is no markup or profit built into the funds. Vanguard's investors or shareholders actually own the firm through their investments in Vanguard funds.

Bogle on Mutual Funds is an excellent book for financially sophisticated people, but beginners can get lost easily in the morass of data and financial terminology. If you're an investment beginner, finish this book and read Malkiel's book, and perhaps my *Mutual Funds For Dummies* book, to help build your knowledge base sufficiently before tackling Bogle's book.

Built to Last: Successful Habits of Visionary Companies

Some people may think that this book is just for the small number of people who want to build a large company, but they're wrong. *Built to Last: Successful Habits of Visionary Companies*, by management consultant James Collins and Stanford Business School Professor Jerry Porras, is an excellent book for all entrepreneurs and people who work in leadership positions in companies, as well as people interested in investing in individual stocks. Rarely does a great book make it to the business best-seller lists, but *Built to Last* did just that.

The book presents the findings from an extensive six years' worth of research into what's behind the success of companies such as 3M, Boeing, Ford, Hewlett-Packard, Motorola, Sony, and Wal-Mart, all of which have achieved great success in their respective industries over many years. The average company in Collins and Porras's study was founded in 1897. In all, the authors tracked 18 extraordinary companies (referred to as the gold medal winners in their respective industries) and compared the traits of these companies with similarly long-lived but less successful peer companies (in the same industry).

Collins and Porras's findings not only yield insight into how to build or identify a great business in which to invest, but also destroy some commonly held myths. For example, some people feel that a great idea is behind every great company. This concept is wrong, and in fact, according to the authors' research, companies founded on the basis of a great idea can lead to a focus on the idea rather than on laying the groundwork to building a great company. Sony's founder, for example, wrote a nine-page philosophical prospectus setting the stage for this great company, yet had few product ideas in his firm's early days. Early products, such as a rice cooker, failed miserably.

Great, visionary companies also are rigid and unyielding when it comes to respecting their core ideologies and principles. On the other hand, such companies tinker and experiment to stimulate positive change and innovation. And despite their often stunning financial success, great companies usually have a higher or equal aspiration to maximizing profits: fulfilling a purpose and being driven by values. Like Bogle's book, this book is packed with insights, information, and examples, so don't expect to absorb all its contents in one reading.

The Pursuit of Happiness: Who Is Happy and Why

Money — investing and amassing wealth — of course, isn't everything. On the road to building wealth, some begin to realize that other parts of their lives — personal relationships and health, for example — are suffering at least in part because of the overemphasis on career and making and accumulating money. A terrific book that talks not only about the relationship between money and happiness but the characteristics of happy people is *The Pursuit of Happiness: Who Is Happy and Why* (Morrow), by David G. Myers, Ph.D.

Myers, a professor of psychology at Michigan's Hope College, has reviewed hundreds of studies on what makes people happy. These studies cover the U.S. and foreign countries. When it comes to money, Myers found that people in other cultures with less financial affluence than the U.S. were just as happy as Americans as long as they had enough money to meet the basic necessities, such as food, shelter, and clothing. Beyond that, Americans reach the point of diminishing returns, he says. "With our needs comfortably met, more money can now buy things we don't need and hardly care about, or if unspent becomes blips on a bank computer or numbers on a stock report," Myers says.

A University of Michigan nationwide survey found that regardless of income level, people who are content with their incomes are much more likely to be happy. Myers says, "Satisfaction isn't so much getting what you want as wanting what you have," adding, "[there are] two ways to be rich: One is to have great wealth. The other is to have few wants."

On your way to building your investment empire, don't forget what's hopefully more important than the girth of your financial net worth:

- ✔ Health
- ✔ Family and friends
- ✔ A fulfilling career
- ✔ Happiness

Chapter 16

Ten Reasons Investing in Collectibles Generates Poor Returns

. . . .

In This Chapter

▶ Collectibles: an object-ionable way to try to make a buck

▶ The risks involved with collectibles

▶ Advice if you want to buy collectibles

. . . .

*E*specially during the 1970s and 1980s, increasing numbers of headlines trumpeted ever-escalating prices for collectibles and near collectibles. One Honus Wagner baseball card sold in 1991 for a whopping $451,000. A year earlier, a single, solitary van Gogh drawing sold for more than $8 million and one of his paintings for more than $82 million. And ponder that during the Reagan White House years, the Metropolitan Museum of Art in New York City paid more than $143,000 for a deck of playing cards, and some collector paid $13,300 at auction for a chamber pot for the 2nd Earl of Warrington of England.

Collectibles are a catchall category for antiques, art, autographs, baseball cards, clocks, coins, comic books, diamonds, dolls, gems, photographs, rare books, rugs, stamps, vintage wine, writing utensils, and a whole host of other items. If you're considering investing in collectibles because you think you'll earn good returns, read the rest of this chapter — hopefully I'll change your mind.

A collectible is just an object

Although some connoisseurs of fine art, antiques, and vintage wine wouldn't like to compare their pastime with buying old playing cards or chamber pots, the bottom line is that collectibles are all simply objects with little intrinsic value. Wine is largely a bunch of old mushed-up grapes. Art — a canvas and some paint that retail would set you back a few bucks. Stamps are a piece of paper, less than an inch square. Baseball cards — heck, my friends and I used to stick these between our bike spokes as kids.

Now, I'm not trying to diminish contributions that artists and others have made to our culture. And I know that some people place a high value on some of these collectibles. But true investments that can make your money grow, such as stocks, real estate, or a small business, are assets that can produce income and profits. Collectibles have little intrinsic value and are thus subject to the whims and speculations of buyers and sellers.

Markups are gargantuan

Buying 100 shares of IBM stock may cost you $100. If you want to sell, you may receive a price of $99.50. In addition to losing the $0.50 per share (which amounts to 0.5 percent), you'll also need to pay a broker a commission. If you're smart and read the earlier chapters of this book, you'll trade stock through a discount broker, where you may pay another 1 to 1.5 percent in trading costs.

Now contrast these costs with the markups on collectibles. The spread between the price a dealer sells to you and then buys the same exact object back from you is often around 100 percent. Sometimes the difference is even greater, particularly if a dealer is the second or third middleman in the chain of purchase.

So, at a minimum, your purchase must typically double in value just to get you back to even. And that may take 10 to 20 years or more!

You don't save money buying at auctions

"But, wait," some people say, "I can save lots of money buying collectibles through an auction house." Typically, the total commissions between buyer and seller in an auction amount to 20 percent. Although much higher than on a stock or mutual fund purchase, 20 percent isn't that much higher than the cost of trading real estate or a small business.

But the bigger problem with auctions is that multiple people bidding on goods tends to drive the price higher, causing you to still pay a high effective markup anyway. This thrill of competition is why dealers love to use auction sales prices to justify the prices they charge in their stores.

Lots of other costs add up

If the markups aren't bad enough, with some collectibles, you incur all sorts of other costs. If you buy more-expensive pieces, you may need to have them appraised. You may have to pay storage and insurance costs as well. And, unlike the markup, you pay some of these fees year after year after year of ownership.

You can get stuck with a pig in a poke

Sometimes, you may overpay even more for a collectible because you don't realize some imperfection or inferiority of an item. Worse, you may buy a forgery. Even reputable dealers have been duped by forgeries.

Your pride and joy can deteriorate over time

Damage from sunlight, humidity, temperatures that are too high or too low, and a whole host of vagaries can ruin the quality of your collectible. Insurance does not cover this type of damage or negligence on your part.

The returns stink

Even ignoring the substantial costs of buying, holding, and selling, the average returns investors have earned from collectibles barely keep up with inflation and are inferior to stock market, real estate, and small business investing.

Objective return data are hard to come by. Never, ever trust such "data" provided by dealers or the many trade rags that boast of hefty annual returns. The best study I've seen comes from Salomon Brothers, an investment banking firm. During the past 20 years, while stocks returned investors an average 13.1 percent per year and conservative bonds 10.2 percent per year, the highest performing collectibles — and the only ones to produce inflation-beating returns — were stamps at 9.1 percent per year and diamonds at 7.9 percent per year.

However, if you factor in the huge markups on buying and selling these collectibles, the returns don't even keep up with inflation.

The best returns collectible investors have enjoyed come from being able to identify, years in advance, items that will *become* popular. Do you think you can do that?

You won't be able to pick tomorrow's stars in advance

You may be the smartest person in the world, but you should know that even most dealers can't tell what's going to rocket to popularity in the next 20 years. Dealers make their profits the same way as other retailers, from the spread or markup on the merchandise they sell. The public and collectors have fickle, quirky tastes, which can't be predicted. Did you know that Pet Rocks or Cabbage Patch dolls were going to be such hits?

Collecting right takes tons of time

You can learn enough about a type of collectible to be a better investor than the average person. But you're going to have to be among the best — perhaps the top 10 percent of such collectors — to have a shot at earning decent returns. To get to this level of expertise, you need to invest thousands of hours reading, researching, and educating yourself.

Tax-wise, collectibles are the odd man out

In 1997 Congress cut taxes on long term capital gains for investments such as stocks and real estate; collectibles, however, were not invited to the party. So even if you do make some money on a collectible you've had for a long time, your gain will be taxed at a higher rate (28 percent maximum) than it would with other investments (18 percent to 20 percent — see Chapter 3).

Nothing is wrong with *spending* money on collectibles, but I don't want you to fool yourself into thinking that they are an investment. You could sink lots of your capital in these nonincome producing, poor return "investments." At their best as investments, collectibles are a way for the wealthy to buy quality stuff that doesn't depreciate.

If you must buy collectibles

- ✔ Do so for your love of the collectible, your desire to enjoy it, or your interest to learn about or master an area.

- ✔ Keep quality items that you and your family have purchased and hope they're someday worth something. Doing so is the simplest way to get into the collectible business. The complete sets of baseball cards I gathered as a youngster are now, 20-plus years later, worth hundreds of dollars to, in one case, $1,000!

- ✔ Buy from the source and cut out the middlemen whenever possible. In some cases, you may be able to buy from the artist, which is what my brother does with most of the pottery he purchases.

- ✔ Check comparables, shop around, and don't be afraid to negotiate. An effective way to negotiate, once you decide what you think you'd like, is to make your offer to the dealer or artist by phone. Because the seller isn't standing right next to you, you don't feel pressured to decide immediately.

- ✔ Ask the dealer who is convinced the item is such a great investment for a written guarantee to rebuy the item from you, if you opt to sell, for at least the same price you paid or higher within five years.

- ✔ A comprehensive resource for researching, buying, selling, maintaining, and improving collectibles is *Kovels' Guide to Selling, Buying, and Fixing Your Antiques and Collectibles* (Crown) by Ralph and Terry Kovel.

Chapter 17

Ten Things to Know When You Consider Selling an Investment

In This Chapter
- Selling for the wrong reasons
- Understanding your investment goals and other big picture issues
- Factoring taxes into your profit

*T*he best investments can and should be held for years and decades. Every year, people sell trillions of dollars' worth of investments. My experience working with and teaching people about investments suggests that too many people sell for the wrong reasons and hold onto investments that they should be selling. In this chapter, I highlight some issues to consider and issues you should weigh when contemplating selling investments.

Which of your investments are good or bad?

Often, people are tempted to sell an investment for the wrong reasons. One natural human tendency is to want to sell investments that have declined in value. Some people fear a further fall, and who wants to be affiliated with a loser? I think this reaction is similar to the phenomenon of piling into the lifeboats when a ship springs a leak.

Take a step back and a deep breath and examine the merits of the investment you're considering selling. If an investment is otherwise still sound, why bail out when prices are down and a sale is going on? What are you going to do with the money? If anything, you should be contemplating buying more of such an investment. Don't make a decision to sell based on your current emotional response, especially to recent news events. If bad news has recently hit, it's old news now. Don't base your investment holdings on such transitory events.

Use the criteria in this book for finding good investments to evaluate the worthiness of your current holdings. If an investment is fundamentally sound, don't sell.

A better reason to sell an investment is that it comes with high fees relative to comparable investments. For example, if you own a bond mutual fund that is socking it to you with fees of 1 percent per year, check out Chapter 8 to discover high-performing, lower-cost funds.

What are your personal preferences and goals?

If you've inherited investments, or your life has changed, your current portfolio may no longer make sense for you. The time that it takes you to manage your portfolio, for example, is a vital matter if you're starved for time or weary of managing a time-consuming investment.

Leo, for example, loved to research, track, and trade individual stocks — until his daughter was born. Then Leo realized how many hours his hobby was taking away from his family, and that realization put his priorities into perspective. Leo now invests in time-friendly mutual funds and doesn't follow them like a hawk.

One of my clients, Mary, loves investing in real estate because she enjoys the challenge of researching, selecting, and managing her properties. She works in a job where she has to put up with lots of controlling, stressed-out bosses. For Mary, real estate isn't just a profitable investment, it also is a way of expressing herself and growing personally.

What does your overall portfolio look like?

A good reason to sell an investment is to allow you to better diversify your portfolio. Suppose that before reading this book, you purchased a restaurant stock every time you read about one. Now your portfolio resembles several bad strip malls. Restaurant stocks comprise 80 percent of your holdings. Or maybe, through your employer, you've accumulated a hefty chunk of stock in your company so that this stock now overwhelms the rest of your investments.

It's time to diversify. Sell off some of the holdings that you have too much of and invest the proceeds in other good investments, such as those recommended in this book. If you think that your employer's stock is going to be a superior investment, staying so weighted down is your gamble. At a minimum, for stocks, see Chapter 6 for how to evaluate a particular stock. But consider the consequences if you're wrong about your employer's stock.

One area where conservative investors often go wrong is with keeping too much of their money in bank accounts, treasury bills, and the like. Read Chapter 3 to come up with an overall investment strategy that fits with the rest of your personal financial situation.

You can trust and educate yourself

You are not a dummy. Before you picked up this book, you may have considered yourself an investing dummy. I didn't, and I still don't, but hopefully you feel less like a dummy after reading this book. If you delegate your investment decision-making to an advisor, you're likely to be disappointed.

Few financial advisors offer objective and knowledgeable advice. Unfortunately, if you're grappling with a selling decision, finding a competent and impartial financial advisor to help with the decision is about as difficult as finding a politician who doesn't accept special interest money. Most financial consultants work on commission, which can cloud their judgment. And among the minority of fee-based advisors, almost all manage money, which creates other conflicts of interest. The more money you give them to invest and manage, the more money these advisors make. Ask them if you should sell your current holdings, and a fee-based advisor who's worth his or her salt will come up with some seemingly sound compelling reasons. If you need advice, turn to a tax or financial advisor who works on an hourly basis.

What are the tax consequences?

When you sell investments held outside a tax-sheltered retirement account, such as an IRA or a 401(k), taxes should be one factor in your decision. (See Chapter 3 to find out about tax rates that apply on the sale of an investment as well as on the distributions investments make.) If the investments are inside retirement accounts, unless you're withdrawing funds from the accounts, taxes aren't an issue because the accounts are sheltered from taxation.

Just because you pay tax on a profit from selling a non-retirement account investment doesn't mean that you should avoid selling. With real estate, you can roll over and defer payment of tax on the profit (see Chapters 9 and 10).

With stocks and mutual funds, things get more complicated because you have the option of specifying which of your shares you're selling. This option makes life more complicated, but you may want to consider specifying what shares you're selling because you may be able to save taxes. If you sell all your shares of a particular security that you own, you need not concern yourself with specifying which shares you're selling.

Which shares cost you more?

When you sell a portion of the shares of a security (for example, stock, bond, or mutual fund) you own, specifying which shares you are selling may be to your tax benefit. Here's an example to show you why you may want to specify selling certain shares — especially those shares that cost you more to buy — so that you can save on your taxes.

Suppose that you own a total of 300 shares of the stock Worldwide Outlandish Wingdings (WOW), and you need to sell 100 shares to pay for a root canal. Suppose further that you bought 100 of these shares a long, long time ago at $2 per share, 100 shares two years ago at $16 per share, and the last 100 shares one year ago at $14 per share. Today, the stock is at $20 per share.

The good tax folks at the IRS allow you to choose which shares you'd like to sell. Electing to sell 100 shares that you purchased at the highest price — in other words, those that you bought for $16 per share two years ago — saves in taxes. (To comply with the tax laws, you must identify the shares you want the broker to sell by the original date of purchase and/or the cost when you sell the shares. The brokerage firm through which you sell the stock should include this information on the confirmation slip you receive for the sale.)

The other method of accounting for which shares are sold is the method the IRS forces you to use if you don't specify before the sale which shares are to be sold — the *first-in-first-out* (FIFO) method. FIFO means that the first shares you sell are simply the first shares that you bought. Not surprisingly, because most stocks appreciate over time, the FIFO method leads to paying more tax sooner. In the case of WOW, the FIFO accounting method leads to the conclusion that the 100 shares you sell are the 100 that you bought long, long ago at the lowly price of $2 per share. Thus, you owe a larger amount of taxes than if you sold the higher-cost shares under the specification method.

Although you save taxes today if you specify selling the shares that you bought more recently at a higher price, remember that when you finally sell the other shares, you'll then owe taxes on the larger profit. The longer you expect to hold these other shares, the greater the value that you'll likely derive from postponing realizing the larger gain and paying more in taxes. If you expect your tax rate to decline in the future, you have another good reason to hold off selling the shares in which you have greater profit.

In case you care — and if you don't, I completely understand — when you sell shares in a mutual fund, the IRS has yet another accounting method, known as the *average cost method,* for figuring your taxable profit or loss when you sell a portion of your holdings in a mutual fund. This method comes in handy if you bought shares in chunks over time or reinvested the fund payouts into purchasing more shares of the fund. As the name suggests, the average cost method allows you to take an average cost for all the shares you bought over time.

Selling investments with hefty profits

Of course, no one likes to pay taxes. But if an investment you own has appreciated in value, someday you will have to pay tax when you sell, unless you plan on passing the investment on to your heirs upon your death. The capital gains tax on appreciated assets is wiped out at death.

Capital gains tax applies when you sell an investment at a higher price than you paid for it. As explained in Chapter 3, your capital gains tax rate may be different than the tax rate you pay on ordinary income (such as from employment earnings or interest on bank savings accounts).

Odds are, the longer you've held securities such as stocks, the greater the capital gain you'll have, because stocks tend to appreciate over time. If all your assets have appreciated greatly, you might resist selling to avoid taxes. However, if you need money for a major purchase, sell what you need and pay the tax. Even if you have to pay state as well as federal taxes totaling some 35 percent of the profit, you'll have lots left. Before you sell, however, do some rough figuring to make sure that you'll have enough money left to accomplish what you want. If you want to sell one investment and reinvest in another, you'll owe tax on the profit unless you're selling and rebuying real estate (see Chapters 9 and 10).

If you hold a number of assets, in order to diversify and meet your other financial goals, give preference to selling your largest holdings with the smallest capital gains. If you have some securities that have profits and some with losses, you can sell some of each in order to offset the profits with the losses.

Selling securities with losses

Perhaps you own some turkeys in your portfolio. If you need to raise cash for some particular reason, you may consider selling some securities at a loss. Losses can be used to offset gains as long as both offsetting securities are held for more than one year (long term) or both are held for less than one year (short term). The IRS makes this delineation because long-term gains and losses are taxed on a different rate schedule than short-term gains and losses (see Chapter 3).

If you need to sell securities at a loss, be advised that you cannot claim more than $3,000 in losses in any one year. If you sell securities with losses totaling more than $3,000 in a year, the losses must be carried over to future tax years. This situation not only creates more tax paperwork, it also delays realizing the value of deducting a tax loss. So try not to have *net losses* (losses + gains) that exceed $3,000 in a year.

Some tax advisors advocate doing year-end tax-loss selling with stocks, bonds, and mutual funds. The logic goes that if you hold a security at a loss, you should sell it, take the tax write-off, and then buy it (or something similar) back.

When selling for tax-loss purposes, be careful of the so-called *wash sale* rules. The IRS will not allow deduction of a loss for a security sale if you buy that same security back within 30 days. As long as you wait 31 or more days, no problem. If you're selling a mutual fund, you can easily sidestep this rule simply by purchasing a fund similar to the one you're selling.

If you own a security that has ceased trading and appears worthless (or you have made a loan that hasn't been repaid), you can probably deduct this loss. Peruse *Taxes For Dummies* for more information on what situations are deductible and how to claim these losses on your annual tax return.

Selling an investment when you don't have a clue about its cost

You may not know what some investments originally cost you or the person who bought them and later gave them to you. If you can't find that original statement, start by calling the firm where the investment was bought. Whether it's a brokerage firm or mutual fund company, it should be able to send you copies of old account statements. You may have to pay a small fee for this service.

Also, increasing numbers of investment firms, especially mutual fund companies, tell you when you sell what the investment cost you. The cost generally calculated is the average cost for the shares that you purchased. See *Taxes For Dummies* for more ideas of what to do when original records aren't available for other assets, such as real estate.

All brokers are not created equal

If you're selling securities, such as stocks and bonds, you need to know that some brokers charge more, in some cases tons more, to sell. Even if the securities you want to sell currently reside at a high-cost brokerage firm, you can have them transferred to a discount brokerage firm. See Chapter 4 to read about the virtues of using a discounter.

The 5th Wave By Rich Tennant

"SELL."

Chapter 18

Ten Ways Your Computer Can Help with Investing

● ●

In This Chapter

▶ Tracking your returns

▶ Planning for your future

▶ Researching investments

▶ Accessing news and publications

▶ Trading online

● ●

*U*nless you live under a rock, you've likely heard that the United States and most parts of the industrialized world are in the midst of a technological revolution. Computers and technology are sweeping the land and are supposed to make our lives more efficient and entertaining.

In the investing world, hundreds of software packages and thousands of World Wide Web sites and online service providers claim to be able to make your investments more profitable and easier to make. As with most other advertising claims, the reality of using your computer for investing and other tasks falls short of the promises and the hype.

In this chapter, I share with you ways your computer may be able to help you with your investing challenges and chores. Throughout this discussion, however, please remember several important issues:

✔ Many very successful investors don't use their computers for their investments.

✔ You may subject yourself to information overload and spend a fair amount of money without much benefit in return.

✔ Don't believe everything you read, especially in the online world where filters and editors are often absent. (Of course, as you can read elsewhere in this book, filters and editors don't in any way guarantee you quality investment advice and information when you read financial periodicals or some books.)

Don't let your computer control your investing decisions

Through your computer, you may be able to improve your investing prowess using software and online services. For those who are technologically challenged, allow me to start with a definition of *software* — it is the information contained on the disks or CD-ROMs that you load onto your computer's hard drive. Good software must be sound and easy to use. Software that helps you make personal investment decisions has the additional need to provide accurate information and, if applicable, well-founded advice.

Which software is best for you depends on what you're trying to accomplish, as well as your level of investment knowledge and expertise. Software can help you with a variety of investing tasks, from tracking your investments to researching, planning, and even placing trades through your computer.

The line between software and online computer services, which access outside data and information via a modem, is beginning to blur. Some software packages allow you to access the online world. If you venture into the online world, please remember the following cautions.

Be careful, be careful, be careful!

Why? First, most of what's on the World Wide Web is advertising. The best stuff on the Web is existing government filings, which are otherwise publicly available. You can usually access these filings a bit faster online. Accessing anything on the lengthy side is painful if you don't have a fast modem. Some of these resources can be accessed other ways. (I explain options later in this chapter.)

Second, when it comes to message board postings and the like, beware of people trying out a second career online who don't know what they are talking about. Heck, everyone makes money, and most people have some experience investing it (more Americans have lots of experience spending it).

Third, be on guard for brokers, with their biases, trolling for clients and trying to change the way people think. (One bias, for example, is that you need a broker to make wise investments.)

Fourth, be careful with how much time and money you spend online. Some of the commercial services charge for every minute you're online.

Tracking your returns

The kingpin of the financial organizing and tracking software is the No. 1 best-selling financial software, Quicken. Most Quicken users use its bill-paying features to write checks via their computer printer or to pay bills electronically. When it comes to investments, Quicken allows you to list and track your investments and returns. To calculate your investment's total returns with the software, however, you must continually enter your investment's dividend (and, for mutual funds, your capital gains distributions) as well as share price changes.

In addition to organizing all your investments into one place, you can track your original purchase price, current market values, and rates of return on your investments. If you have accounts at numerous investments firms, Quicken can reduce the clutter and complications involved in tracking your investing kingdom. Consolidating your investments at an investment company, for example, a discount broker (some of the larger mutual fund companies have discount brokerage divisions as well) can accomplish the same things for you without you having to invest hours in learning software and entering data. See the comparison of discount brokers in Chapter 6.

Software packages comparable to Quicken are Microsoft Money and Managing Your Money. So if your new computer happens to come with one of these packages preinstalled, give it a whirl. Over the years, these three packages have come to be more and more alike.

Planning for retirement

Creating a retirement plan is a great way to get yourself motivated to start saving money. However, unless you were an applied math major in college, coming up with a useful plan with a pencil and a calculator is a complex task. There are so many things to factor in: expected rates of investment return, inflation, tax brackets, savings rates, social security benefits, retirement ages, pension benefits, life expectancies. . . and on it goes.

So if you've got a computer or access to one, let your computer assist you. A number of investment and software companies offer retirement planning programs designed to do just that. My two favorites are **Quicken Financial Planner** ($39.95, 800-446-8848, also available through software retailers) and **Vanguard's Retirement Planner** ($15, 800-876-1840, only available through Vanguard).

Both programs make it easy for you to test out different scenarios, which is probably their most valuable feature. Tinker with any variable — the inflation rate, for example, or your desired retirement income — and you can quickly see how that change affects your whole retirement plan.

Quicken's retirement program allows a little more detail in your plan. Besides looking at all the factors mentioned above, Quicken lets you plan for multiple income changes over your lifetime as well as major one-time financial events such as selling your house. Vanguard's package does a better job explaining and illustrating the risks of investing in the stock and bond markets.

If you're already in retirement or near retirement, check out the **Vanguard Retirement Manager**, which does a good job helping you to making your nest egg last during your golden years.

Researching your investments

Investment research software packages usually separate investment beginners (and others who don't want to spend a lot of their time managing their money) from those who enjoy wallowing in data and conducting primary research. If you already have a plan in mind and just want to get on with investing, you can go straight to the market and invest your money. But even if you don't want to conduct more-specific research, some of these packages, discussed later in the section, can also help you conduct transactions online for your investment accounts and track your investment's performance.

Investment software packages do not lack information and research. In fact, you'll probably have the problem of sifting through too much data and differentiating the best from the mediocre and downright awful. And unless cost is no object, you need to be careful that you don't spend too much of your loot simply accessing the information.

Before you plunge into the data jungle and try to become the next Peter Lynch or Warren Buffett and pick individual stocks, be honest about your reasons for wanting to research. Some investors fool themselves into believing that their research will help them to beat the markets. Few investors, even so-called professionals, ever do. Witness the fact that over long time periods (ten-plus years), mutual funds that invest in a fixed market index, such as the Standard & Poor's 500, outperform three-quarters of their actively managed peers thanks to the former's lower operating expenses (see Chapter 8).

If you like to invest in individual securities, the Value Line Investment Survey for Windows helps with researching individual stocks using the data provided by the Value Line Investment Survey, discussed in Chapter 6. This software package lets you sift through Value Line's data very efficiently. You can also use it to track your stock portfolio. A two-month introductory offer costs $55, and an annual subscription costs $595 for monthly updates. The software is only available from Value Line at 800-654-0508.

Accessing news and publications

If you want "content," as they call it in the online world, you gotta open up your wallet. Just as a good book costs you money, so, too, does accessing magazines and other financial periodicals online. The two online services with extensive financial content and Internet access are America Online and CompuServe.

America Online (AOL)

AOL, the largest of the online services, is user-friendly and carries lots of business news, indexed by topic for easy retrieval. You can search current news, for example, for articles on specific investments or companies you're interested in. Financial and economic news and financial market highlights are provided as well, in case you want to check on recent market happenings.

AOL offers articles from many financial and general interest magazines, including *Consumer Reports, Business Week, Worth, Time, Investor's Business Daily,* and a number of major newspapers. In some forums, you also can search past articles on a particular topic.

Like just about everyone else in the online world, AOL (800-827-6364) has gone to the flat rate pricing system: $19.95 per month for unlimited access time. If, however, you're pretty sure you won't be a junkie, you can sign up for the light usage plan: $4.95 per month for 3 hours of online time, with additional time costing $2.50 per hour.

CompuServe

CompuServe is the other major player in the online world when it comes to financial content. News related to investments can be obtained through *Associated Press Online* (a basic service) or the more expensive *Business News* or *Executive News Service.* These latter two services give you access to thousands of articles and allow you to set up criteria for searching the news databases. The *Magazine Database Plus* can be helpful, but it's relatively expensive to use. You can retrieve the full text of articles from more than 140 magazines, including many financial magazines. Lots of information is available, but you pay $1.50 for each article, plus the connect time for the search. The *Business Database Plus* has articles from more than 500 specialized business magazines, trade journals, and newspapers, and the database has archives that go back five years.

CompuServe costs $9.95 a month for 5 hours of basic services; additional time is billed at a rate of $2.95 per hour. Most of its better stuff is considered part of its premium services and is charged at $4.80 an hour for most modem speeds. Additional charges apply for investment quotes, portfolio valuation, and executive news service. To order CompuServe's software, call 800-848-8990.

Dow Jones News/Retrieval

Another online service worth checking out is the Dow Jones News/Retrieval. In addition to offering access to most major regional newspapers and hundreds of magazines, you can also peruse the Dow Jones Newswire and various international newswires, plus a wire service reporting on business-related government activity. You can also make use of a clipping service that can collect articles as they are written for particular topics of your choosing.

Everything you do through Dow Jones News/Retrieval costs money. Most articles cost $2.95 per access. They offer a service called the *Private Investor Edition,* which provides you with ten hours of usage per month for $29.95. This flat-rate service is not available weekdays between 6 a.m. and 7 p.m. and offers far fewer publications. You can reach Dow Jones at 800-522-3567.

Reuters Money Network

Another online package worth considering is Reuters Money Network, which is a relatively low-cost option that allows users to access research reports on stocks and bonds from Standard & Poor's, financial news from Dow Jones, Reuters, and various financial periodicals for a fixed monthly fee ranging from $10 to $20. For an extra monthly fee, you can use its Personalized News Clipping Service, which culls articles from a number of publications on your specific portfolio. This service may save you the time and hassle of subscribing to publications to track news items on your investments (800-346-2024).

Telescan

If you want to do more-comprehensive screening of individual stocks, the Telescan System allows you to perform stock searches using dozens of variables, such as historic and projected earnings, valuation, asset and liability, and other financial measures. Telescan is relatively easy to use and graphically pleasing. Telescan also allows you to quickly and easily obtain pricing charts for individual securities and mutual funds for up to the past 20 years.

The big drawback to Telescan is the price tag. The cost of the basic software package (called the Analyzer Module) is $199, and that doesn't include the monthly charges for online time, which run from $9.95 for an hour on up to $300 for unlimited access. Supplementary services to the basic package all cost you extra: for example, the Mutual Fund Search, which lets you sort through funds by adjustable search criteria, costs $100. Not a program for the casual investor. 800-324-8246.

Finally, for all sorts of Securities and Exchange Commission filings made by companies (such as annual reports, 10-Ks, and the like, all discussed in Chapter 6), visit the Web site `http://www.sec.gov`. Alternatively, you may call the individual companies you're interested in and have them mail you the desired material.

Trading online

Many of the discount brokers I discuss in Chapter 6 offer online trading capabilities. The two largest discount brokers, Charles Schwab and Fidelity Investments, offer software packages that not only provide access to investment research and the ability to track the performance of your accounts but also offer the ability to trade through your brokerage account at these firms. Both Schwab's StreetSmart and Fidelity's On-line Xpress+ (also known as FOX) provide free real-time quotes and up-to-date information on your investments held through your brokerage account. One of the useful features of these packages is that you can invest in and track both mutual funds and individual securities. Fidelity and Schwab reward your using your PC to trade, instead of their live personnel, by giving you a discount off their regular transaction fee schedule.

Both software programs can also provide you with a direct link to subscription-based market research services. Through *FOX,* you can log on to Reuter's Money Network and Telescan's Tipnet. *StreetSmart* supports accesss to Reuter's Money Network, Dow Jones News/Retrieval, and Standard and Poor's MarketScope. Of course, you pay extra for these added goodies.

Schwab's *StreetSmart* is available for both Windows and Macintosh ($39, 800-334-4455). Fidelity's *On-line Xpress+* is for Windows only (free, 800-544-7272).

A handful of deep discount brokers also allow trading through the commercial online services. eTrade (800-786-2575) for example, for a flat fee of $19.95, will buy or sell up to 5,000 shares of stock. You can place a trade through eTrade through your computer (America Online, CompuServe, or through direct access) or via touch-tone phone. For $34.95, you can place a trade through a live broker. Other traditional discounters have begun to offer similar services. For example, Charles Schwab now offers e.Schwab, which charges $29.95 per trade for the first 1,000 shares. (For more information on discount brokers, see Chapter 6.)

Index

(continued)

(continued)

(continued)

Notes

Notes

Notes

Notes

Notes

Notes

Notes

Notes

Notes

Discover Dummies Online!

The Dummies Web Site is your fun and friendly online resource for the latest information about ...*For Dummies*® books and your favorite topics. The Web site is the place to communicate with us, exchange ideas with other ...*For Dummies* readers, chat with authors, and have fun!

Ten Fun and Useful Things You Can Do at www.dummies.com

1. Win free ...*For Dummies* books and more!
2. Register your book and be entered in a prize drawing.
3. Meet your favorite authors through the IDG Books Author Chat Series.
4. Exchange helpful information with other ...*For Dummies* readers.
5. Discover other great ...*For Dummies* books you must have!
6. Purchase Dummieswear™ exclusively from our Web site.
7. Buy ...*For Dummies* books online.
8. Talk to us. Make comments, ask questions, get answers!
9. Download free software.
10. Find additional useful resources from authors.

Link directly to these ten fun and useful things at
http://www.dummies.com/10useful

For other technology titles from IDG Books Worldwide, go to
www.idgbooks.com

Not on the Web yet? It's easy to get started with *Dummies 101*®: *The Internet For Windows*®*95* or *The Internet For Dummies*®, 4th Edition, at local retailers everywhere.

Find other ...*For Dummies* books on these topics:
Business • Career • Databases • Food & Beverage • Games • Gardening • Graphics
Hardware • Health & Fitness • Internet and the World Wide Web • Networking
Office Suites • Operating Systems • Personal Finance • Pets • Programming • Recreation
Sports • Spreadsheets • Teacher Resources • Test Prep • Word Processing

IDG BOOKS WORLDWIDE BOOK REGISTRATION

We want to hear from you!

Register This Book and Win!

Visit **http://my2cents.dummies.com** to register this book and tell us how you liked it!

- ✔ Get entered in our monthly prize giveaway.

- ✔ Give us feedback about this book — tell us what you like best, what you like least, or maybe what you'd like to ask the author and us to change!

- ✔ Let us know any other ...*For Dummies* topics that interest you.

Your feedback helps us determine what books to publish, tells us what coverage to add as we revise our books, and lets us know whether we're meeting your needs as a ...*For Dummies* reader. You're our most valuable resource, and what you have to say is important to us!

Not on the Web yet? It's easy to get started with *Dummies 101*®: *The Internet For Windows*® *95* or *The Internet For Dummies*®, 4th Edition, at local retailers everywhere.

Or let us know what you think by sending us a letter at the following address:

...*For Dummies* Book Registration
Dummies Press
7260 Shadeland Station, Suite 100
Indianapolis, IN 46256
Fax 317-596-5498

BUSINESS AND GENERAL REFERENCE BOOK SERIES FROM IDG

COMPUTER BOOK SERIES FROM IDG